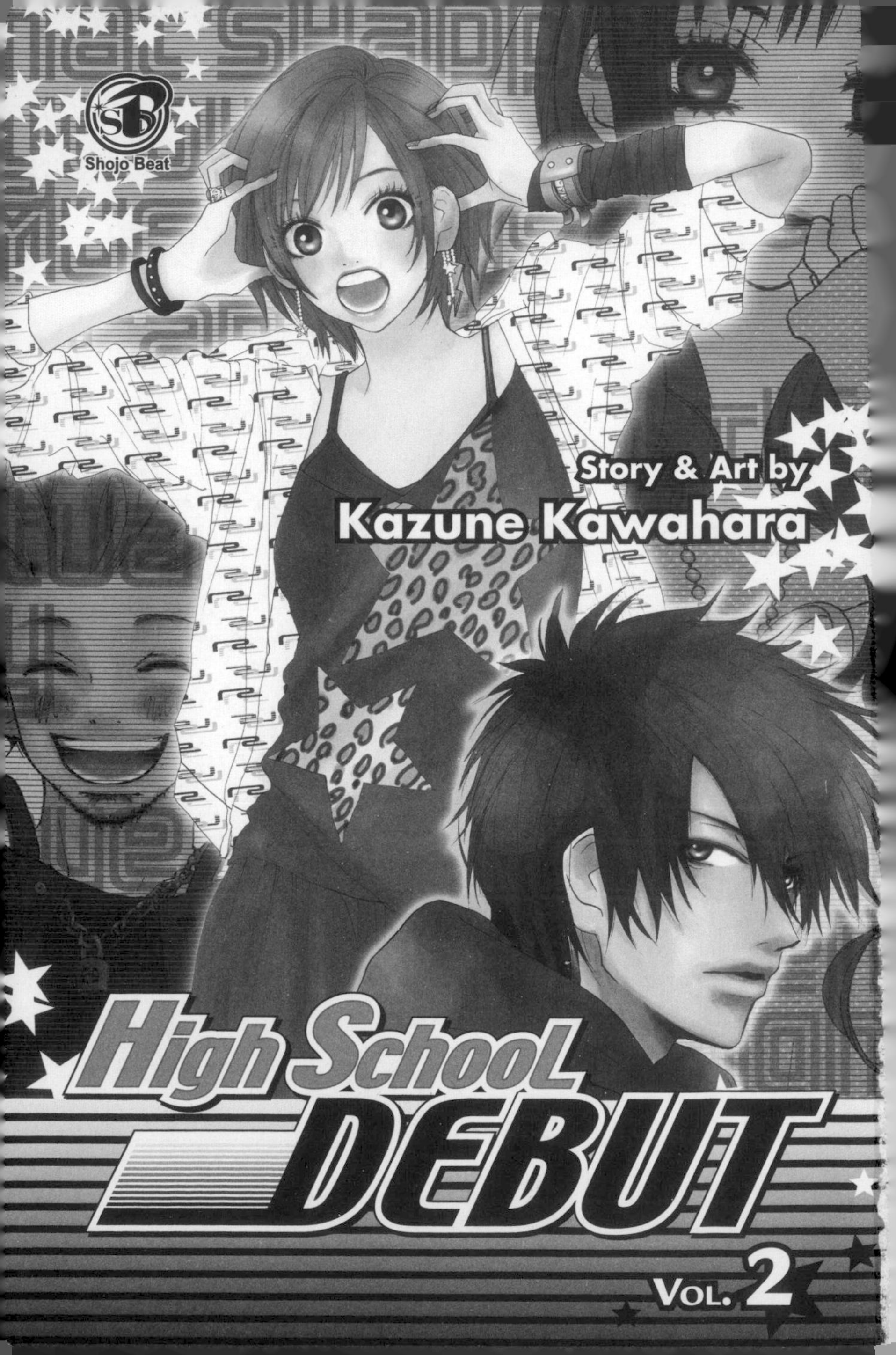
Shojo Beat
Story & Art by
Kazune Kawahara
High School
DEBUT
Vol. 2

Contents

Story Thus Far...

High school freshman Haruna was a sporty girl and an ace player for her softball team back in junior high. Now that she's in high school, she wants to give her all to finding true love instead! Unfortunately, all her efforts are in vain as she can't even get a boy interested in her. Luckily, she bumps into Yoh, a guy who knows all about what makes girls popular with guys. At first he refuses to become Haruna's "love coach," partly because he had a bad experience with his ex-girlfriend and has become disillusioned with girls and being popular. When he sees Haruna's determination, however, Yoh changes his mind and decides to be her coach after all!

Haruna's delighted when she gets hit on for the first time in her life, but she becomes quite shocked when she realizes she's been deceived. Trying to take her mind off things at the batting center, she bumps into Yoh's friend Fumiya, who cheers her up. Haruna then starts to think of Fumiya as more than a friend...

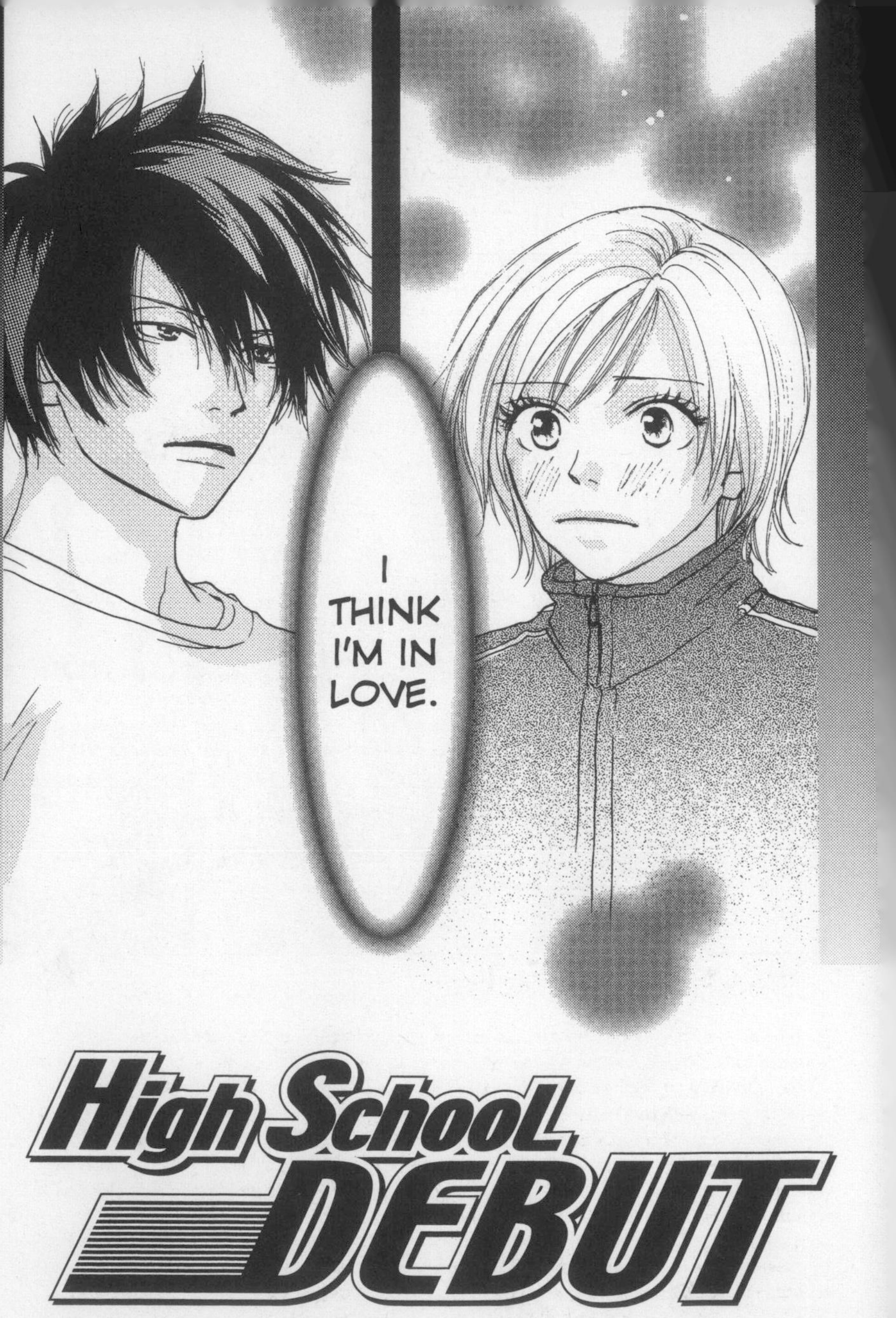
I THINK I'M IN LOVE.

High School DEBUT

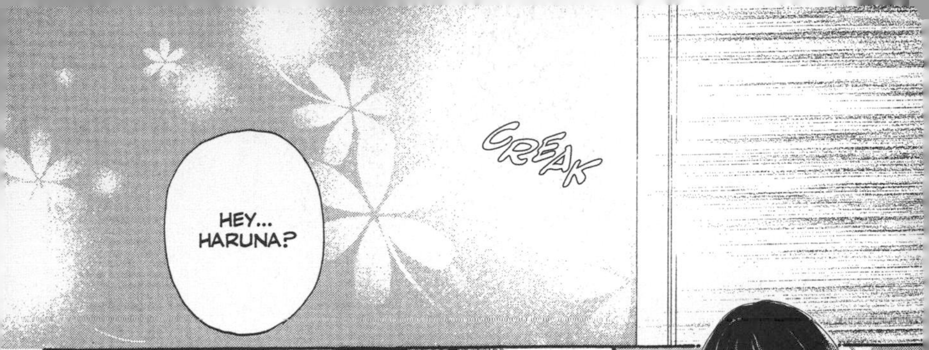
CREAK
HEY... HARUNA?
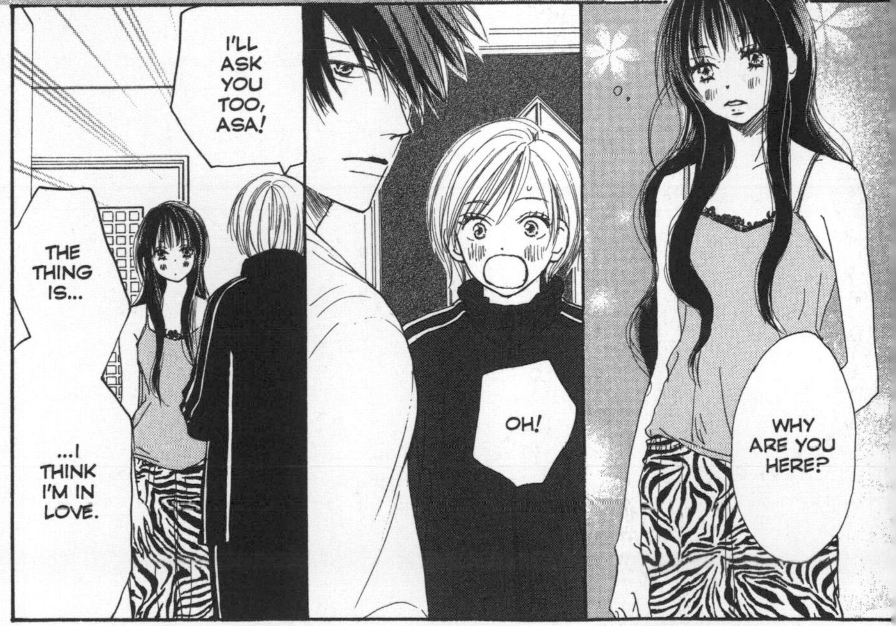
WHY ARE YOU HERE?
OH!
I'LL ASK YOU TOO, ASA!
THE THING IS...
...I THINK I'M IN LOVE.
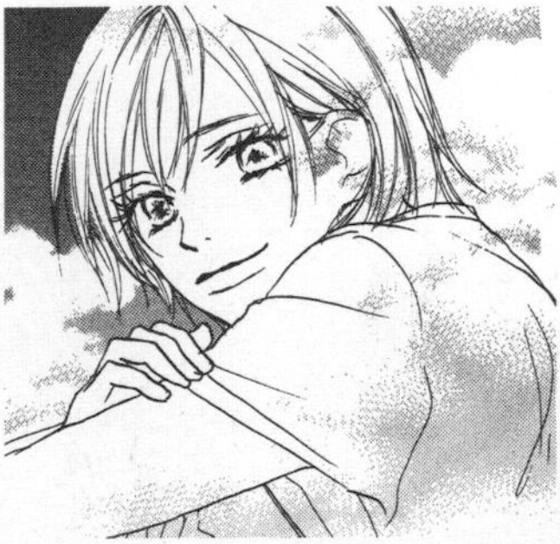

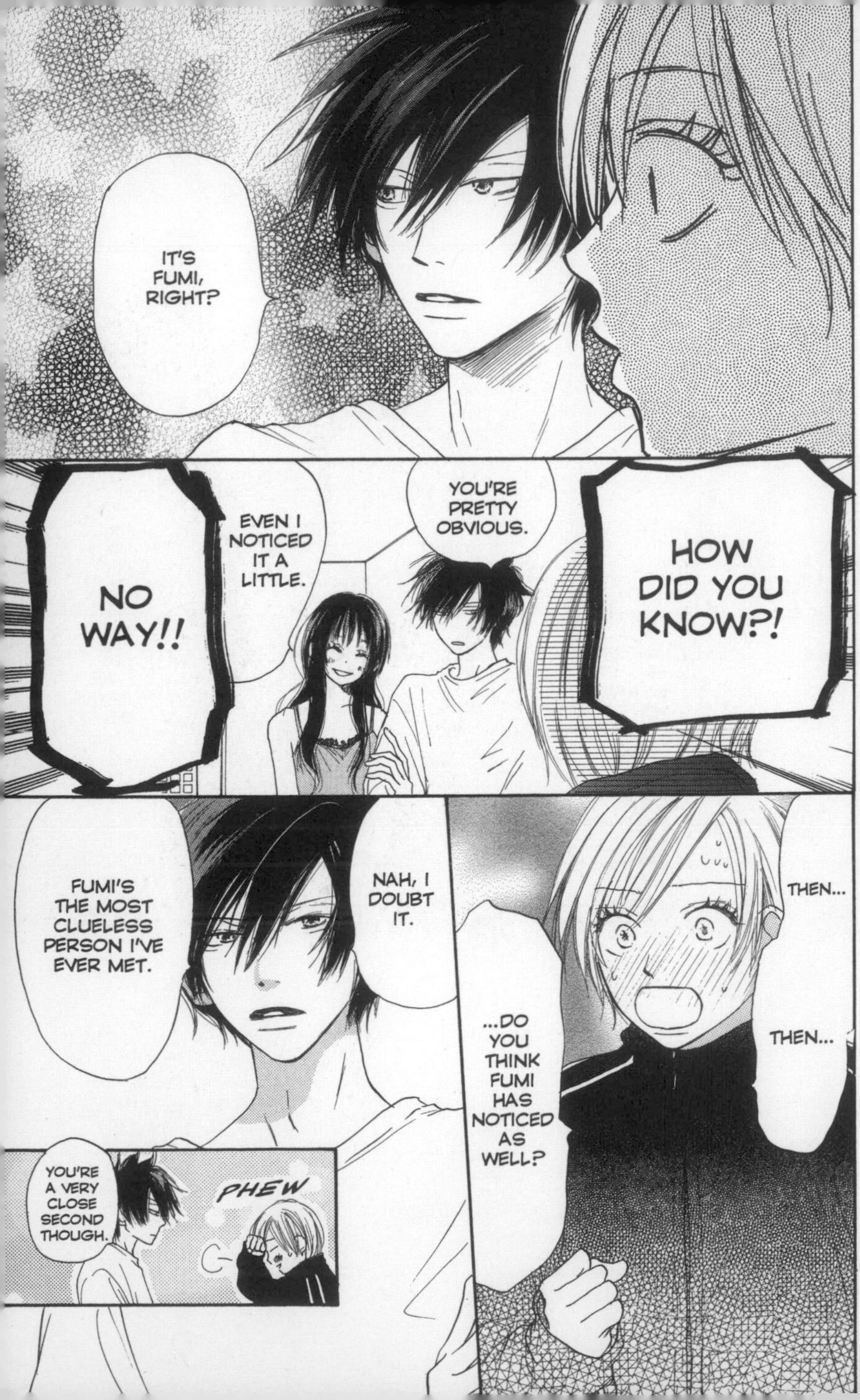
IT'S FUMI, RIGHT?
HOW DID YOU KNOW?!
YOU'RE PRETTY OBVIOUS.
EVEN I NOTICED IT A LITTLE.
NO WAY!!
THEN...
THEN...
...DO YOU THINK FUMI HAS NOTICED AS WELL?
NAH, I DOUBT IT.
FUMI'S THE MOST CLUELESS PERSON I'VE EVER MET.
PHEW
YOU'RE A VERY CLOSE SECOND THOUGH.

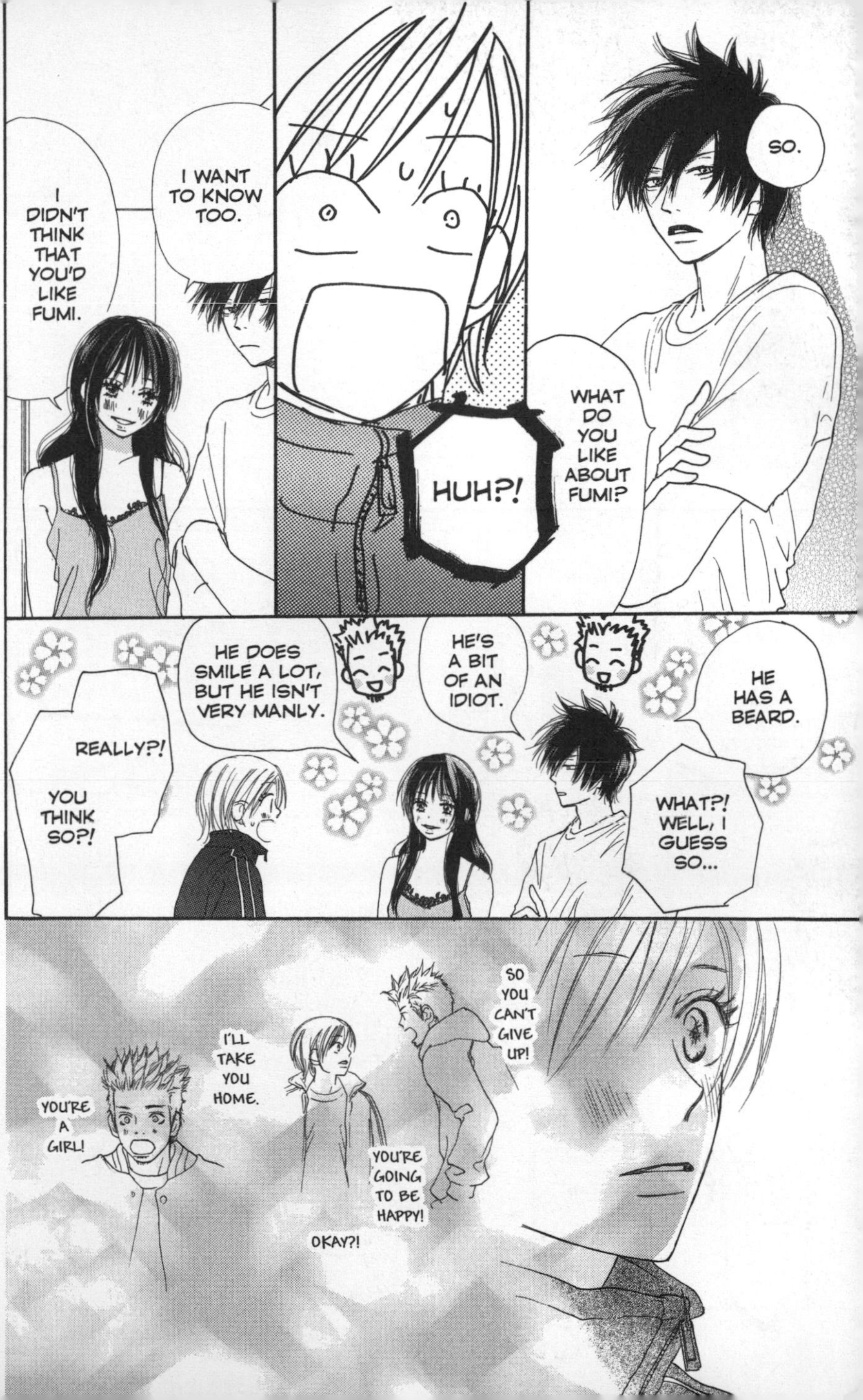
SO.
WHAT DO YOU LIKE ABOUT FUMI?
HUH?!
I WANT TO KNOW TOO.
I DIDN'T THINK THAT YOU'D LIKE FUMI.
HE HAS A BEARD.
WHAT?! WELL, I GUESS SO...
HE'S A BIT OF AN IDIOT.
HE DOES SMILE A LOT, BUT HE ISN'T VERY MANLY.
REALLY?!
YOU THINK SO?!
SO YOU CAN'T GIVE UP!
YOU'RE GOING TO BE HAPPY!
OKAY?!
I'LL TAKE YOU HOME.
YOU'RE A GIRL!

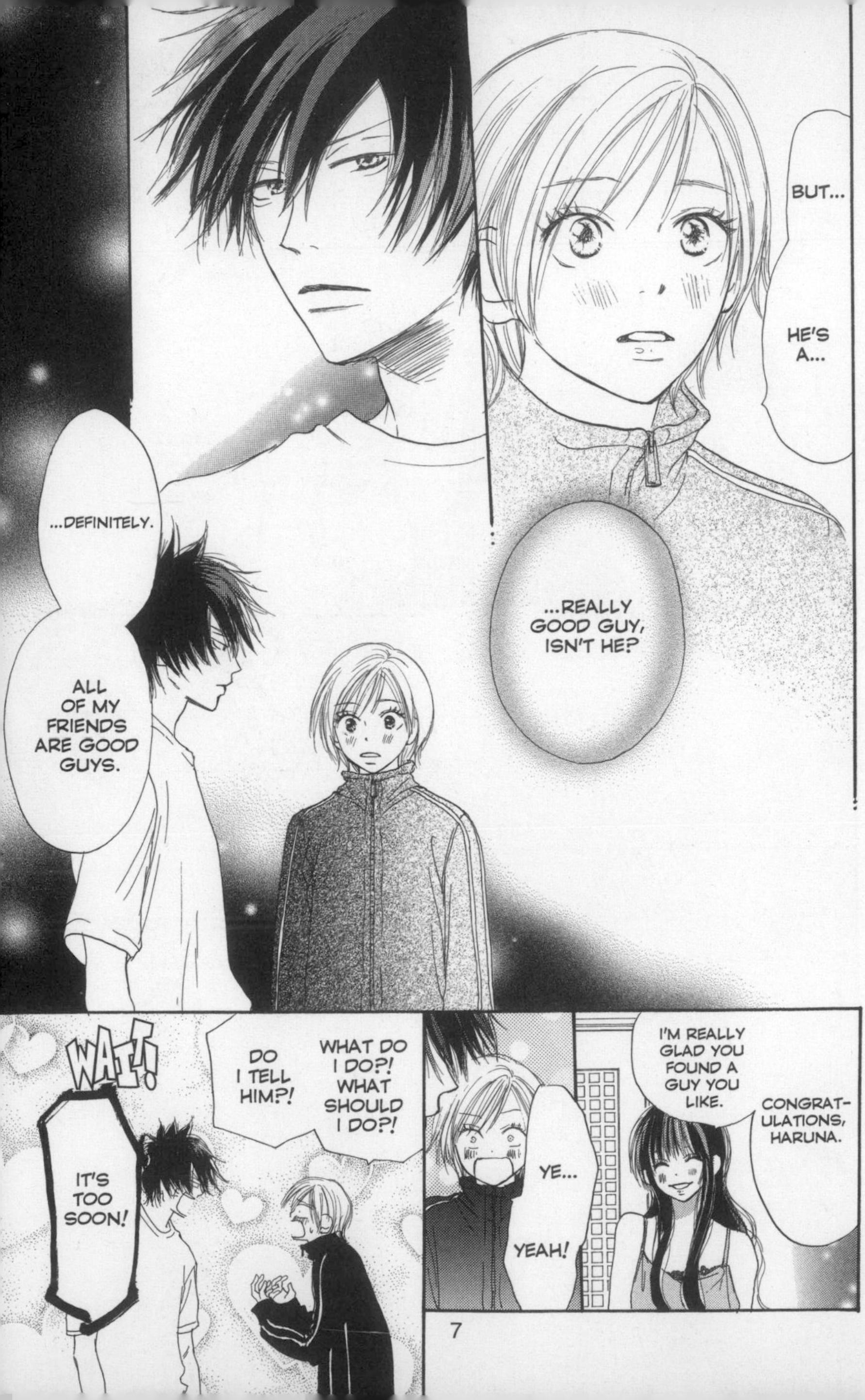
BUT...
HE'S A...
...REALLY GOOD GUY, ISN'T HE?
...DEFINITELY.
ALL OF MY FRIENDS ARE GOOD GUYS.
I'M REALLY GLAD YOU FOUND A GUY YOU LIKE.
CONGRAT-ULATIONS, HARUNA.
YE...
YEAH!
WHAT DO I DO?! WHAT SHOULD I DO?!
DO I TELL HIM?!
WAIT!
IT'S TOO SOON!

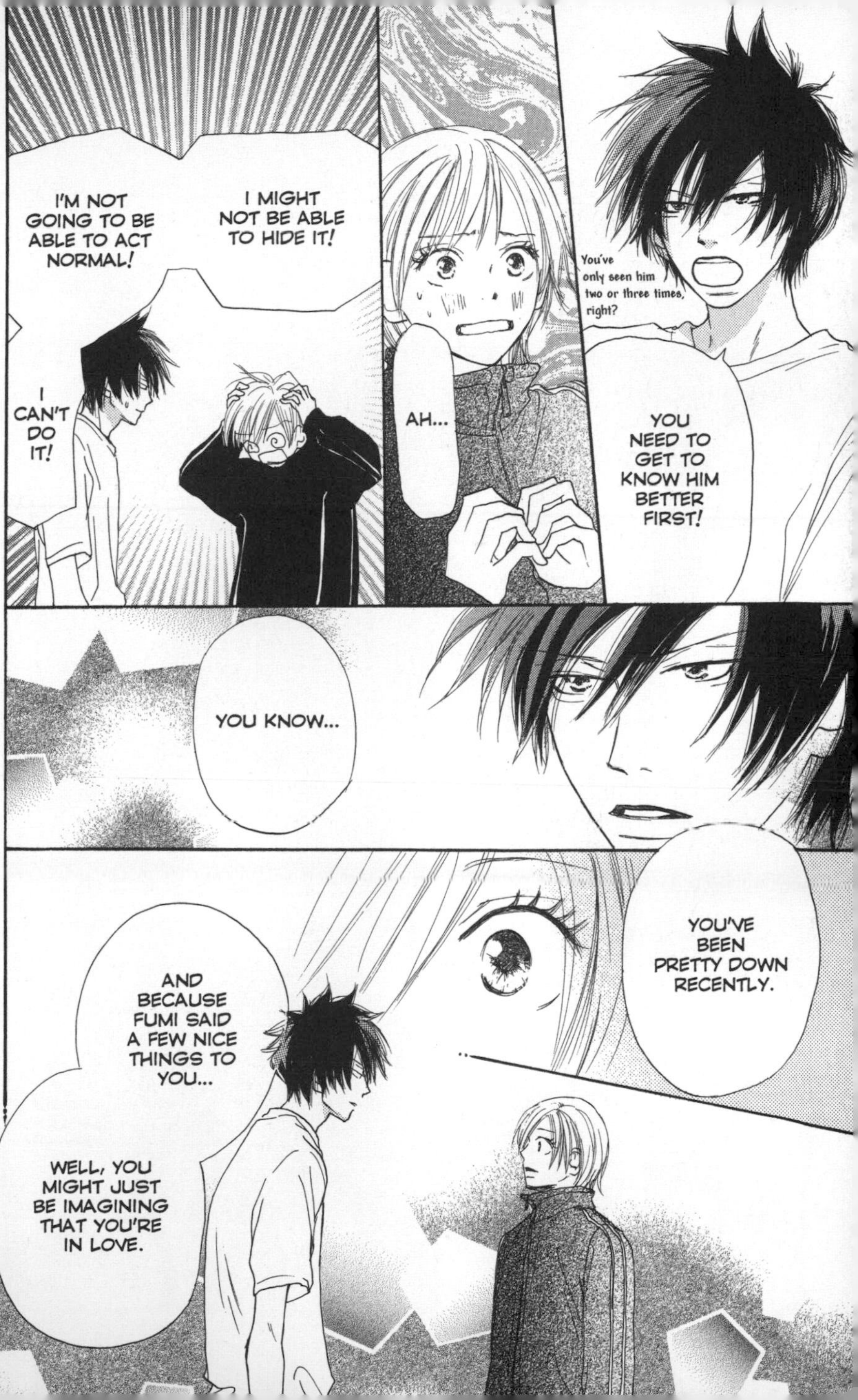
You've only seen him two or three times, right?
YOU NEED TO GET TO KNOW HIM BETTER FIRST!
AH...
I MIGHT NOT BE ABLE TO HIDE IT!
I'M NOT GOING TO BE ABLE TO ACT NORMAL!
I CAN'T DO IT!
YOU KNOW...
YOU'VE BEEN PRETTY DOWN RECENTLY.
...
AND BECAUSE FUMI SAID A FEW NICE THINGS TO YOU...
WELL, YOU MIGHT JUST BE IMAGINING THAT YOU'RE IN LOVE.

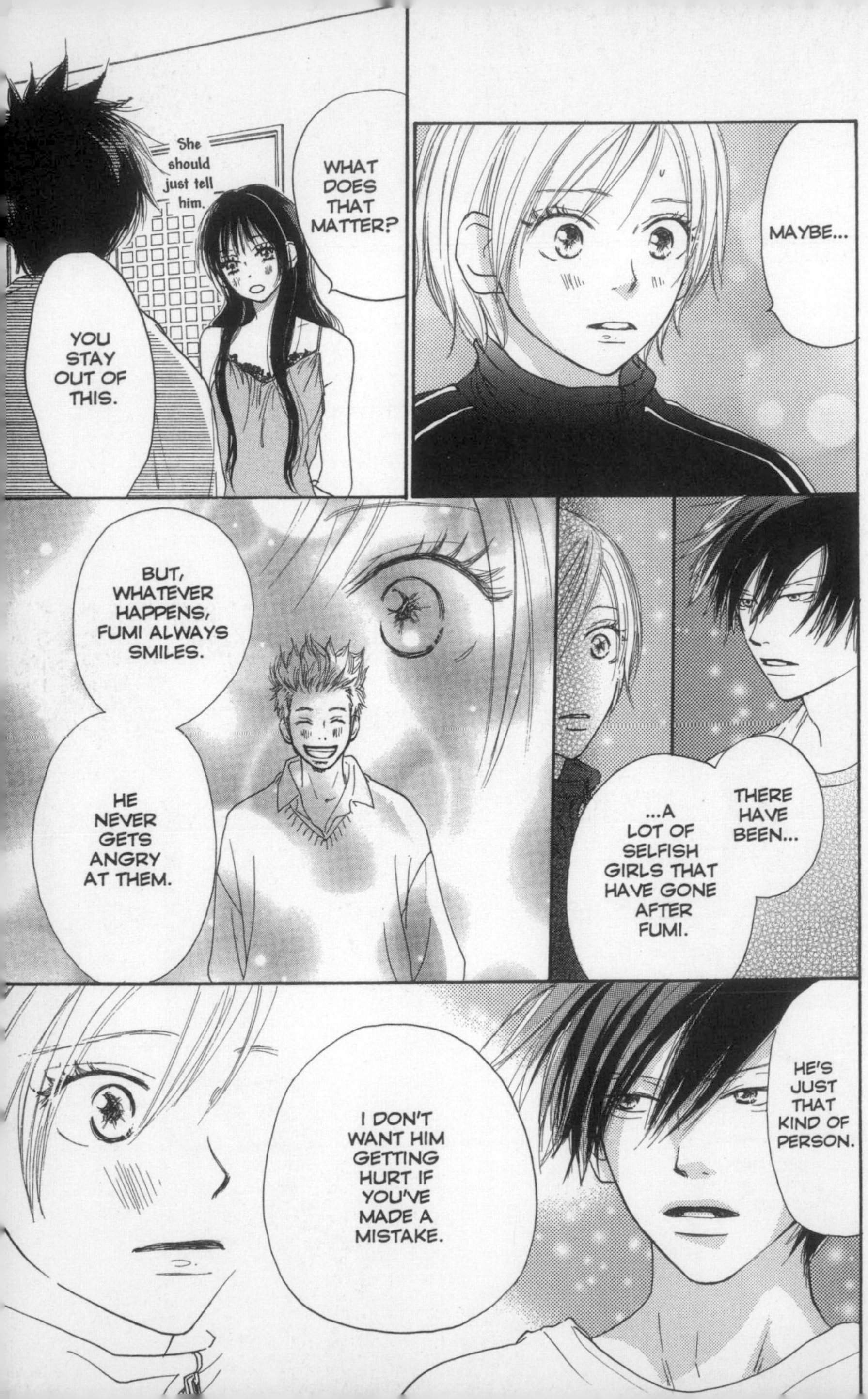
MAYBE...
WHAT DOES THAT MATTER?
She should just tell him.
YOU STAY OUT OF THIS.
THERE HAVE BEEN...
...A LOT OF SELFISH GIRLS THAT HAVE GONE AFTER FUMI.
BUT, WHATEVER HAPPENS, FUMI ALWAYS SMILES.
HE NEVER GETS ANGRY AT THEM.
HE'S JUST THAT KIND OF PERSON.
I DON'T WANT HIM GETTING HURT IF YOU'VE MADE A MISTAKE.

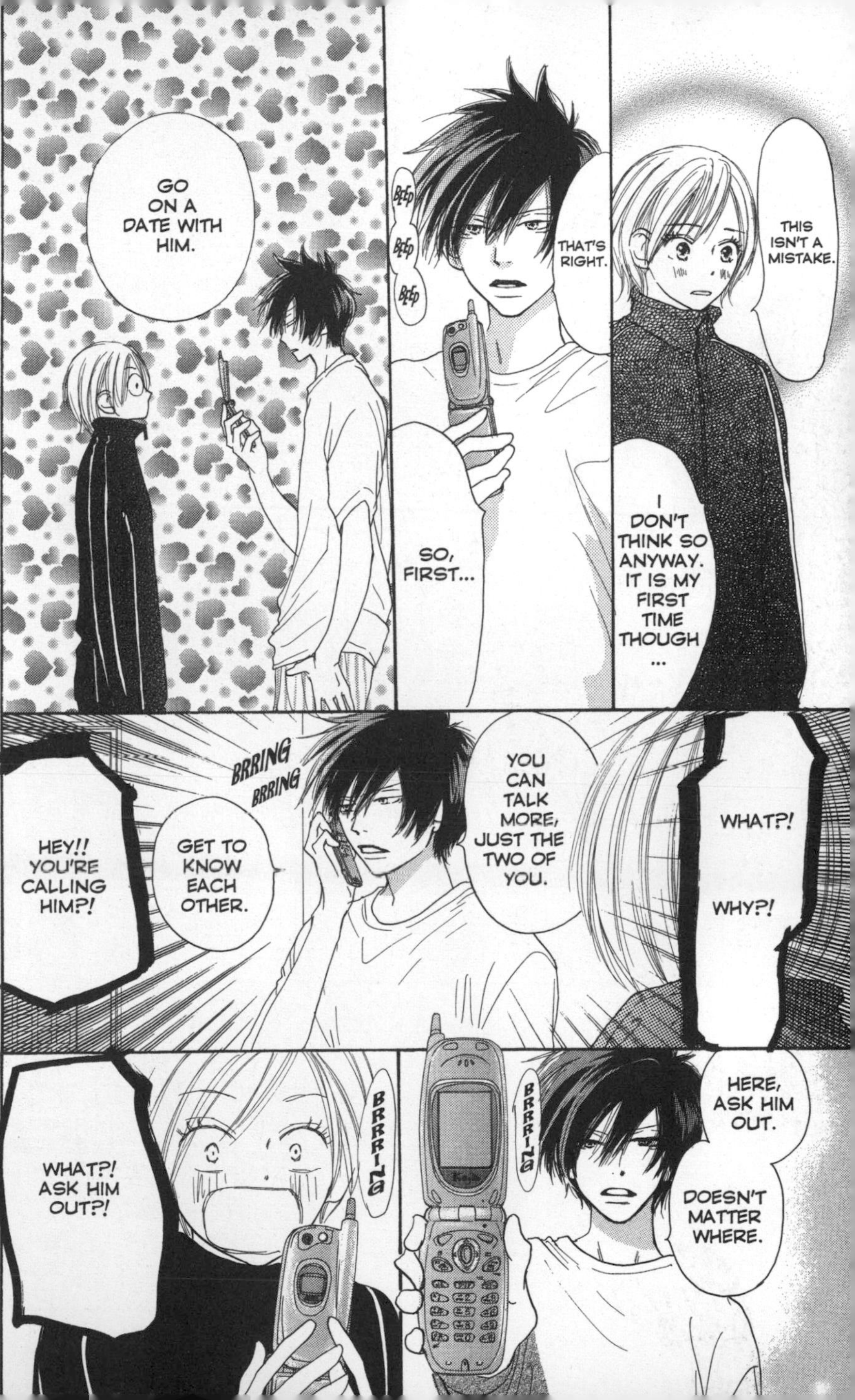
THIS ISN'T A MISTAKE.
I DON'T THINK SO ANYWAY. IT IS MY FIRST TIME THOUGH...
THAT'S RIGHT.
BEEP
BEEP
BEEP
SO, FIRST...
GO ON A DATE WITH HIM.
WHAT?!
WHY?!
YOU CAN TALK MORE, JUST THE TWO OF YOU.
BRRING
BRRING
GET TO KNOW EACH OTHER.
HEY!! YOU'RE CALLING HIM?!
HERE, ASK HIM OUT.
DOESN'T MATTER WHERE.
BRRRING
BRRRING
WHAT?! ASK HIM OUT?!

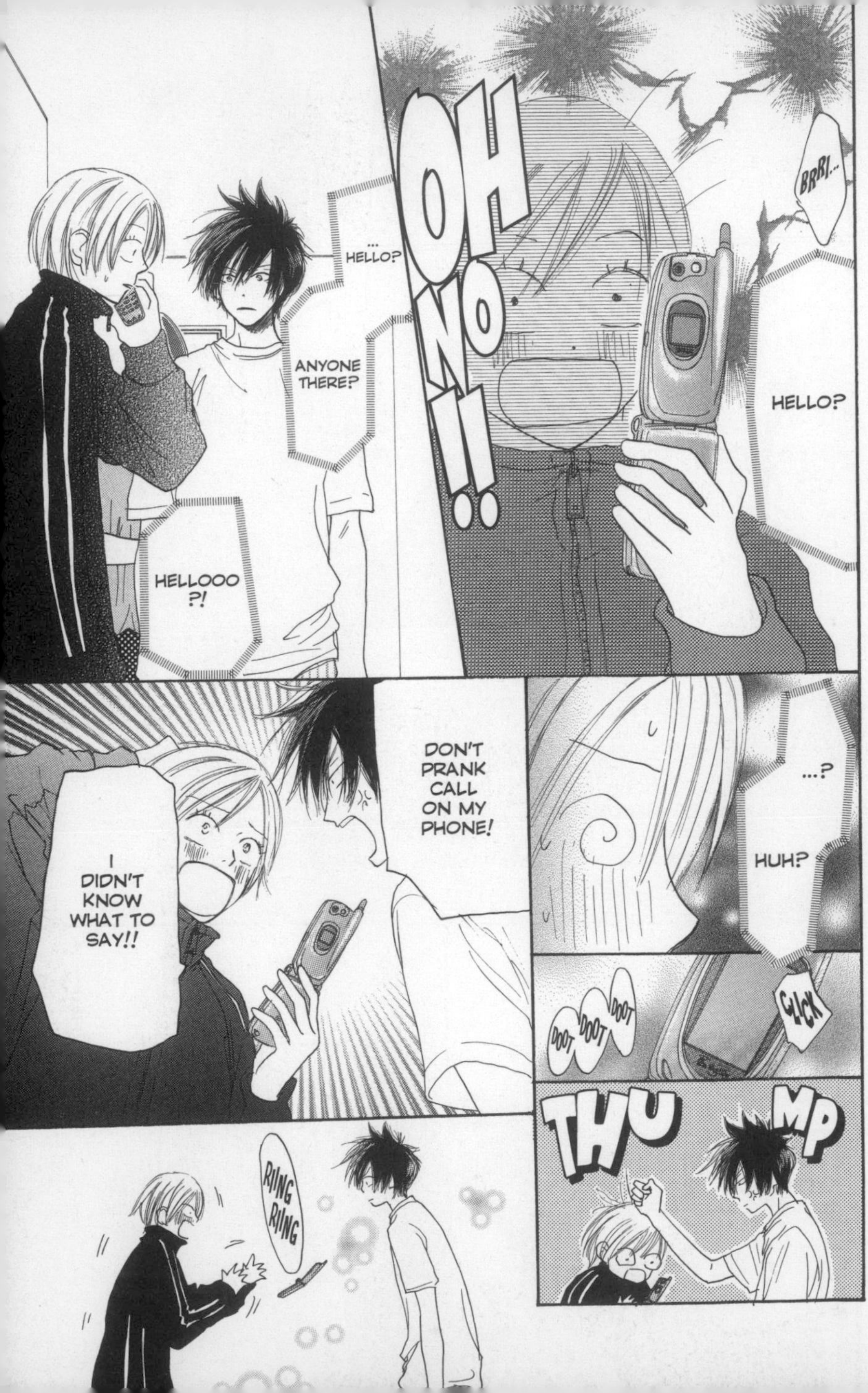
BRRI...
HELLO?
OH NO!!!!
... HELLO?
ANYONE THERE?
HELLOOO ?!
...?
HUH?
CLICK
DOOT DOOT DOOT
THUMP
DON'T PRANK CALL ON MY PHONE!
I DIDN'T KNOW WHAT TO SAY!!
RIING RIING

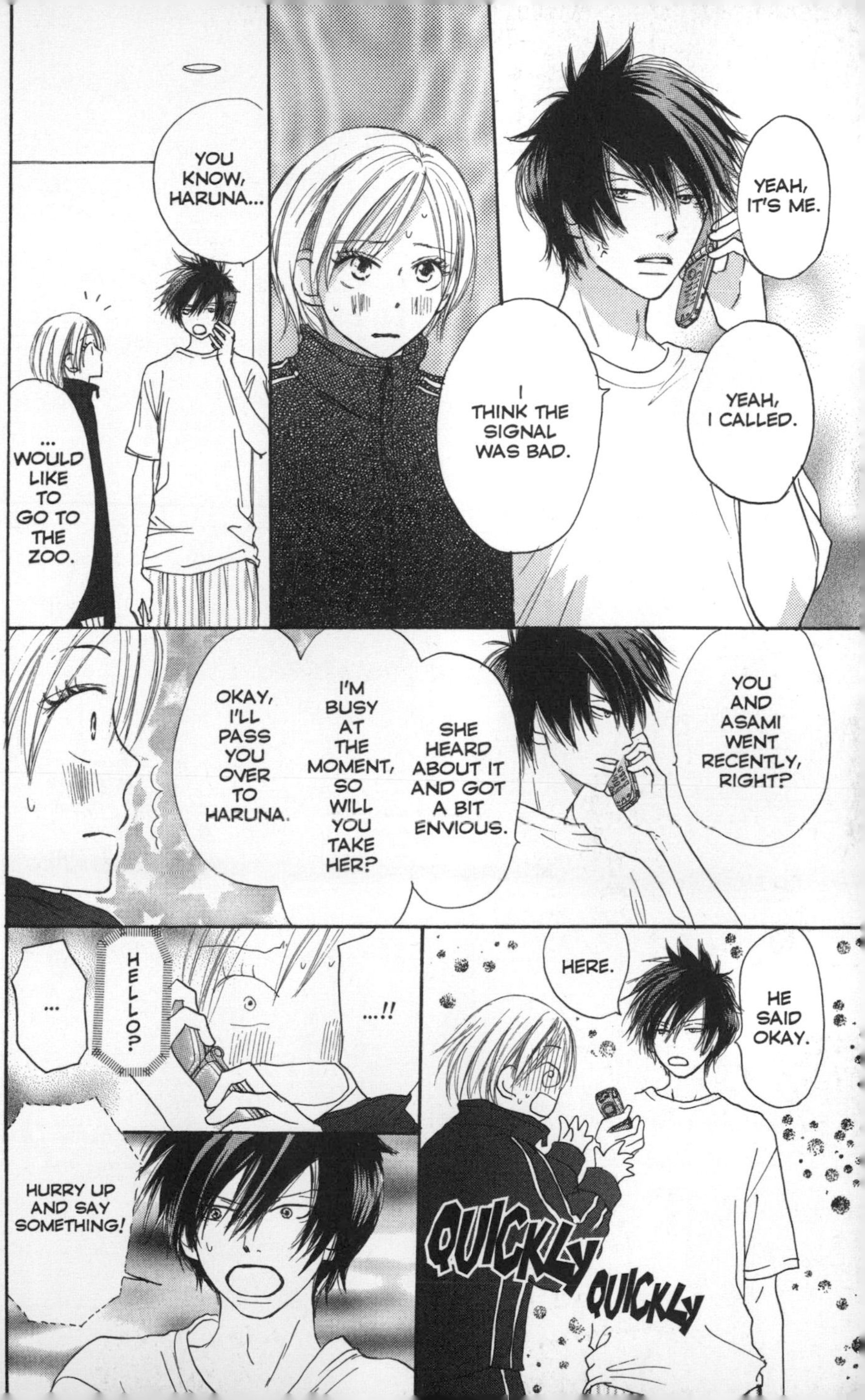

YEAH, IT'S ME.
YEAH, I CALLED.
I THINK THE SIGNAL WAS BAD.
YOU KNOW, HARUNA...
...WOULD LIKE TO GO TO THE ZOO.
YOU AND ASAMI WENT RECENTLY, RIGHT?
SHE HEARD ABOUT IT AND GOT A BIT ENVIOUS.
I'M BUSY AT THE MOMENT, SO WILL YOU TAKE HER?
OKAY, I'LL PASS YOU OVER TO HARUNA.
HE SAID OKAY.
HERE.
QUICKLY
QUICKLY
...!!
HELLO?
...
HURRY UP AND SAY SOMETHING!

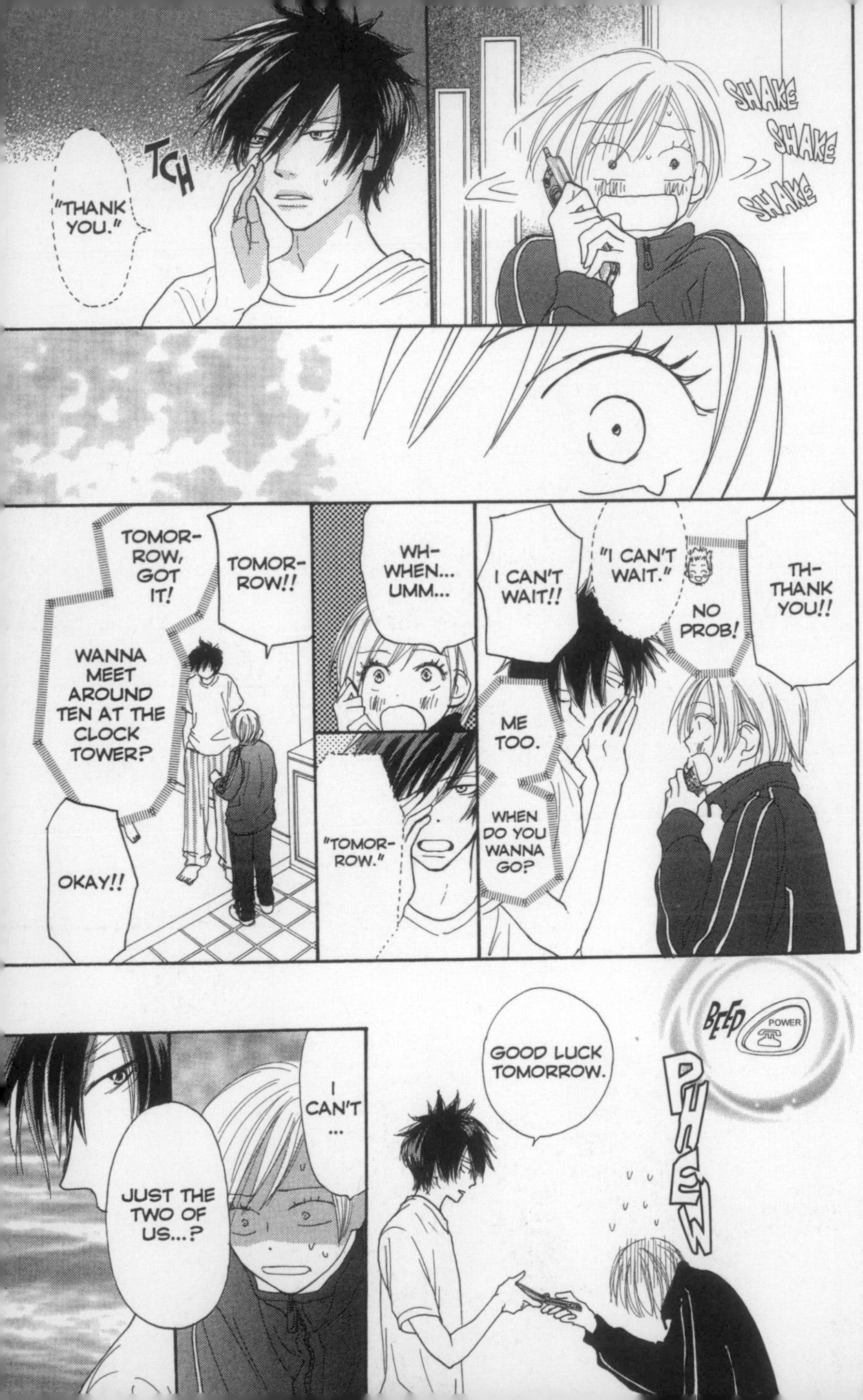
SHAKE
SHAKE
SHAKE
TCH
"THANK YOU."
TH- THANK YOU!!
"I CAN'T WAIT."
NO PROB!
I CAN'T WAIT!!
ME TOO.
WHEN DO YOU WANNA GO?
WH- WHEN... UMM...
"TOMOR-ROW."
TOMOR-ROW!!
TOMOR-ROW, GOT IT!
WANNA MEET AROUND TEN AT THE CLOCK TOWER?
OKAY!!
BEEP
POWER
GOOD LUCK TOMORROW.
PHEW
I CAN'T ...
JUST THE TWO OF US...?

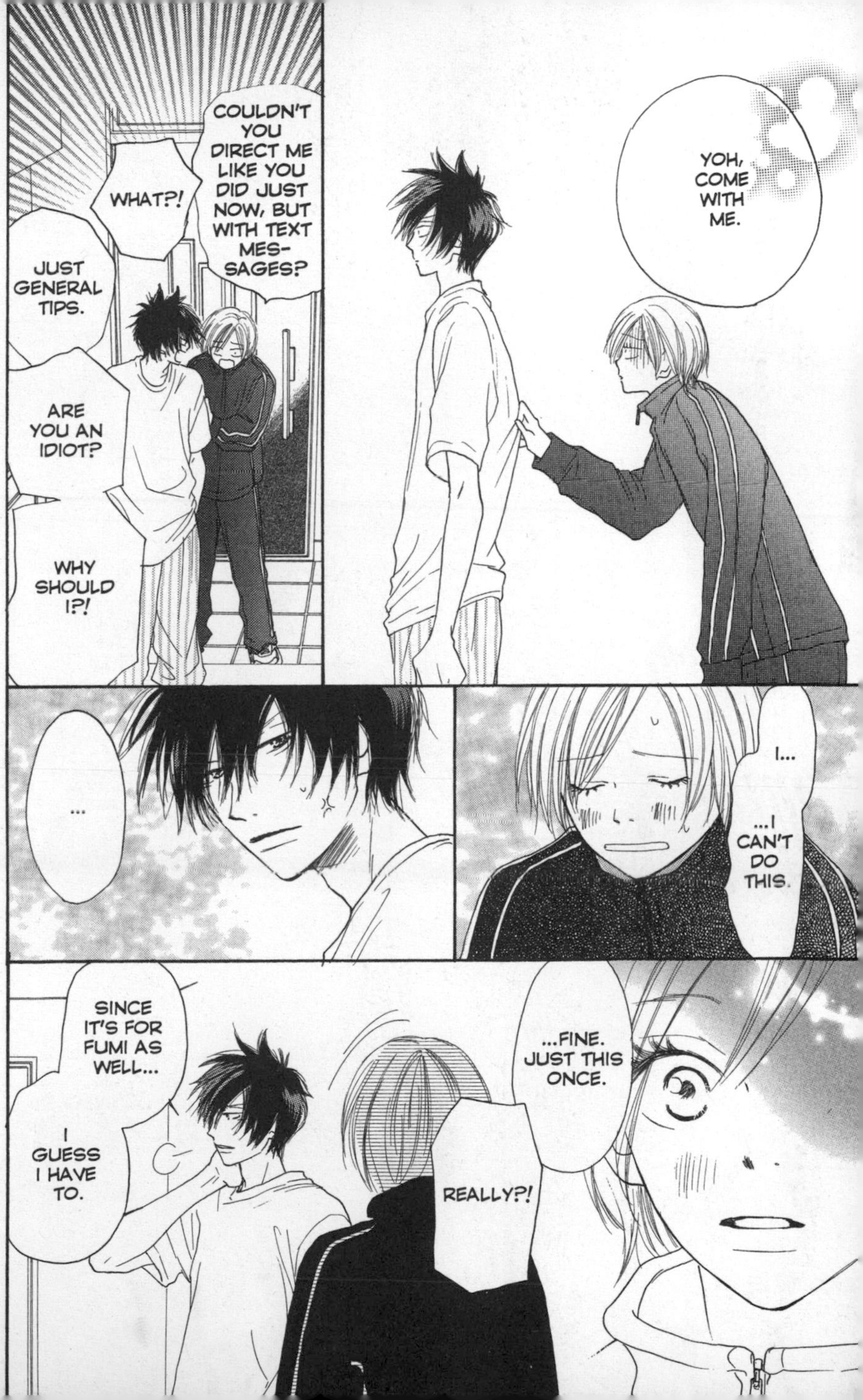
YOH, COME WITH ME.
COULDN'T YOU DIRECT ME LIKE YOU DID JUST NOW, BUT WITH TEXT MES-SAGES?
WHAT?!
JUST GENERAL TIPS.
ARE YOU AN IDIOT?
WHY SHOULD I?!
I...
...I CAN'T DO THIS.
...
...FINE. JUST THIS ONCE.
REALLY?!
SINCE IT'S FOR FUMI AS WELL...
I GUESS I HAVE TO.

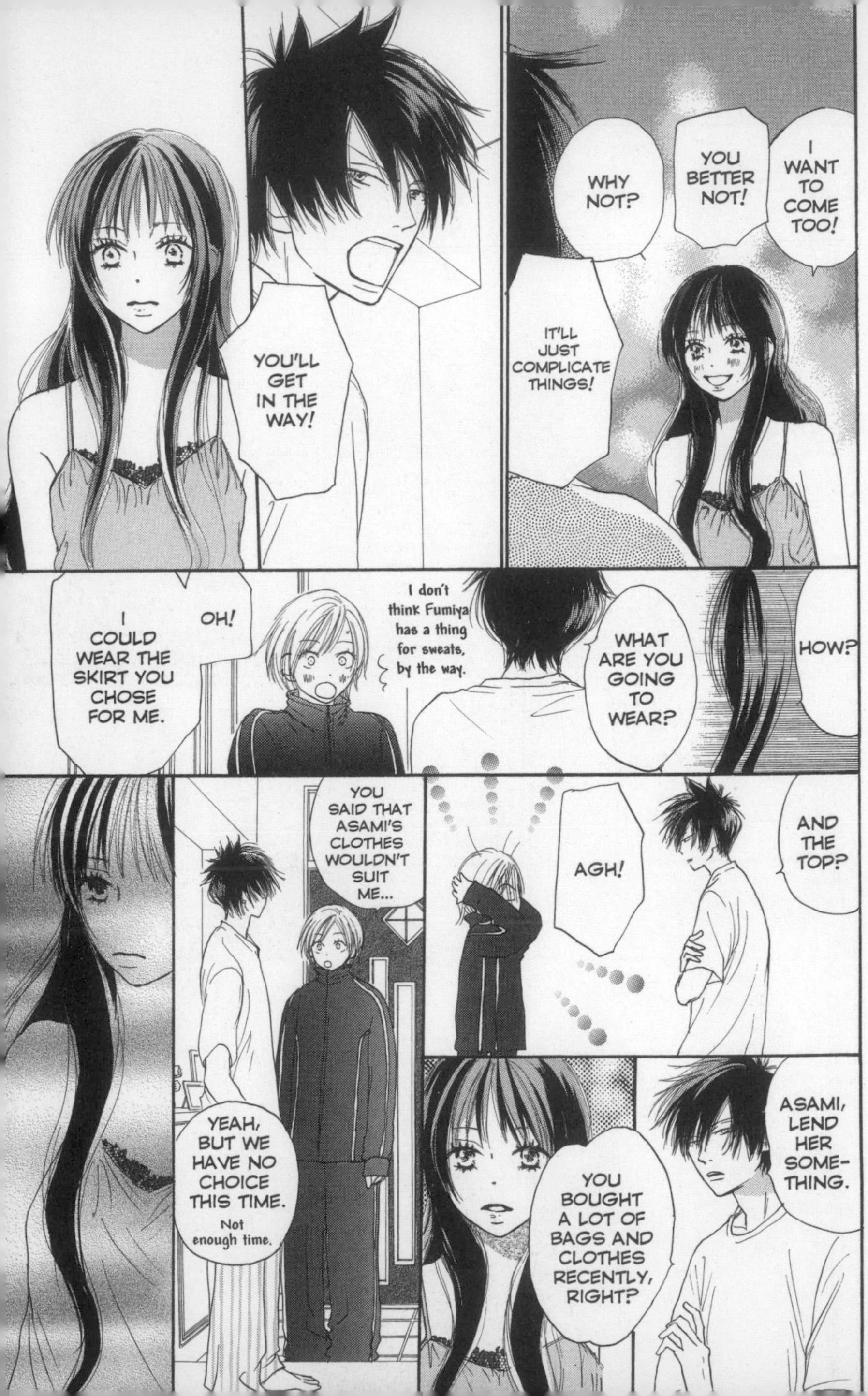
I WANT TO COME TOO!
YOU BETTER NOT!
WHY NOT?
IT'LL JUST COMPLICATE THINGS!
YOU'LL GET IN THE WAY!
HOW?
WHAT ARE YOU GOING TO WEAR?
I don't think Fumiya has a thing for sweats, by the way.
OH!
I COULD WEAR THE SKIRT YOU CHOSE FOR ME.
AND THE TOP?
AGH!
ASAMI, LEND HER SOME-THING.
YOU BOUGHT A LOT OF BAGS AND CLOTHES RECENTLY, RIGHT?
YOU SAID THAT ASAMI'S CLOTHES WOULDN'T SUIT ME...
YEAH, BUT WE HAVE NO CHOICE THIS TIME.
Not enough time.

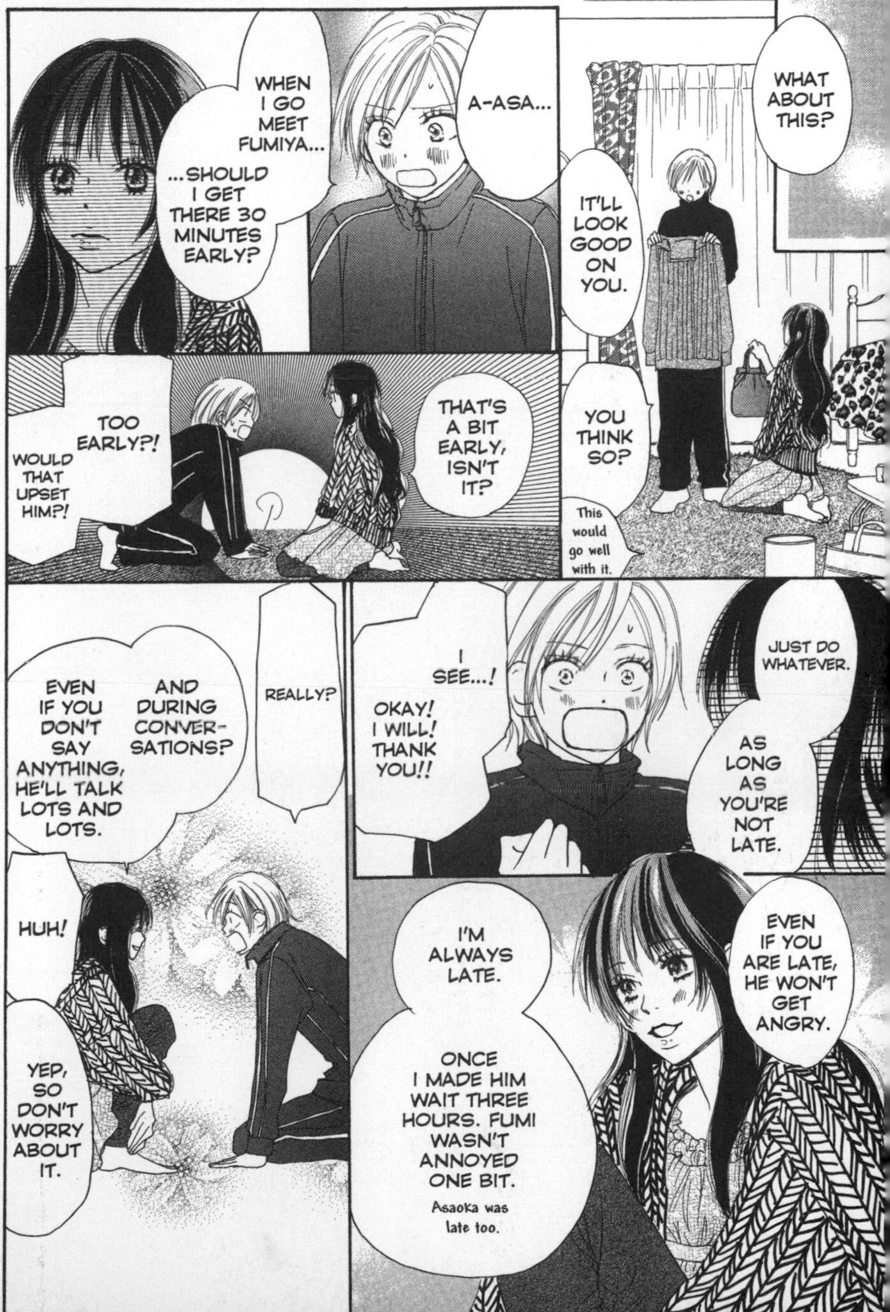
WHAT ABOUT THIS?
IT'LL LOOK GOOD ON YOU.
YOU THINK SO?
This would go well with it.
A-ASA...
WHEN I GO MEET FUMIYA...
...SHOULD I GET THERE 30 MINUTES EARLY?
THAT'S A BIT EARLY, ISN'T IT?
TOO EARLY?!
WOULD THAT UPSET HIM?!
JUST DO WHATEVER.
AS LONG AS YOU'RE NOT LATE.
I SEE...!
OKAY! I WILL! THANK YOU!!
EVEN IF YOU ARE LATE, HE WON'T GET ANGRY.
I'M ALWAYS LATE.
ONCE I MADE HIM WAIT THREE HOURS. FUMI WASN'T ANNOYED ONE BIT.
Asaoka was late too.
REALLY?
AND DURING CONVER-SATIONS?
EVEN IF YOU DON'T SAY ANYTHING, HE'LL TALK LOTS AND LOTS.
HUH!
YEP, SO DON'T WORRY ABOUT IT.

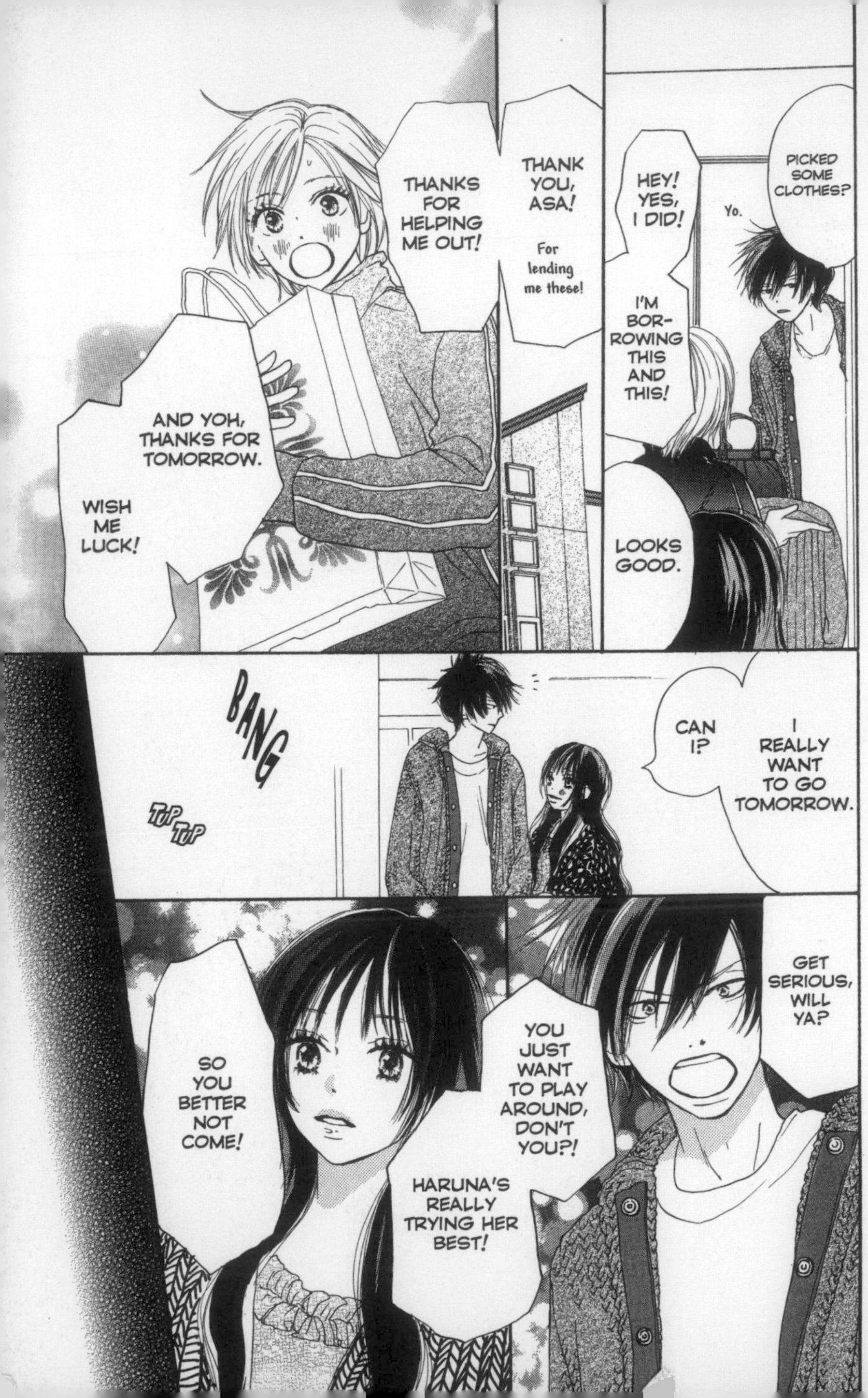
PICKED SOME CLOTHES?
Yo.
HEY! YES, I DID!
I'M BOR-ROWING THIS AND THIS!
LOOKS GOOD.
THANK YOU, ASA!
For lending me these!
THANKS FOR HELPING ME OUT!
AND YOH, THANKS FOR TOMORROW.
WISH ME LUCK!
I REALLY WANT TO GO TOMORROW.
CAN I?
BANG
TOP TOP
GET SERIOUS, WILL YA?
YOU JUST WANT TO PLAY AROUND, DON'T YOU?!
HARUNA'S REALLY TRYING HER BEST!
SO YOU BETTER NOT COME!

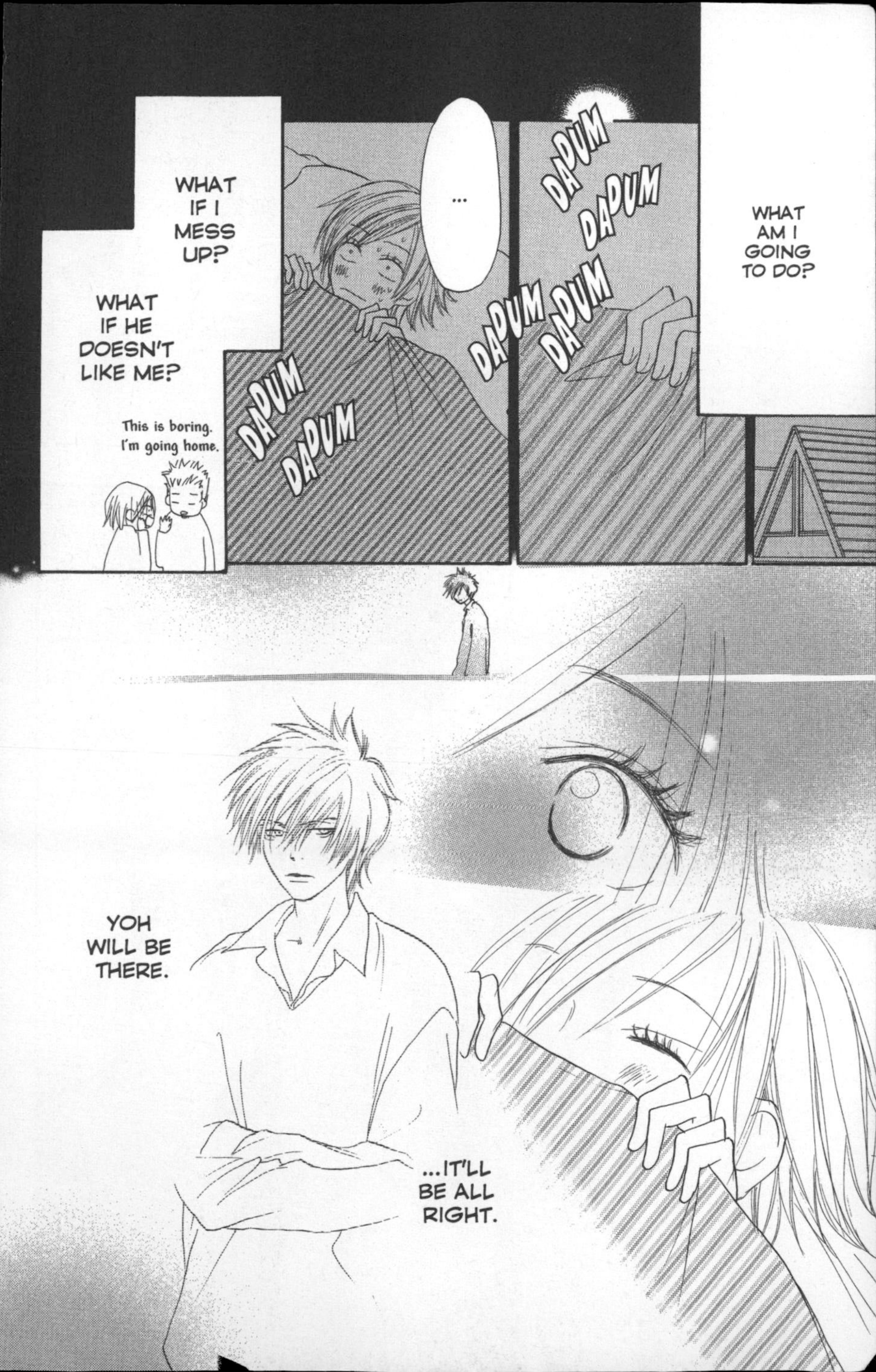

WHAT AM I GOING TO DO?
DADUM
DADUM
DADUM
DADUM
...
DADUM
DADUM
WHAT IF I MESS UP?
WHAT IF HE DOESN'T LIKE ME?
This is boring. I'm going home.
YOH WILL BE THERE.
...IT'LL BE ALL RIGHT.

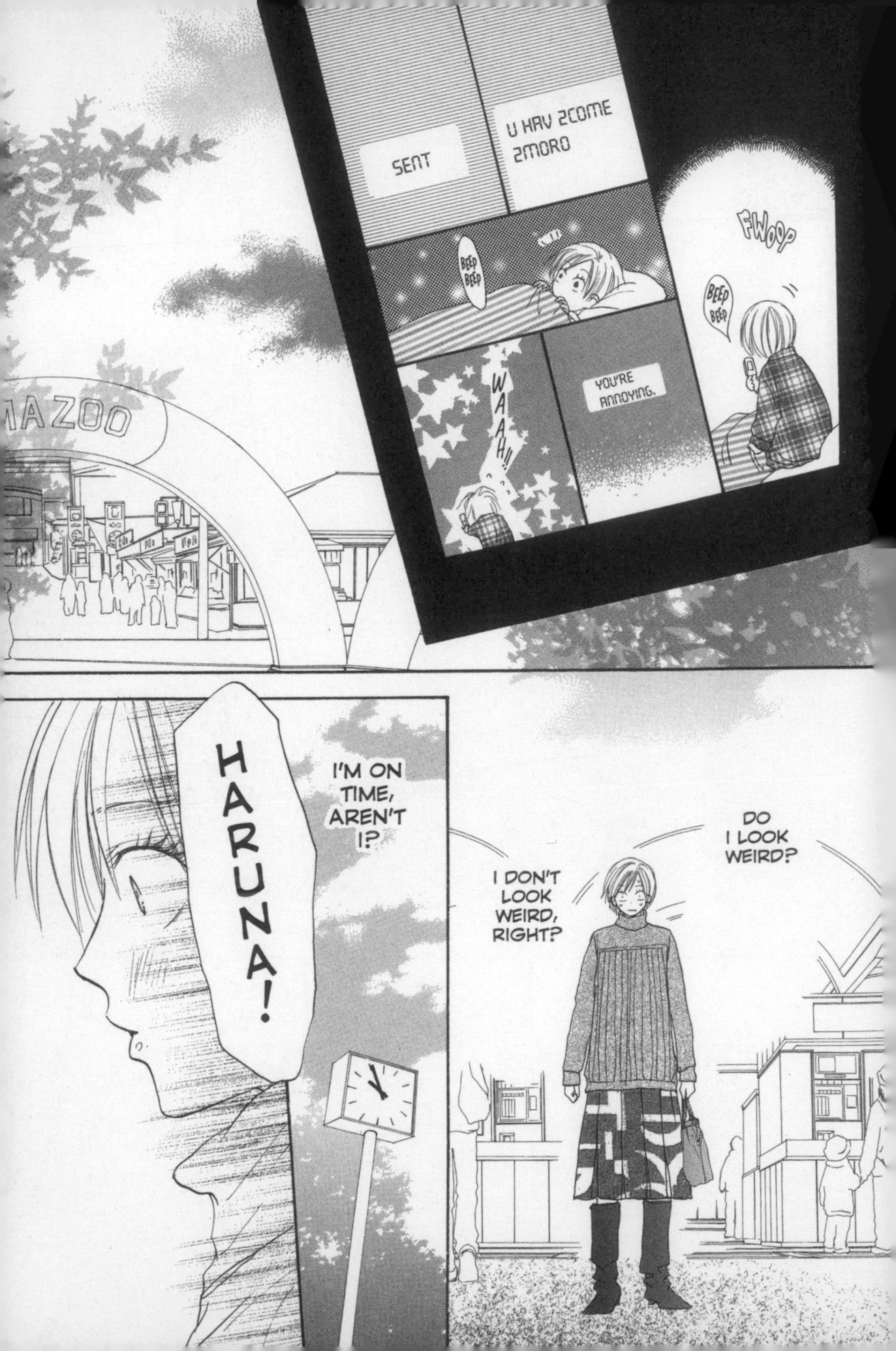
U HAV 2COME 2MORO
SENT
FWOOP
BEEP BEEP
BEEP BEEP
YOU'RE ANNOYING.
WAAAH!!
MAZOO
DO I LOOK WEIRD?
I DON'T LOOK WEIRD, RIGHT?
I'M ON TIME, AREN'T I?
HARUNA!

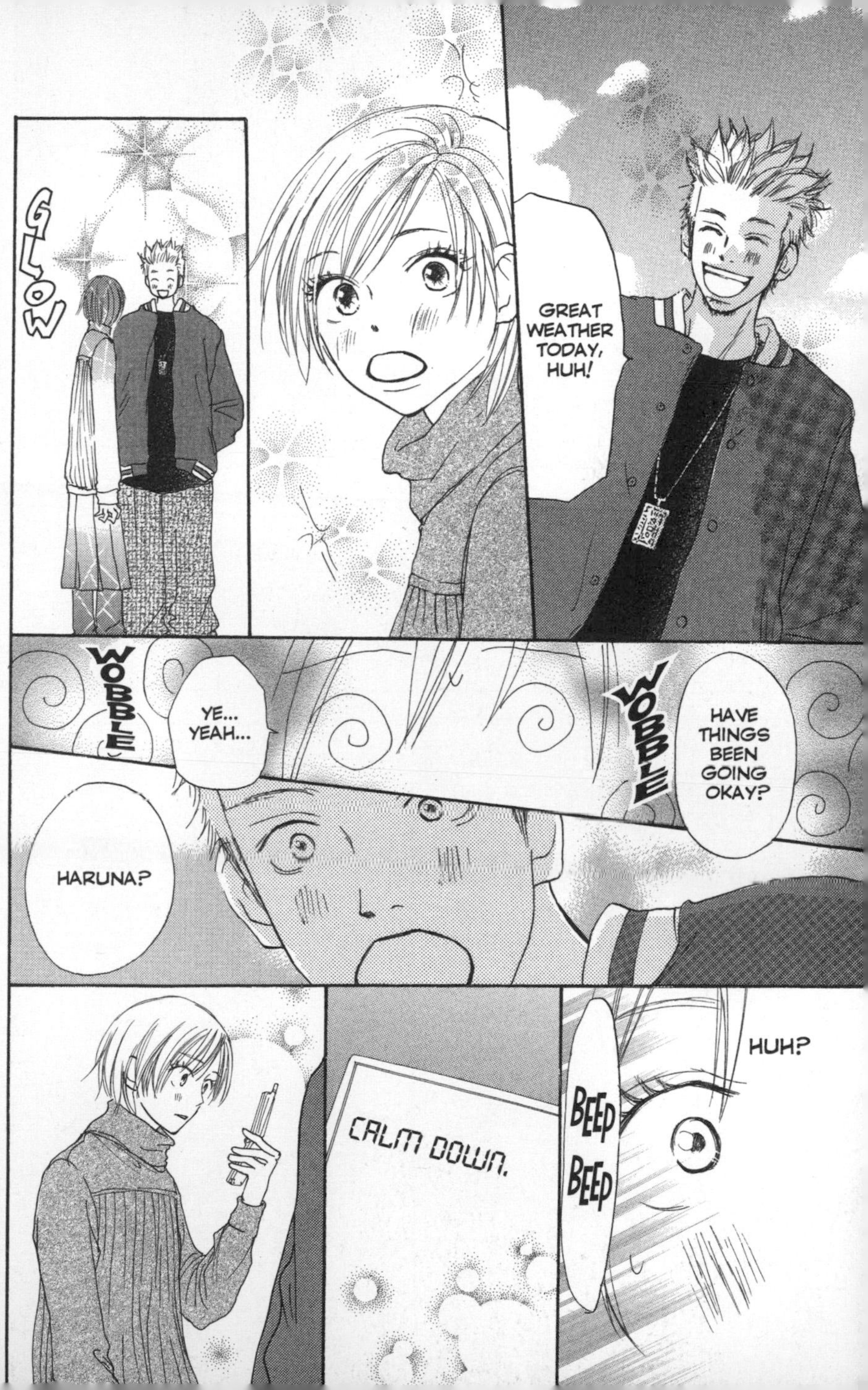
GREAT WEATHER TODAY, HUH!
GLOW
WOBBLE
HAVE THINGS BEEN GOING OKAY?
YE... YEAH...
WOBBLE
HARUNA?
HUH?
BEEP BEEP
CALM DOWN.

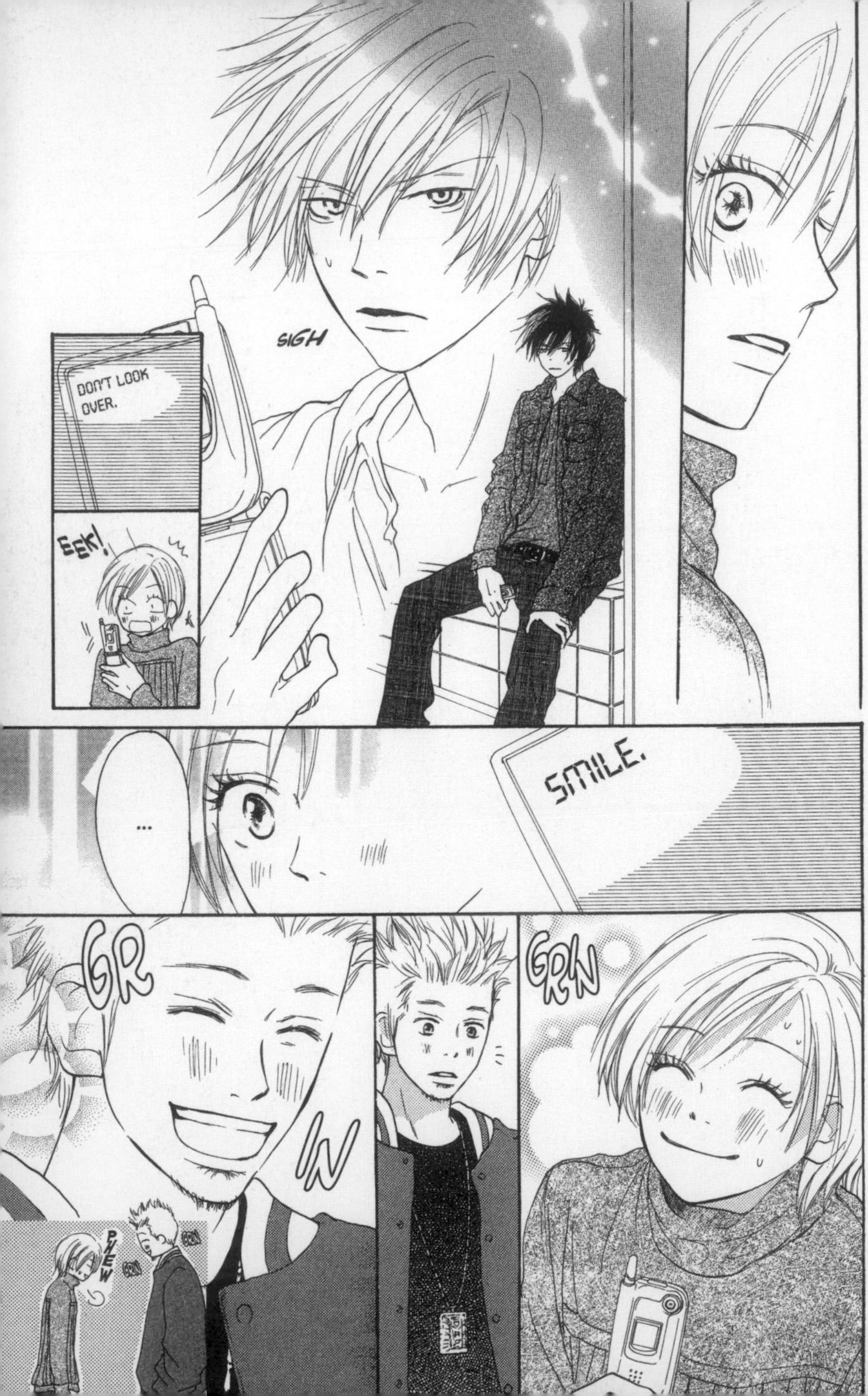

SIGH
DON'T LOOK OVER.
EEK!
SMILE.
...
GRIN
GRIN
PHEW
GRIN

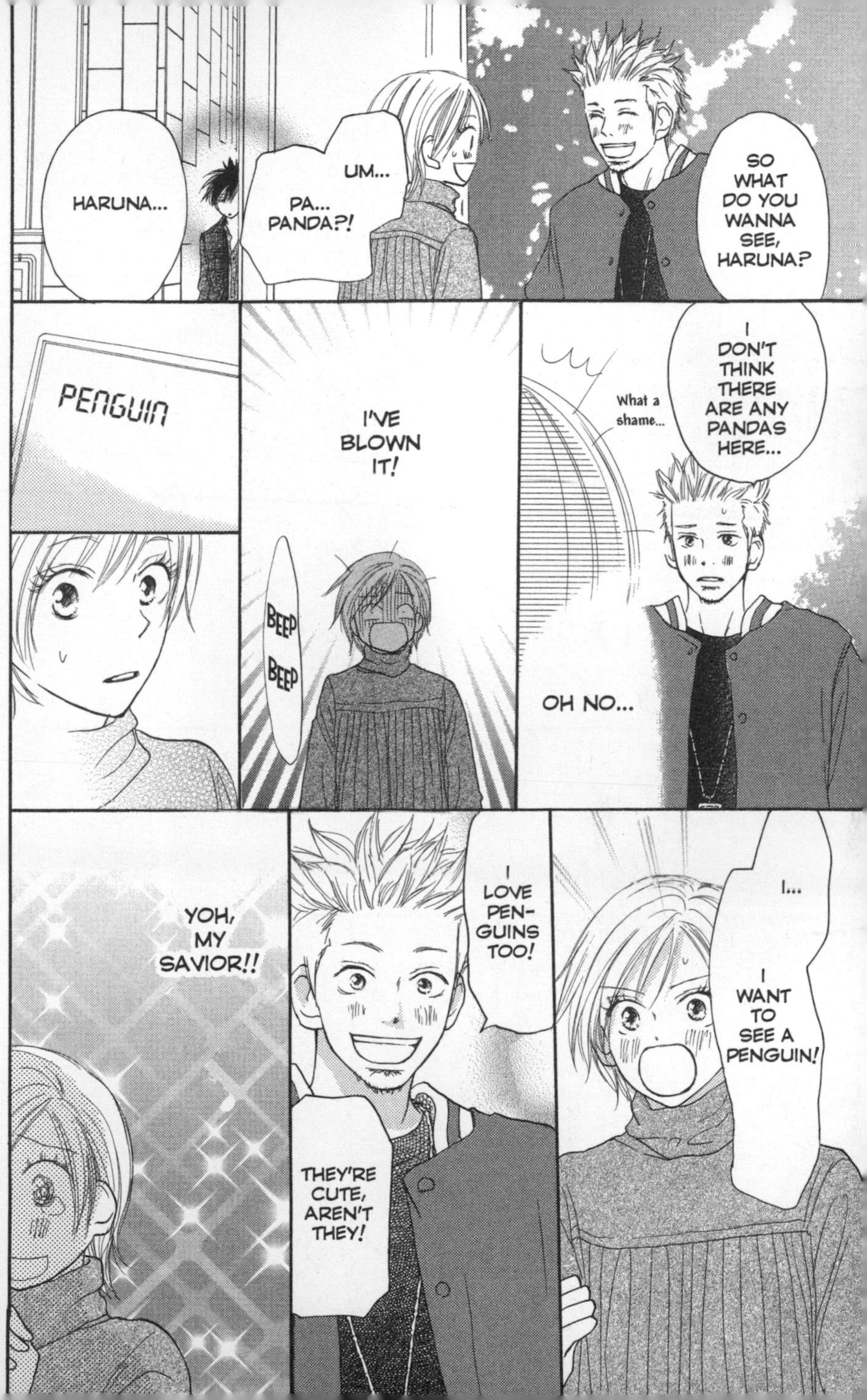
SO WHAT DO YOU WANNA SEE, HARUNA?
UM... PA... PANDA?!
HARUNA...
I DON'T THINK THERE ARE ANY PANDAS HERE...
What a shame...
OH NO...
I'VE BLOWN IT!
BEEP BEEP
PENGUIN
I... I WANT TO SEE A PENGUIN!
I LOVE PEN-GUINS TOO!
THEY'RE CUTE, AREN'T THEY!
YOH, MY SAVIOR!!

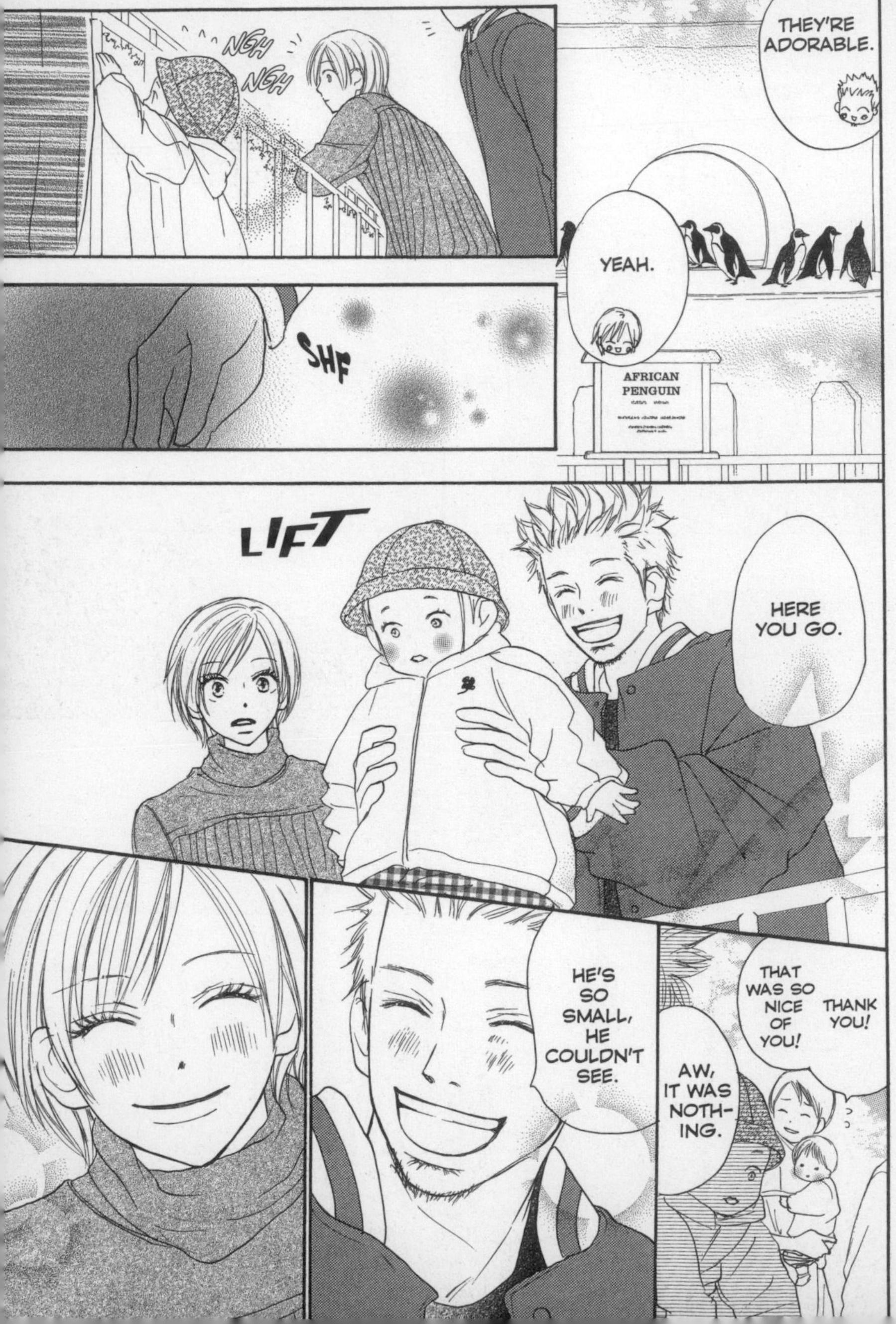
THEY'RE ADORABLE.
YEAH.
AFRICAN PENGUIN
NGH NGH
SHF
LIFT
HERE YOU GO.
THANK YOU!
THAT WAS SO NICE OF YOU!
AW, IT WAS NOTHING.
HE'S SO SMALL, HE COULDN'T SEE.

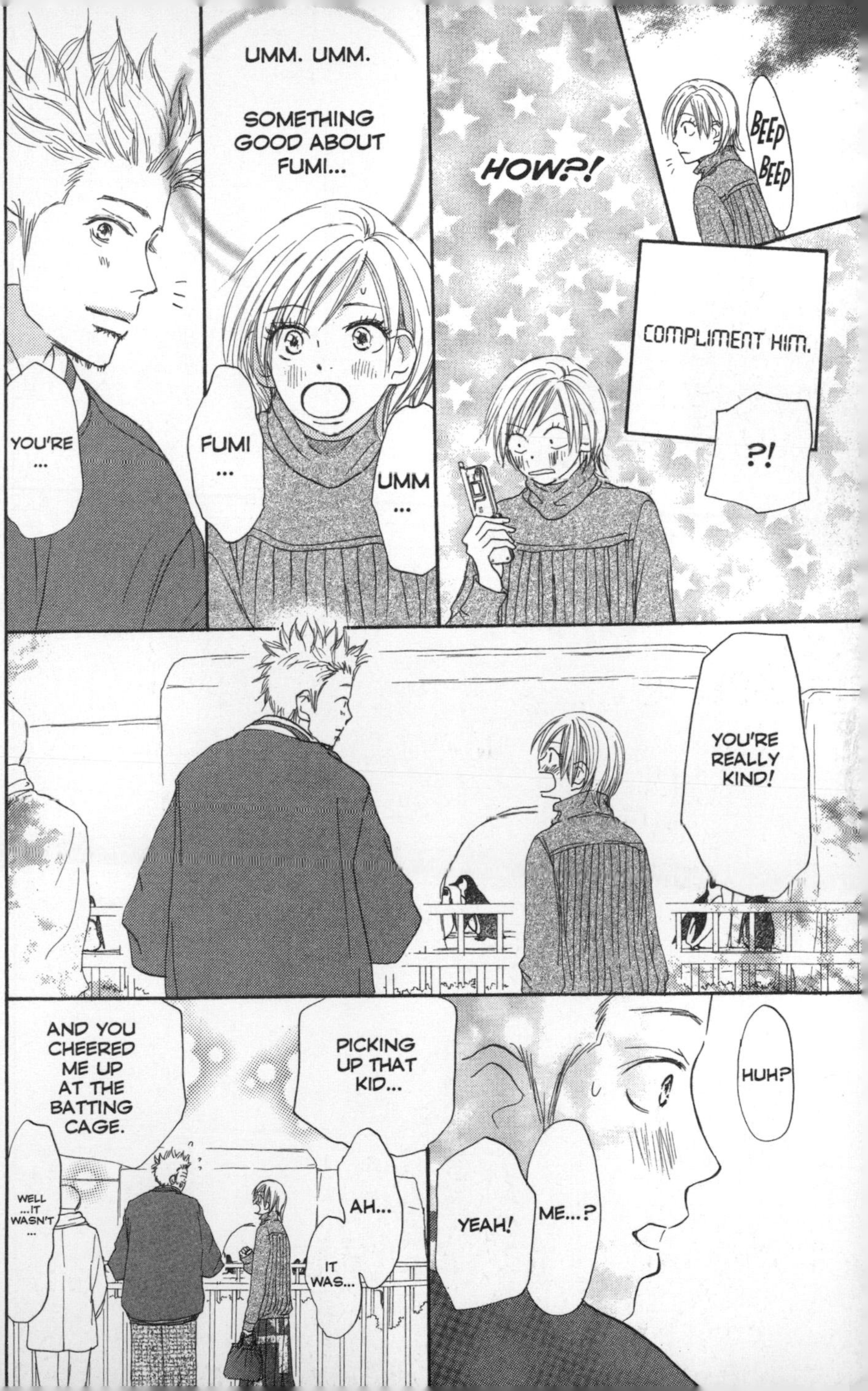
BEEP BEEP
COMPLIMENT HIM.
?!
HOW?!
UMM. UMM.
SOMETHING GOOD ABOUT FUMI...
UMM ...
FUMI ...
YOU'RE ...
YOU'RE REALLY KIND!
HUH?
ME...?
YEAH!
PICKING UP THAT KID...
AND YOU CHEERED ME UP AT THE BATTING CAGE.
AH...
IT WAS...
WELL ...IT WASN'T ...

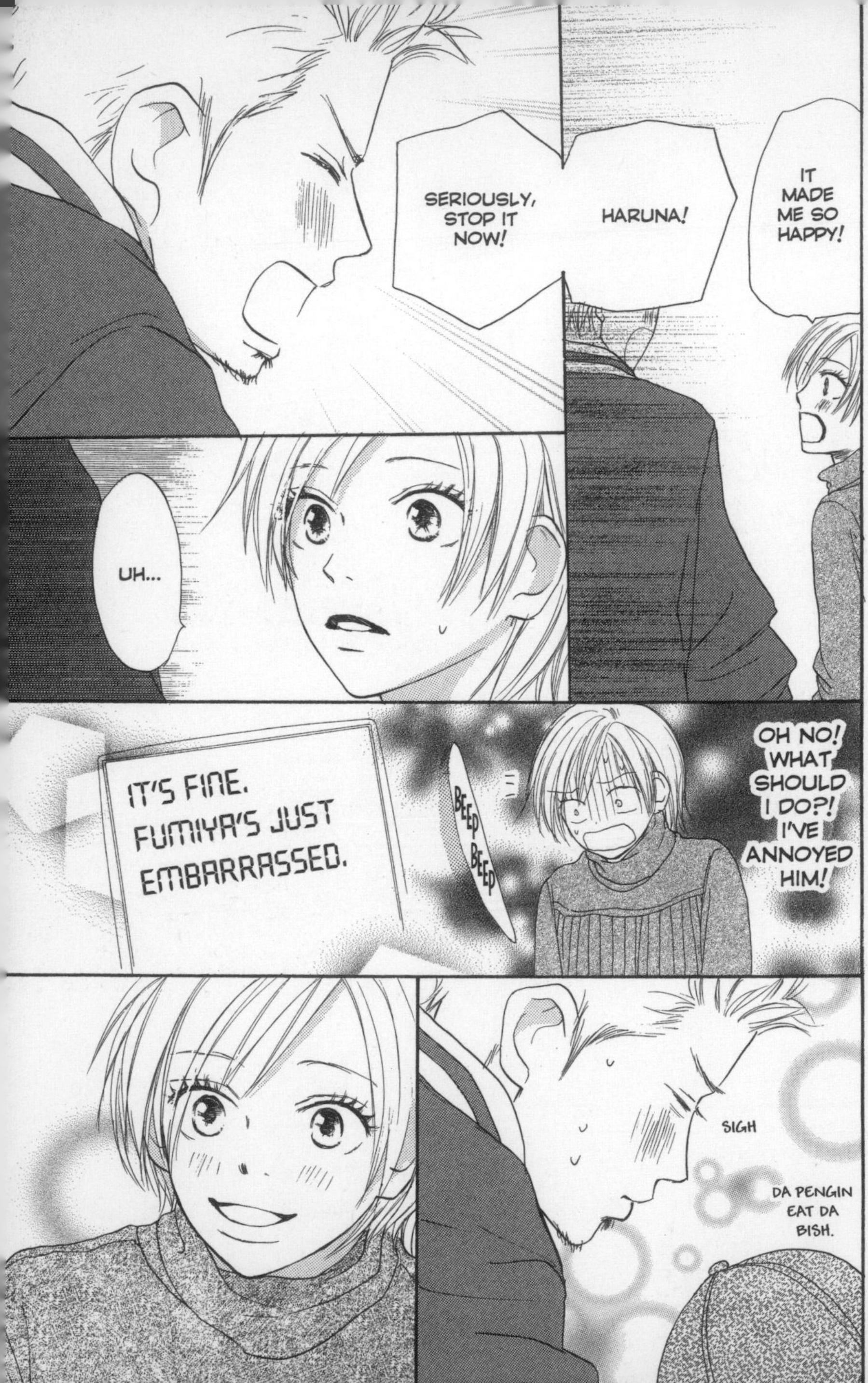
IT MADE ME SO HAPPY!
HARUNA!
SERIOUSLY, STOP IT NOW!
UH...
OH NO! WHAT SHOULD I DO?! I'VE ANNOYED HIM!
BEEP BEEP
IT'S FINE. FUMIYA'S JUST EMBARRASSED.
SIGH
DA PENGIN EAT DA BISH.

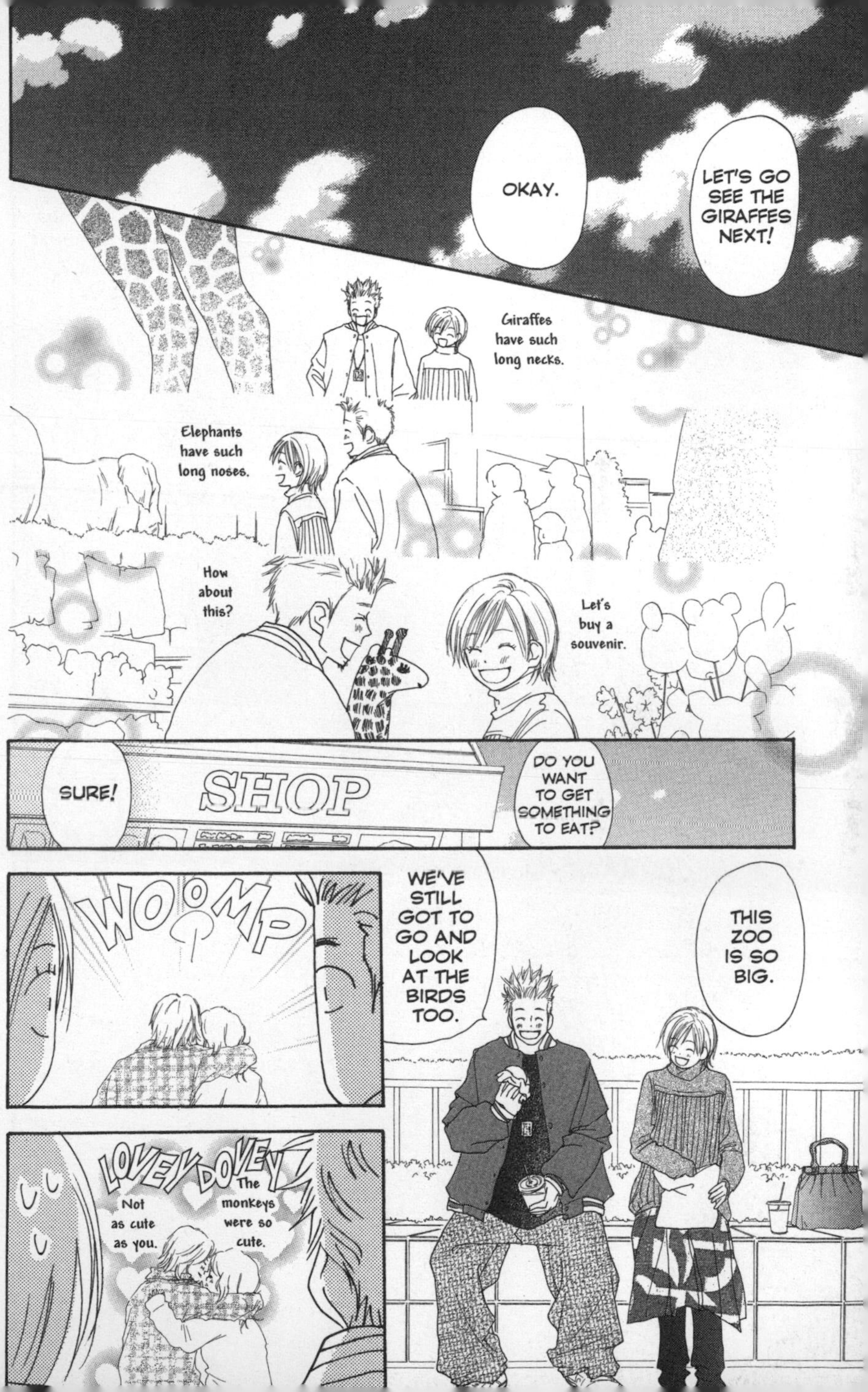
LET'S GO SEE THE GIRAFFES NEXT!
OKAY.
Giraffes have such long necks.
Elephants have such long noses.
Let's buy a souvenir.
How about this?
DO YOU WANT TO GET SOMETHING TO EAT?
SHOP
SURE!
THIS ZOO IS SO BIG.
WE'VE STILL GOT TO GO AND LOOK AT THE BIRDS TOO.
WOOMP
LOVEY DOVEY
The monkeys were so cute.
Not as cute as you.

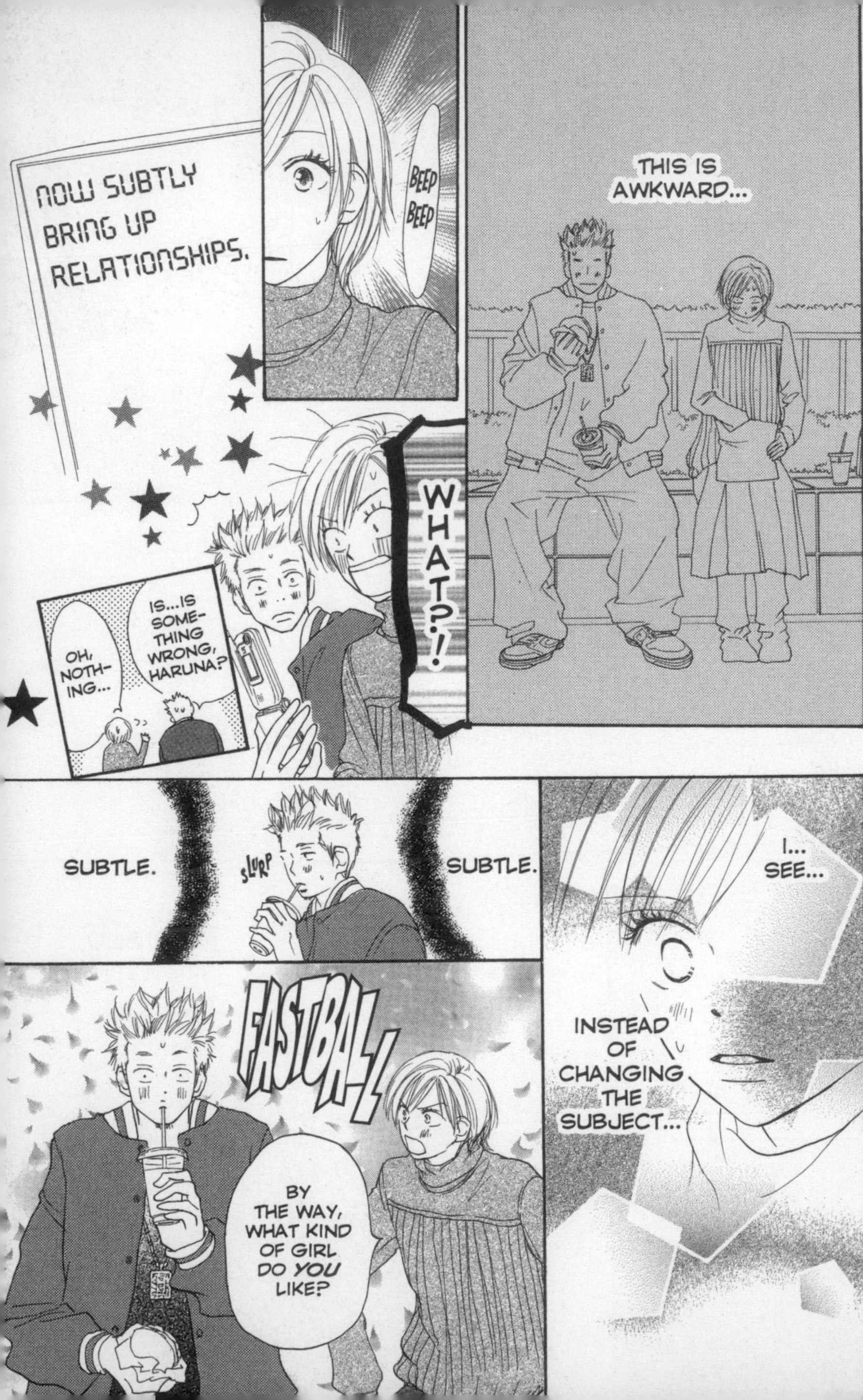
THIS IS AWKWARD...
BEEP BEEP
NOW SUBTLY BRING UP RELATIONSHIPS.
WHAT?!
IS...IS SOME-THING WRONG, HARUNA?
OH, NOTHING...
I... SEE...
INSTEAD OF CHANGING THE SUBJECT...
SUBTLE.
SLURP
SUBTLE.
FASTBALL
BY THE WAY, WHAT KIND OF GIRL DO YOU LIKE?

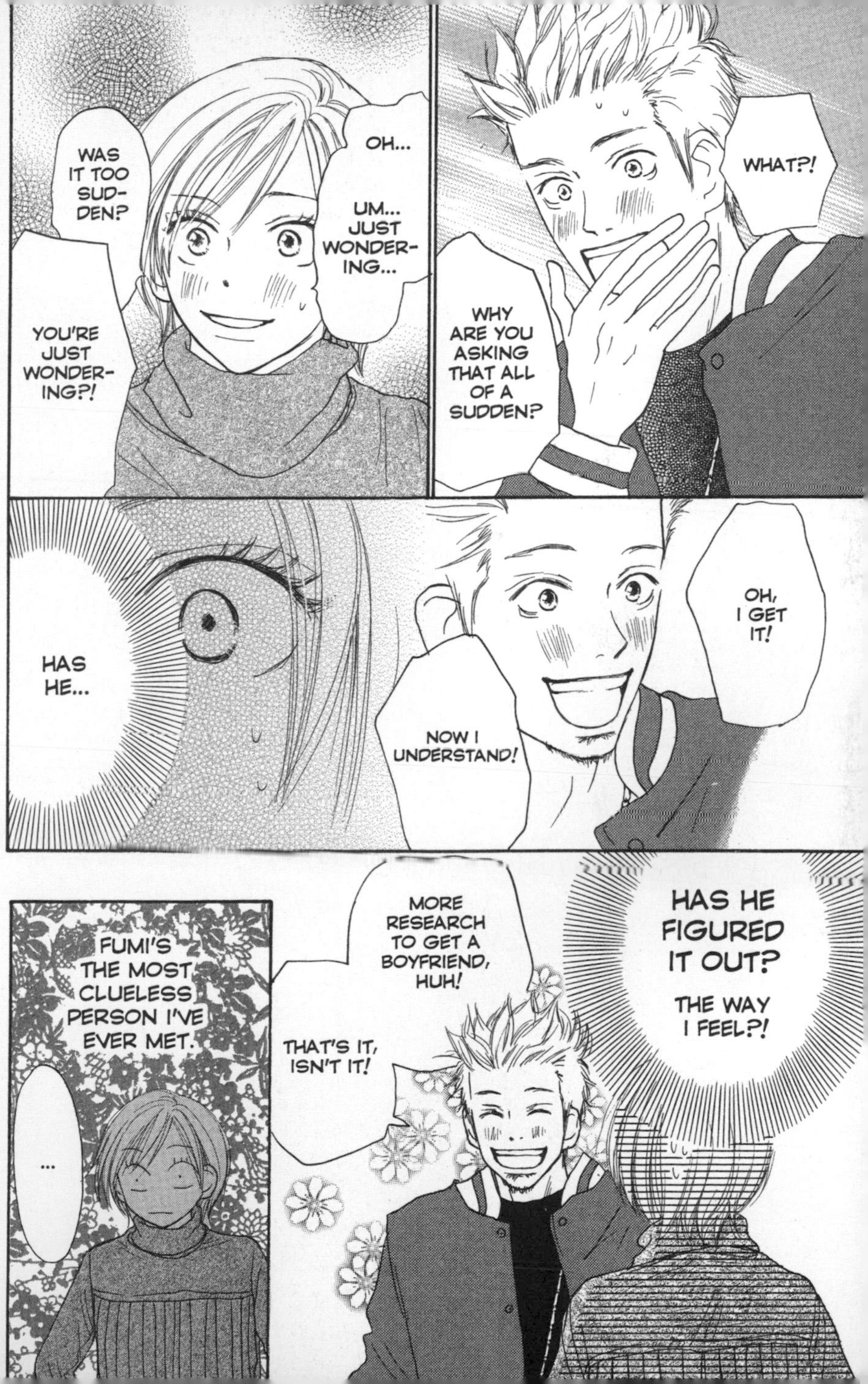
WHAT?!
WHY ARE YOU ASKING THAT ALL OF A SUDDEN?
OH...
UM... JUST WONDERING...
WAS IT TOO SUD-DEN?
YOU'RE JUST WONDER-ING?!
OH, I GET IT!
NOW I UNDERSTAND!
HAS HE...
HAS HE FIGURED IT OUT?
THE WAY I FEEL?!
MORE RESEARCH TO GET A BOYFRIEND, HUH!
THAT'S IT, ISN'T IT!
FUMI'S THE MOST CLUELESS PERSON I'VE EVER MET.
...

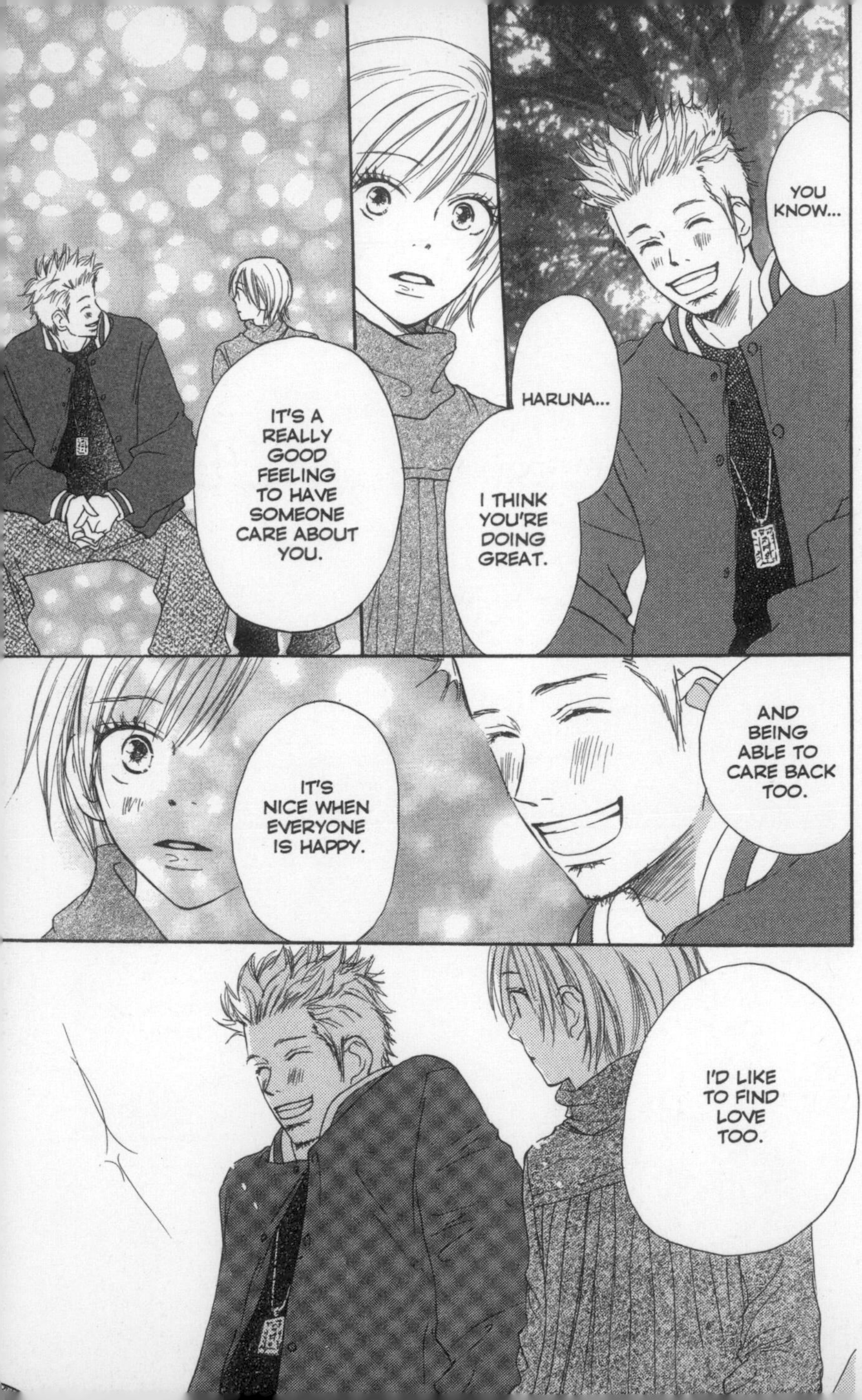
YOU KNOW...
HARUNA...
I THINK YOU'RE DOING GREAT.
IT'S A REALLY GOOD FEELING TO HAVE SOMEONE CARE ABOUT YOU.
AND BEING ABLE TO CARE BACK TOO.
IT'S NICE WHEN EVERYONE IS HAPPY.
I'D LIKE TO FIND LOVE TOO.

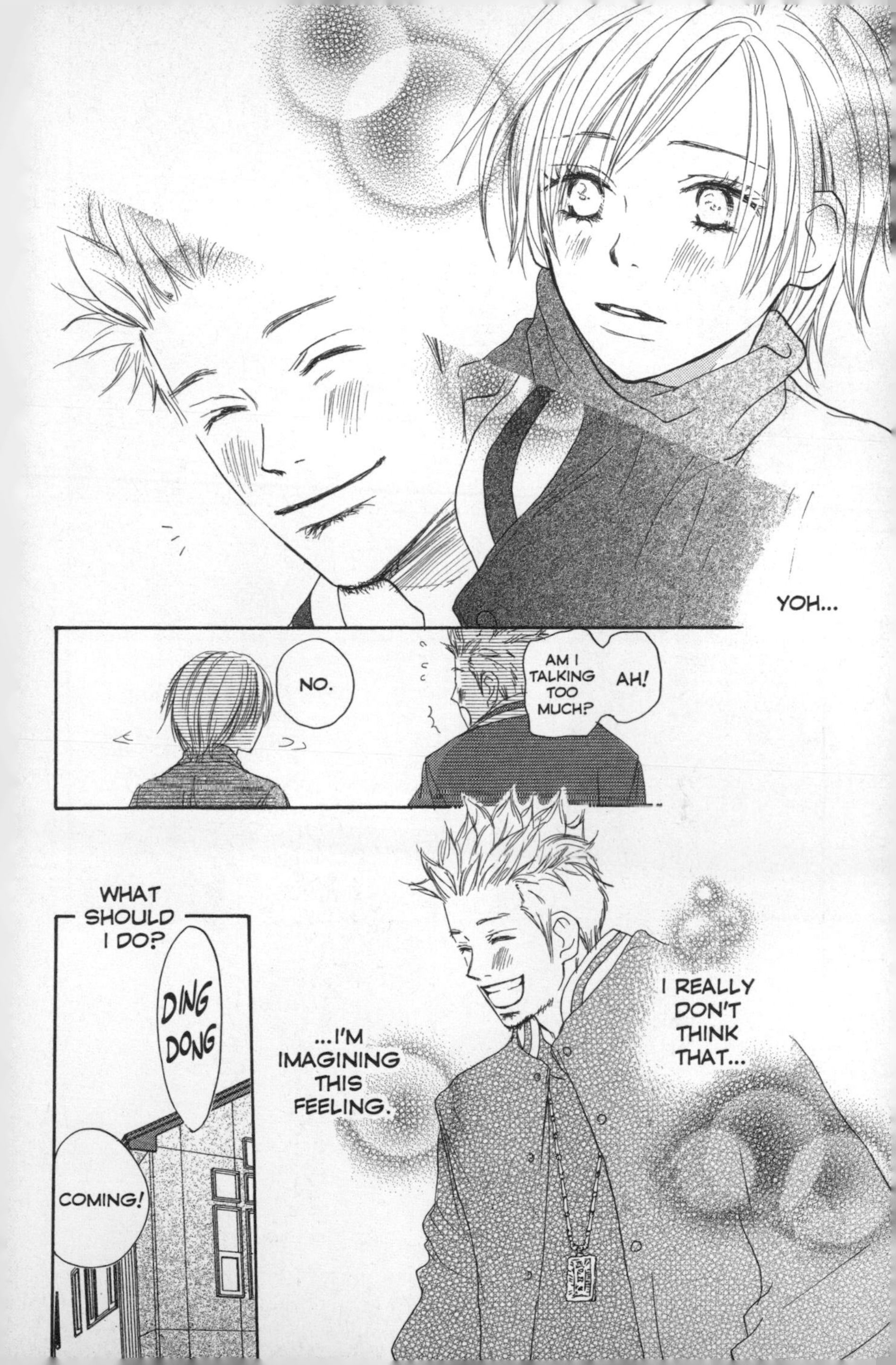

YOH...
AH!
AM I TALKING TOO MUCH?
NO.
I REALLY DON'T THINK THAT...
...I'M IMAGINING THIS FEELING.
WHAT SHOULD I DO?
DING DONG
COMING!

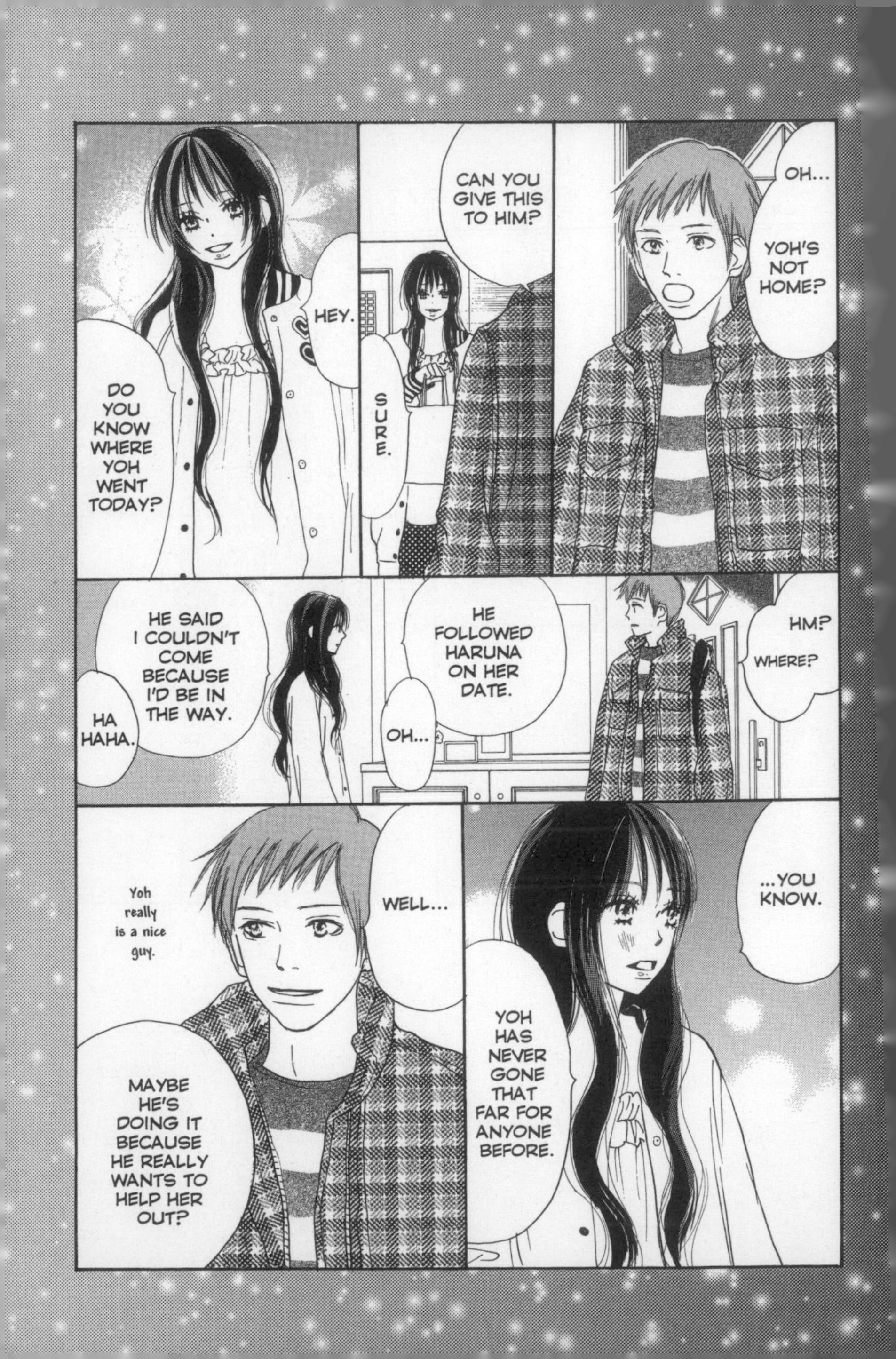
OH...
YOH'S NOT HOME?
CAN YOU GIVE THIS TO HIM?
SURE.
HEY.
DO YOU KNOW WHERE YOH WENT TODAY?
HM?
WHERE?
HE FOLLOWED HARUNA ON HER DATE.
OH...
HE SAID I COULDN'T COME BECAUSE I'D BE IN THE WAY.
HA HAHA.
...YOU KNOW.
YOH HAS NEVER GONE THAT FAR FOR ANYONE BEFORE.
WELL...
Yoh really is a nice guy.
MAYBE HE'S DOING IT BECAUSE HE REALLY WANTS TO HELP HER OUT?

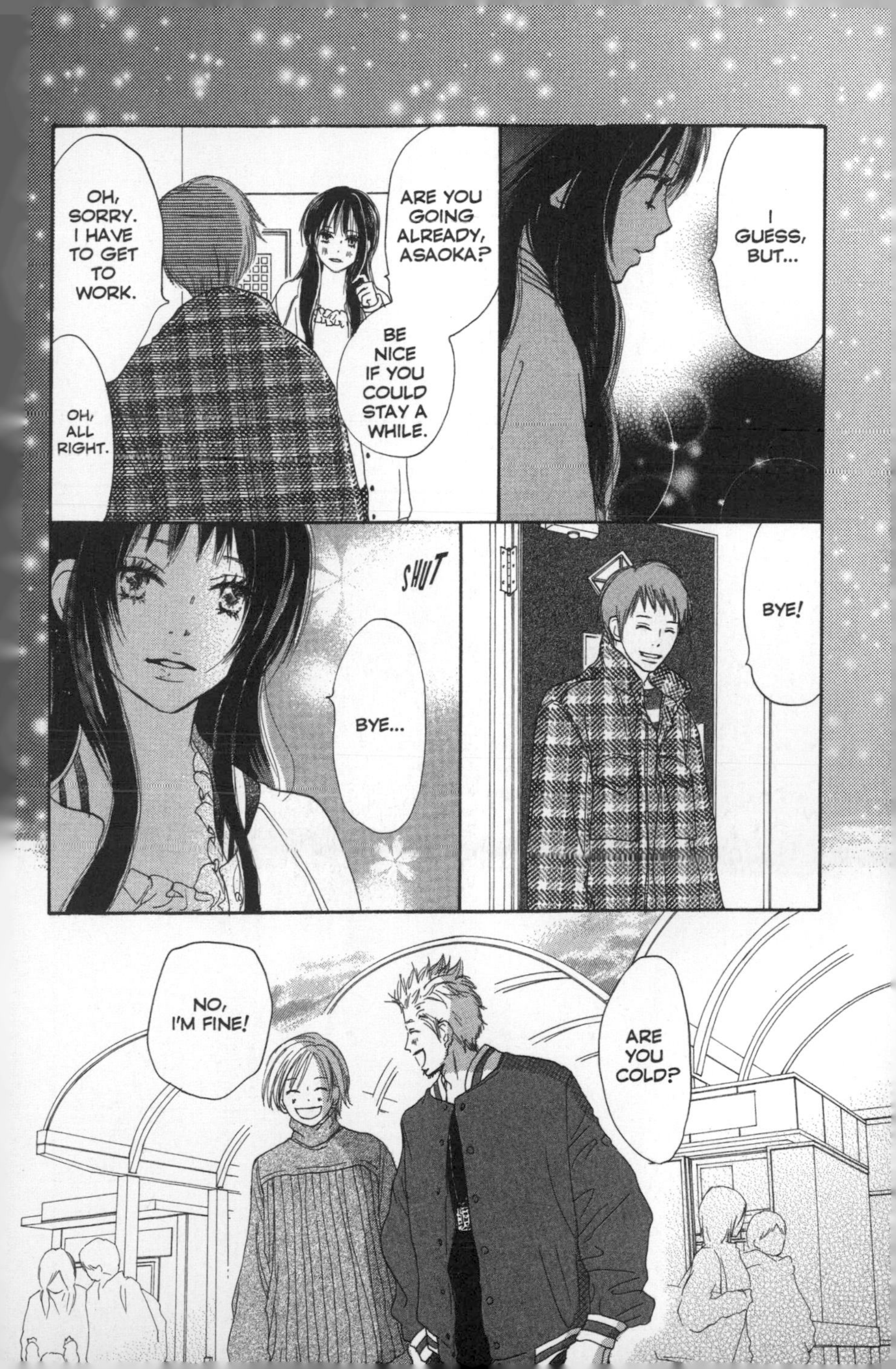
I GUESS, BUT...
ARE YOU GOING ALREADY, ASAOKA?
OH, SORRY. I HAVE TO GET TO WORK.
BE NICE IF YOU COULD STAY A WHILE.
OH, ALL RIGHT.
BYE!
SHUT
BYE...
ARE YOU COLD?
NO, I'M FINE!

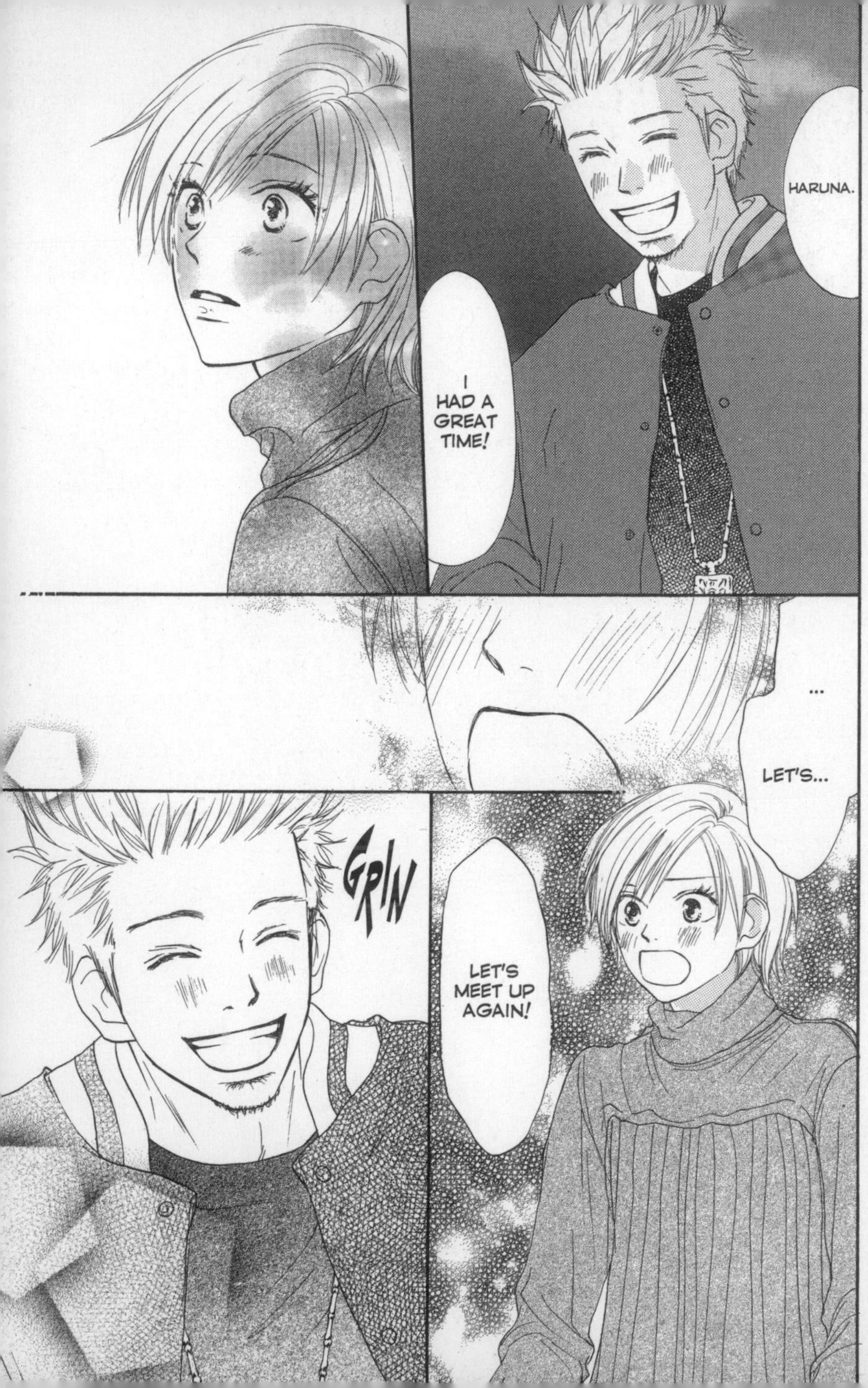
HARUNA.
I HAD A GREAT TIME!
...
LET'S...
LET'S MEET UP AGAIN!
GRIN

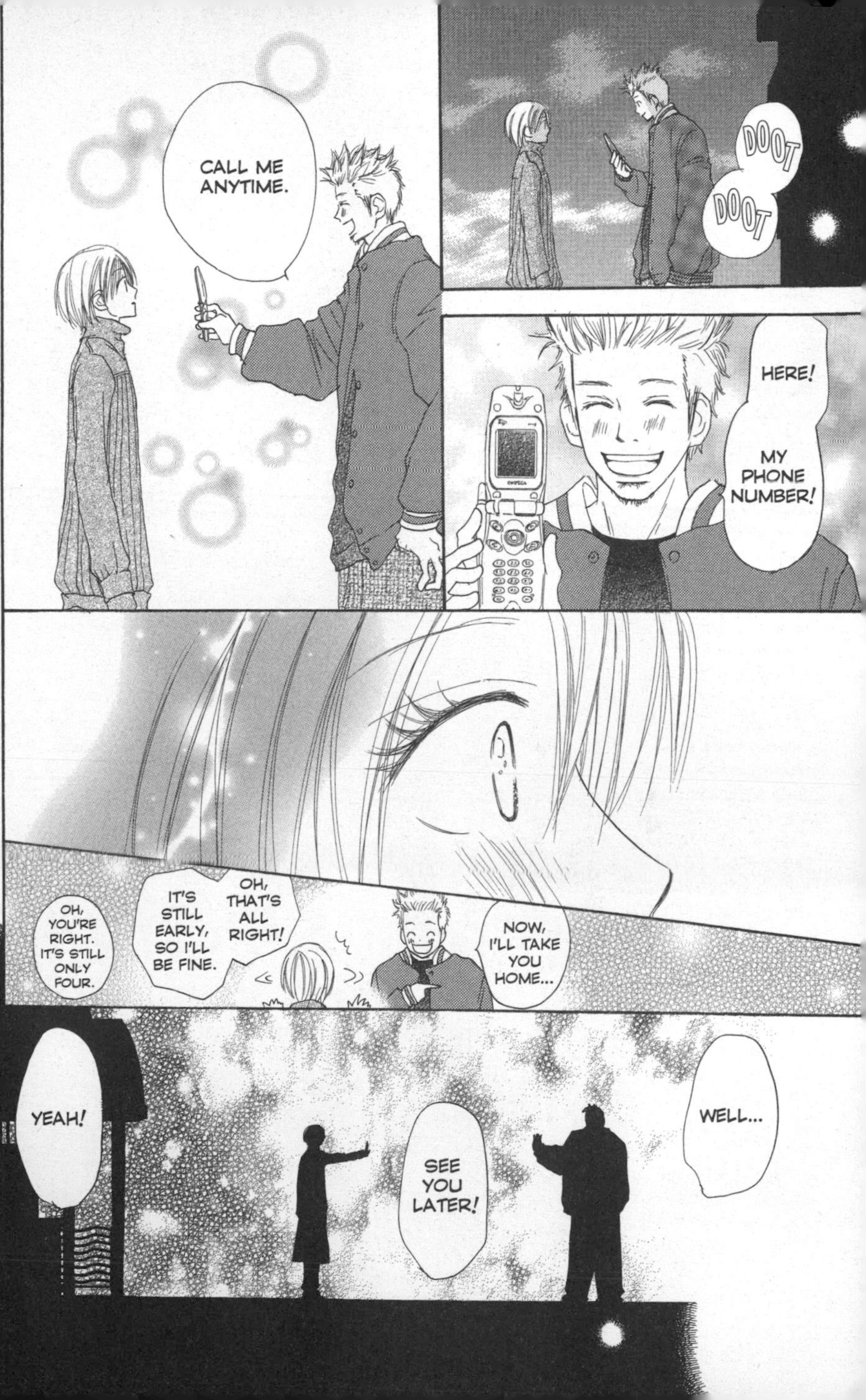
DOOT
DOOT
HERE!
MY PHONE NUMBER!
CALL ME ANYTIME.
NOW, I'LL TAKE YOU HOME...
OH, THAT'S ALL RIGHT!
IT'S STILL EARLY, SO I'LL BE FINE.
OH, YOU'RE RIGHT. IT'S STILL ONLY FOUR.
WELL...
SEE YOU LATER!
YEAH!

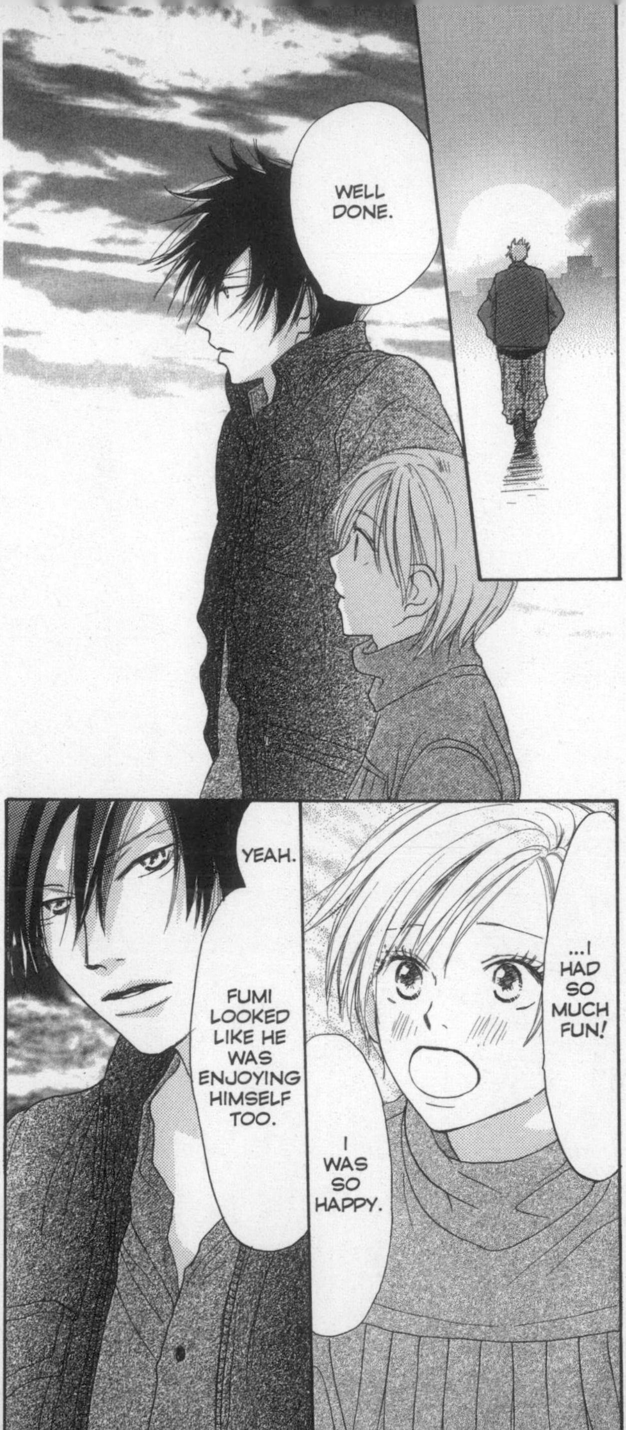
WELL DONE.
...I HAD SO MUCH FUN!
I WAS SO HAPPY.
FUMI LOOKED LIKE HE WAS ENJOYING HIMSELF TOO.
YEAH.

1

Hello. It's the terribly forgetful Kawahara here. I was watching T.V. today. They said that the reason for early forgetfulness was bad kidneys and that I should drink sword bean tea. I'll go get some tomorrow. What if it makes me come up with some great ideas for manga? Something that would make me really concentrate every day. Or allow me to finish something in one day! I would drink anything... I would eat anything...

This is unrelated, but when I was small, I was really picky. Spinach was the only vegetable I'd really eat. I had lots of likes and dislikes, but I really loved to eat spinach and drink milk.

The milk I got for lunch was never enough.

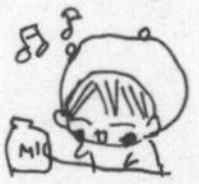

At home, they'll always give me milk instead of water unless I say something.

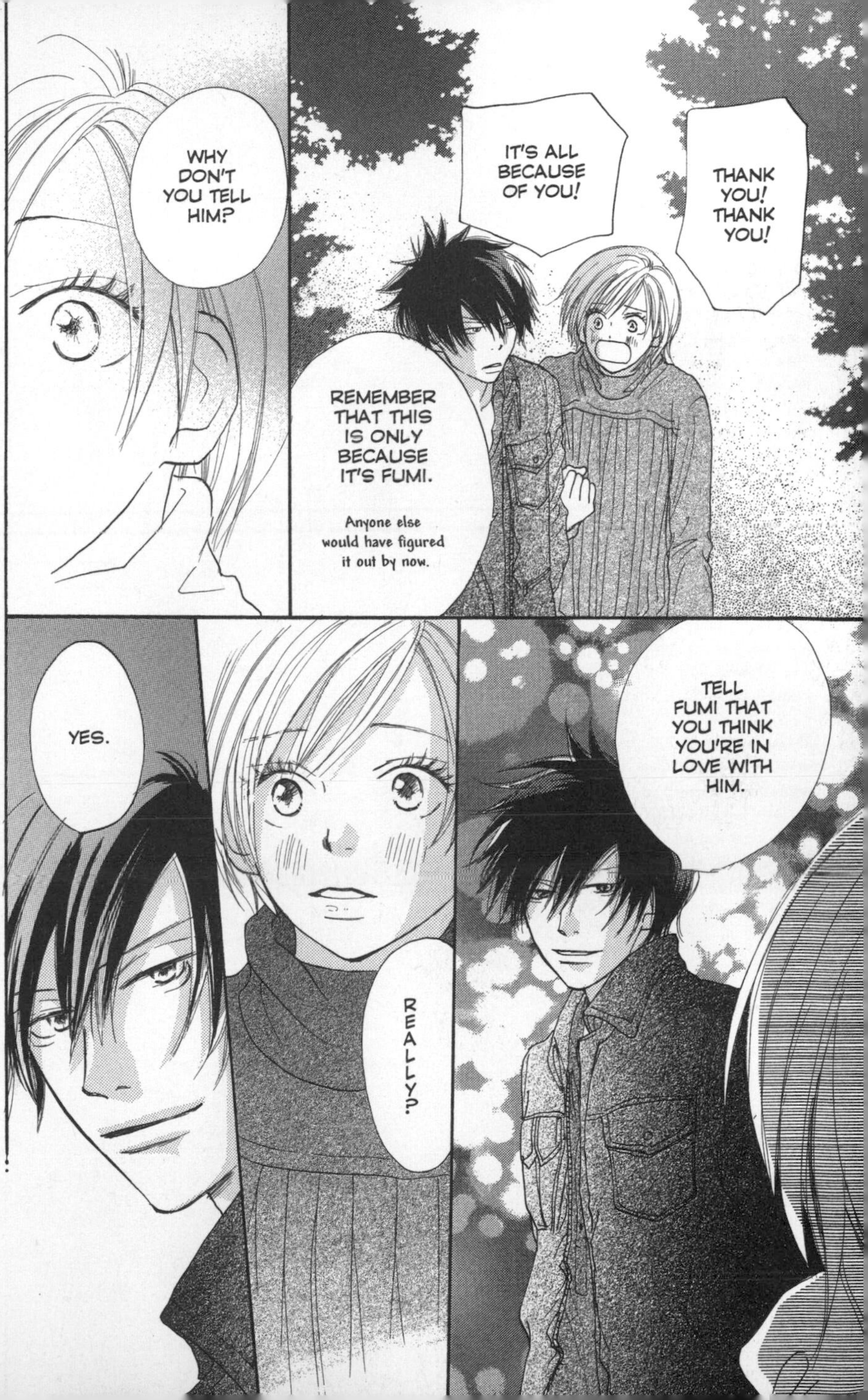
THANK YOU! THANK YOU!
IT'S ALL BECAUSE OF YOU!
REMEMBER THAT THIS IS ONLY BECAUSE IT'S FUMI.
Anyone else would have figured it out by now.
WHY DON'T YOU TELL HIM?
TELL FUMI THAT YOU THINK YOU'RE IN LOVE WITH HIM.
REALLY?
YES.

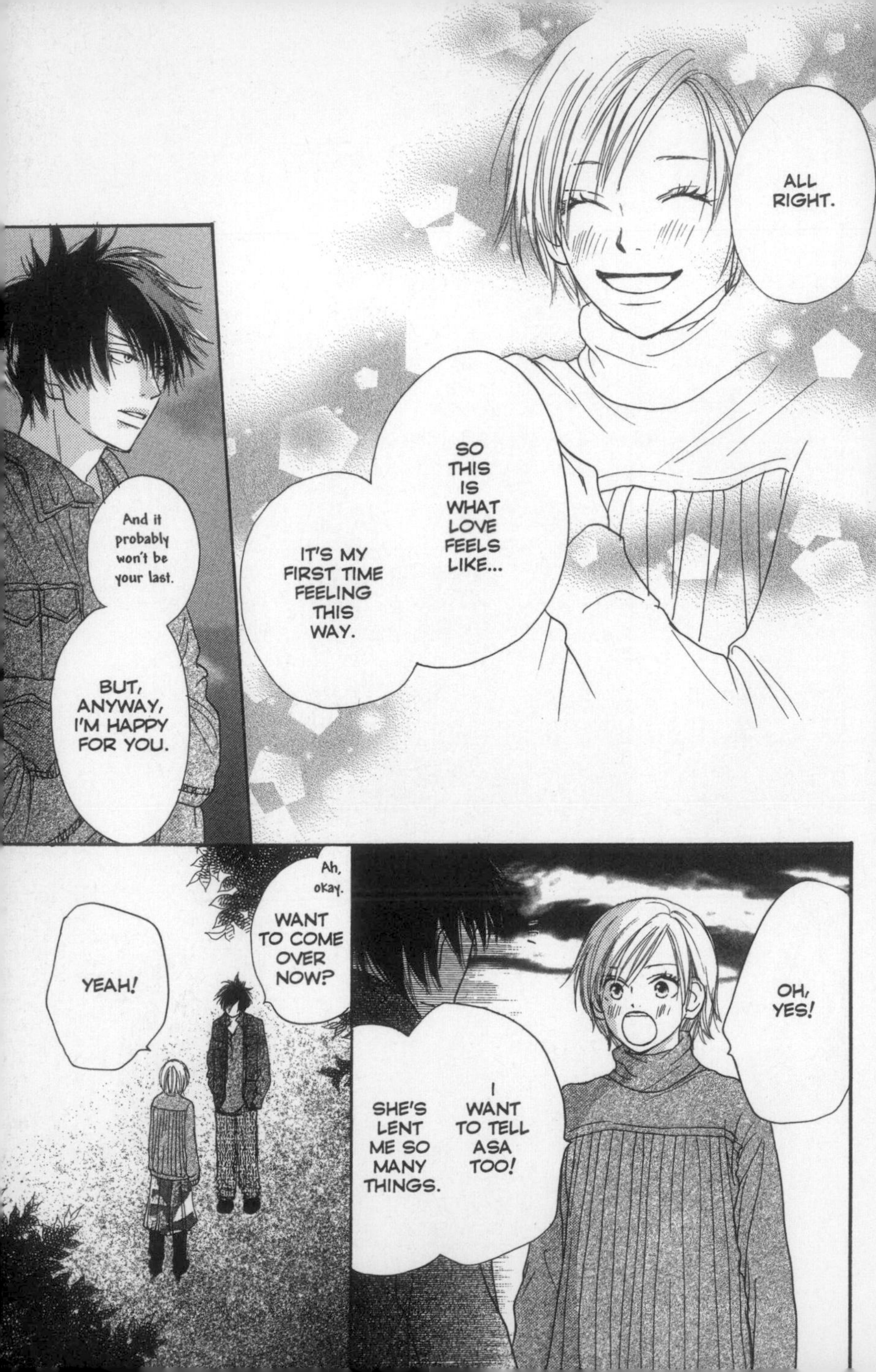

ALL RIGHT.
SO THIS IS WHAT LOVE FEELS LIKE...
IT'S MY FIRST TIME FEELING THIS WAY.
And it probably won't be your last.
BUT, ANYWAY, I'M HAPPY FOR YOU.
OH, YES!
I WANT TO TELL ASA TOO!
SHE'S LENT ME SO MANY THINGS.
Ah, okay.
WANT TO COME OVER NOW?
YEAH!

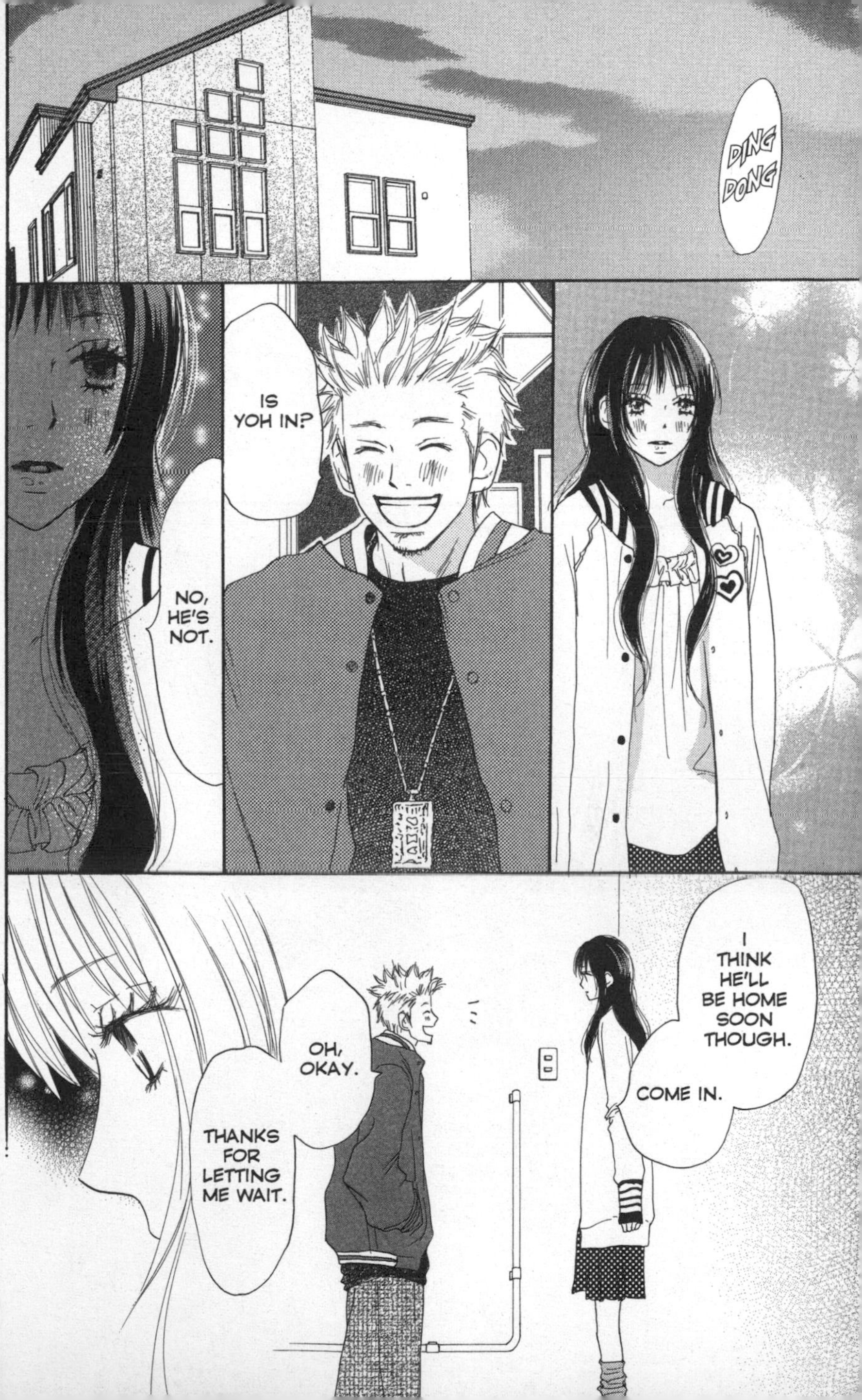
DING DONG
IS YOH IN?
NO, HE'S NOT.
I THINK HE'LL BE HOME SOON THOUGH.
COME IN.
OH, OKAY.
THANKS FOR LETTING ME WAIT.

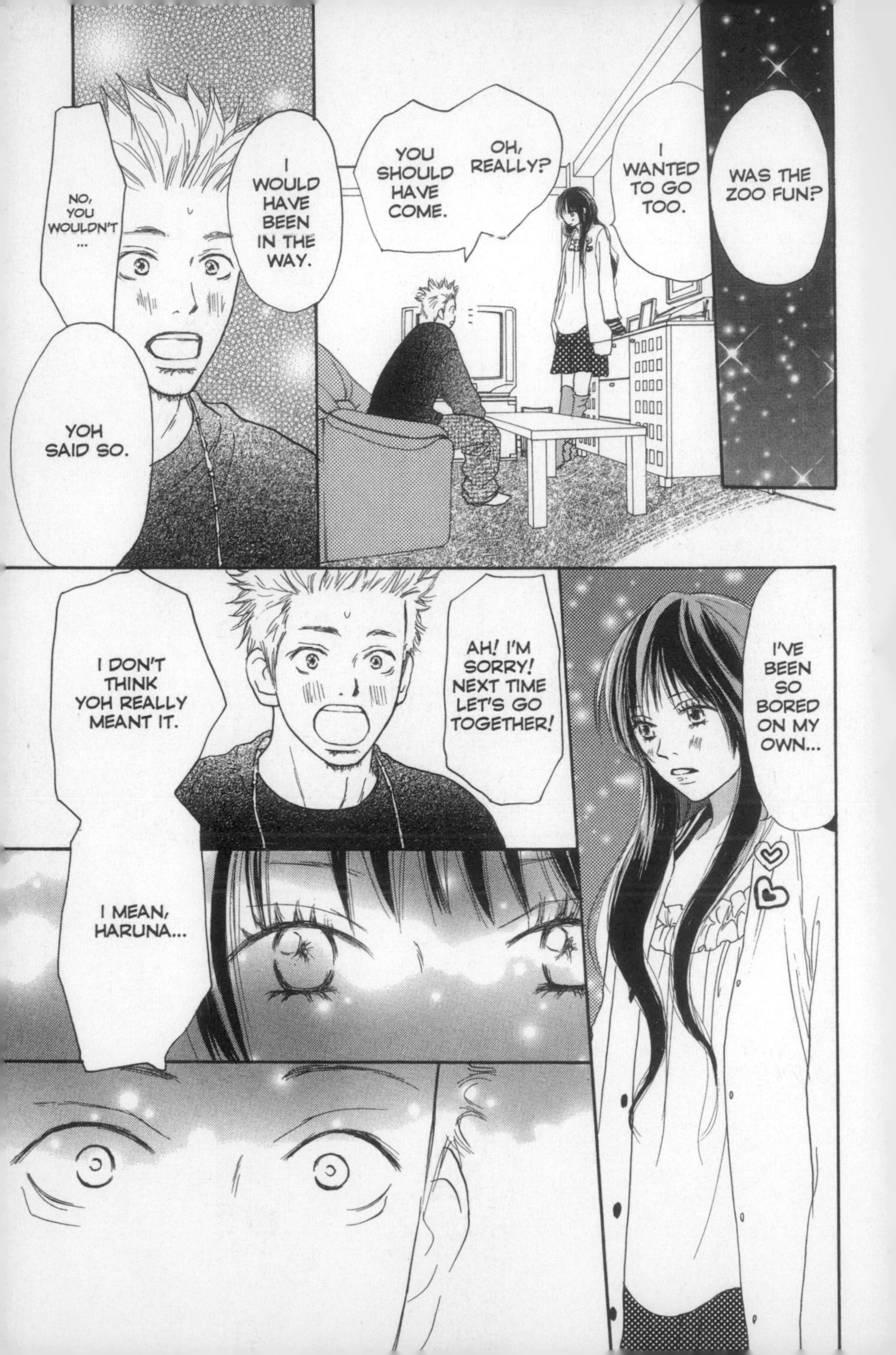
WAS THE ZOO FUN?
I WANTED TO GO TOO.
OH, REALLY?
YOU SHOULD HAVE COME.
I WOULD HAVE BEEN IN THE WAY.
NO, YOU WOULDN'T ...
YOH SAID SO.
I'VE BEEN SO BORED ON MY OWN...
AH! I'M SORRY! NEXT TIME LET'S GO TOGETHER!
I DON'T THINK YOH REALLY MEANT IT.
I MEAN, HARUNA...

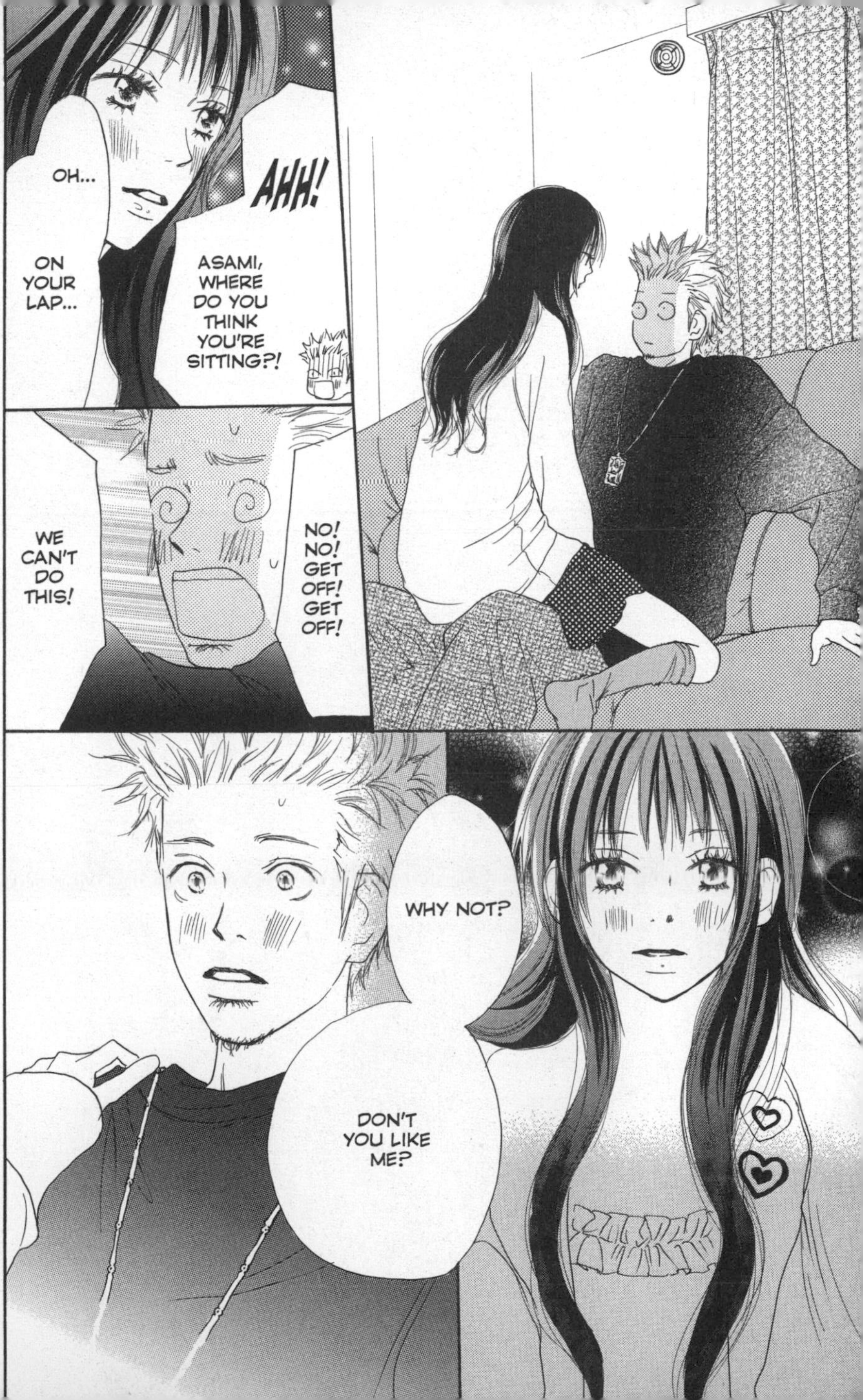

AHH!
ASAMI, WHERE DO YOU THINK YOU'RE SITTING?!
OH...
ON YOUR LAP...
NO! NO! GET OFF! GET OFF!
WE CAN'T DO THIS!
WHY NOT?
DON'T YOU LIKE ME?

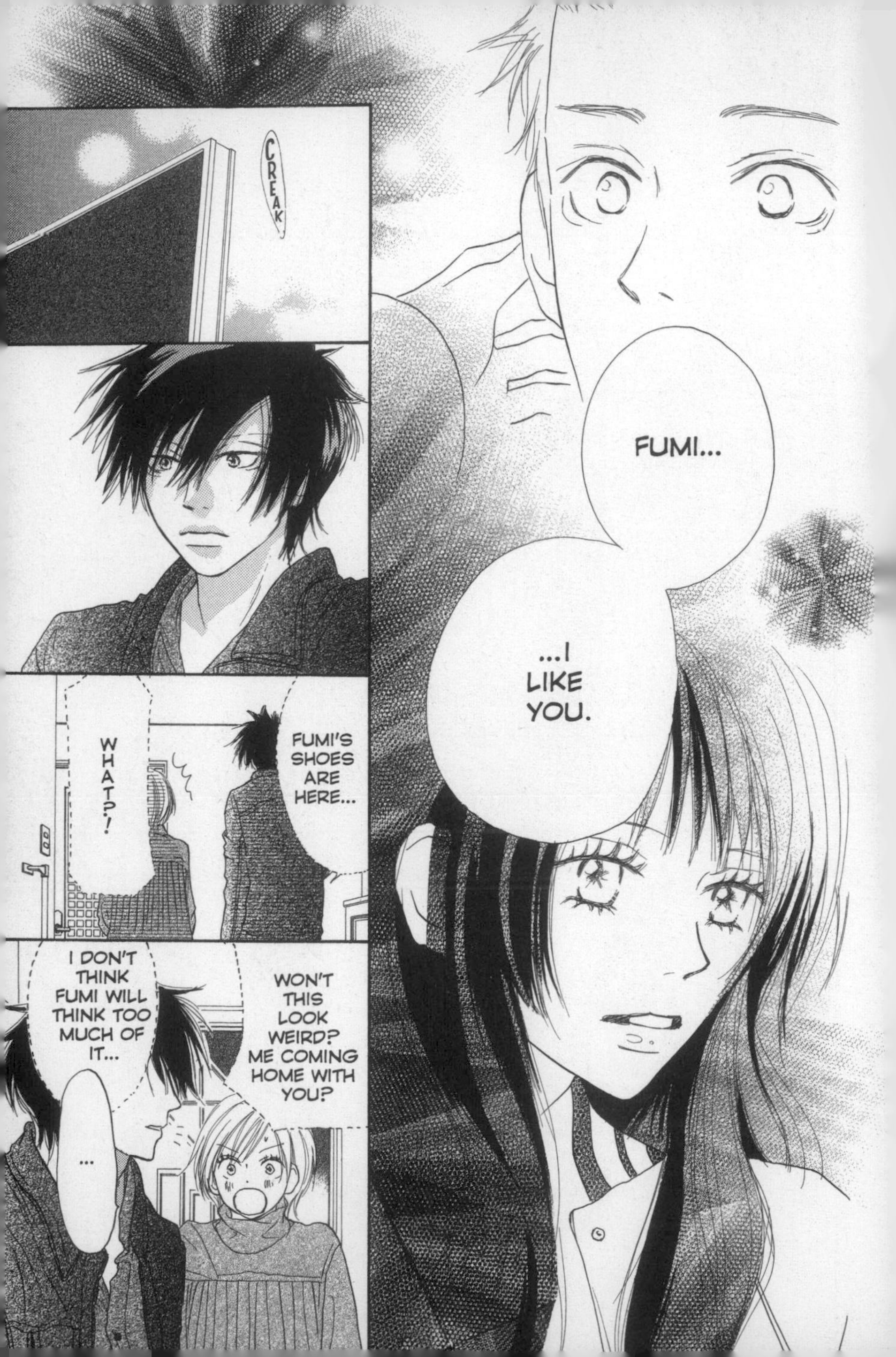
FUMI...
...I LIKE YOU.
CREAK
FUMI'S SHOES ARE HERE...
WHAT?!
WON'T THIS LOOK WEIRD? ME COMING HOME WITH YOU?
I DON'T THINK FUMI WILL THINK TOO MUCH OF IT...
...

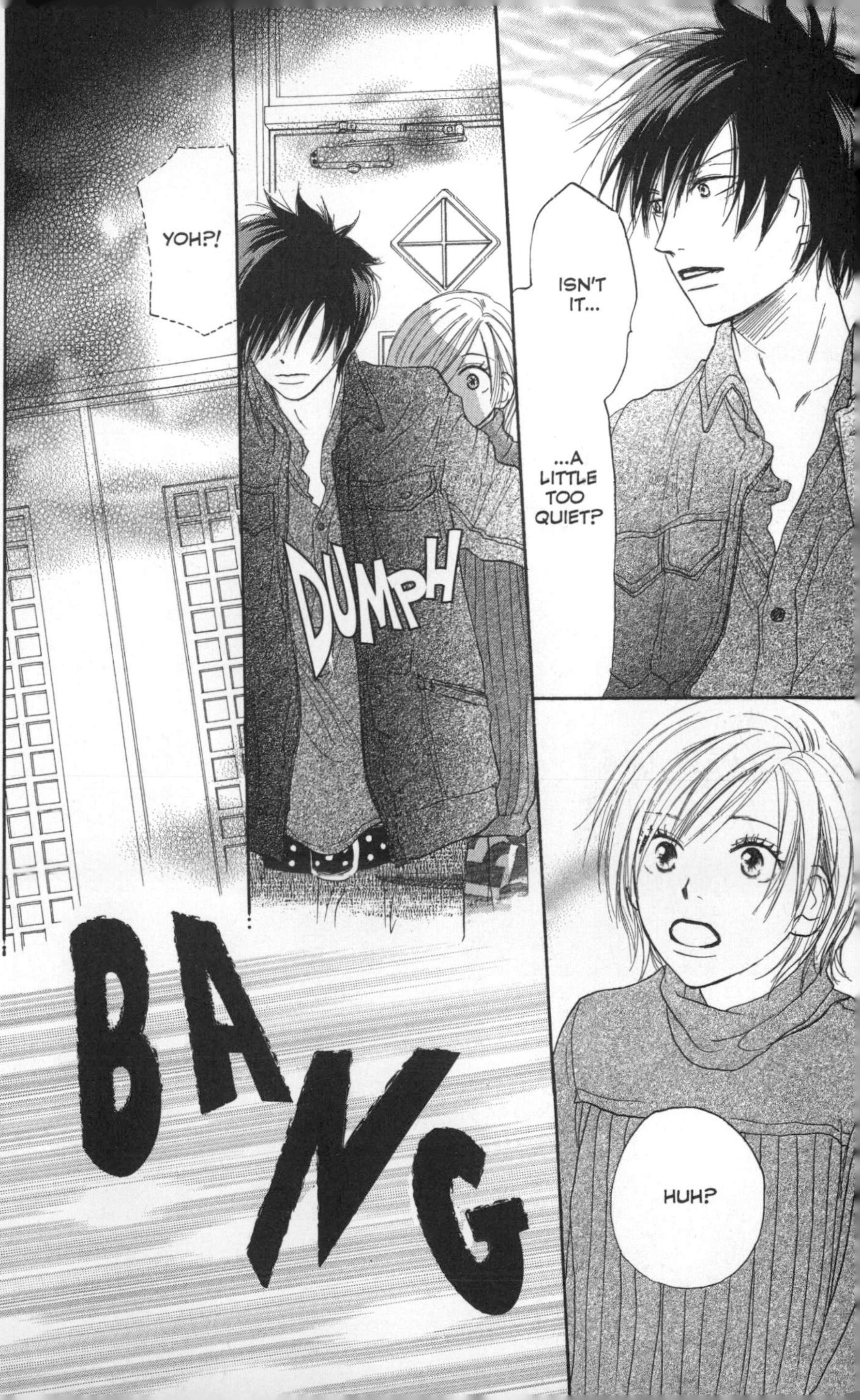
ISN'T IT...
...A LITTLE TOO QUIET?
HUH?
DUMPH
YOH?!
BANG

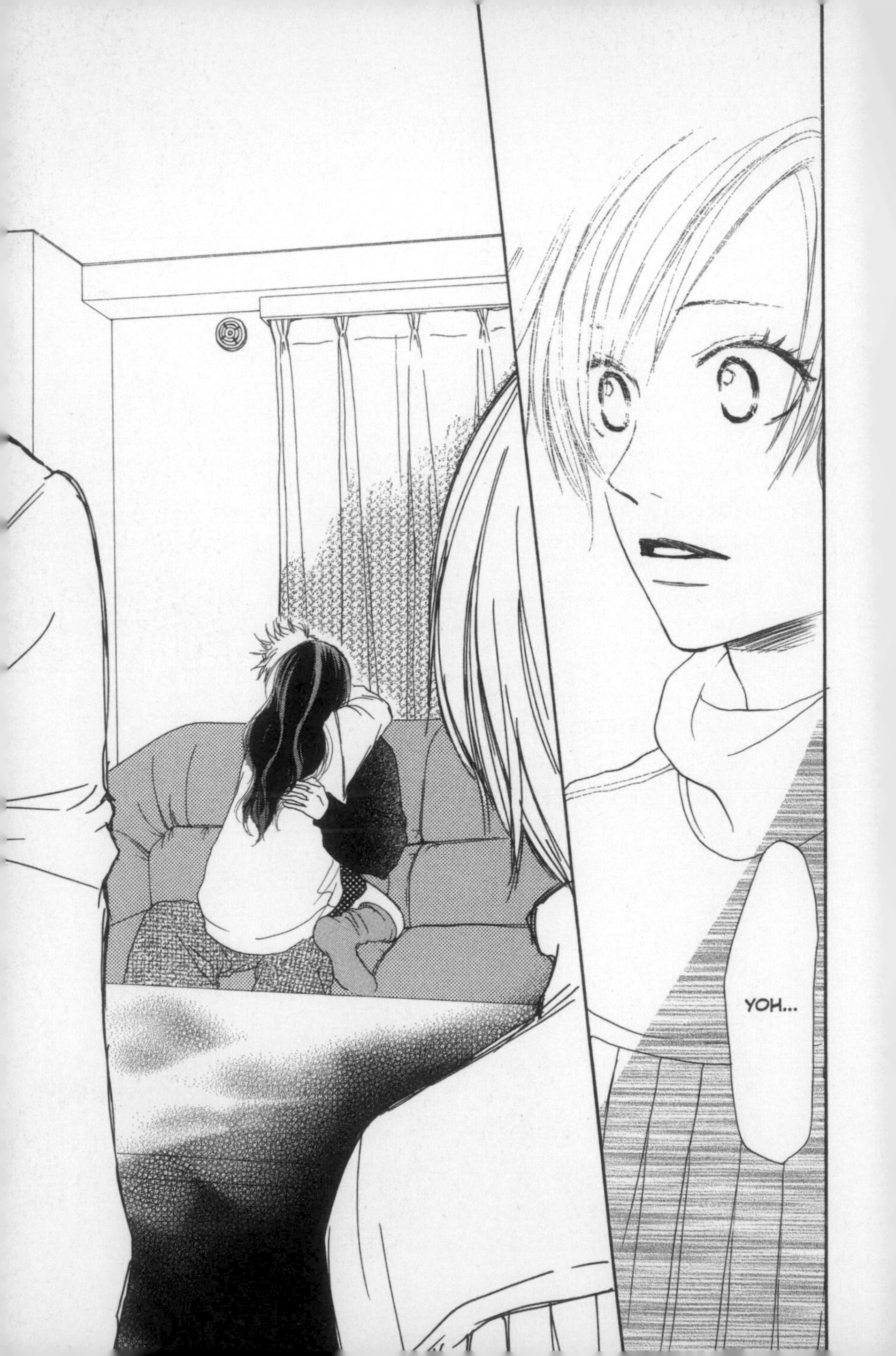
YOH...

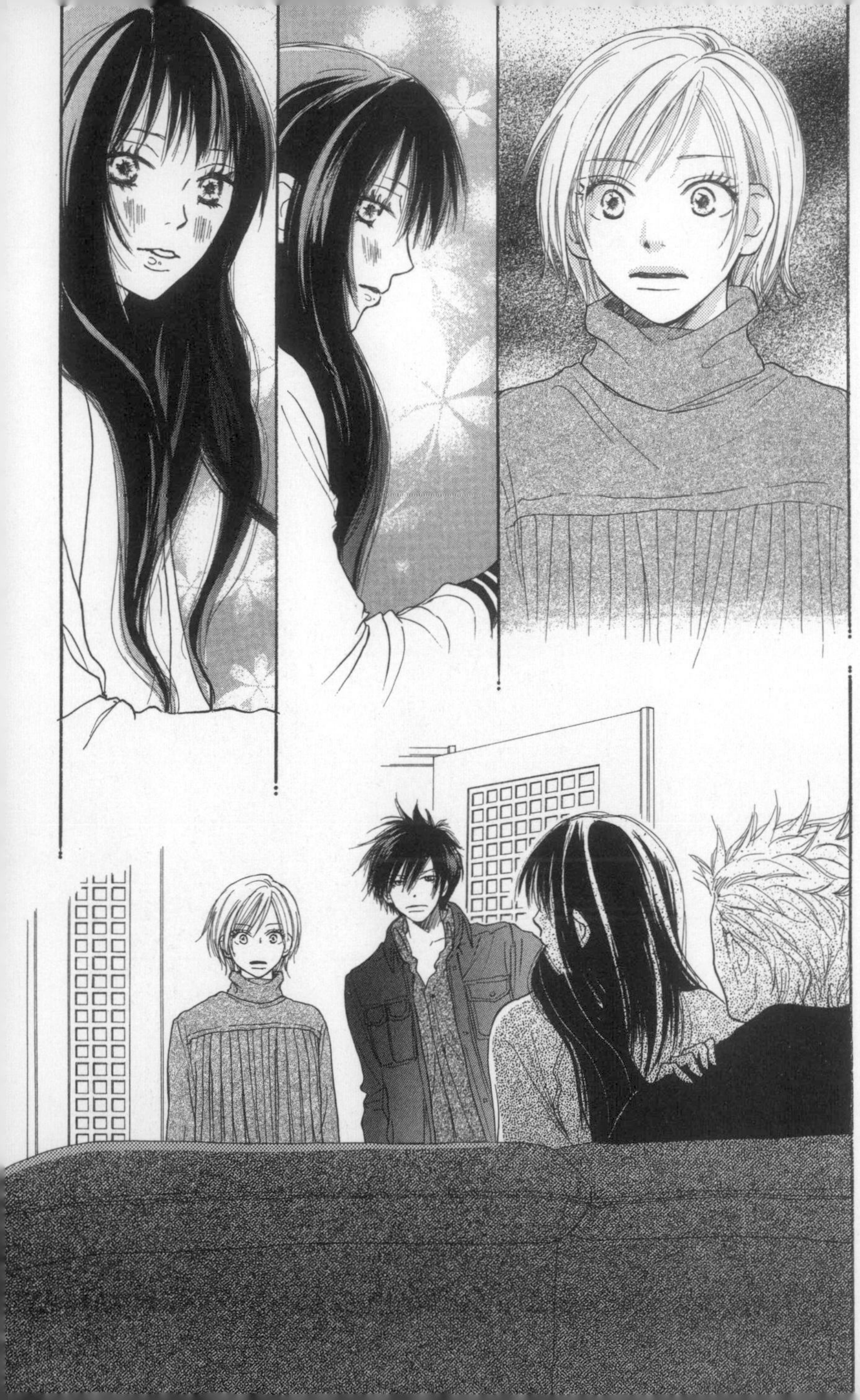

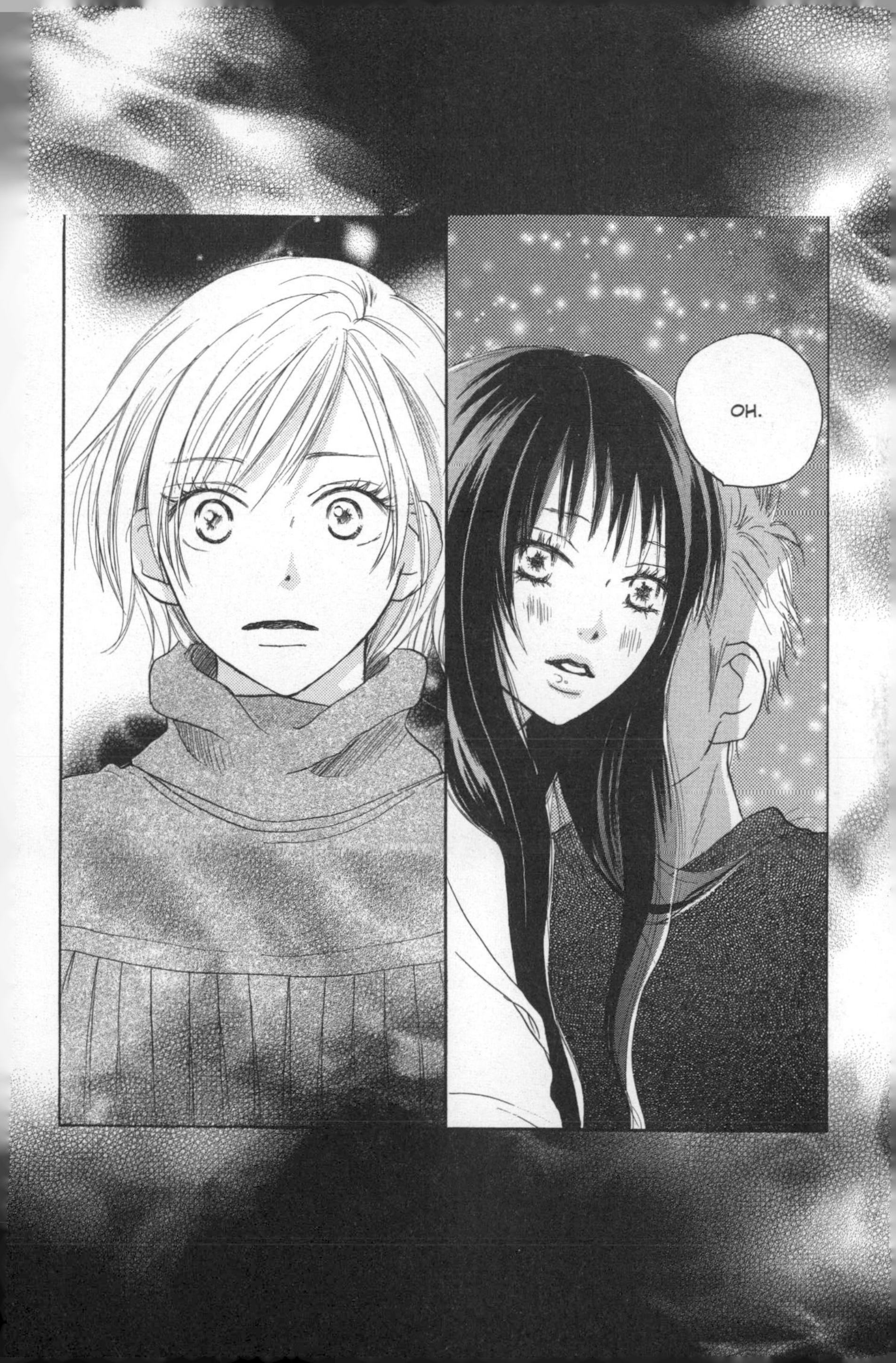
OH.

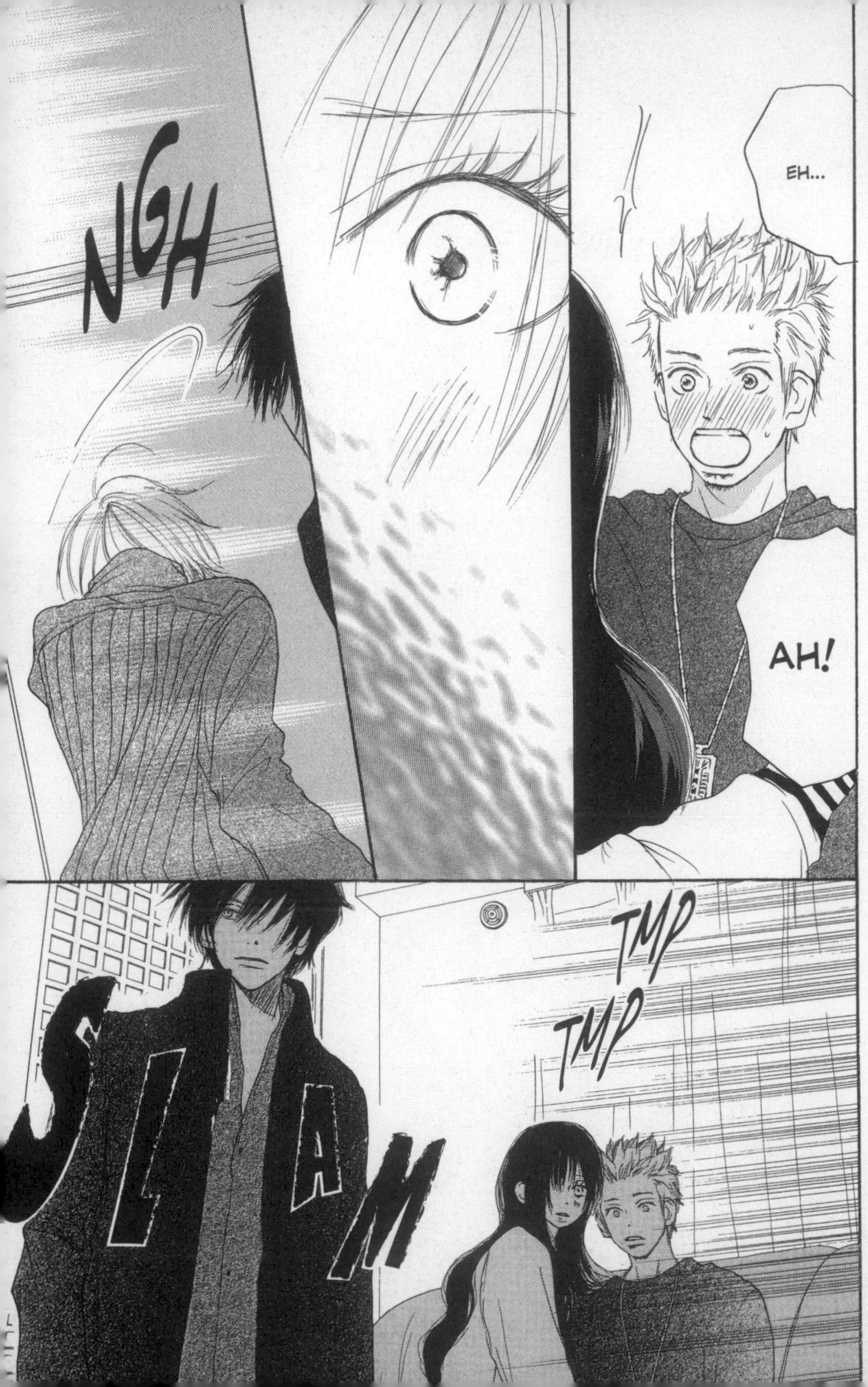
EH...
AH!
NGH
TMP
TMP
SLAM

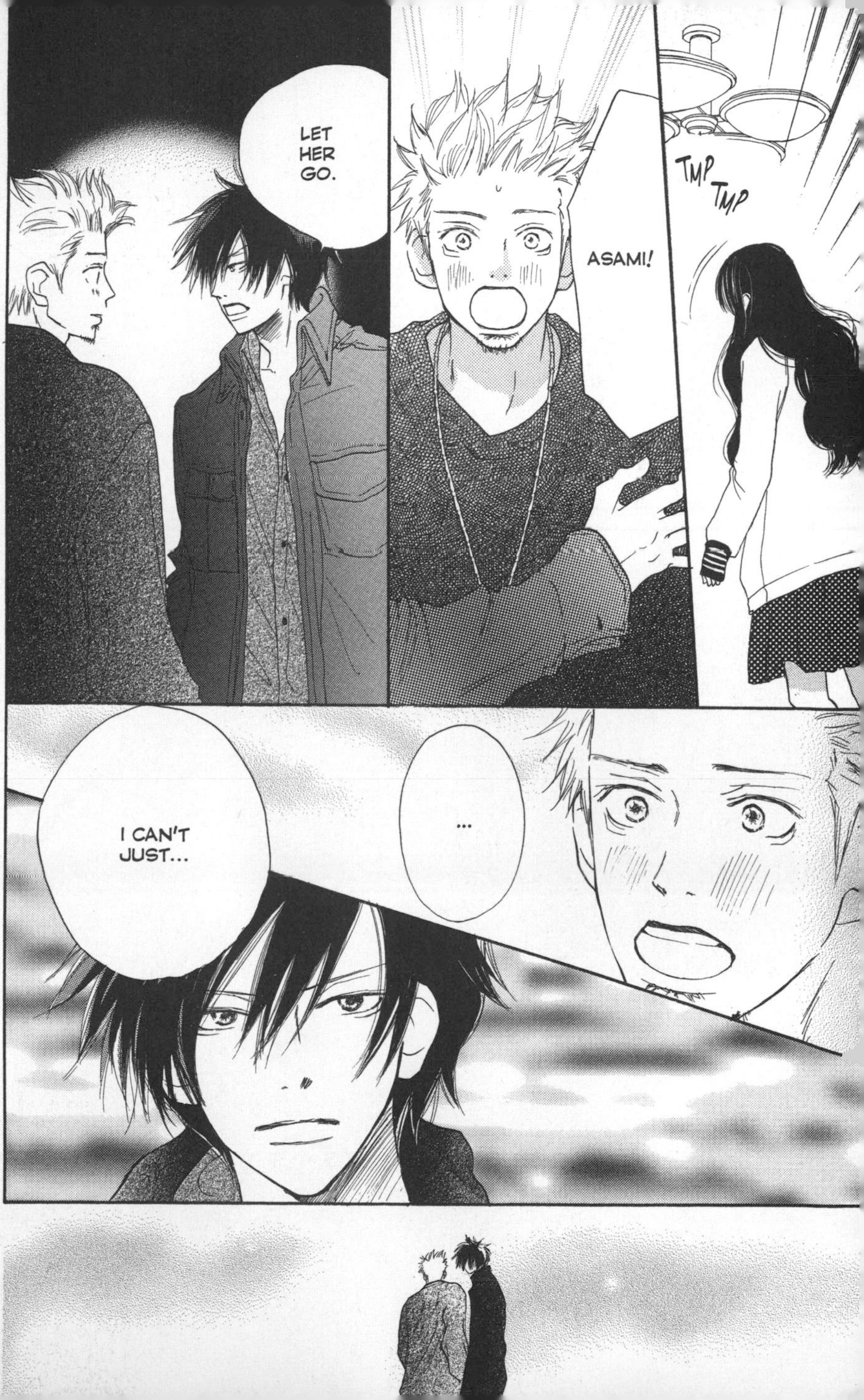
TMP TMP
ASAMI!
LET HER GO.
...
I CAN'T JUST...

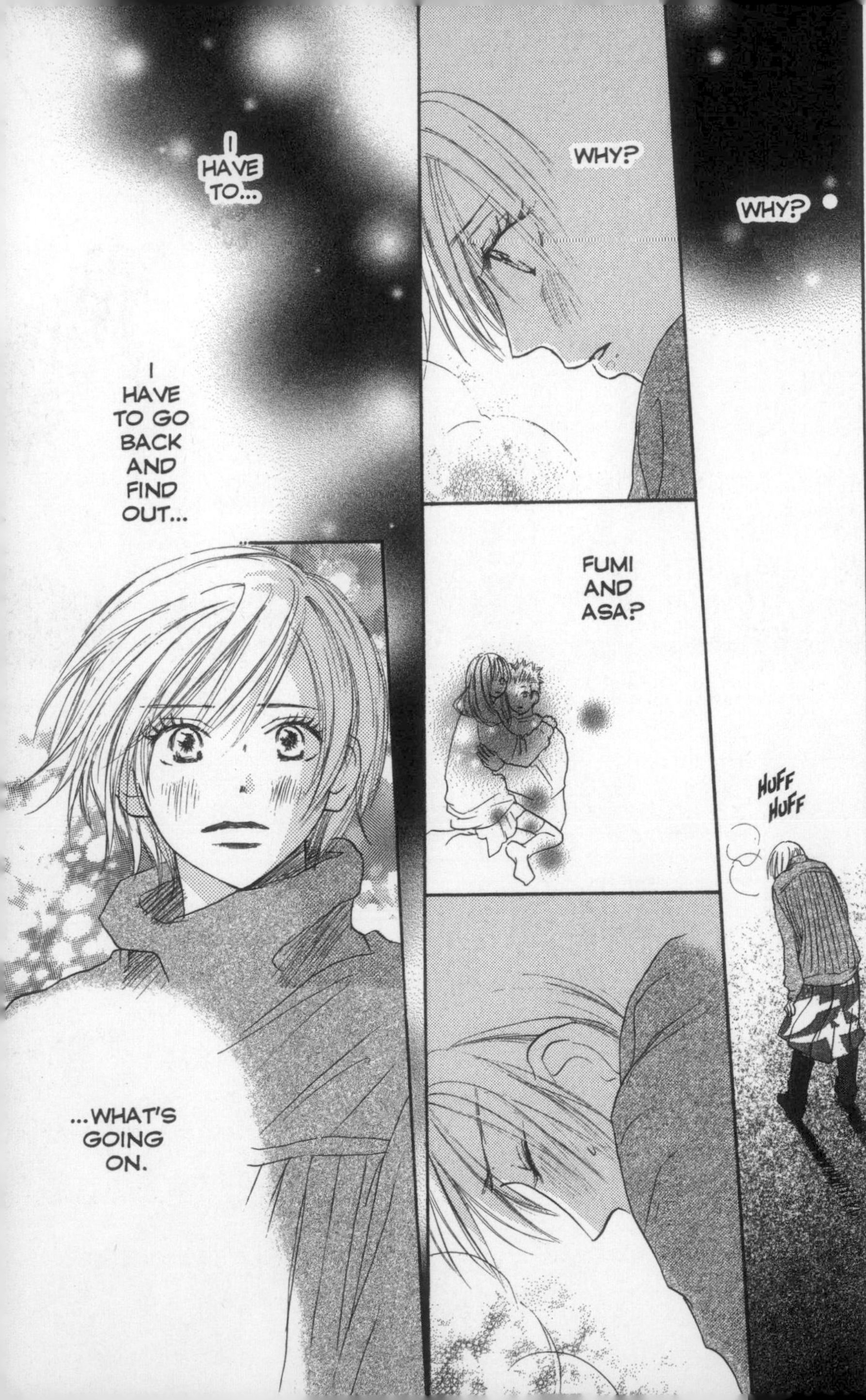
WHY?
HUFF HUFF
WHY?
FUMI AND ASA?
I HAVE TO...
I HAVE TO GO BACK AND FIND OUT...
...WHAT'S GOING ON.

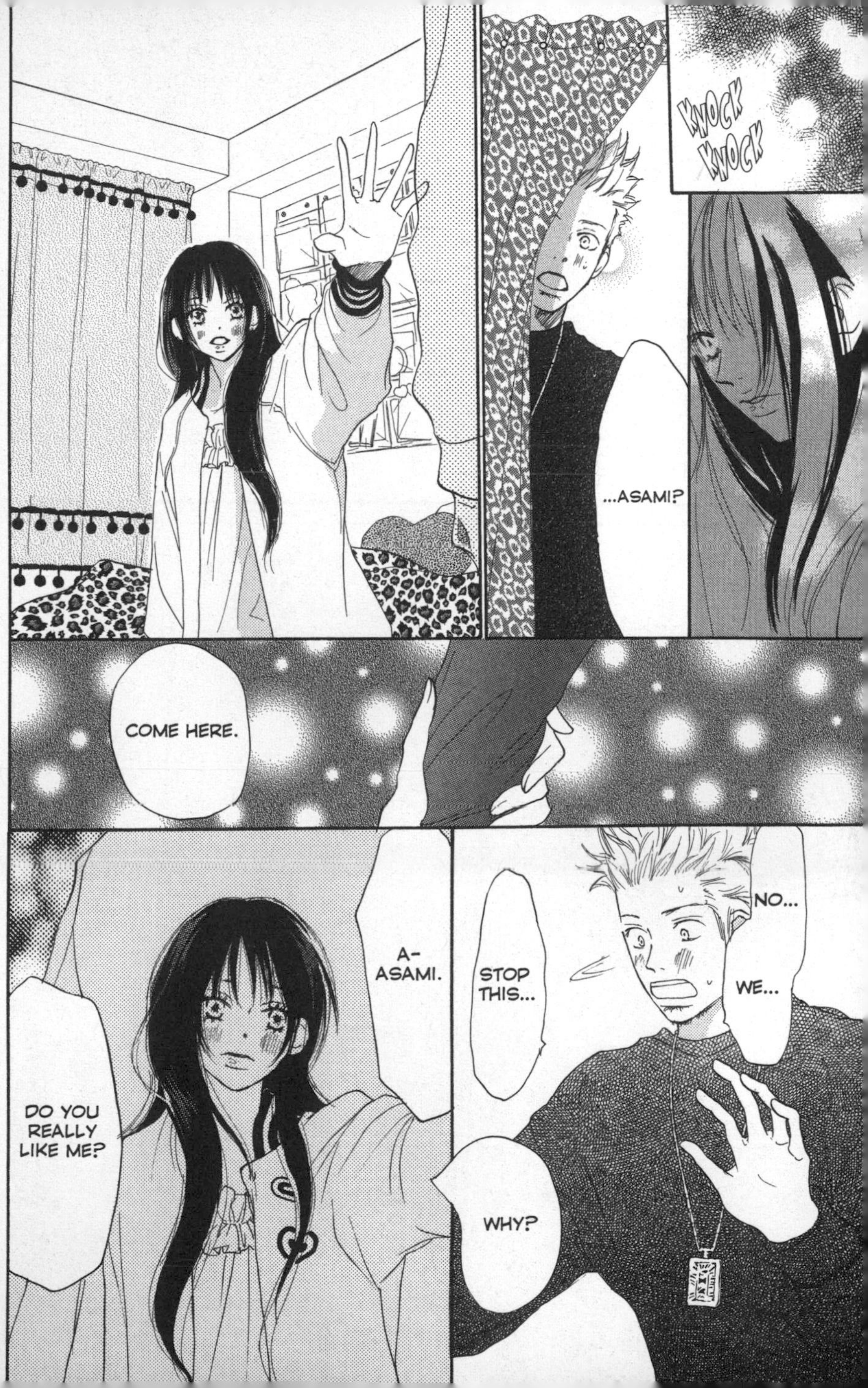
KNOCK KNOCK
...ASAMI?
COME HERE.
NO...
WE...
STOP THIS...
WHY?
A-ASAMI.
DO YOU REALLY LIKE ME?

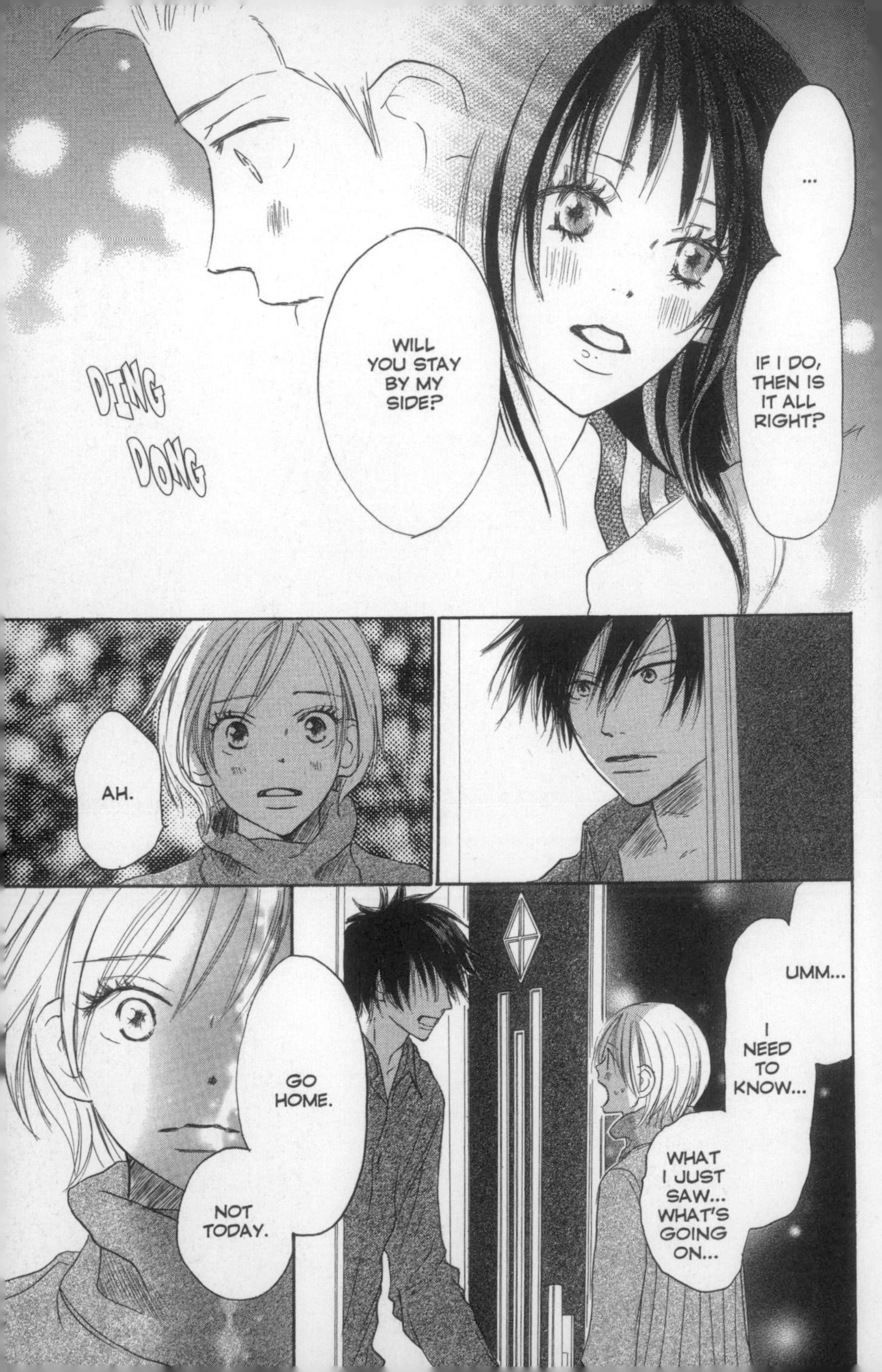
...
IF I DO, THEN IS IT ALL RIGHT?
WILL YOU STAY BY MY SIDE?
DING DONG
AH.
UMM...
I NEED TO KNOW...
WHAT I JUST SAW... WHAT'S GOING ON...
GO HOME.
NOT TODAY.

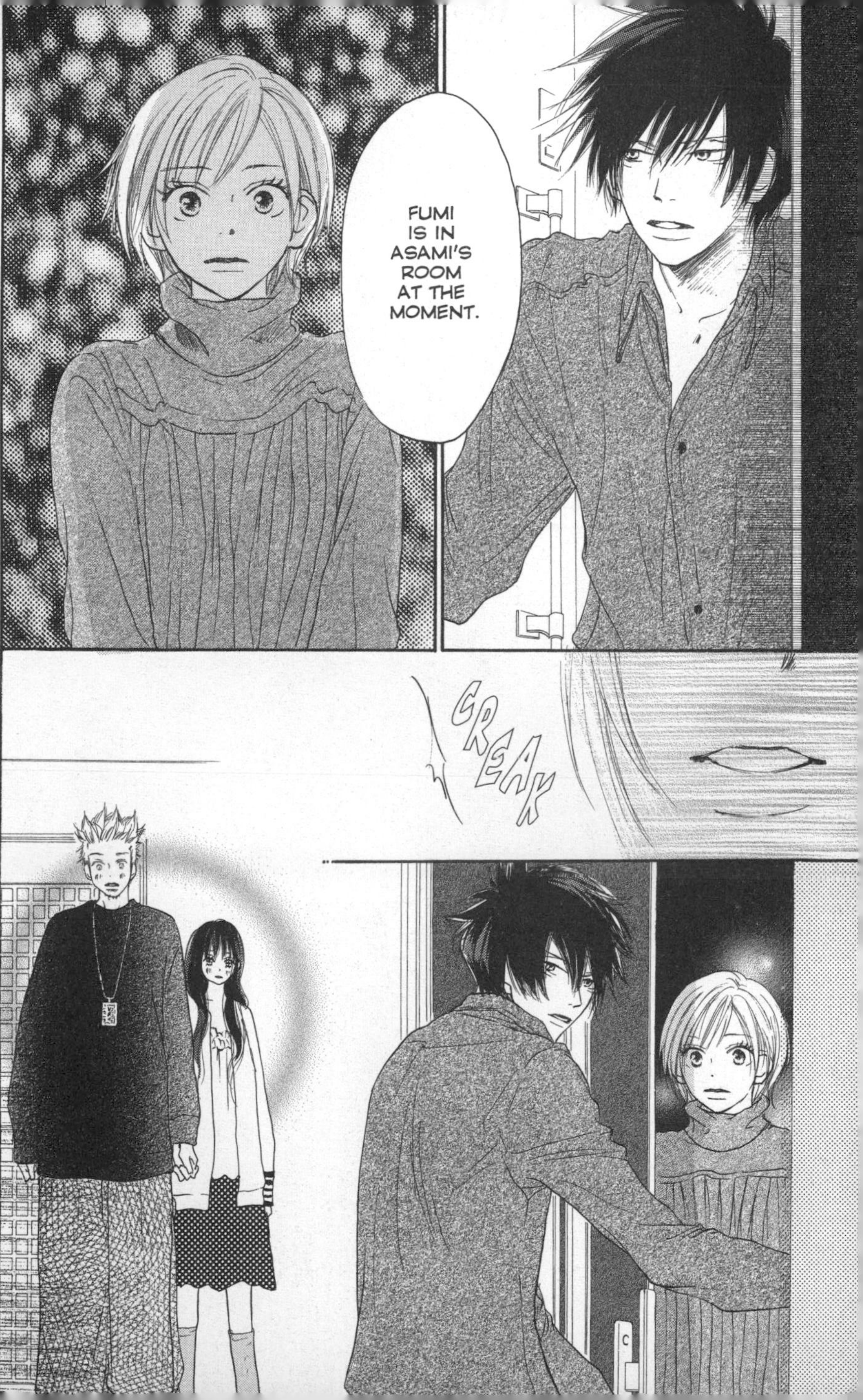
FUMI IS IN ASAMI'S ROOM AT THE MOMENT.
CREAK

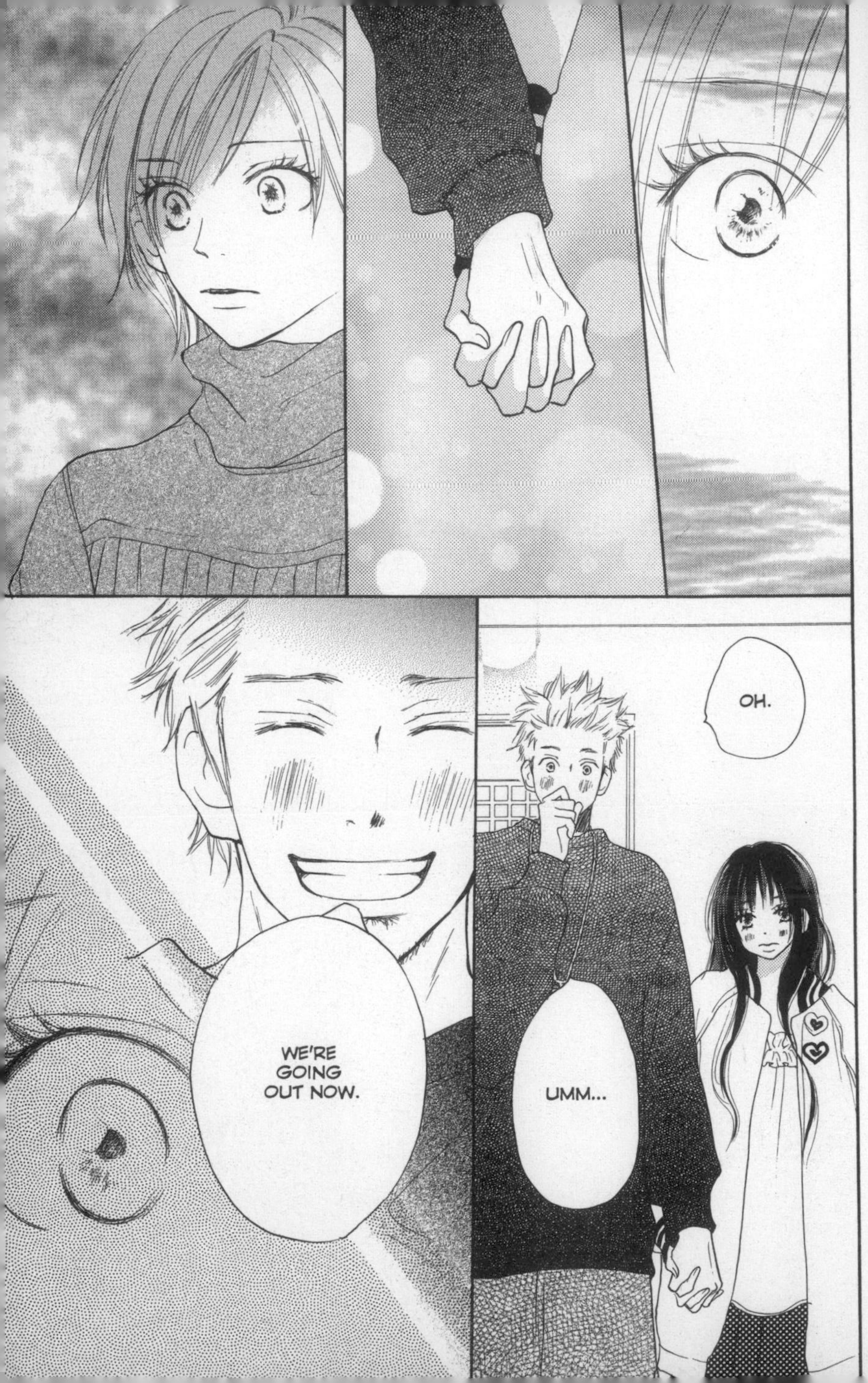
OH.
UMM...
WE'RE GOING OUT NOW.

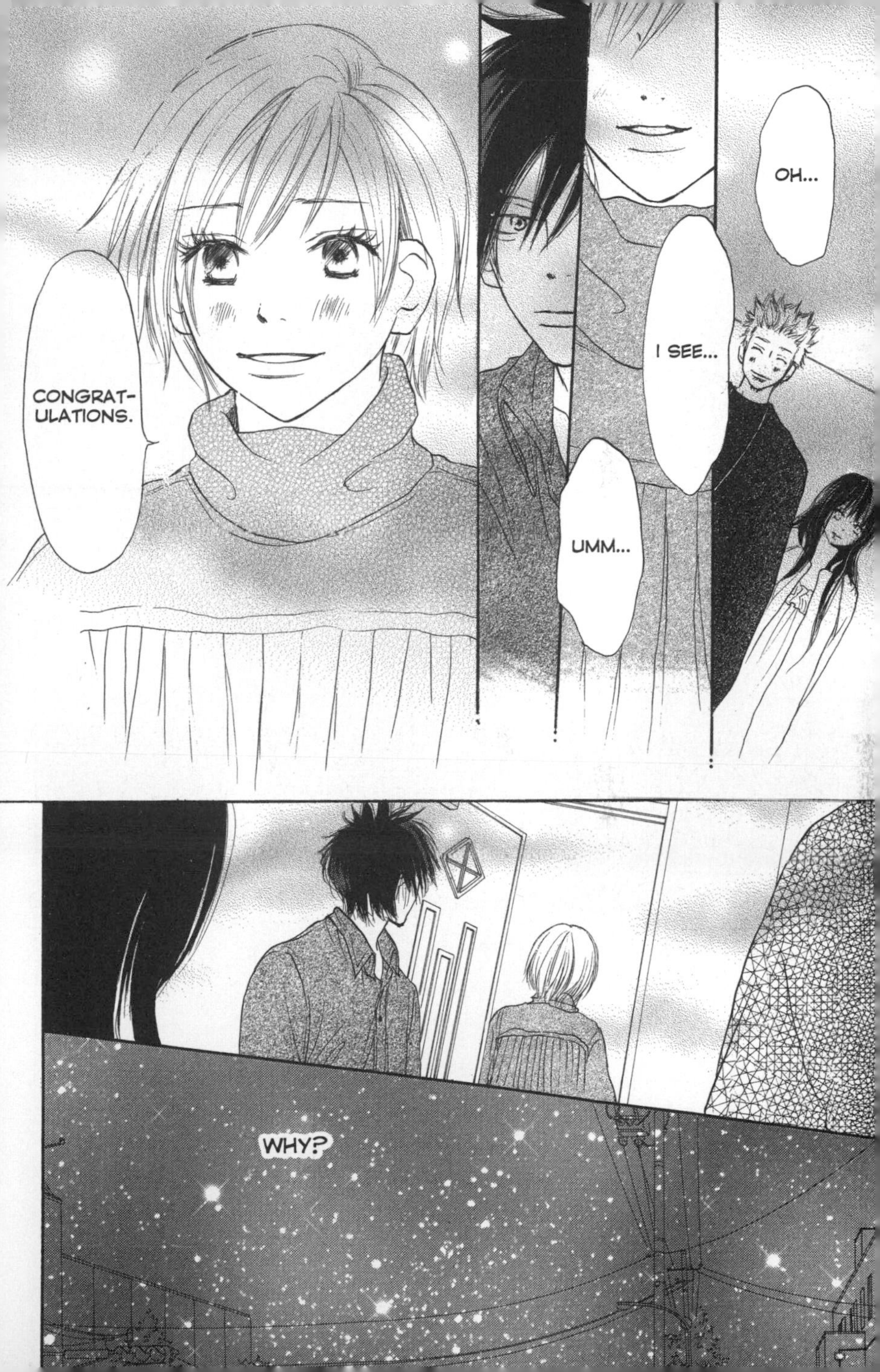
OH...
I SEE...
UMM...
CONGRAT-
ULATIONS.
WHY?

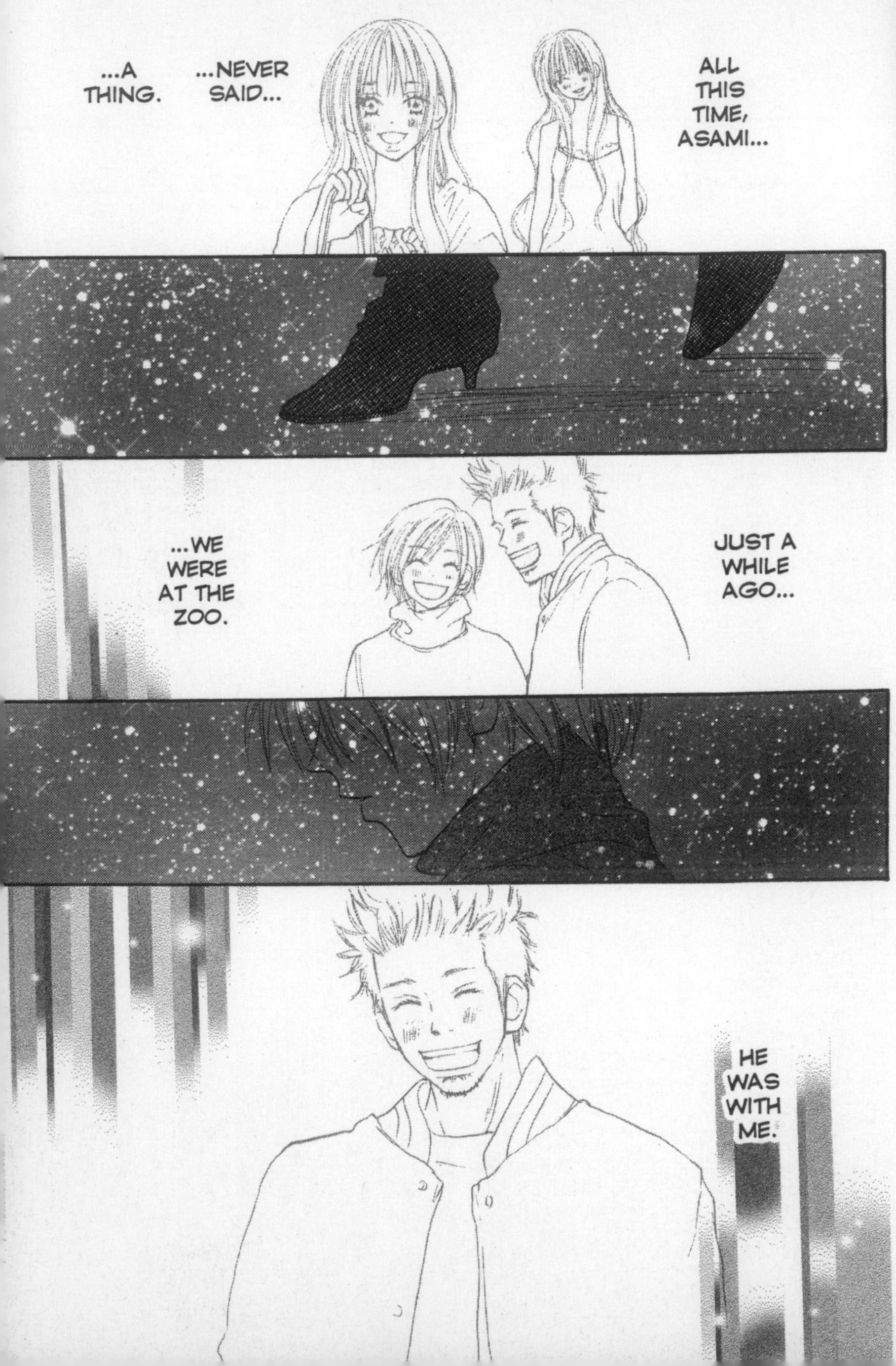
ALL THIS TIME, ASAMI...
...NEVER SAID...
...A THING.
JUST A WHILE AGO...
...WE WERE AT THE ZOO.
HE WAS WITH ME.

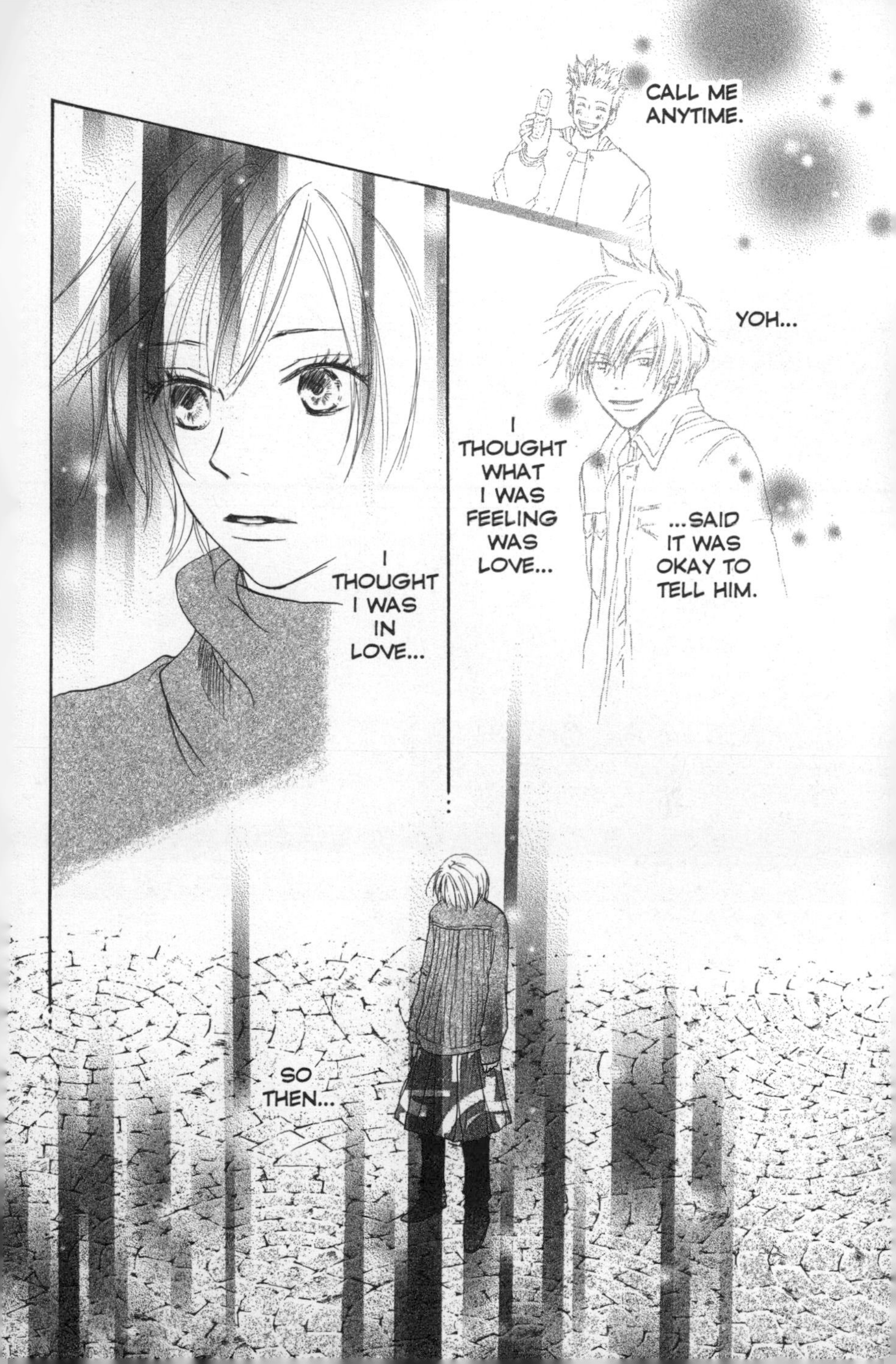
CALL ME ANYTIME.
YOH...
...SAID IT WAS OKAY TO TELL HIM.
I THOUGHT WHAT I WAS FEELING WAS LOVE...
I THOUGHT I WAS IN LOVE...
SO THEN...

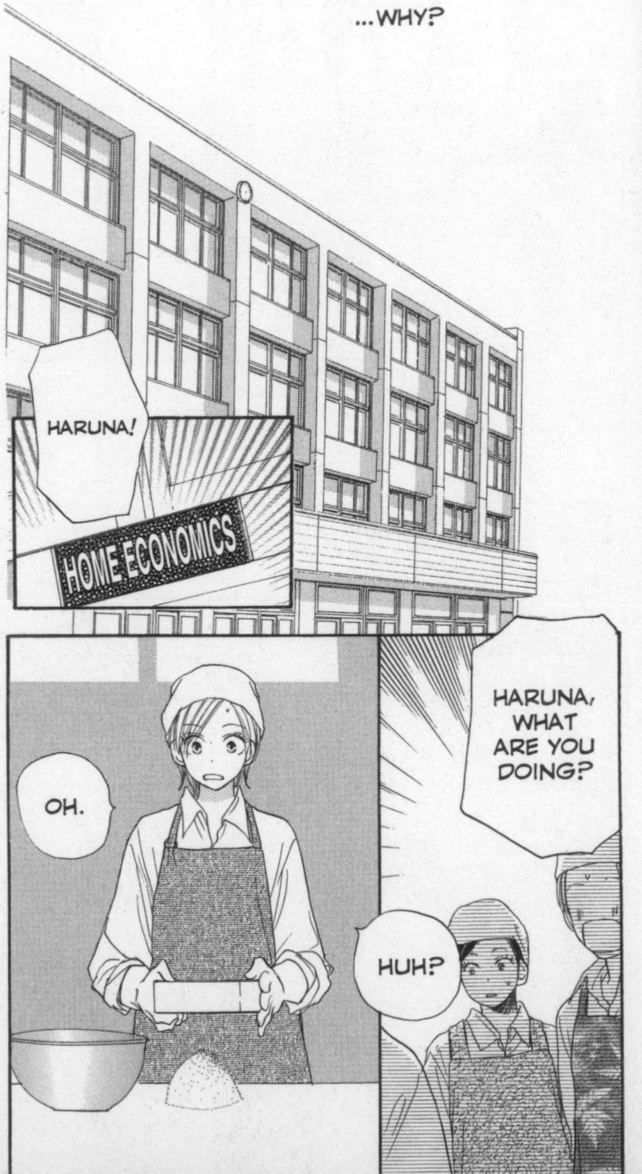
...WHY?
HARUNA!
HOME ECONOMICS
HARUNA, WHAT ARE YOU DOING?
HUH?
OH.

2

It's not an exciting story, but I lose a lot of things and get stuff stolen all the time. My bike often gets stolen. It's happened four times now. Last time, a neighbor downstairs told me.

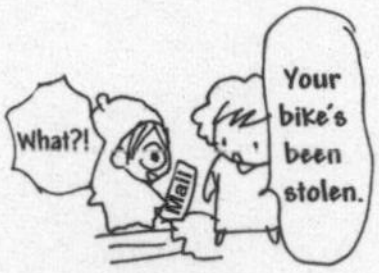
What?!
Mail
Your bike's been stolen.

When I went to look at where I'd left my bike, I saw that it was true.

So I've decided to give up now. I walk. No one has stolen my car yet though...

Also, I often lose my train pass.

Subway 3300 ← This thing.

I've lost five cards in all. I lose it when I put it in my pocket, go to town, and come home. Argh...I wonder why...I wonder if drinking that tea will stop this from happening?

That's it for today. I'll keep working hard! Hope to see you again soon!

Kazune Kawahara
2004

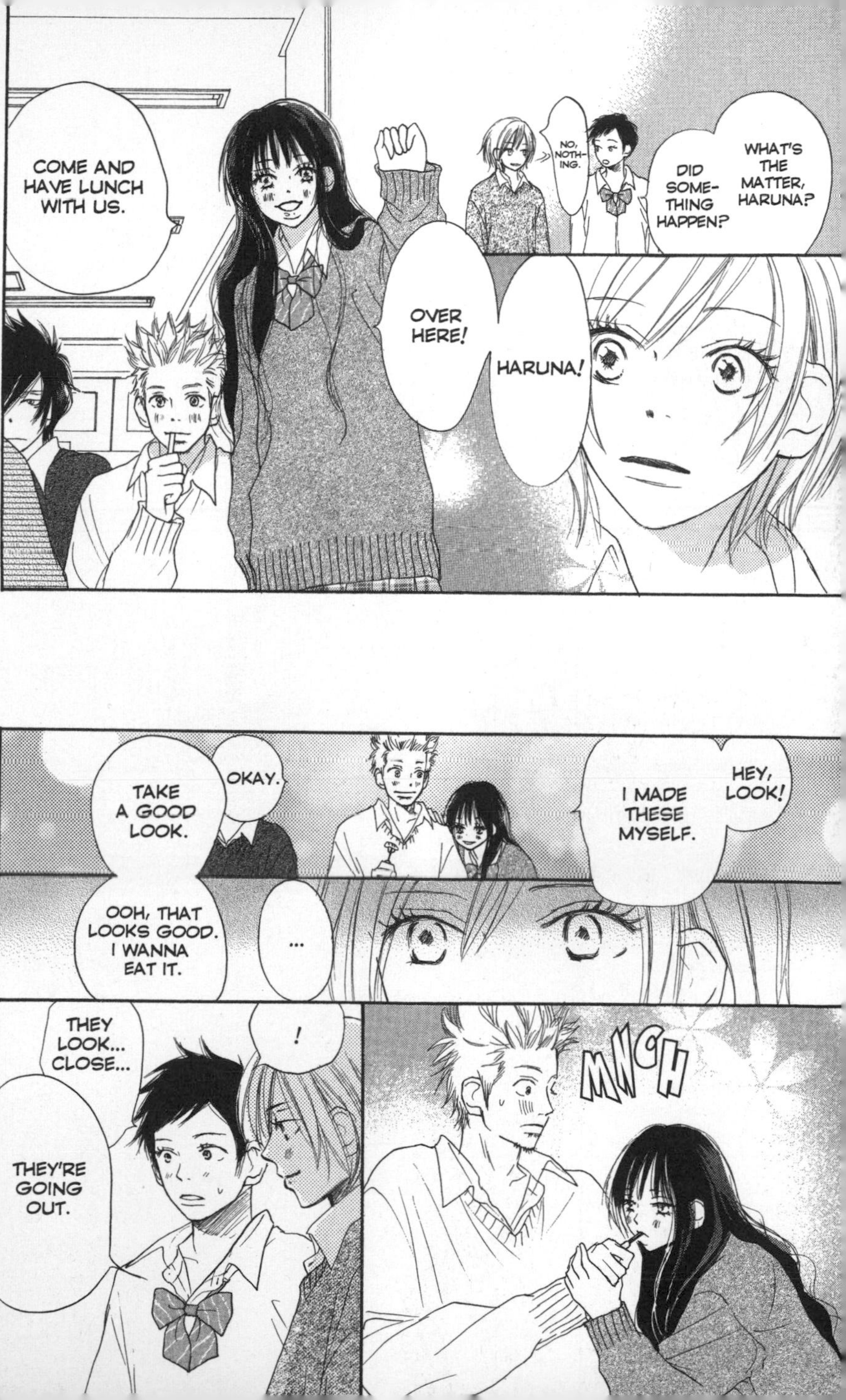
WHAT'S THE MATTER, HARUNA?
DID SOMETHING HAPPEN?
NO, NOTHING.
HARUNA!
OVER HERE!
COME AND HAVE LUNCH WITH US.
HEY, LOOK!
I MADE THESE MYSELF.
OKAY.
TAKE A GOOD LOOK.
...
OOH, THAT LOOKS GOOD. I WANNA EAT IT.
MNCH
!
THEY LOOK... CLOSE...
THEY'RE GOING OUT.

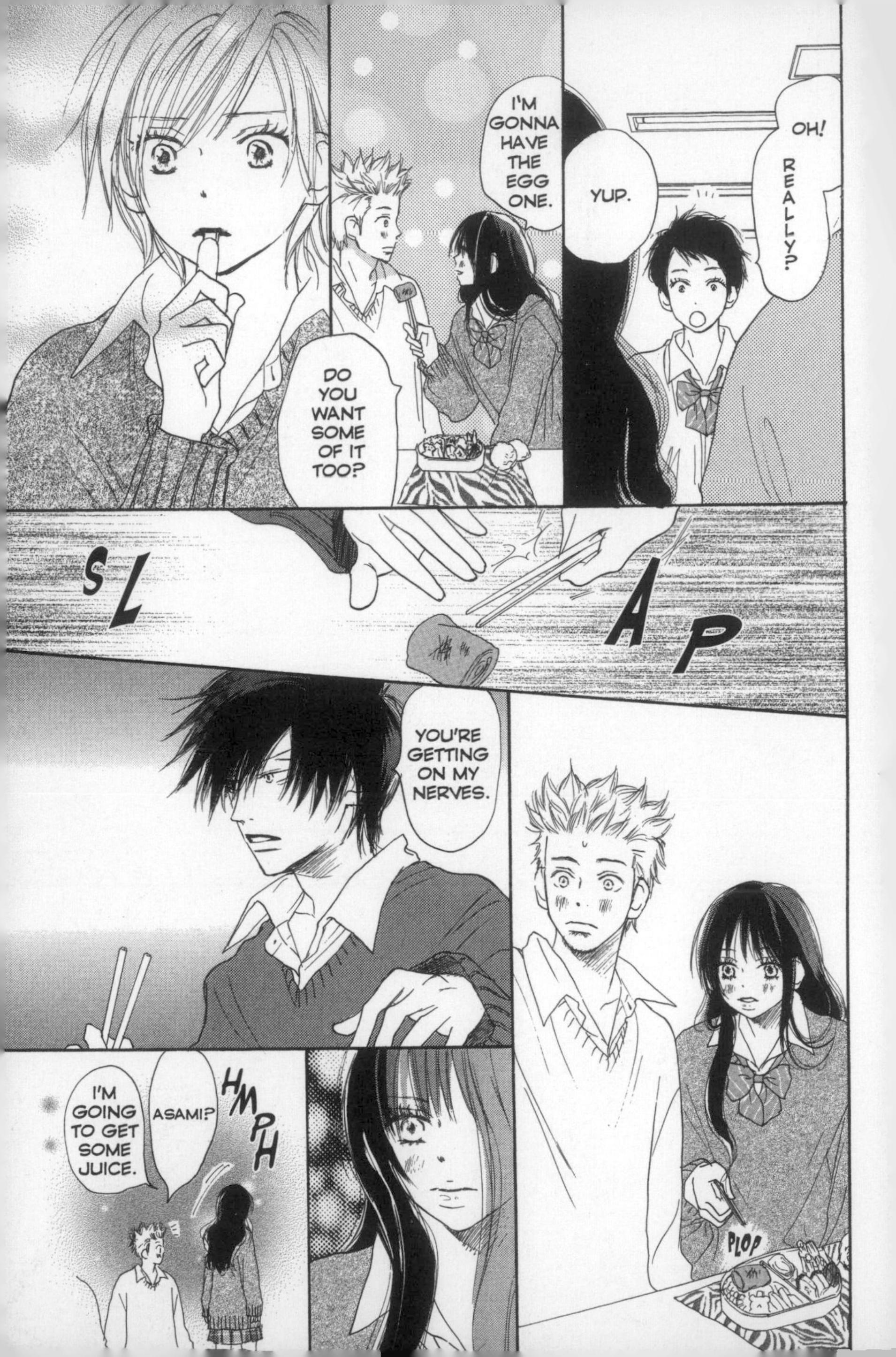
OH! REALLY?
YUP.
I'M GONNA HAVE THE EGG ONE.
DO YOU WANT SOME OF IT TOO?
SLAP
PLOP
YOU'RE GETTING ON MY NERVES.
HMPH
ASAMI?
I'M GOING TO GET SOME JUICE.

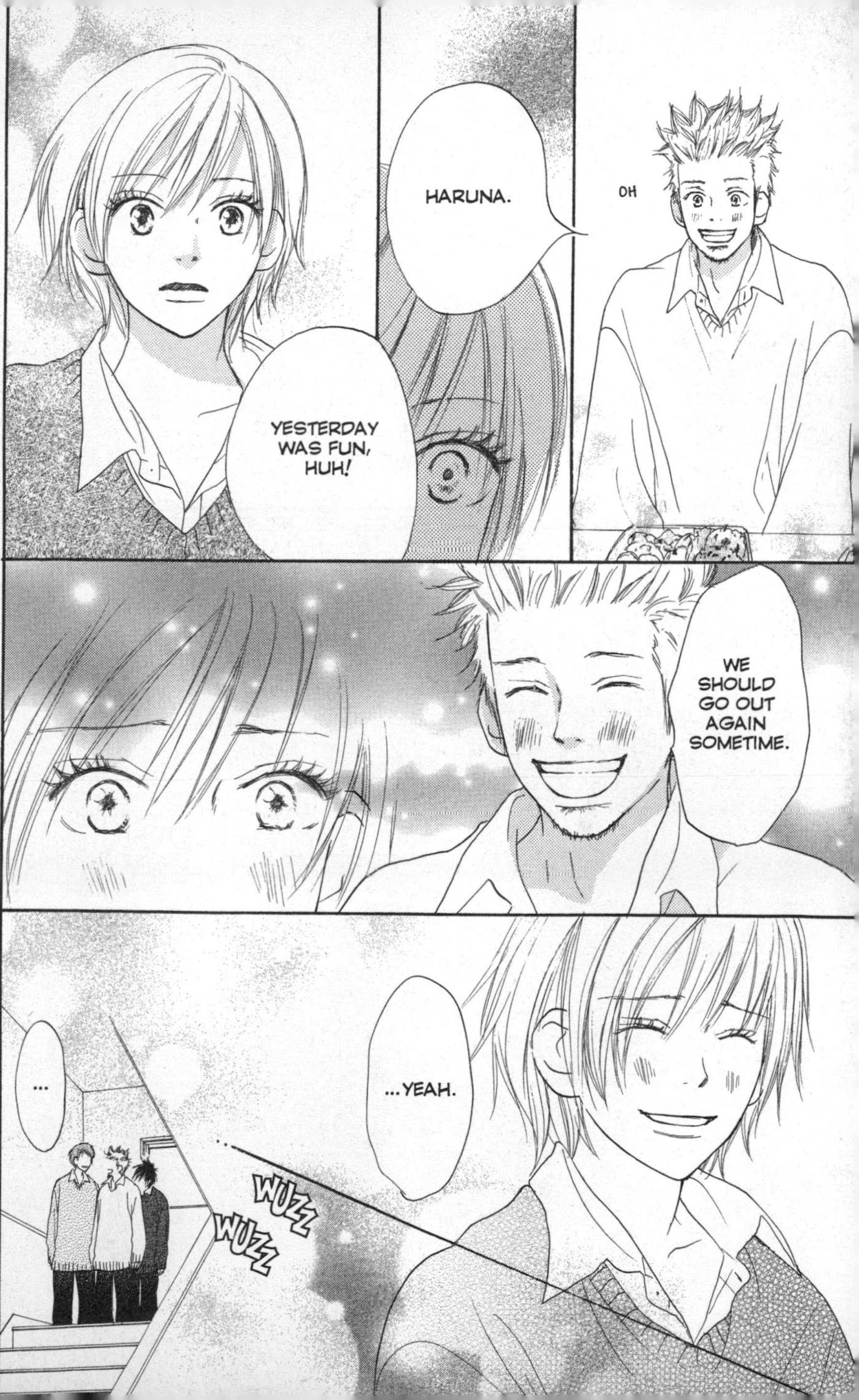
OH
HARUNA.
YESTERDAY WAS FUN, HUH!
WE SHOULD GO OUT AGAIN SOMETIME.
...YEAH.
...
WUZZ WUZZ

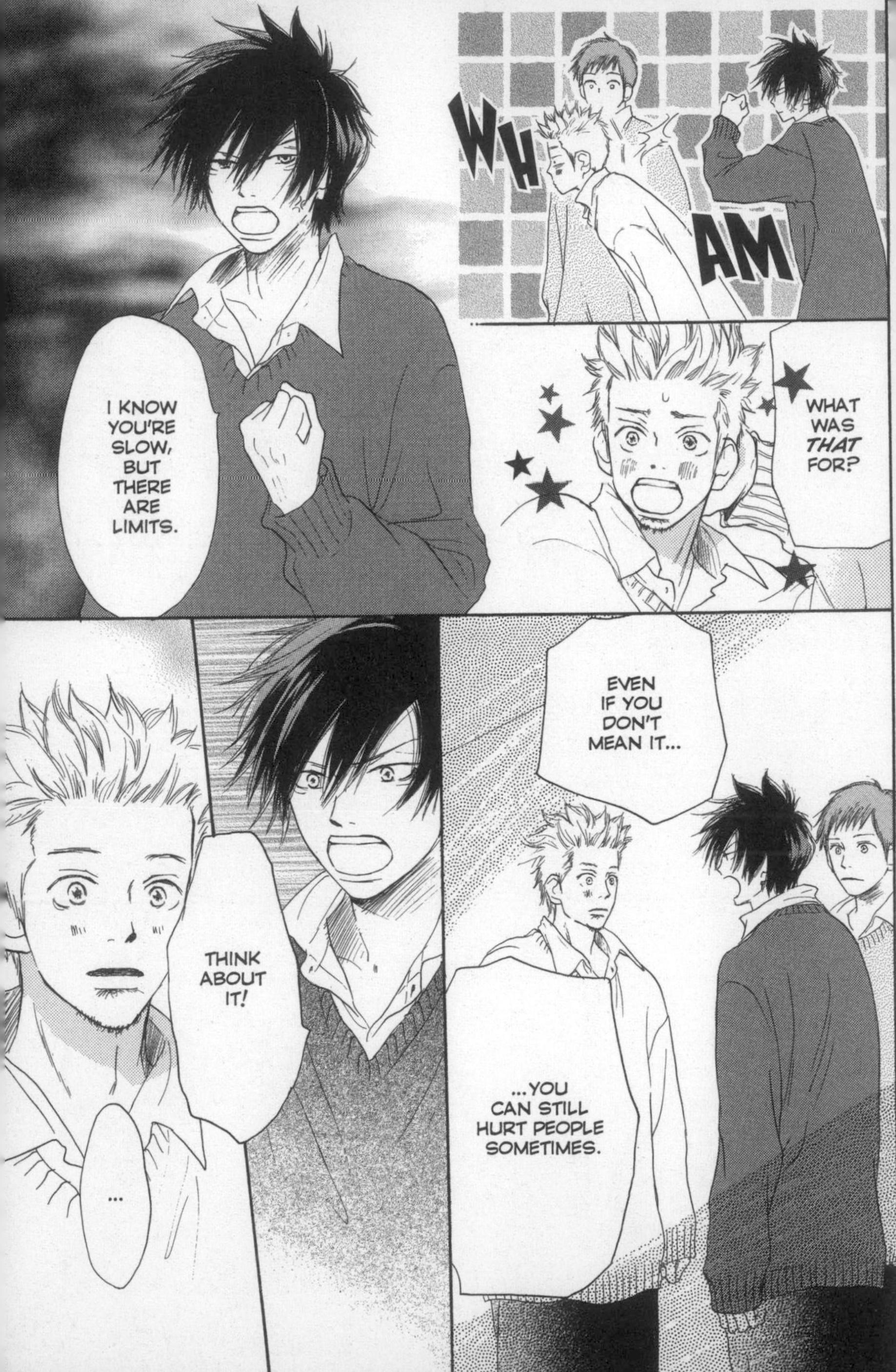
WHAM
WHAT WAS *THAT* FOR?
I KNOW YOU'RE SLOW, BUT THERE ARE LIMITS.
EVEN IF YOU DON'T MEAN IT...
...YOU CAN STILL HURT PEOPLE SOMETIMES.
THINK ABOUT IT!
...

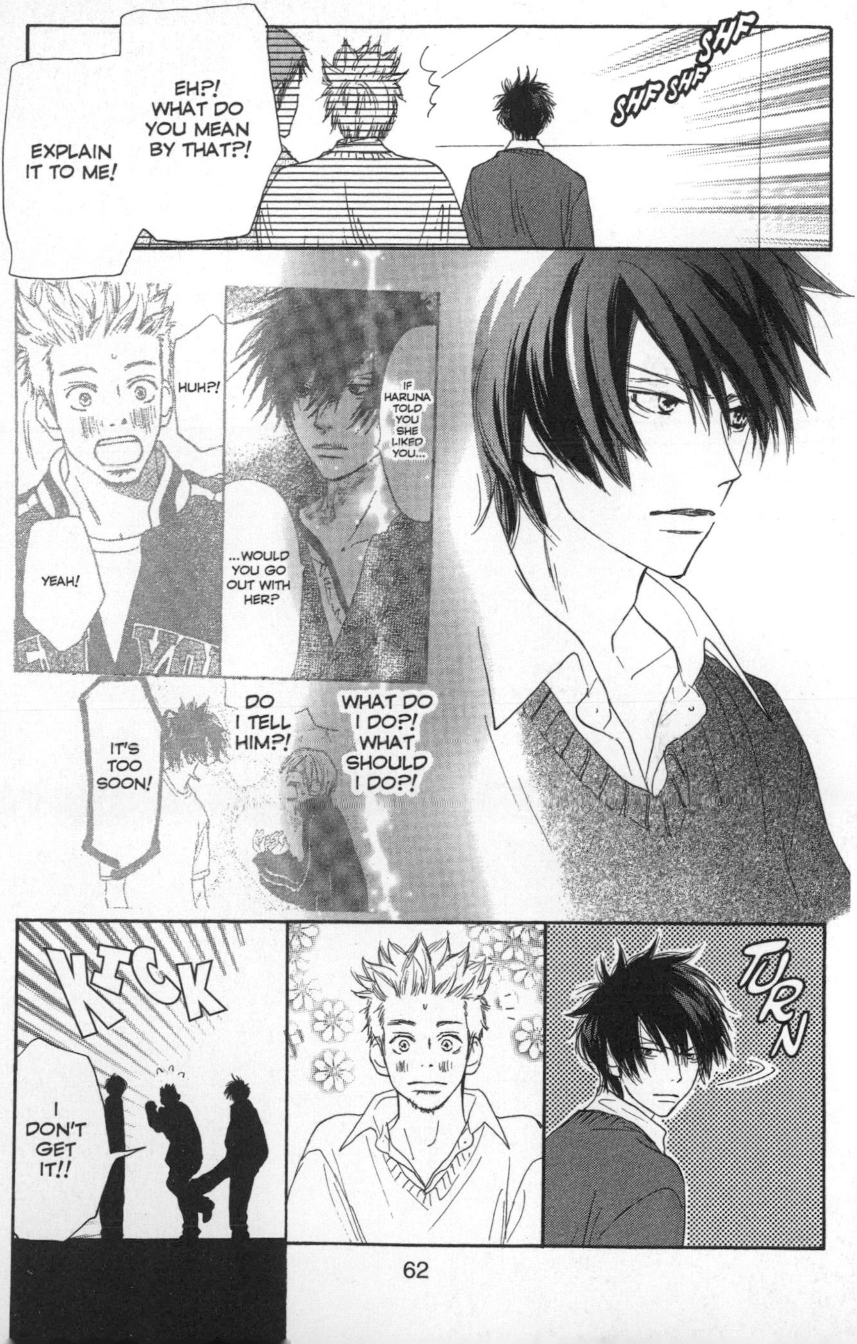
SHF SHF SHF
EH?! WHAT DO YOU MEAN BY THAT?!
EXPLAIN IT TO ME!
IF HARUNA TOLD YOU SHE LIKED YOU...
...WOULD YOU GO OUT WITH HER?
HUH?!
YEAH!
WHAT DO I DO?! WHAT SHOULD I DO?!
DO I TELL HIM?!
IT'S TOO SOON!
TURN
KICK
I DON'T GET IT!!

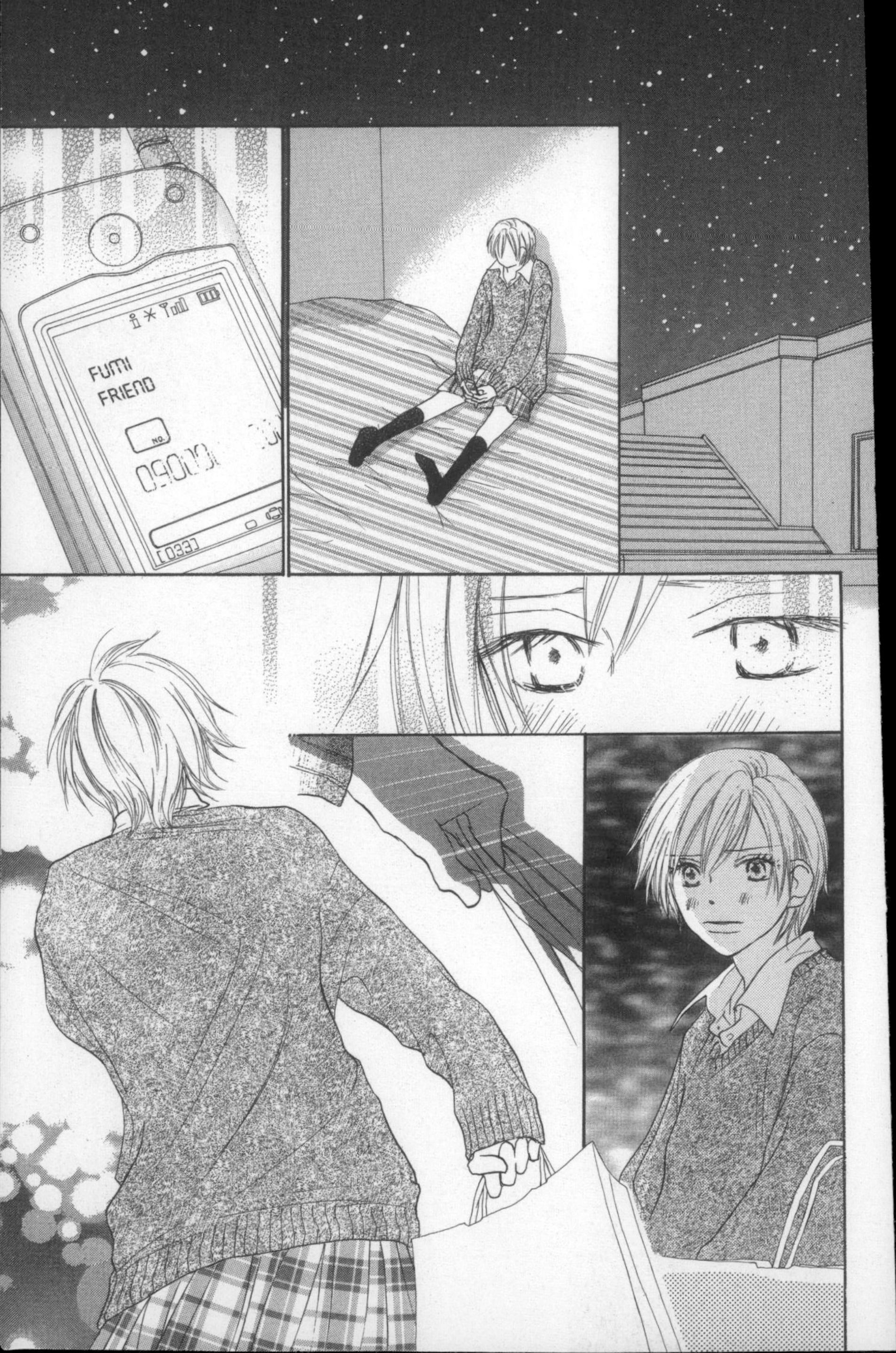
FUMI
FRIEND

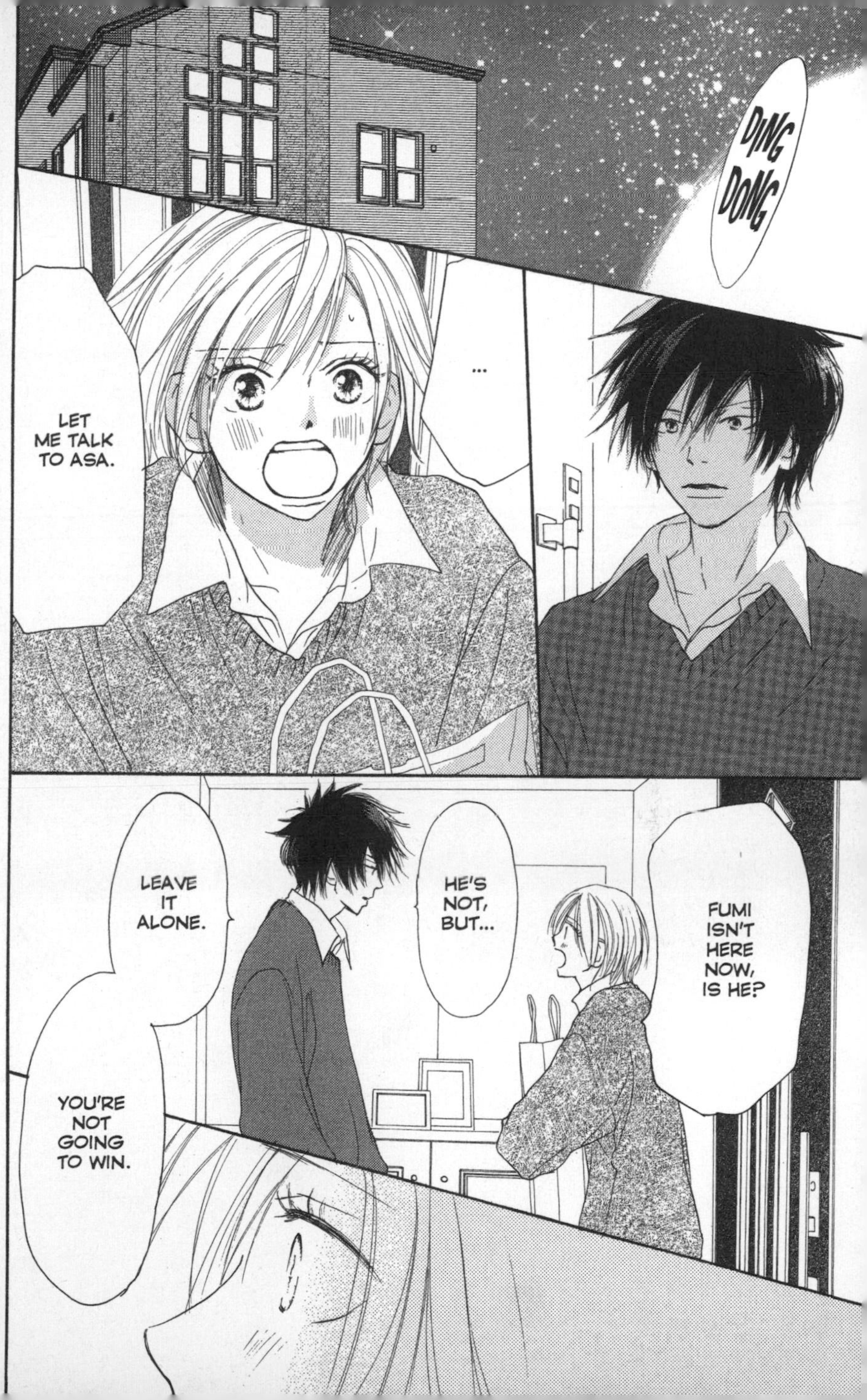
DING DONG
...
LET ME TALK TO ASA.
FUMI ISN'T HERE NOW, IS HE?
HE'S NOT, BUT...
LEAVE IT ALONE.
YOU'RE NOT GOING TO WIN.

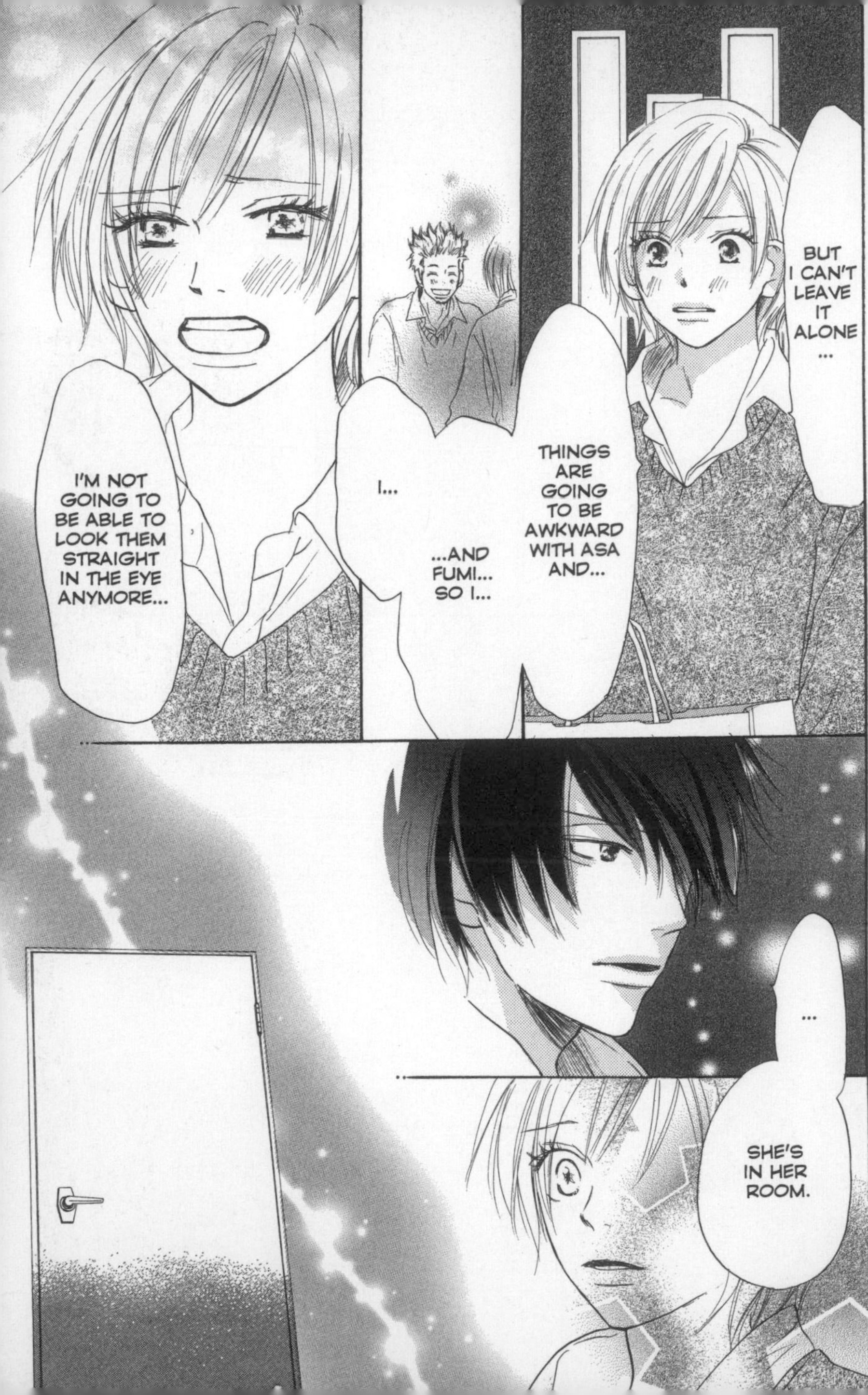
BUT I CAN'T LEAVE IT ALONE...
THINGS ARE GOING TO BE AWKWARD WITH ASA AND...
...AND FUMI... SO I...
I...
I'M NOT GOING TO BE ABLE TO LOOK THEM STRAIGHT IN THE EYE ANYMORE...
...
SHE'S IN HER ROOM.

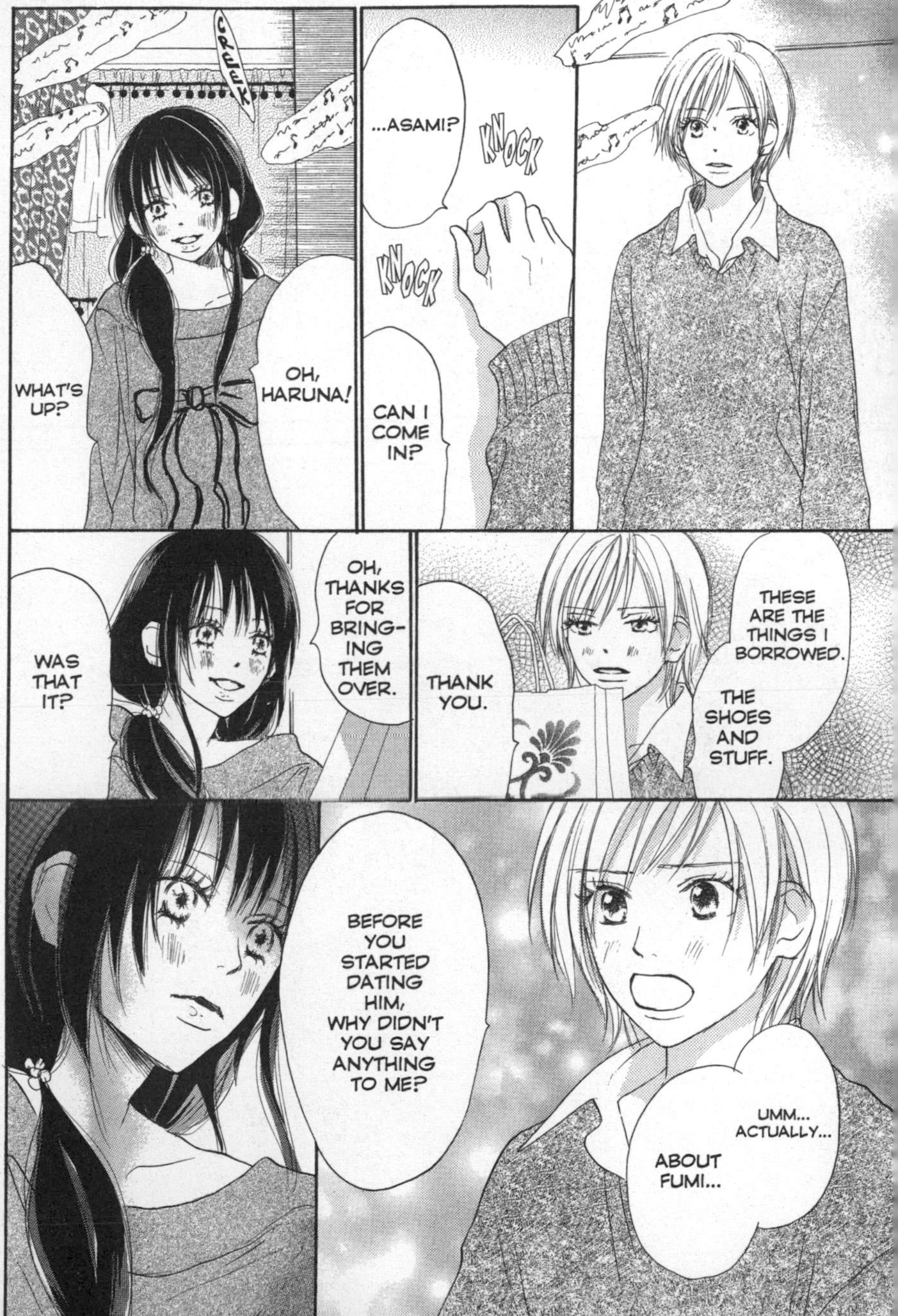
...ASAMI?
KNOCK
KNOCK
CAN I COME IN?
CREEK
OH, HARUNA!
WHAT'S UP?
THESE ARE THE THINGS I BORROWED.
THE SHOES AND STUFF.
THANK YOU.
OH, THANKS FOR BRING-ING THEM OVER.
WAS THAT IT?
UMM... ACTUALLY...
ABOUT FUMI...
BEFORE YOU STARTED DATING HIM, WHY DIDN'T YOU SAY ANYTHING TO ME?

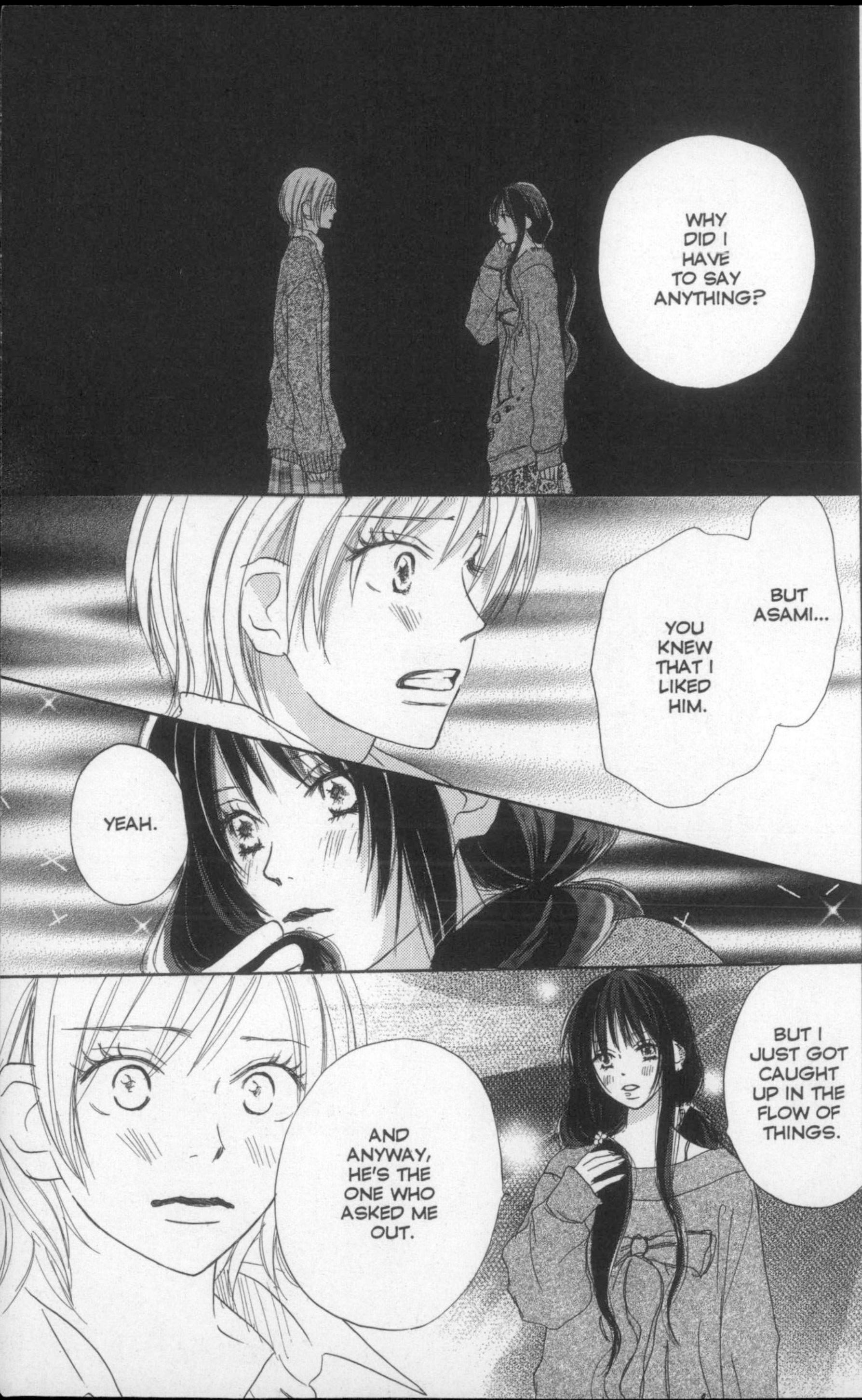
WHY DID I HAVE TO SAY ANYTHING?
BUT ASAMI...
YOU KNEW THAT I LIKED HIM.
YEAH.
BUT I JUST GOT CAUGHT UP IN THE FLOW OF THINGS.
AND ANYWAY, HE'S THE ONE WHO ASKED ME OUT.

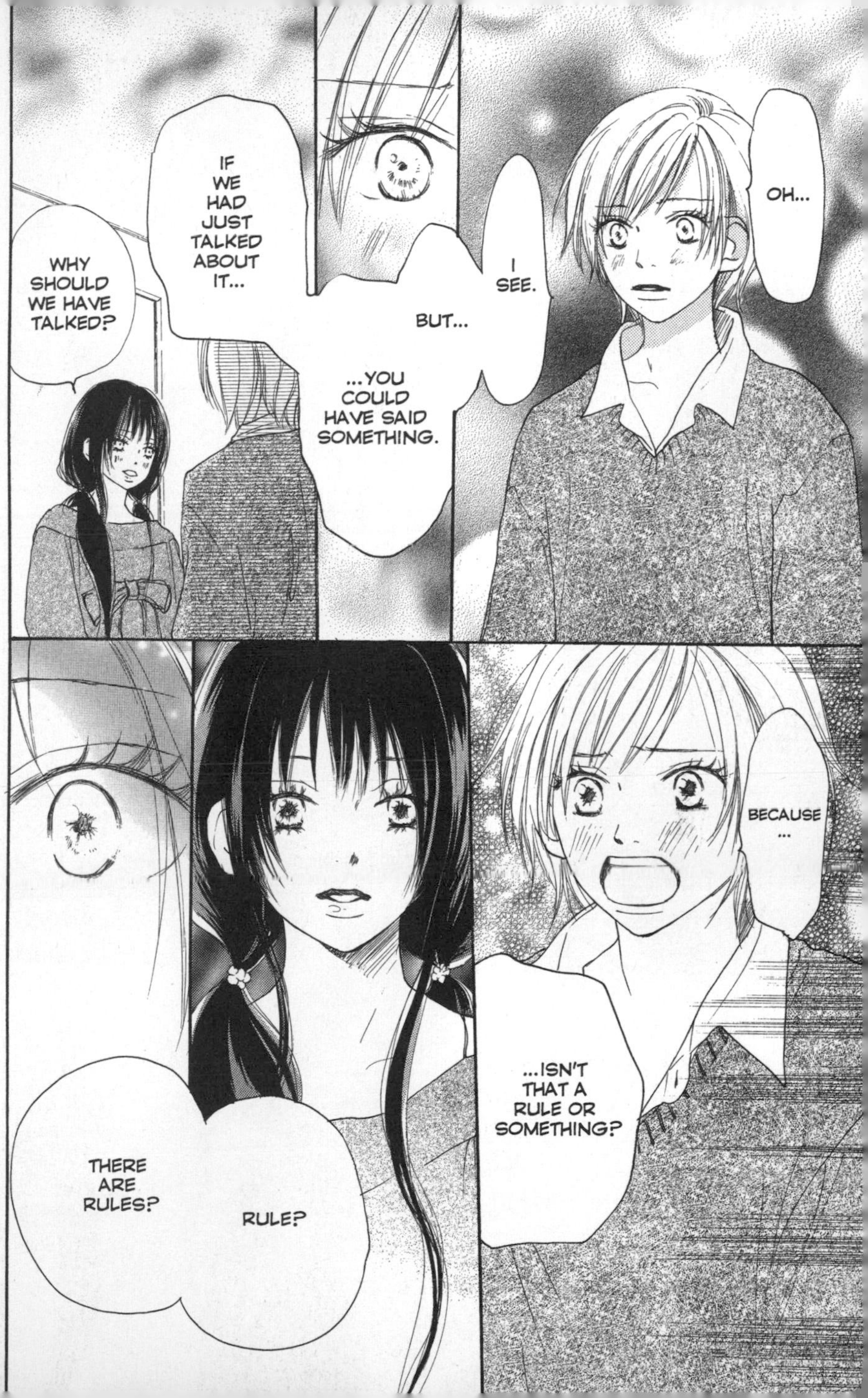
OH...
I SEE.
BUT...
...YOU COULD HAVE SAID SOMETHING.
IF WE HAD JUST TALKED ABOUT IT...
WHY SHOULD WE HAVE TALKED?
BECAUSE...
...ISN'T THAT A RULE OR SOMETHING?
RULE?
THERE ARE RULES?

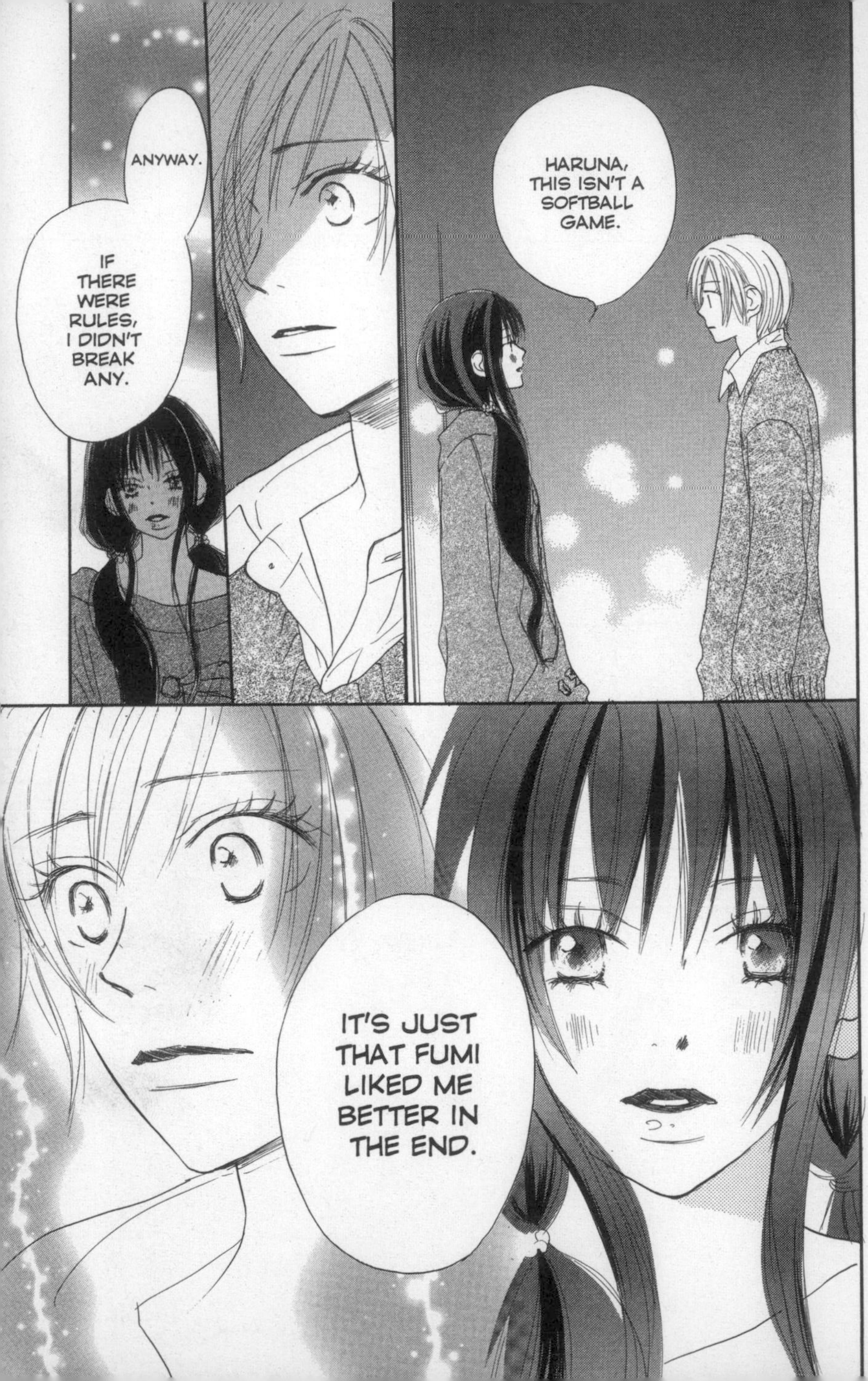
HARUNA, THIS ISN'T A SOFTBALL GAME.
ANYWAY.
IF THERE WERE RULES, I DIDN'T BREAK ANY.
IT'S JUST THAT FUMI LIKED ME BETTER IN THE END.

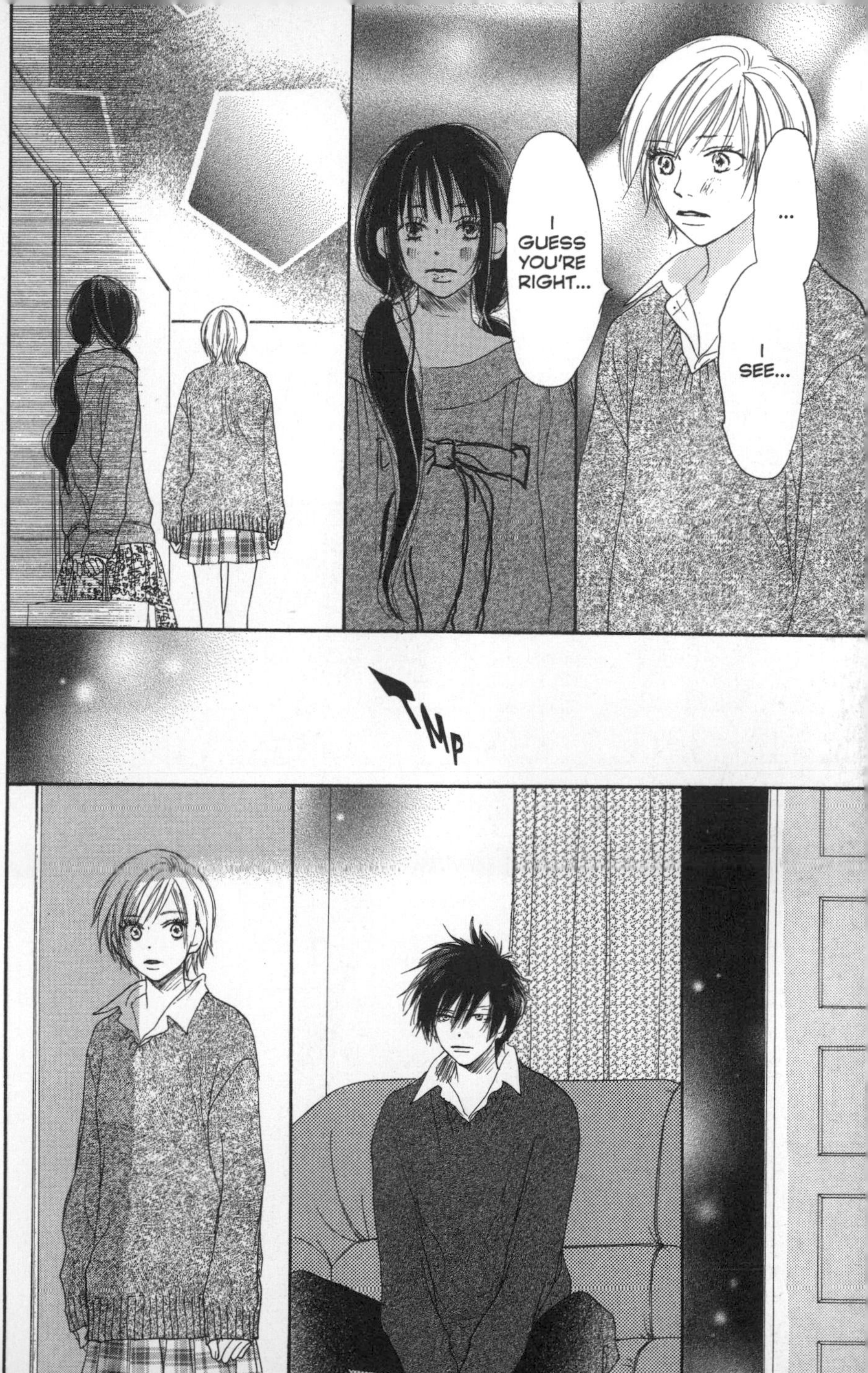
...
I SEE...
I GUESS YOU'RE RIGHT...
TMP

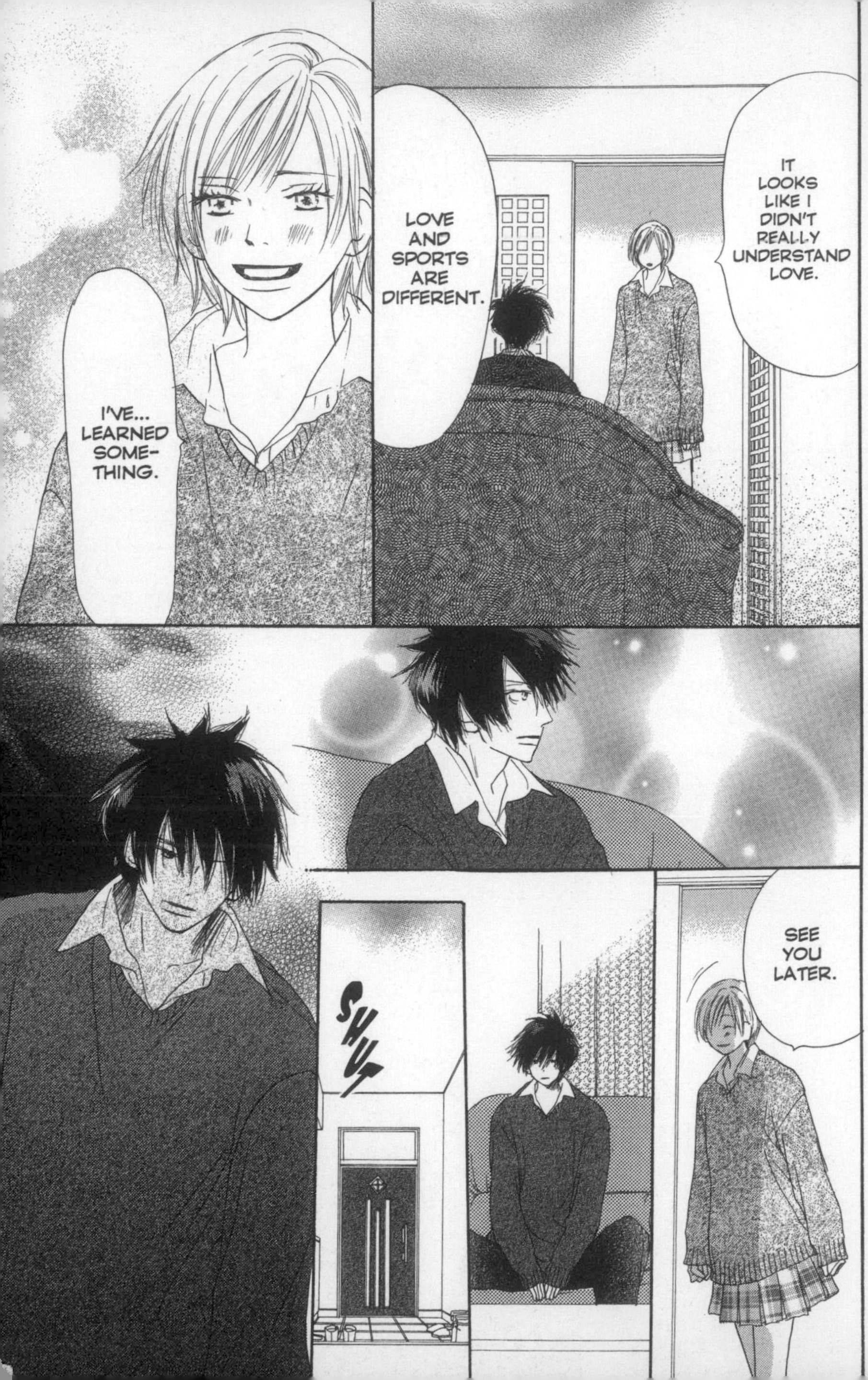
IT LOOKS LIKE I DIDN'T REALLY UNDERSTAND LOVE.
LOVE AND SPORTS ARE DIFFERENT.
I'VE... LEARNED SOME-THING.
SEE YOU LATER.
SHUT

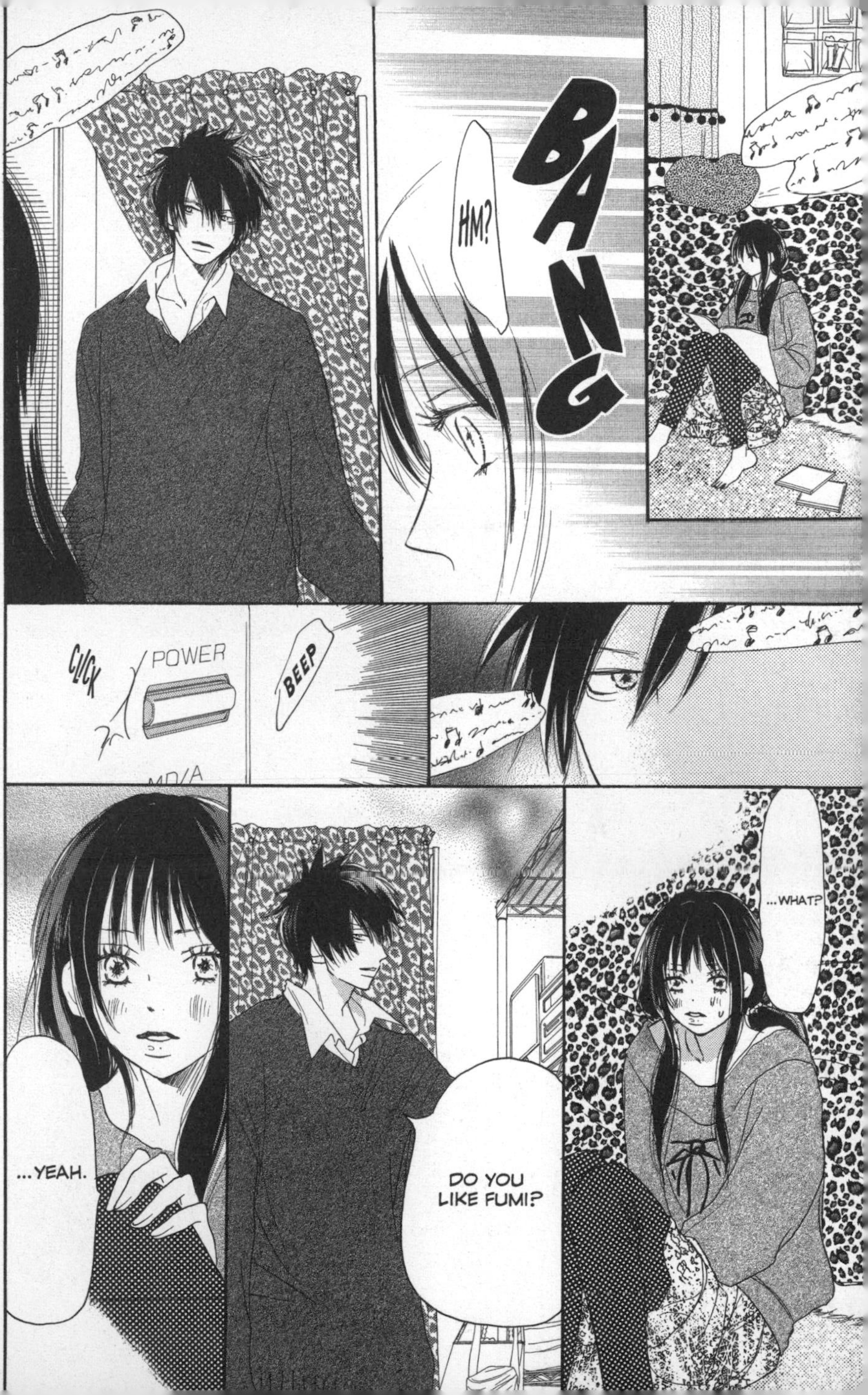
BANG
HM?
BEEP
POWER
CLICK
MD/A
...WHAT?
DO YOU LIKE FUMI?
...YEAH.

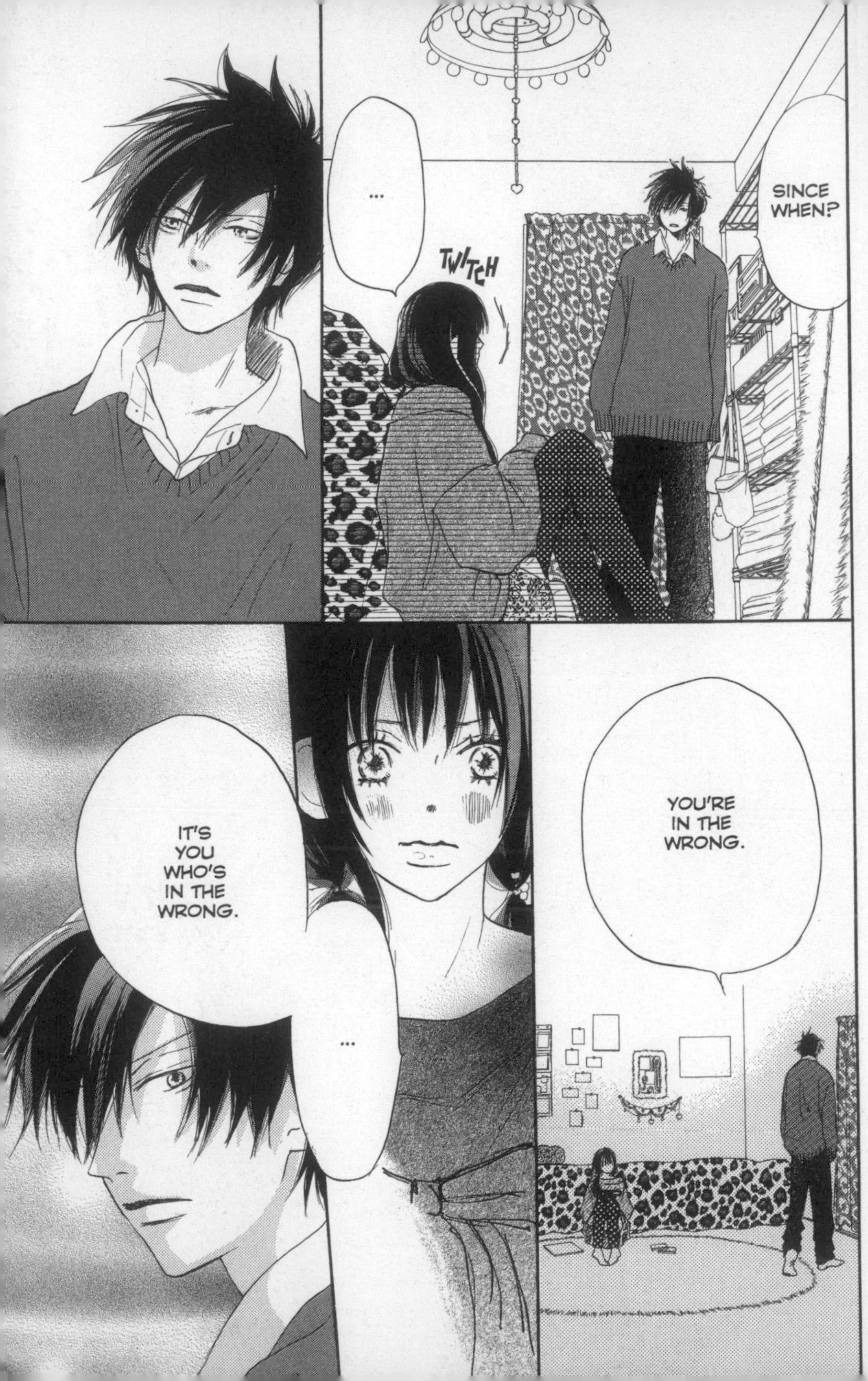
SINCE WHEN?
...
TWITCH
YOU'RE IN THE WRONG.
IT'S YOU WHO'S IN THE WRONG.
...

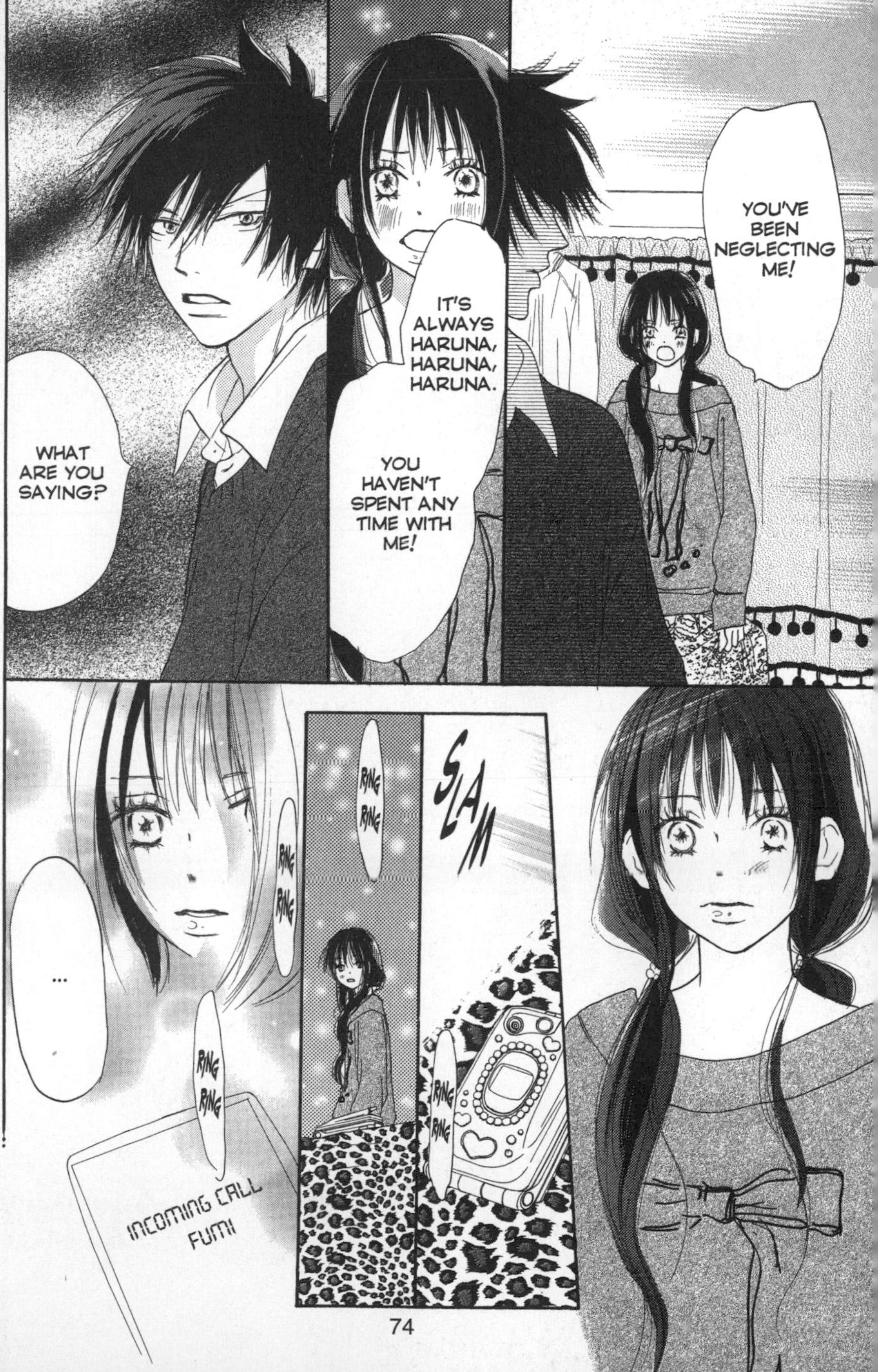
YOU'VE BEEN NEGLECTING ME!
IT'S ALWAYS HARUNA, HARUNA, HARUNA.
YOU HAVEN'T SPENT ANY TIME WITH ME!
WHAT ARE YOU SAYING?
SLAM
RING RING
RING RING
RING RING
...
RING RING
INCOMING CALL FUMI

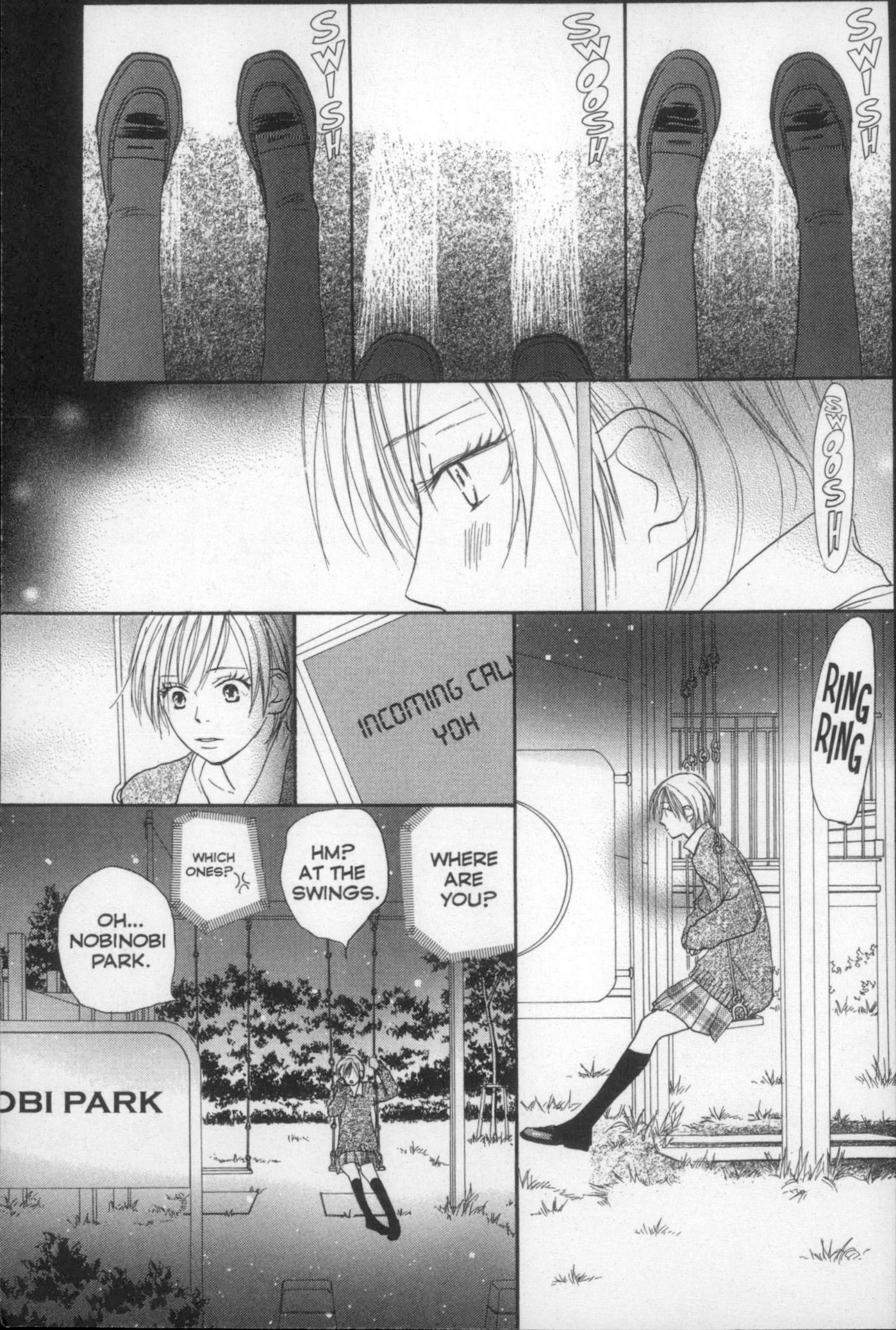
SWISH
SWOOSH
SWISH
SWOOSH
RING RING
INCOMING CAL
YOH
WHERE ARE YOU?
HM? AT THE SWINGS.
WHICH ONES?
OH... NOBINOBI PARK.
OBI PARK

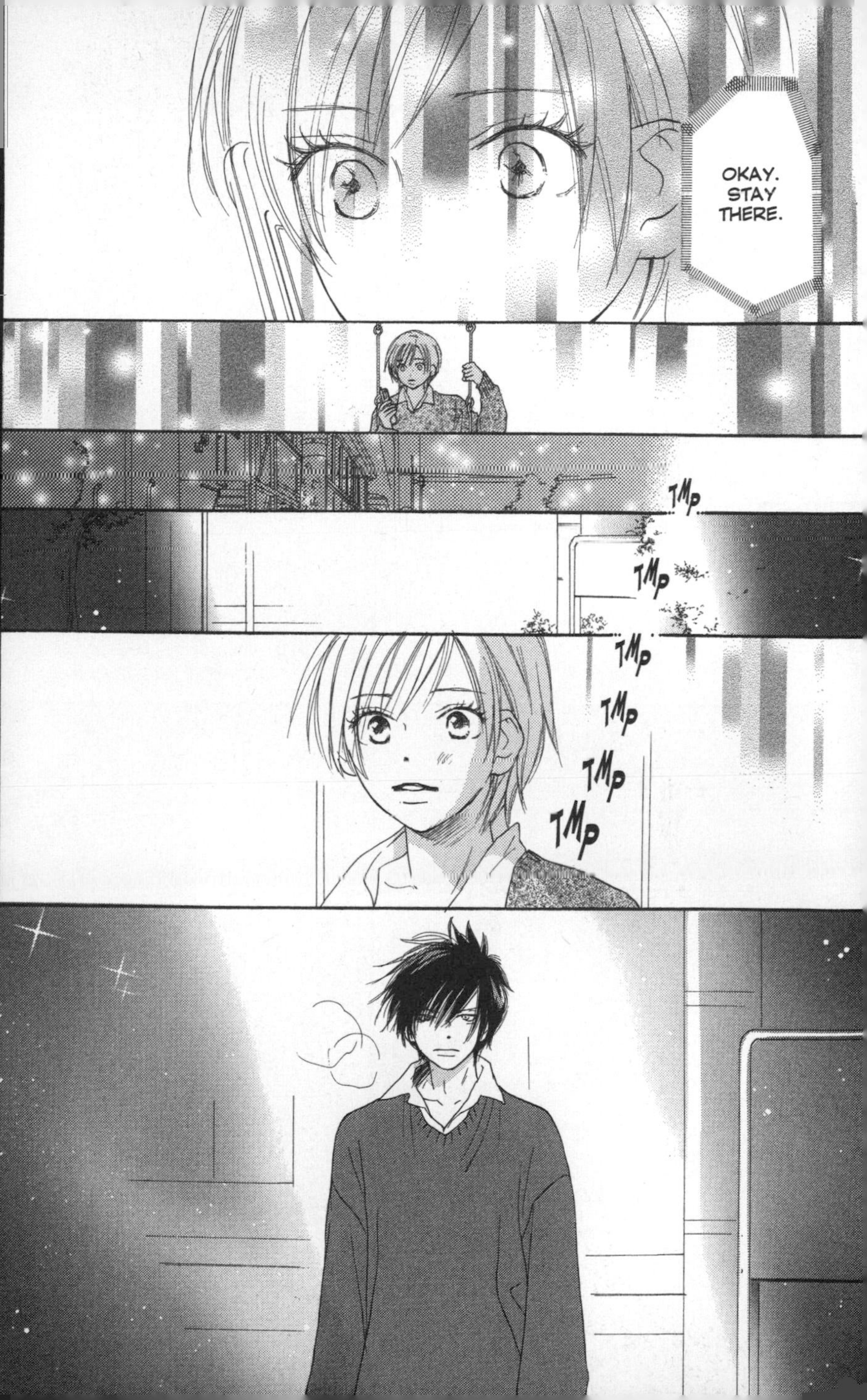
OKAY. STAY THERE.
TMP
TMP
TMP
TMP
TMP
TMP

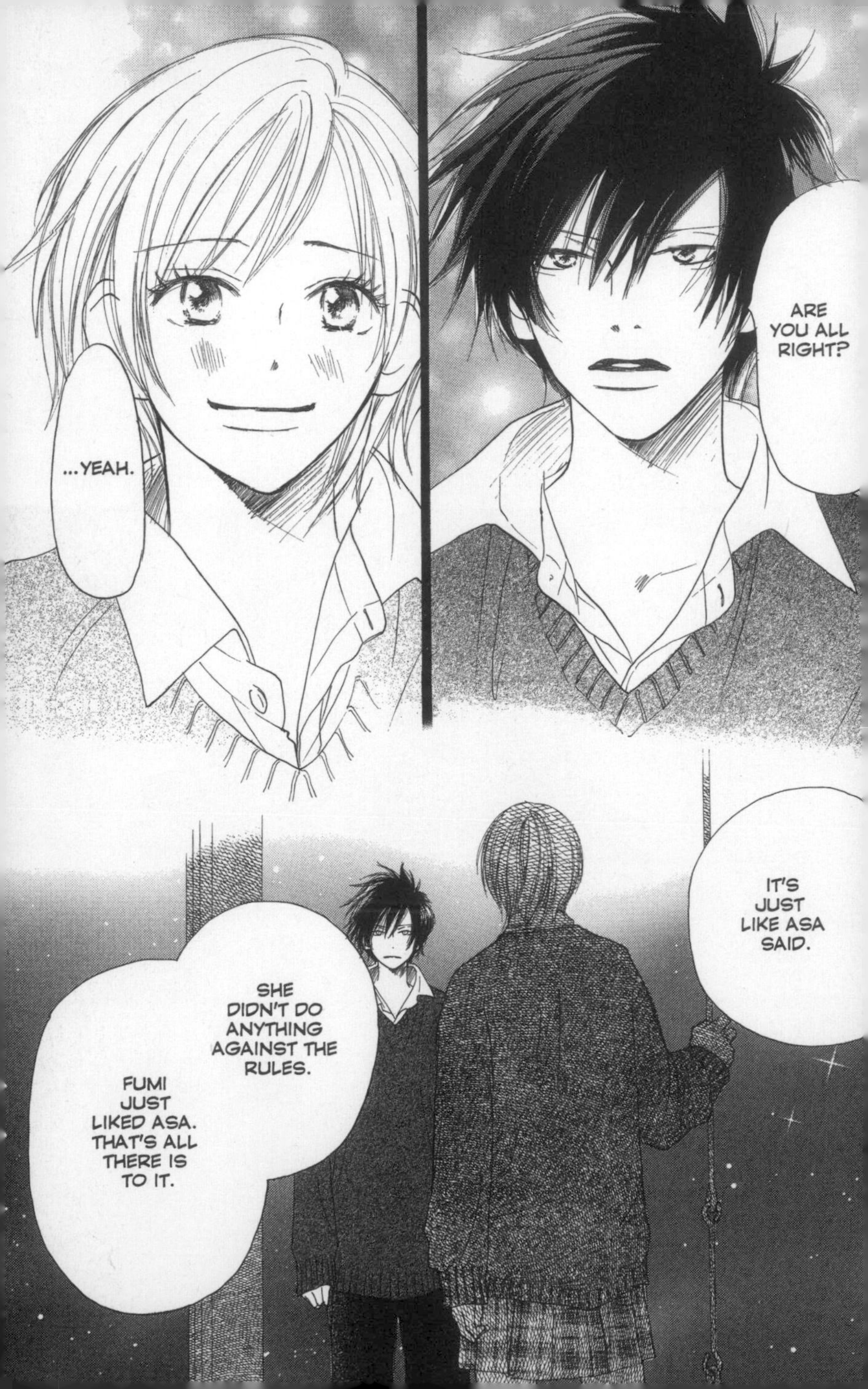
ARE YOU ALL RIGHT?
...YEAH.
IT'S JUST LIKE ASA SAID.
SHE DIDN'T DO ANYTHING AGAINST THE RULES.
FUMI JUST LIKED ASA. THAT'S ALL THERE IS TO IT.

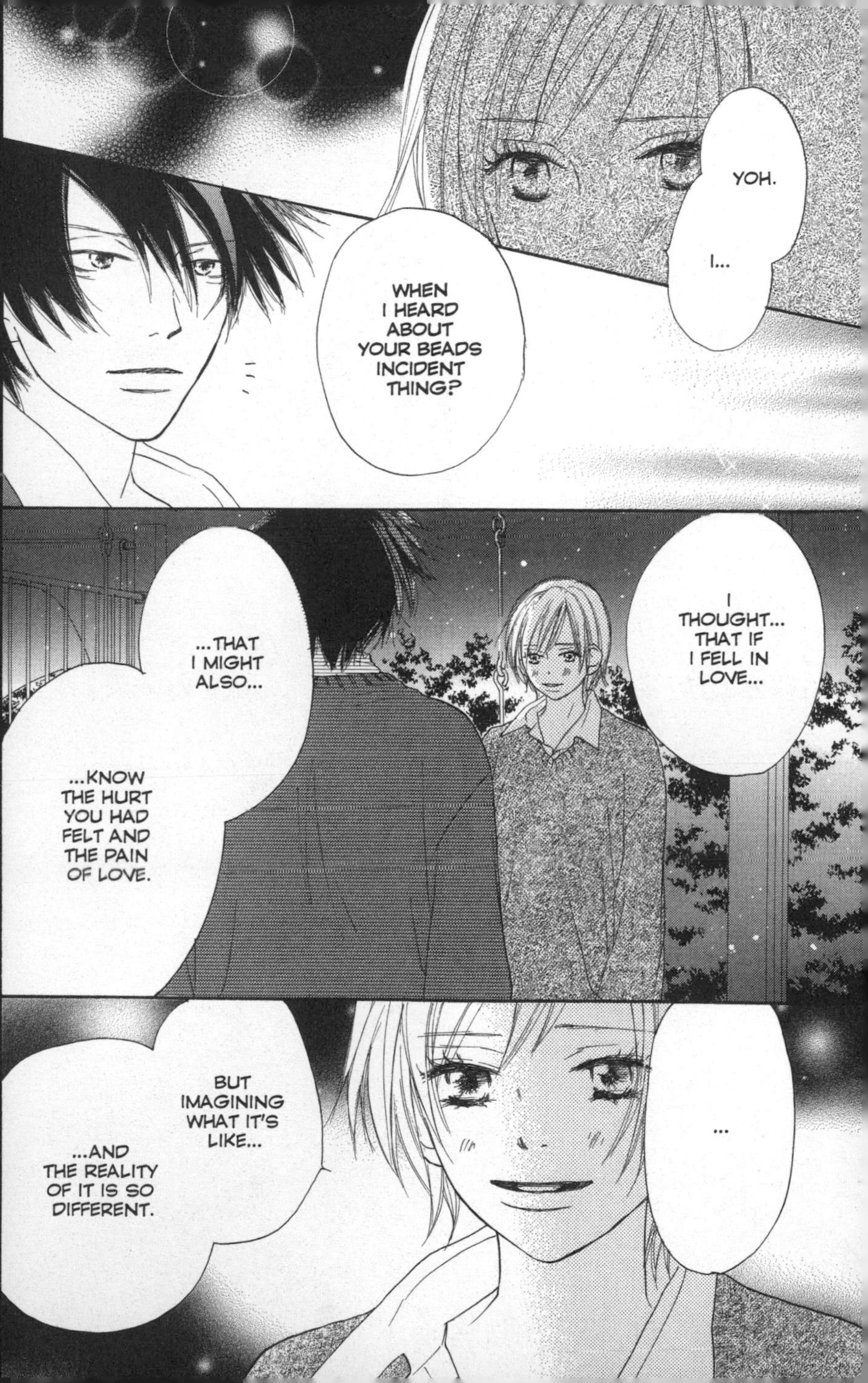
YOH.
I...
WHEN I HEARD ABOUT YOUR BEADS INCIDENT THING?
I THOUGHT... THAT IF I FELL IN LOVE...
...THAT I MIGHT ALSO...
...KNOW THE HURT YOU HAD FELT AND THE PAIN OF LOVE.
...
BUT IMAGINING WHAT IT'S LIKE...
...AND THE REALITY OF IT IS SO DIFFERENT.

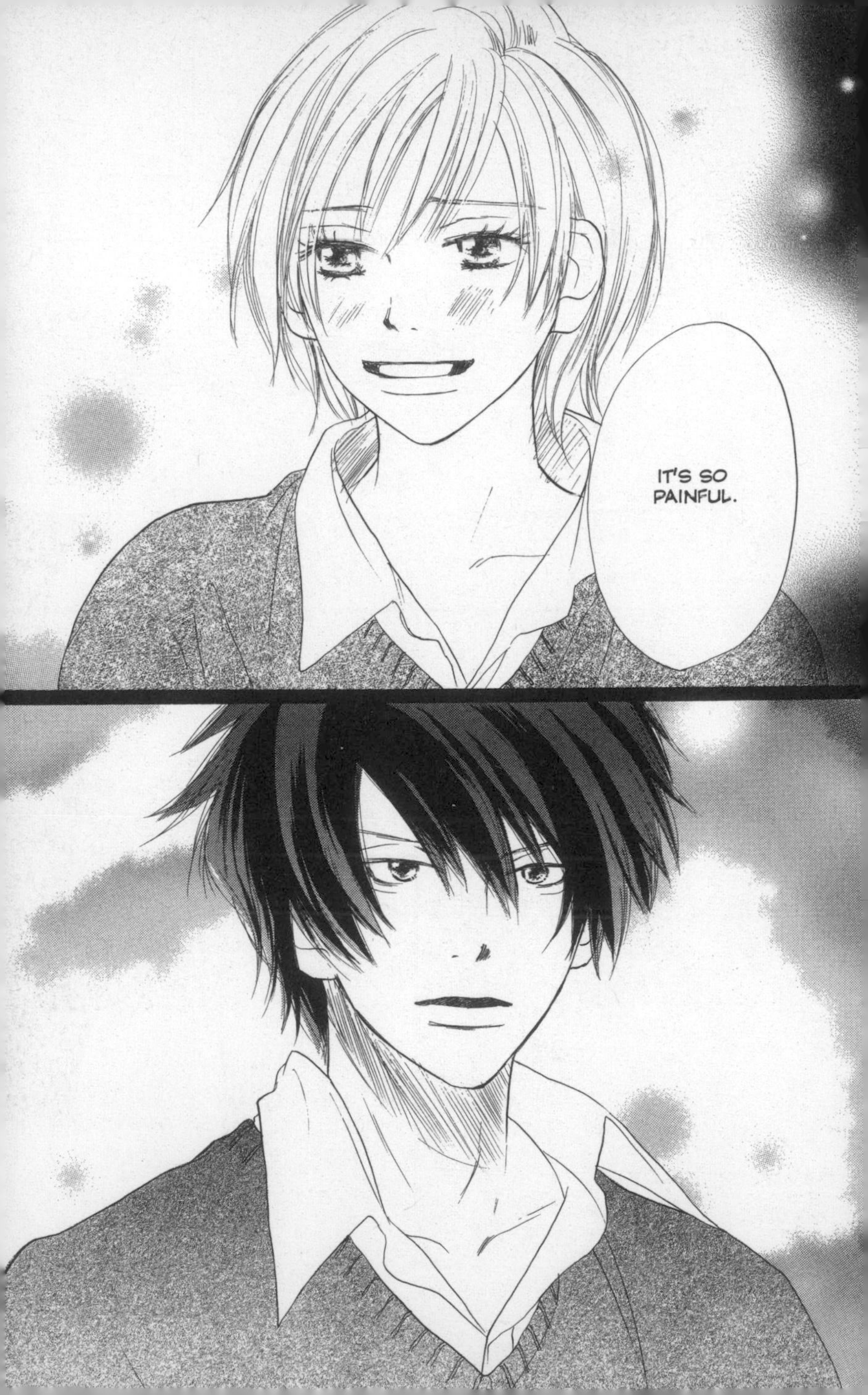
IT'S SO PAINFUL.

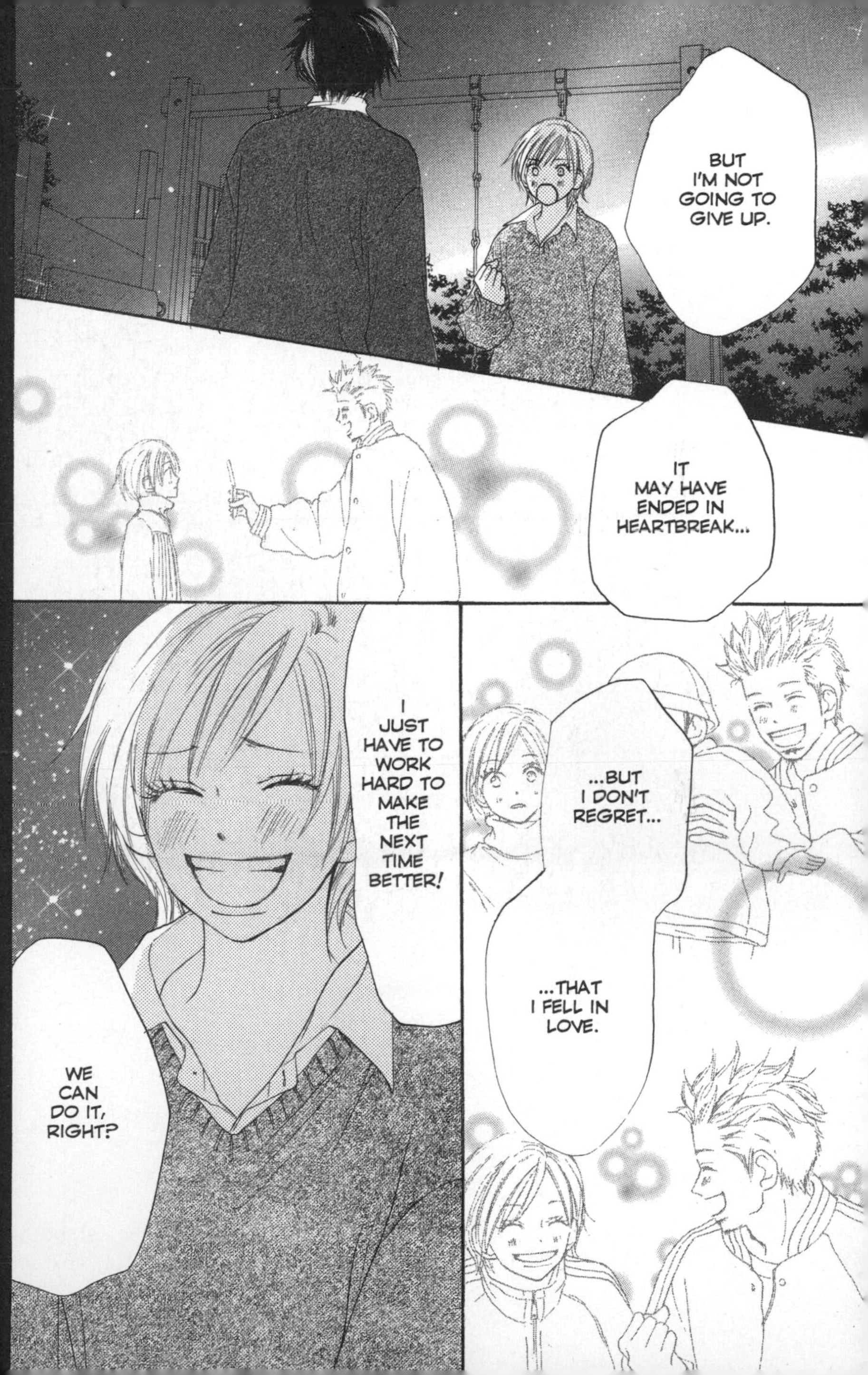
BUT I'M NOT GOING TO GIVE UP.
IT MAY HAVE ENDED IN HEARTBREAK...
...BUT I DON'T REGRET...
...THAT I FELL IN LOVE.
I JUST HAVE TO WORK HARD TO MAKE THE NEXT TIME BETTER!
WE CAN DO IT, RIGHT?

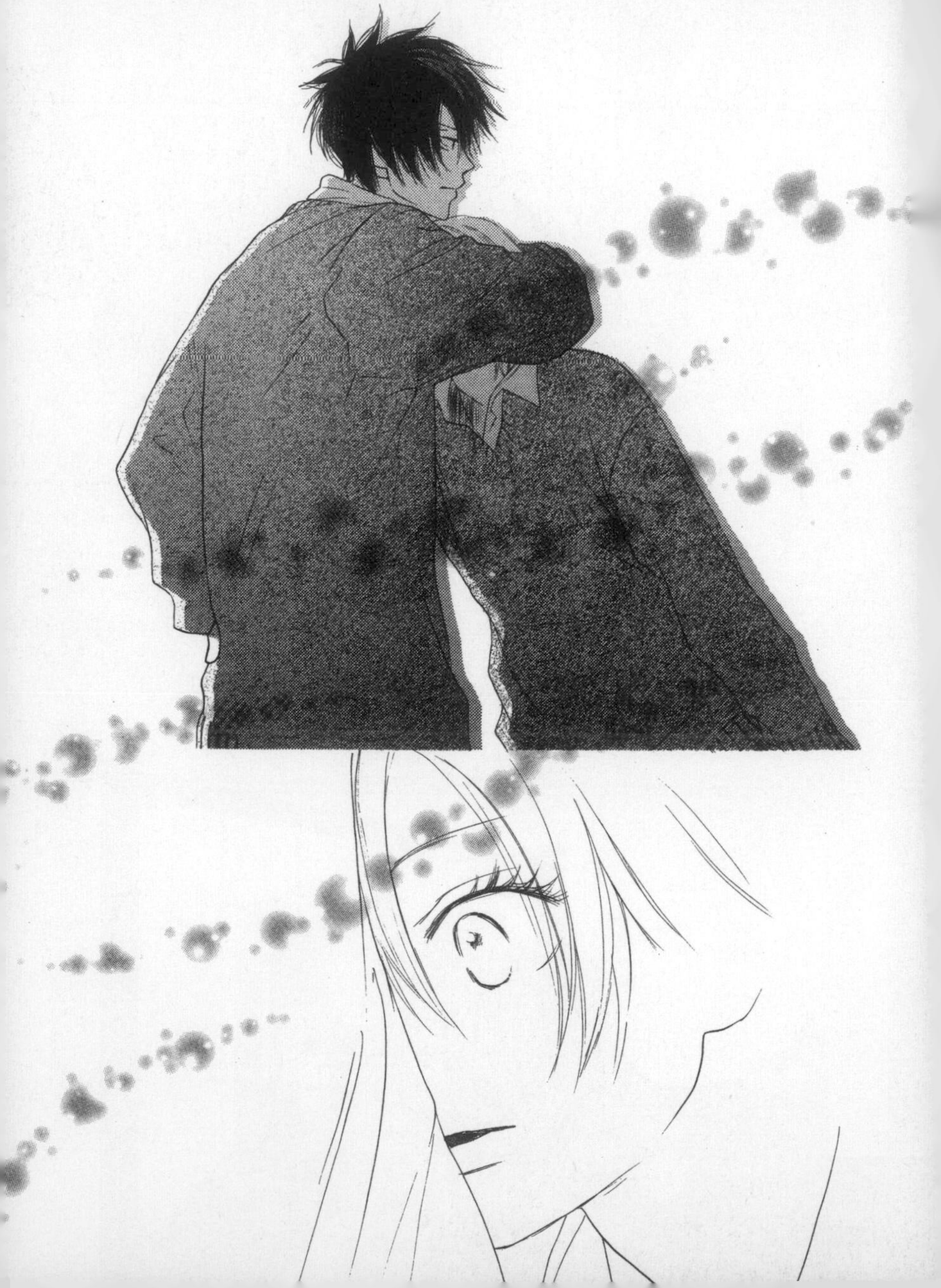

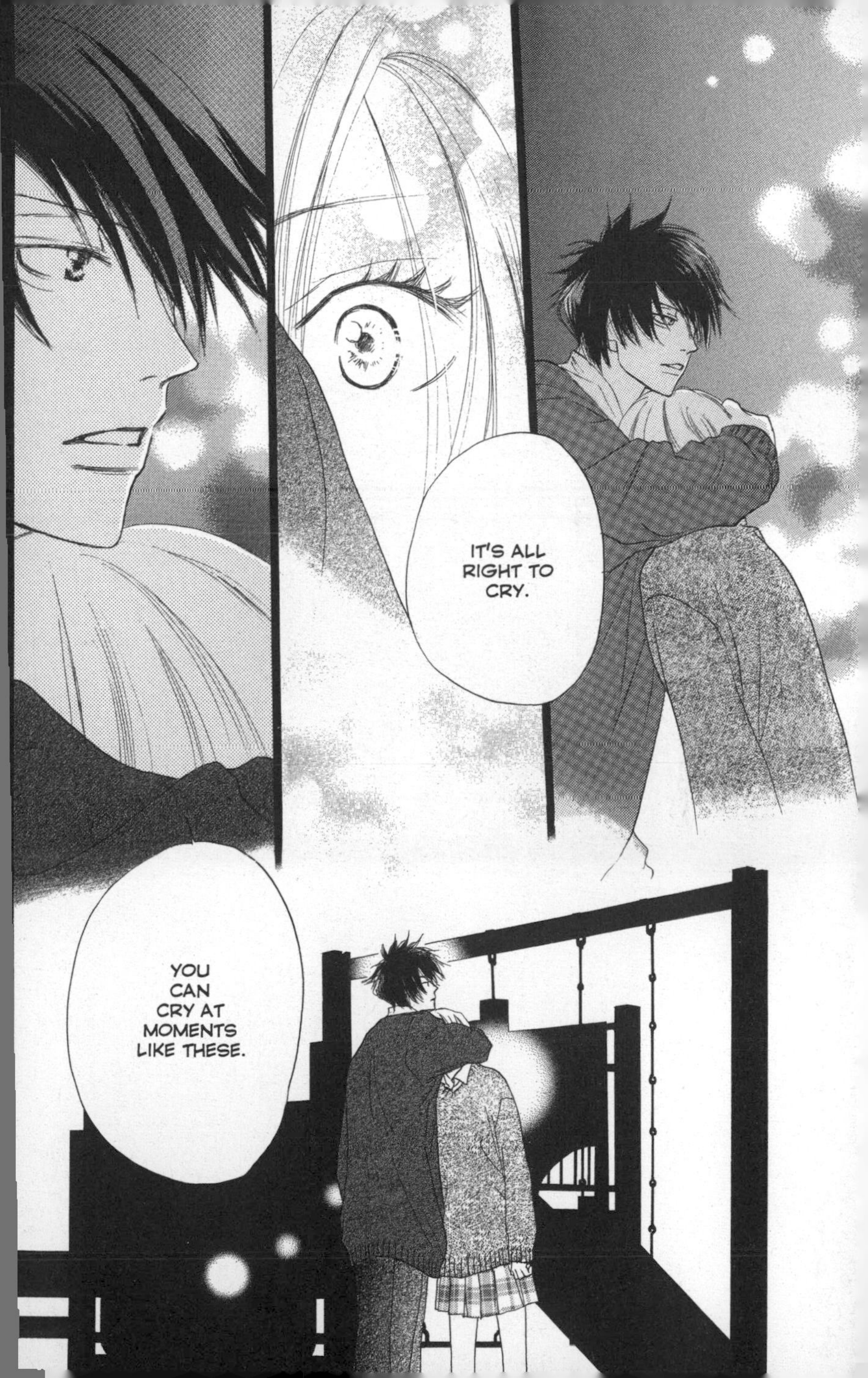
IT'S ALL RIGHT TO CRY.
YOU CAN CRY AT MOMENTS LIKE THESE.

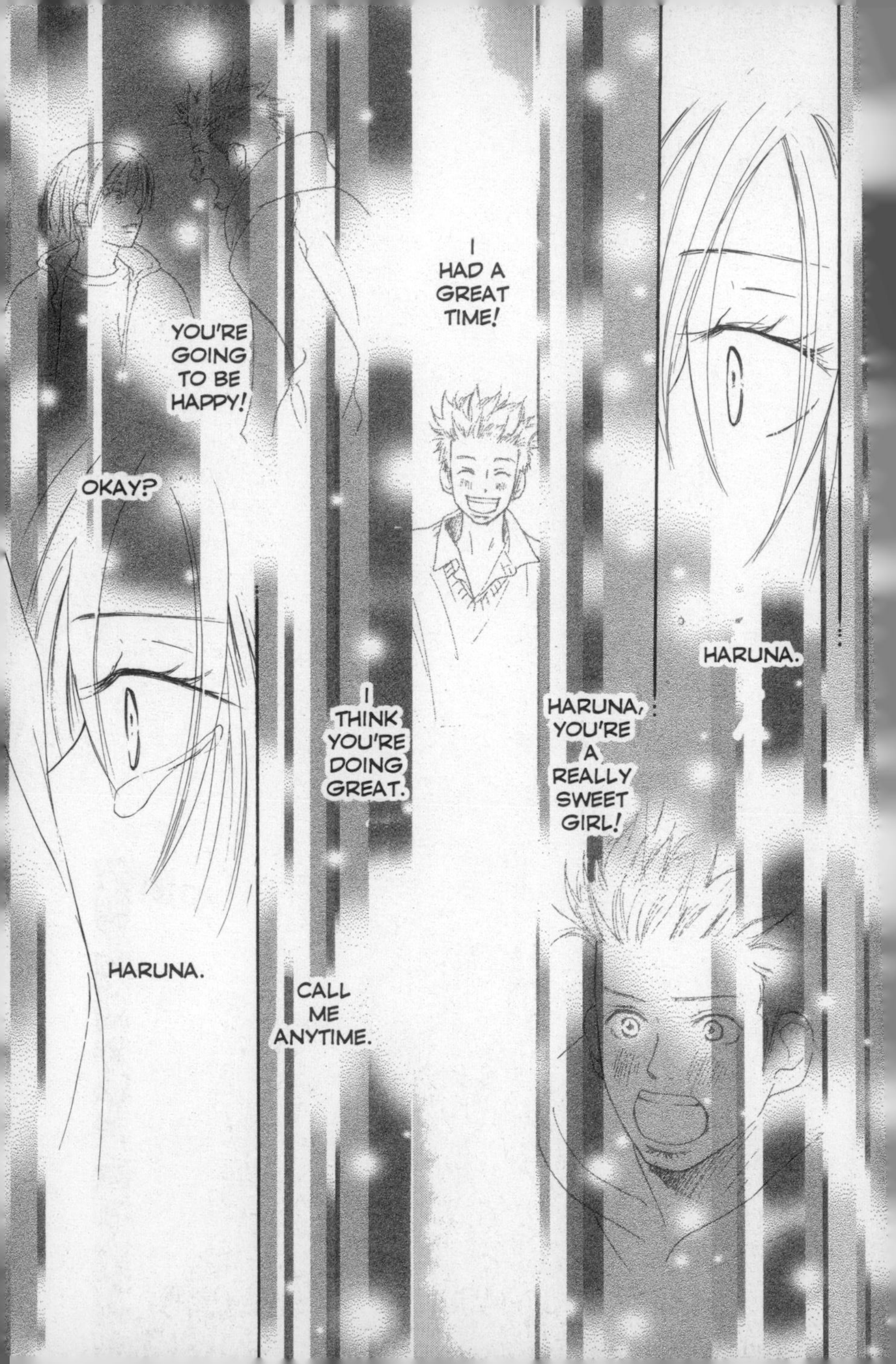
HARUNA.
HARUNA, YOU'RE A REALLY SWEET GIRL!
I HAD A GREAT TIME!
I THINK YOU'RE DOING GREAT.
CALL ME ANYTIME.
YOU'RE GOING TO BE HAPPY!
OKAY?
HARUNA.

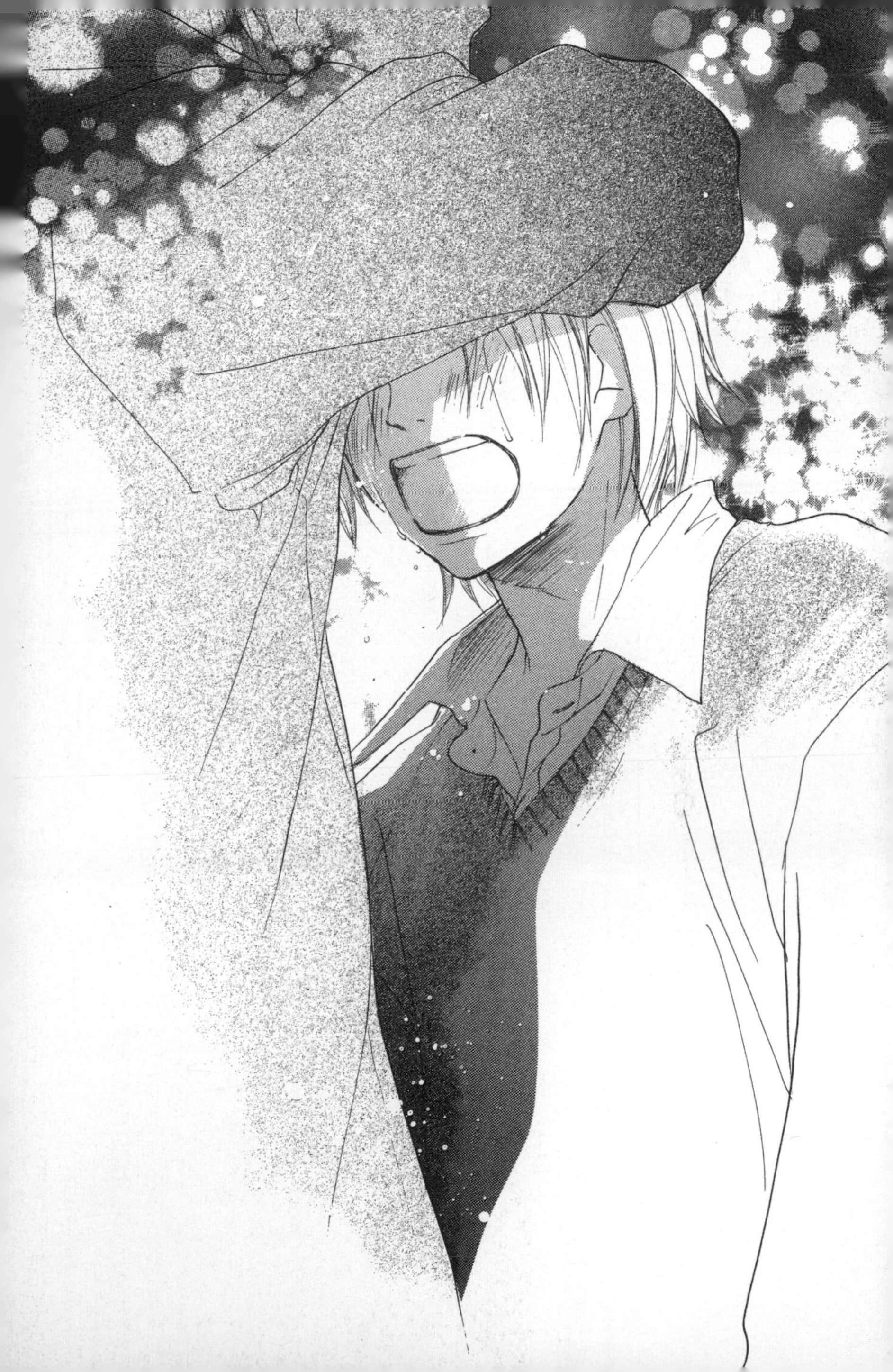

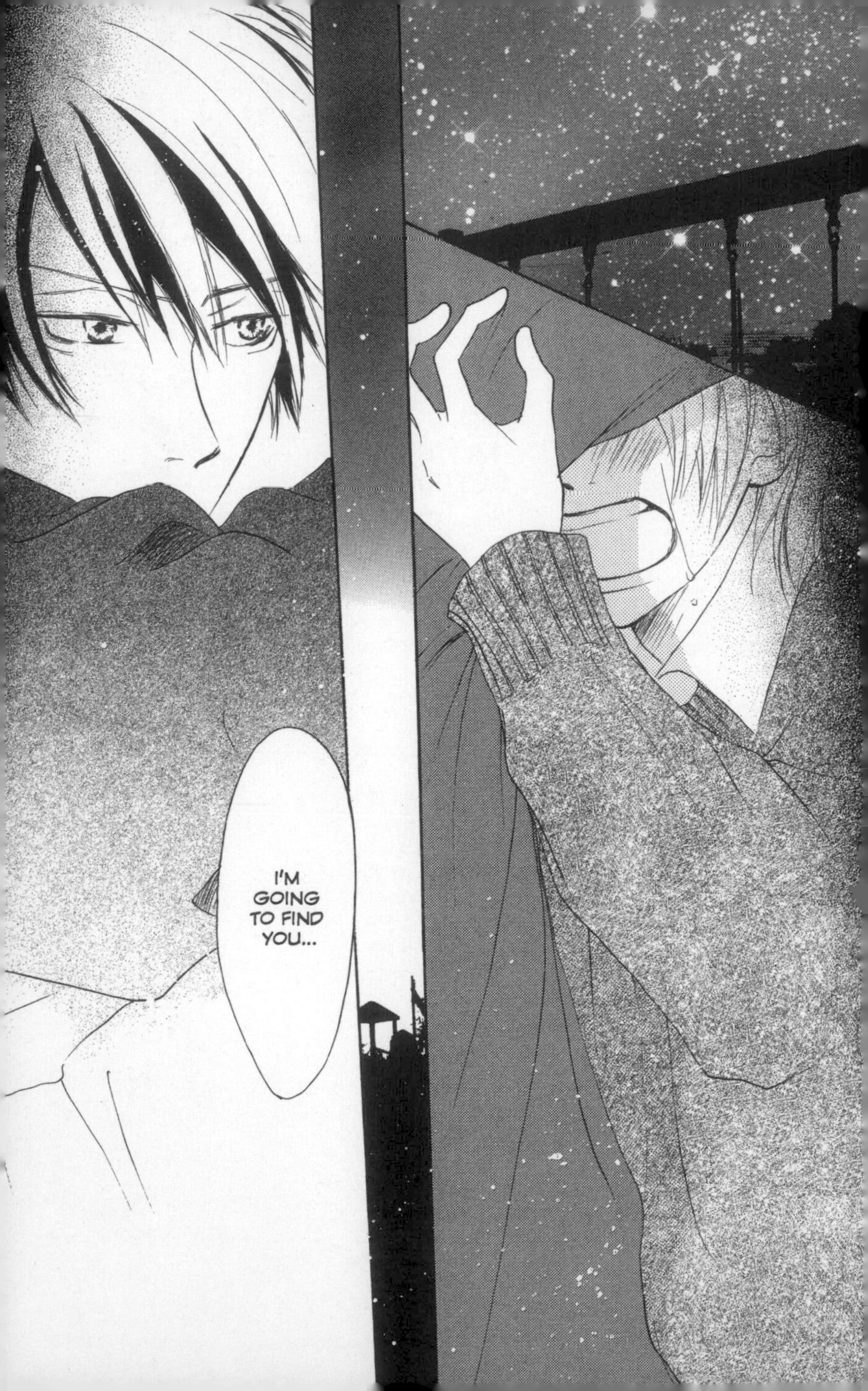
I'M GOING TO FIND YOU...

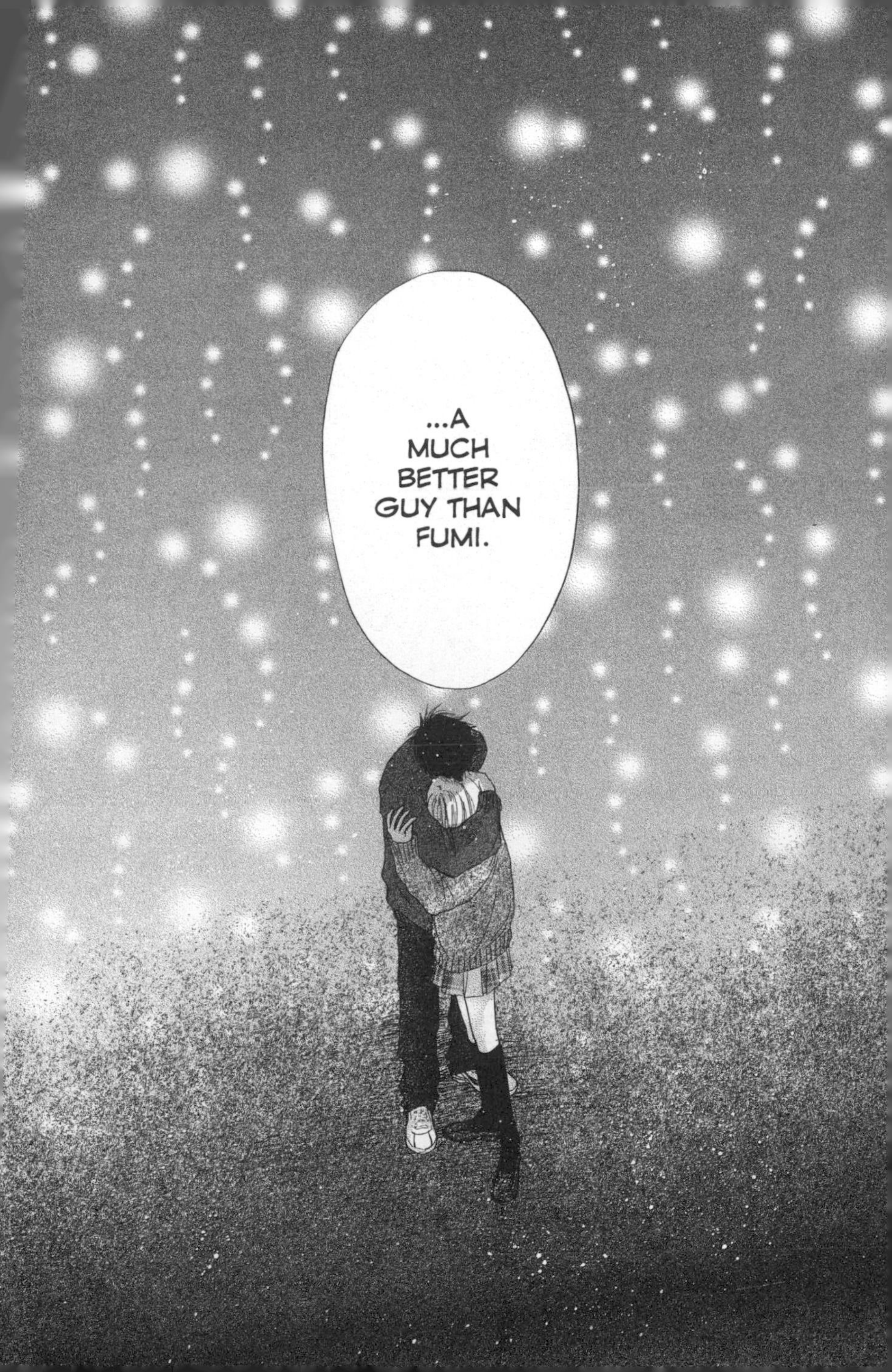
...A MUCH BETTER GUY THAN FUMI.

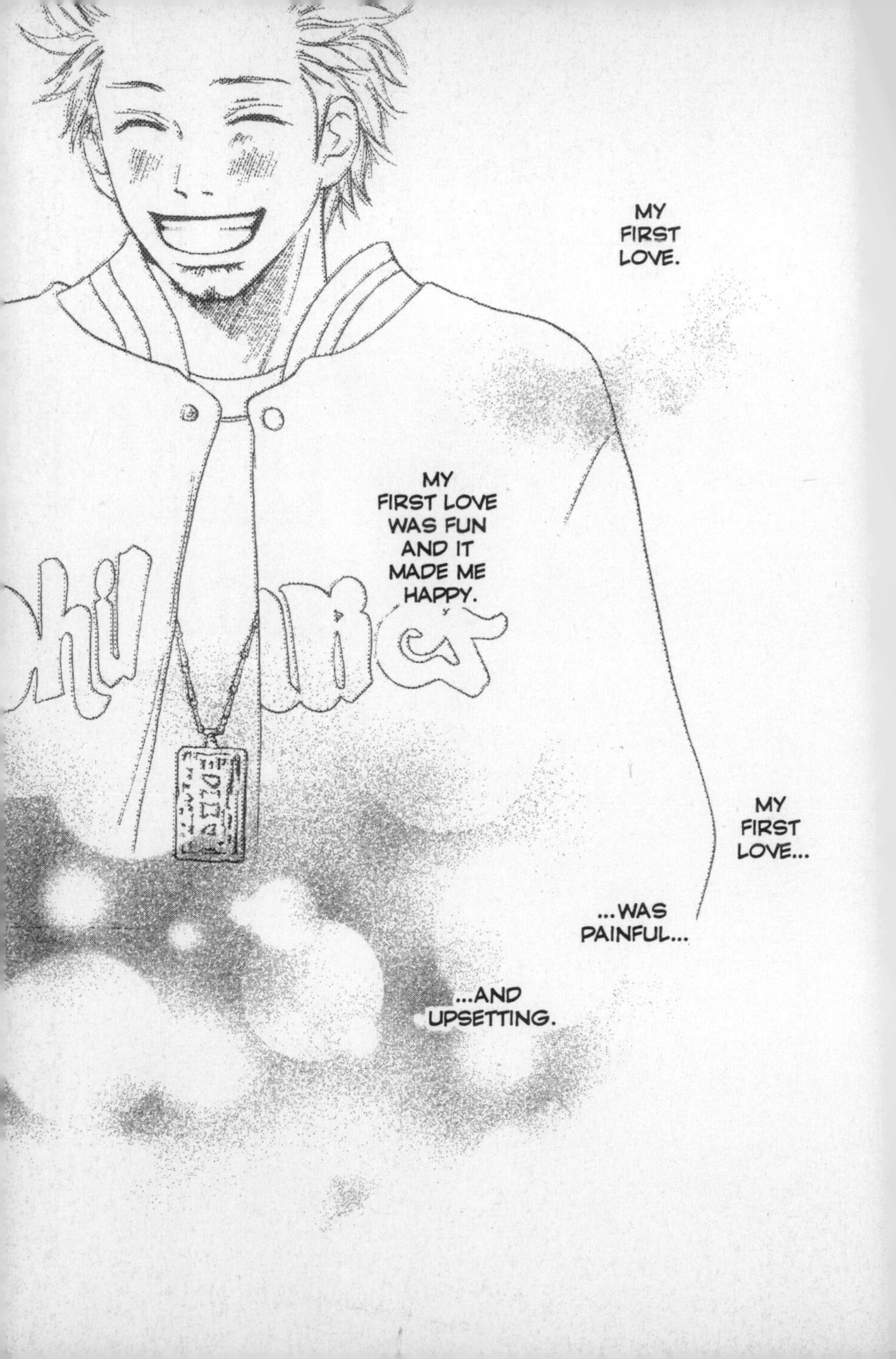
MY FIRST LOVE.
MY FIRST LOVE WAS FUN AND IT MADE ME HAPPY.
MY FIRST LOVE...
...WAS PAINFUL...
...AND UPSETTING.

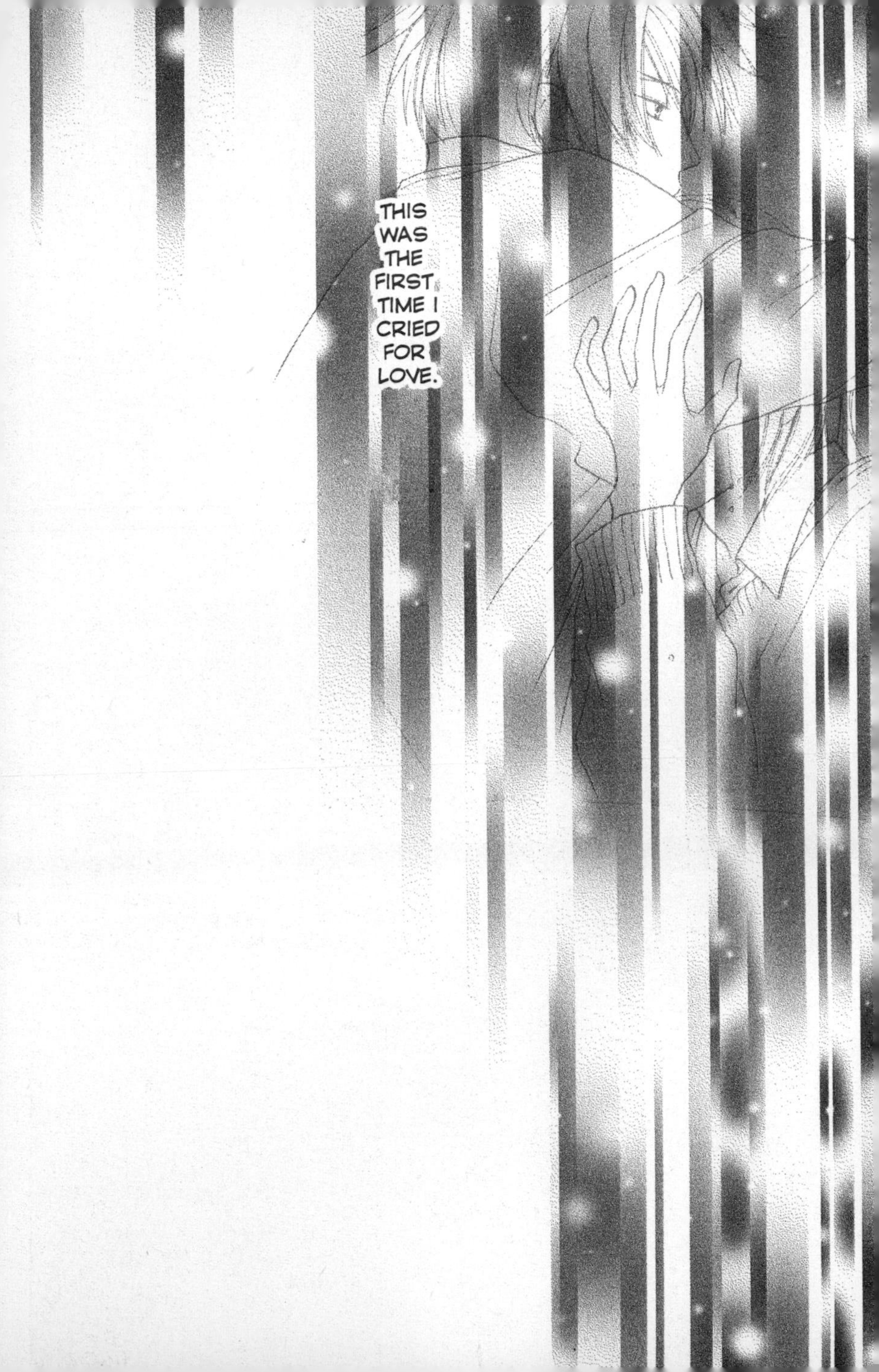
THIS WAS THE FIRST TIME I CRIED FOR LOVE.

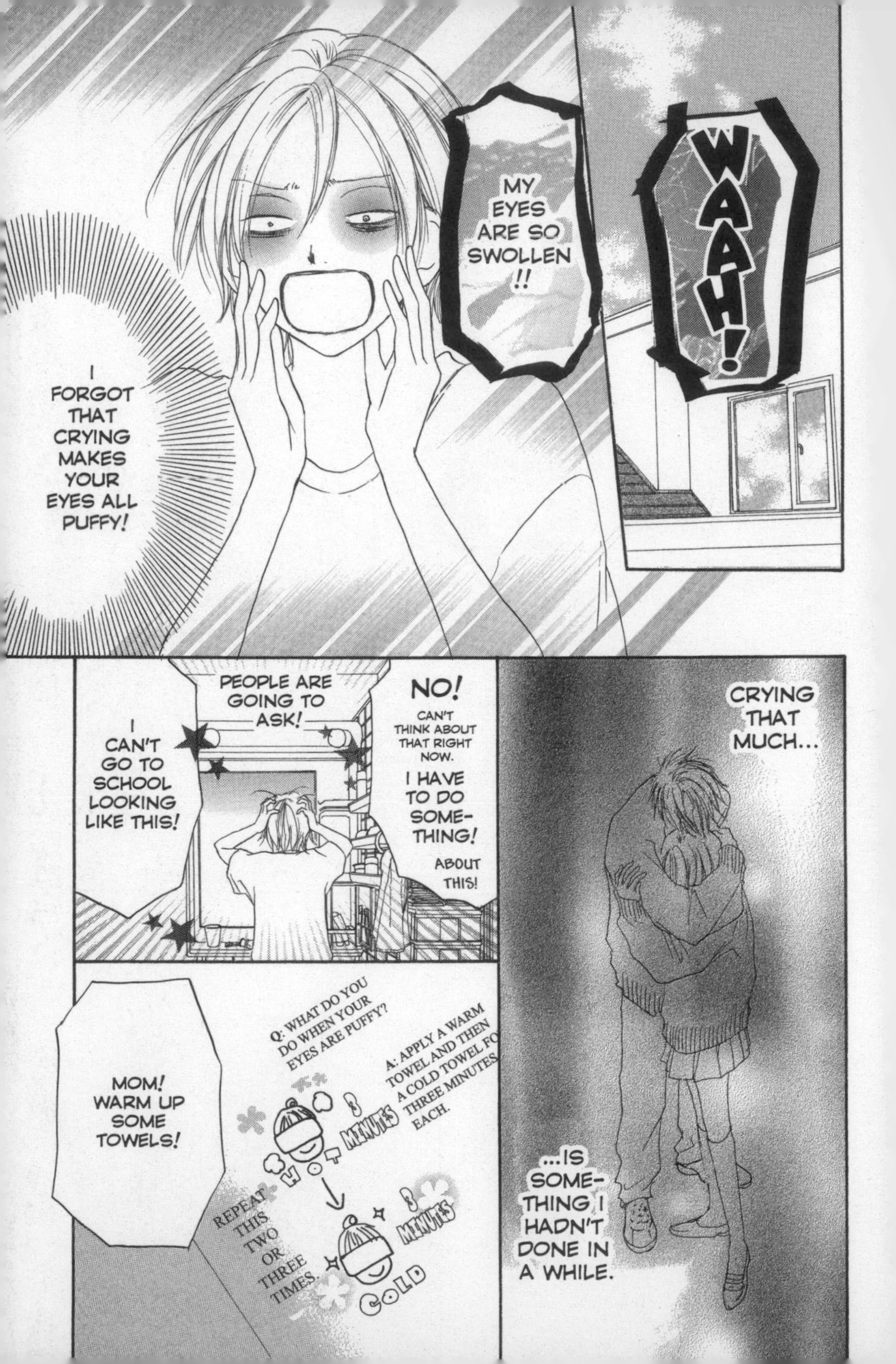
WAAH!
MY EYES ARE SO SWOLLEN!!
I FORGOT THAT CRYING MAKES YOUR EYES ALL PUFFY!
CRYING THAT MUCH...
...IS SOMETHING I HADN'T DONE IN A WHILE.
NO!
CAN'T THINK ABOUT THAT RIGHT NOW.
I HAVE TO DO SOMETHING!
ABOUT THIS!
PEOPLE ARE GOING TO ASK!
I CAN'T GO TO SCHOOL LOOKING LIKE THIS!
A: APPLY A WARM TOWEL AND THEN A COLD TOWEL FOR THREE MINUTES EACH.
Q: WHAT DO YOU DO WHEN YOUR EYES ARE PUFFY?
3 MINUTES
HOT
3 MINUTES
COLD
REPEAT THIS TWO OR THREE TIMES.
MOM! WARM UP SOME TOWELS!

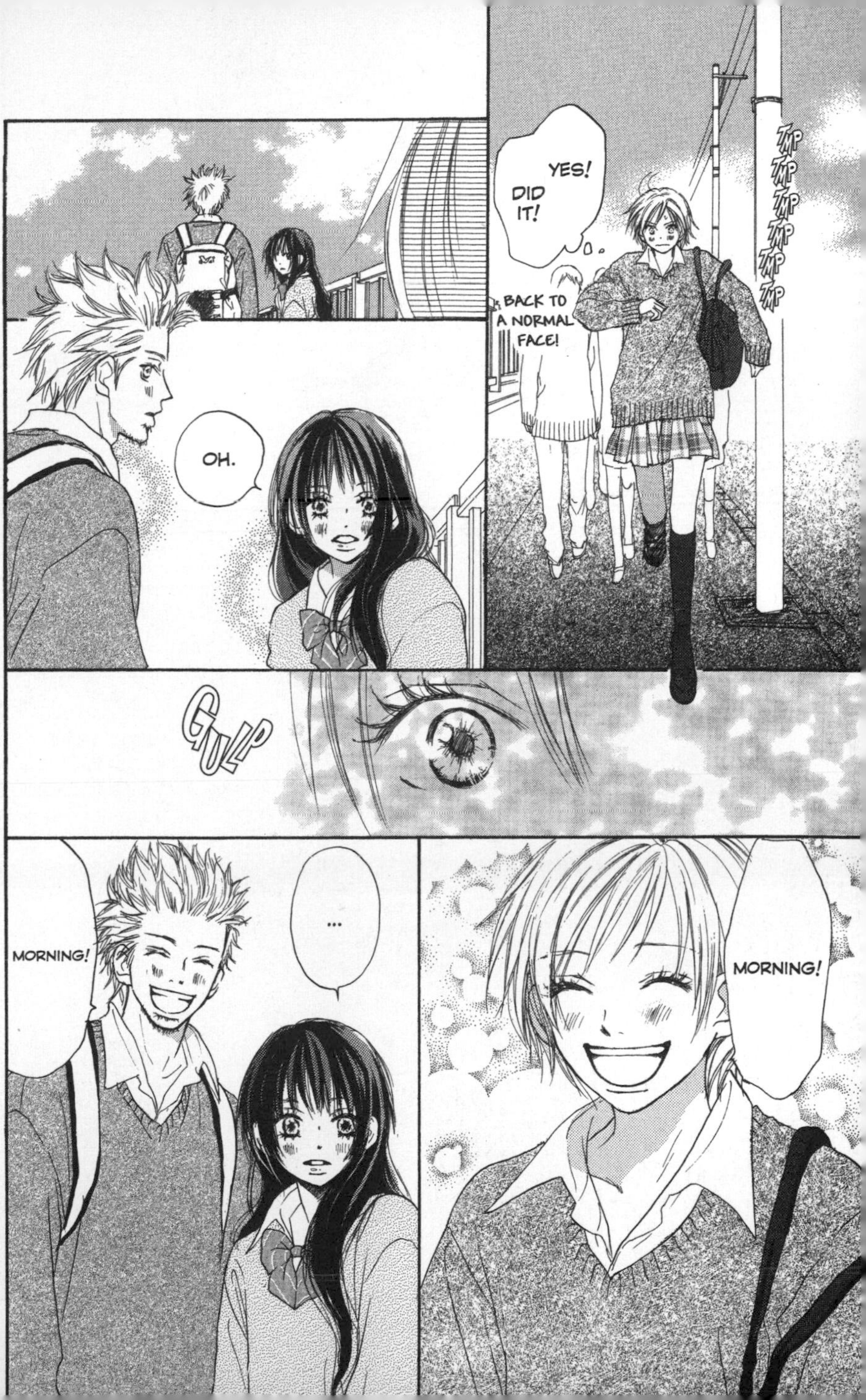
TMP TMP TMP TMP TMP TMP
YES! DID IT!
BACK TO A NORMAL FACE!
OH.
GULP
MORNING!
...
MORNING!

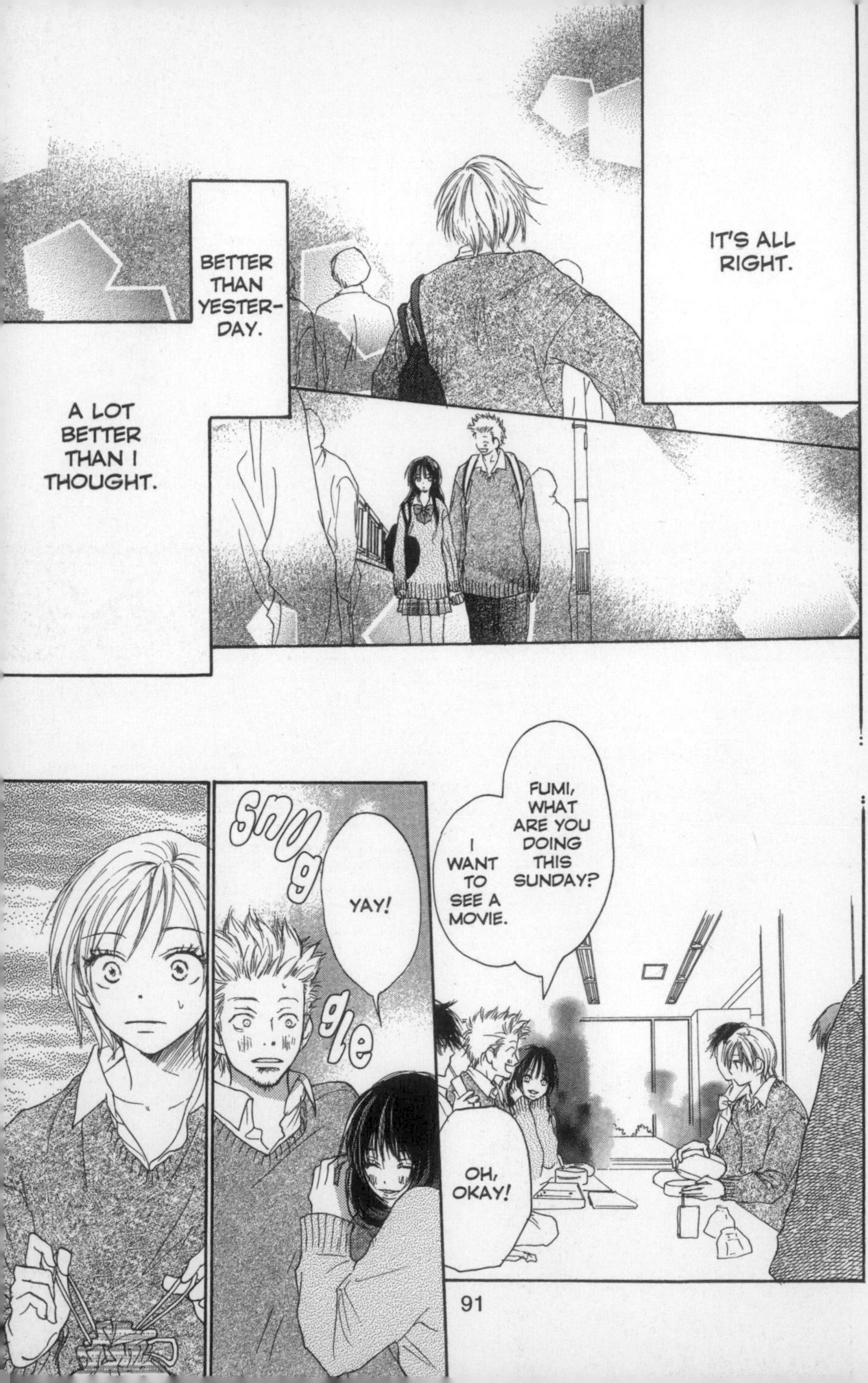
IT'S ALL RIGHT.
BETTER THAN YESTER-DAY.
A LOT BETTER THAN I THOUGHT.
FUMI, WHAT ARE YOU DOING THIS SUNDAY?
I WANT TO SEE A MOVIE.
OH, OKAY!
YAY!
snuggle

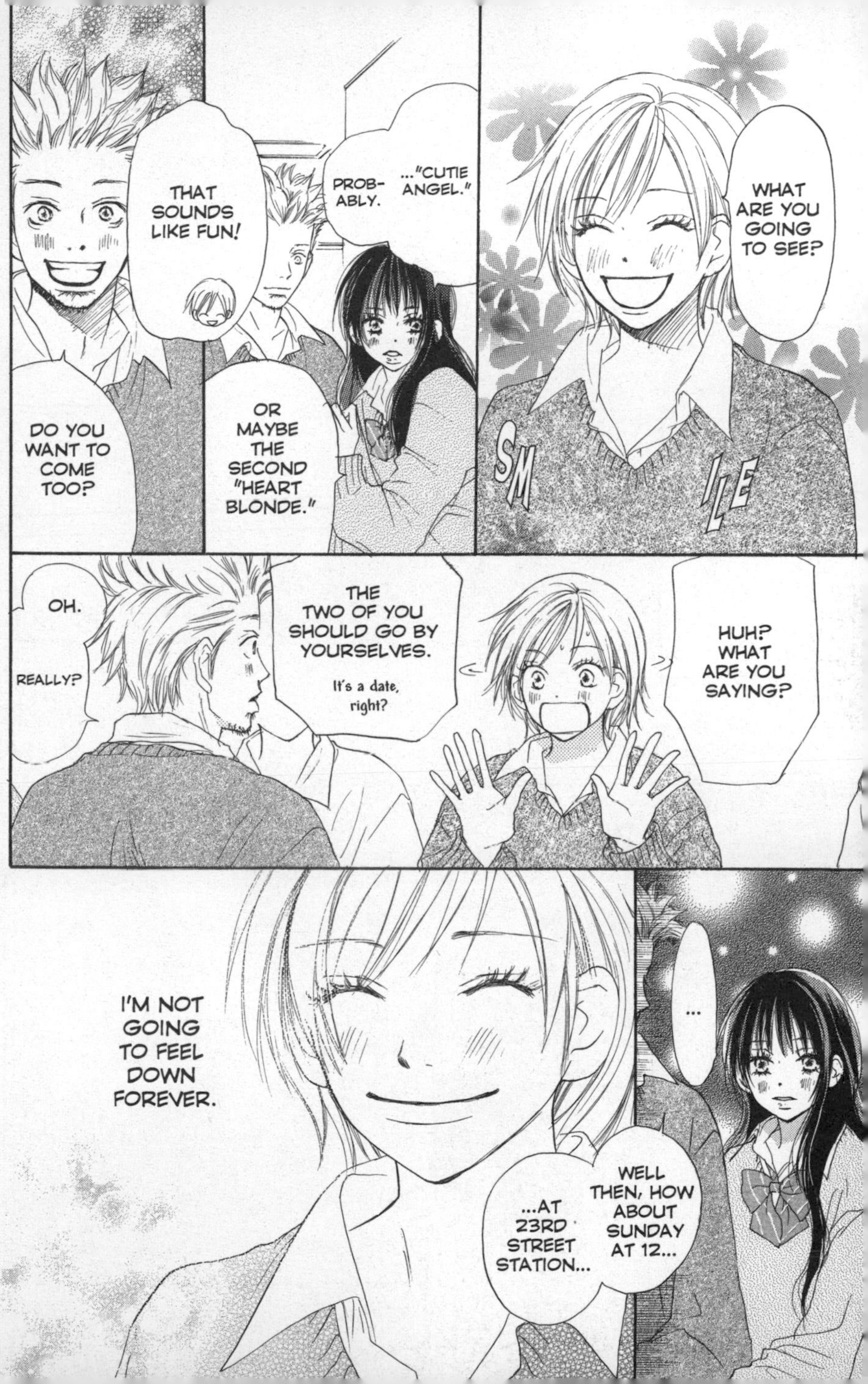
WHAT ARE YOU GOING TO SEE?
SMILE
..."CUTIE ANGEL."
PROB-ABLY.
OR MAYBE THE SECOND "HEART BLONDE."
THAT SOUNDS LIKE FUN!
DO YOU WANT TO COME TOO?
HUH? WHAT ARE YOU SAYING?
THE TWO OF YOU SHOULD GO BY YOURSELVES.
It's a date, right?
OH.
REALLY?
...
I'M NOT GOING TO FEEL DOWN FOREVER.
WELL THEN, HOW ABOUT SUNDAY AT 12...
...AT 23RD STREET STATION...

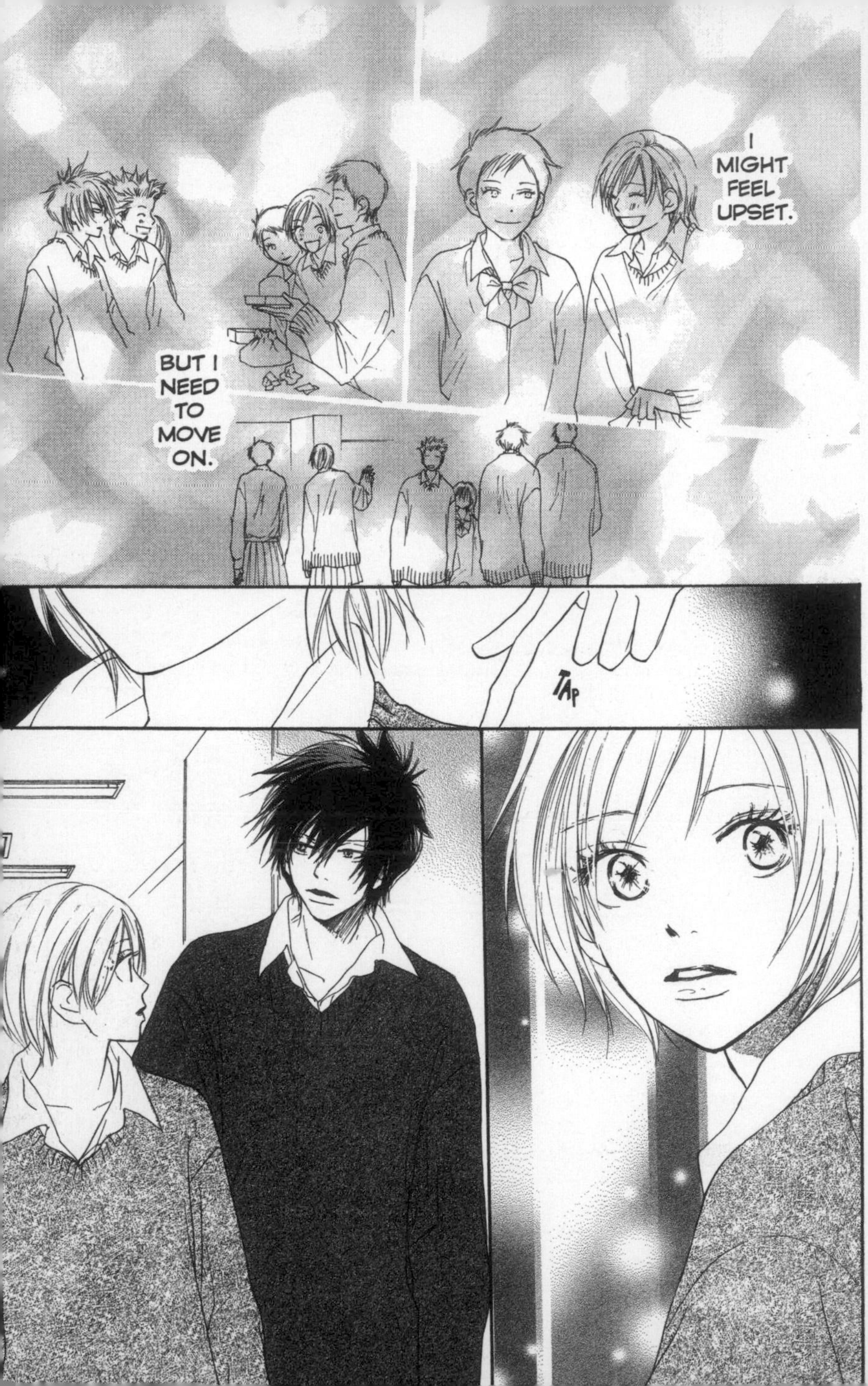
I MIGHT FEEL UPSET.
BUT I NEED TO MOVE ON.
TAP

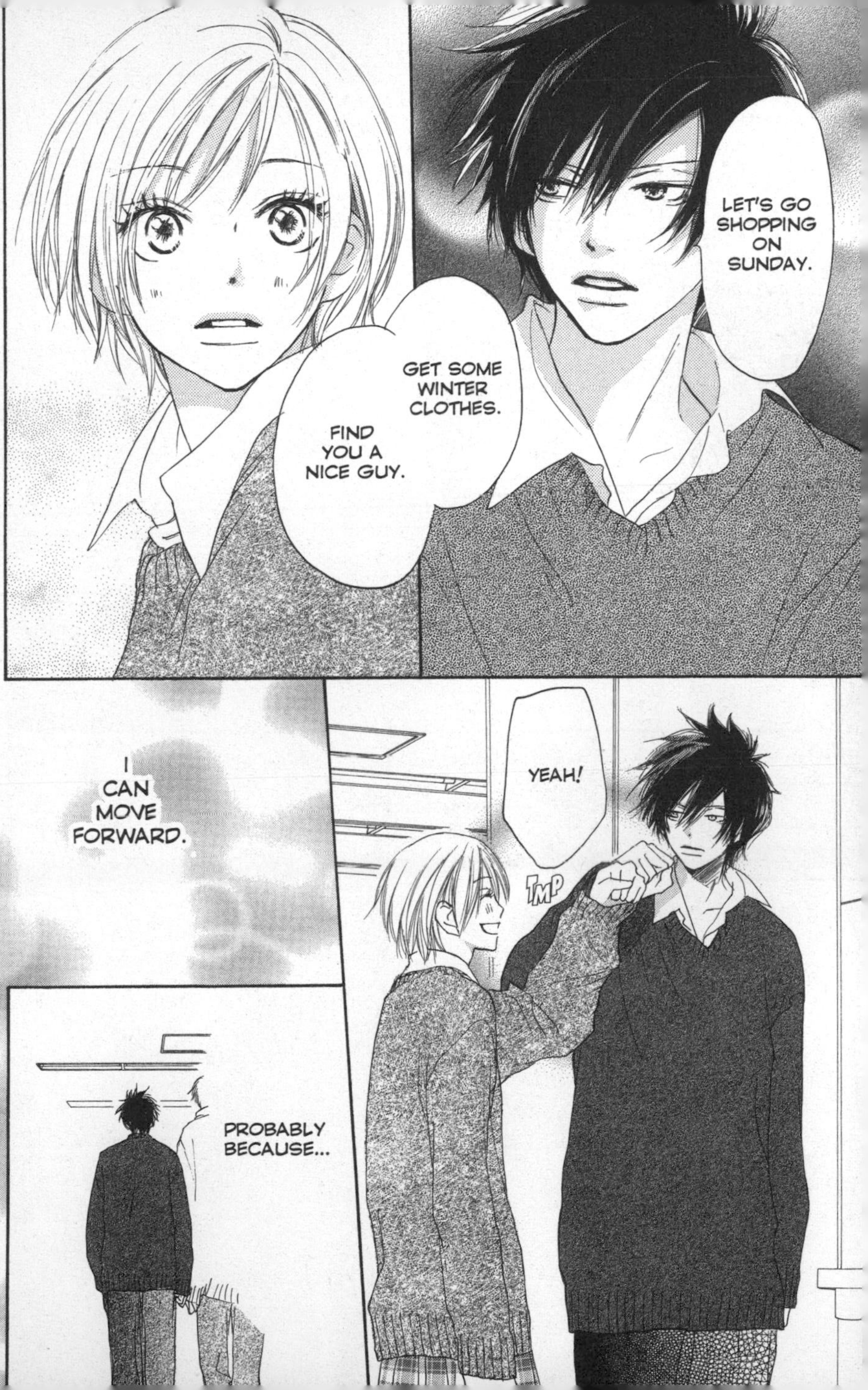
LET'S GO SHOPPING ON SUNDAY.
GET SOME WINTER CLOTHES.
FIND YOU A NICE GUY.
YEAH!
TMP
I CAN MOVE FORWARD.
PROBABLY BECAUSE...

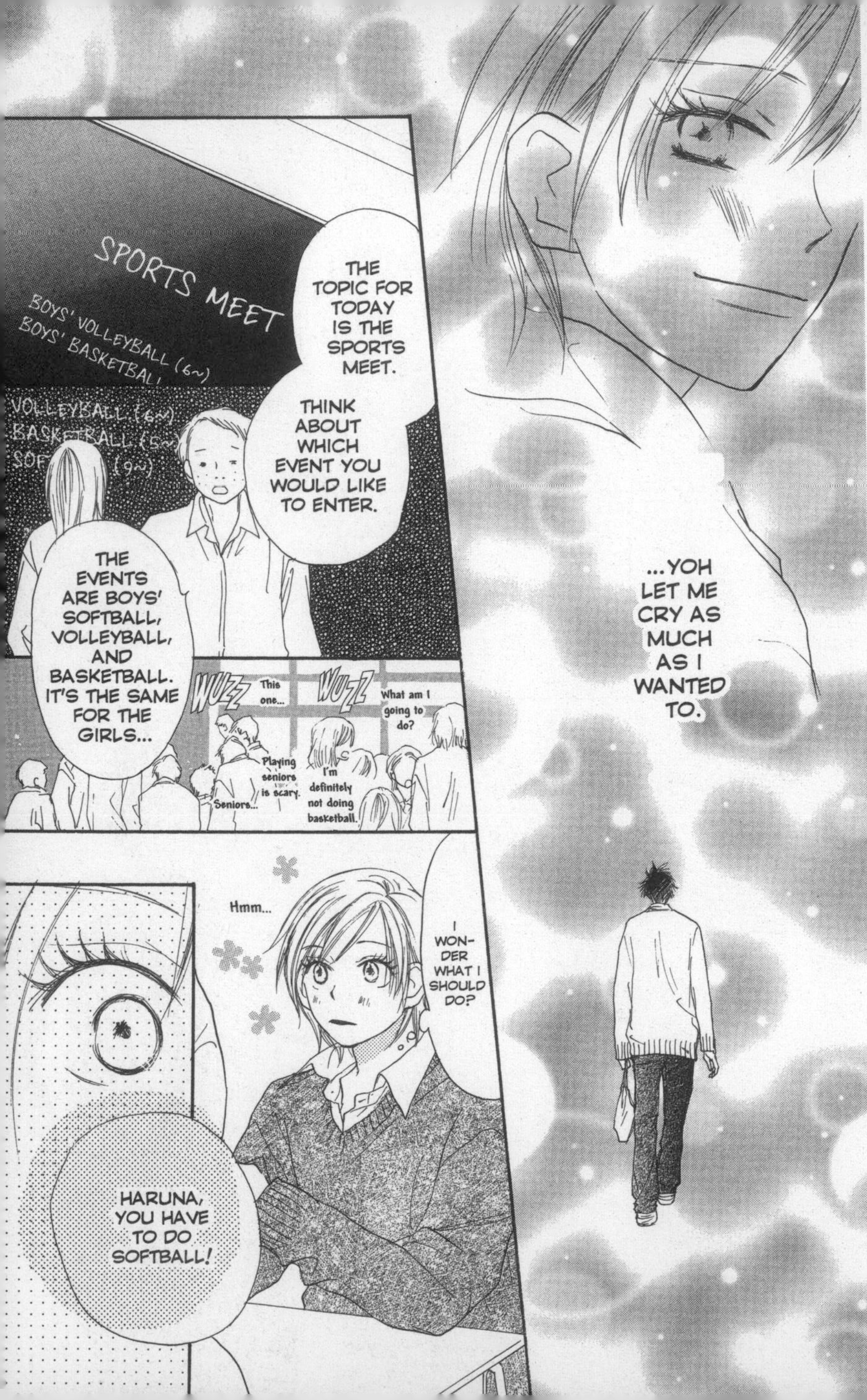
...YOH LET ME CRY AS MUCH AS I WANTED TO.
SPORTS MEET
BOYS' VOLLEYBALL (6~)
BOYS' BASKETBALL
VOLLEYBALL (6~)
BASKETBALL (5~)
THE TOPIC FOR TODAY IS THE SPORTS MEET.
THINK ABOUT WHICH EVENT YOU WOULD LIKE TO ENTER.
THE EVENTS ARE BOYS' SOFTBALL, VOLLEYBALL, AND BASKETBALL. IT'S THE SAME FOR THE GIRLS...
What am I going to do?
WUZZ
This one...
WUZZ
I'm definitely not doing basketball.
Playing seniors is scary.
Seniors...
I WONDER WHAT I SHOULD DO?
Hmm...
HARUNA, YOU HAVE TO DO SOFTBALL!

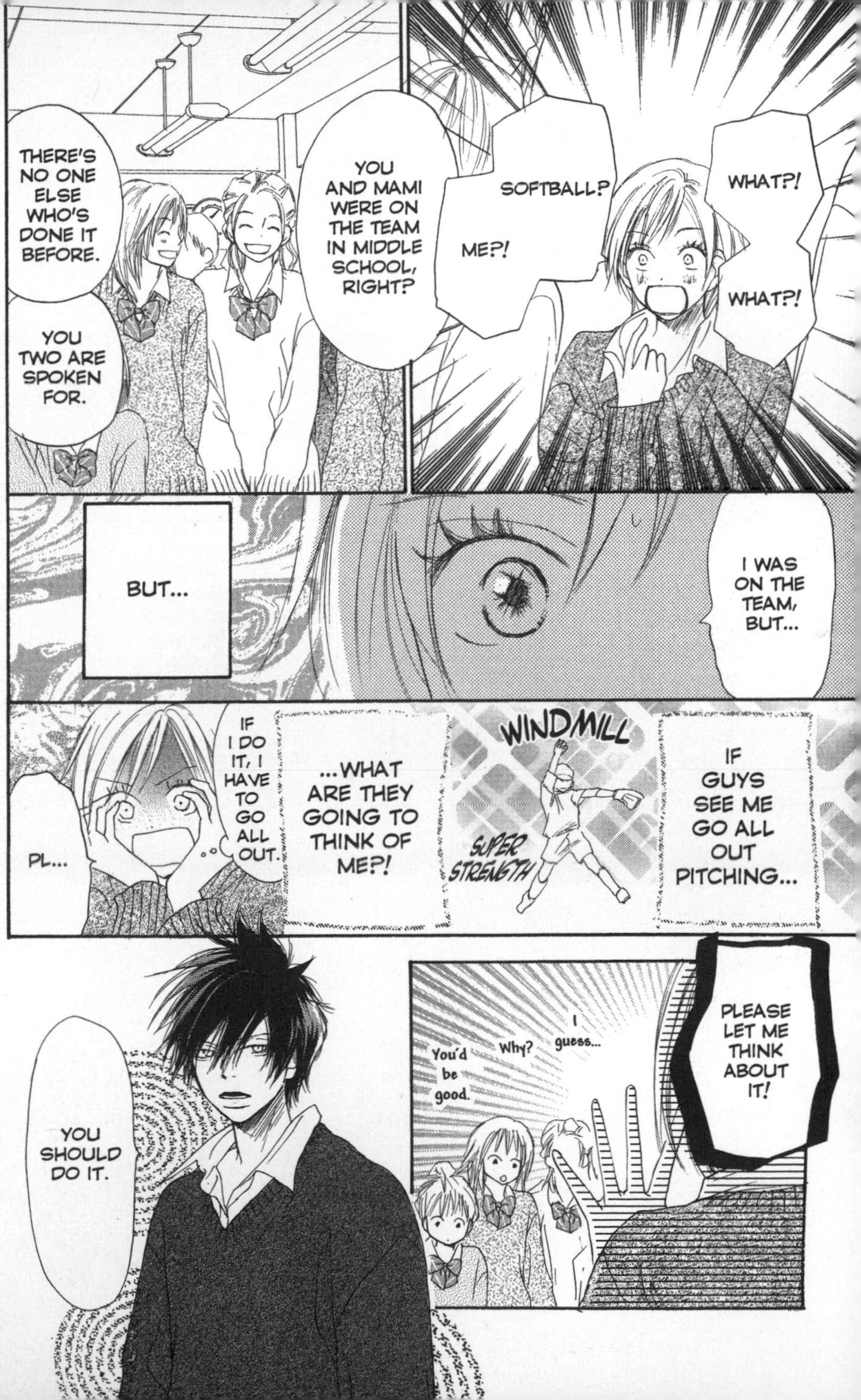
WHAT?!
WHAT?!
SOFTBALL?
ME?!
YOU AND MAMI WERE ON THE TEAM IN MIDDLE SCHOOL, RIGHT?
THERE'S NO ONE ELSE WHO'S DONE IT BEFORE.
YOU TWO ARE SPOKEN FOR.
I WAS ON THE TEAM, BUT...
BUT...
IF GUYS SEE ME GO ALL OUT PITCHING...
WINDMILL
SUPER STRENGTH
...WHAT ARE THEY GOING TO THINK OF ME?!
IF I DO IT, I HAVE TO GO ALL OUT.
PL...
PLEASE LET ME THINK ABOUT IT!
I guess...
Why?
You'd be good.
YOU SHOULD DO IT.

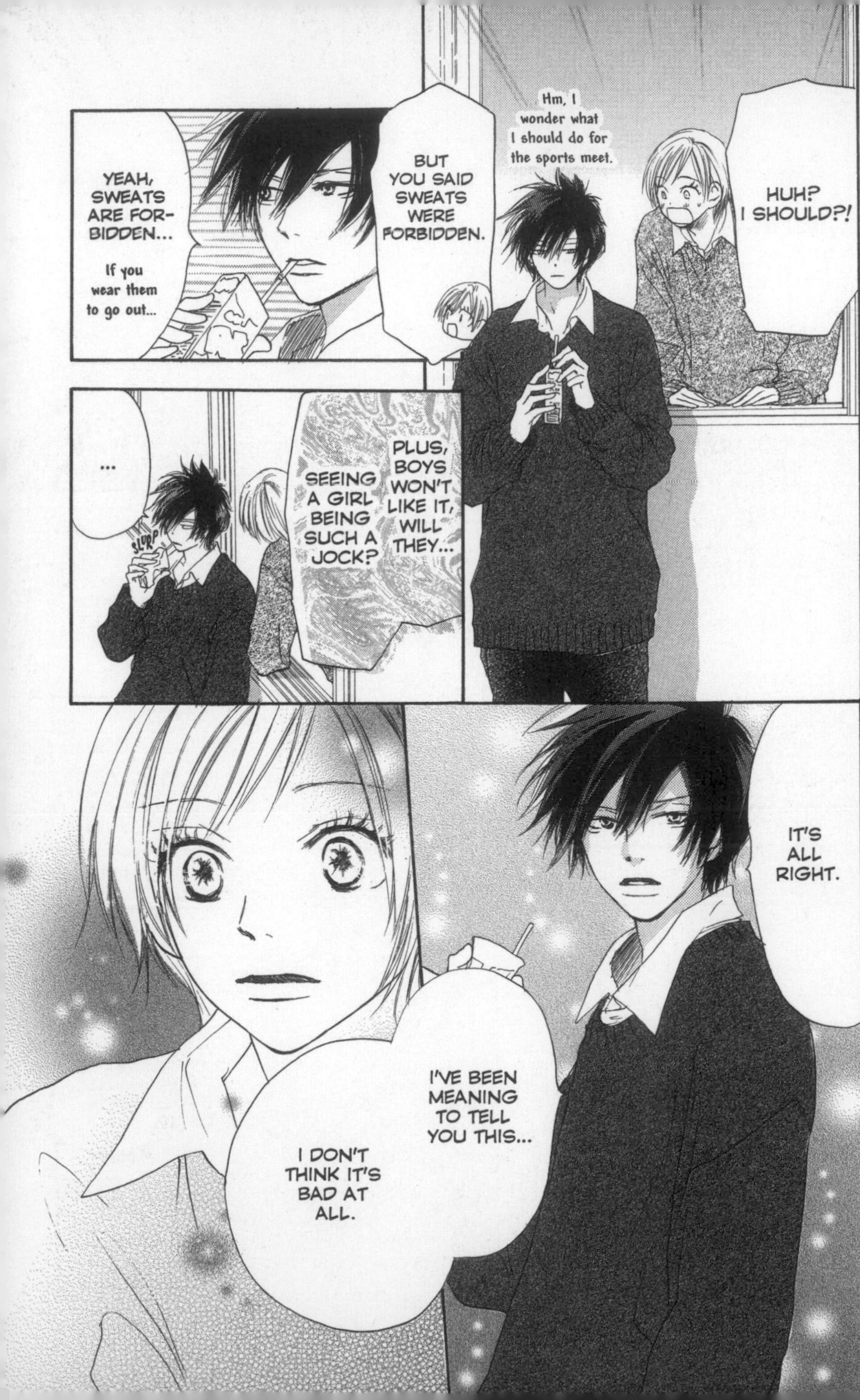
Hm, I wonder what I should do for the sports meet.
HUH? I SHOULD?!
BUT YOU SAID SWEATS WERE FORBIDDEN.
YEAH, SWEATS ARE FORBIDDEN...
If you wear them to go out...
PLUS, BOYS WON'T LIKE IT, WILL THEY...
SEEING A GIRL BEING SUCH A JOCK?
SLURP
...
IT'S ALL RIGHT.
I'VE BEEN MEANING TO TELL YOU THIS...
I DON'T THINK IT'S BAD AT ALL.

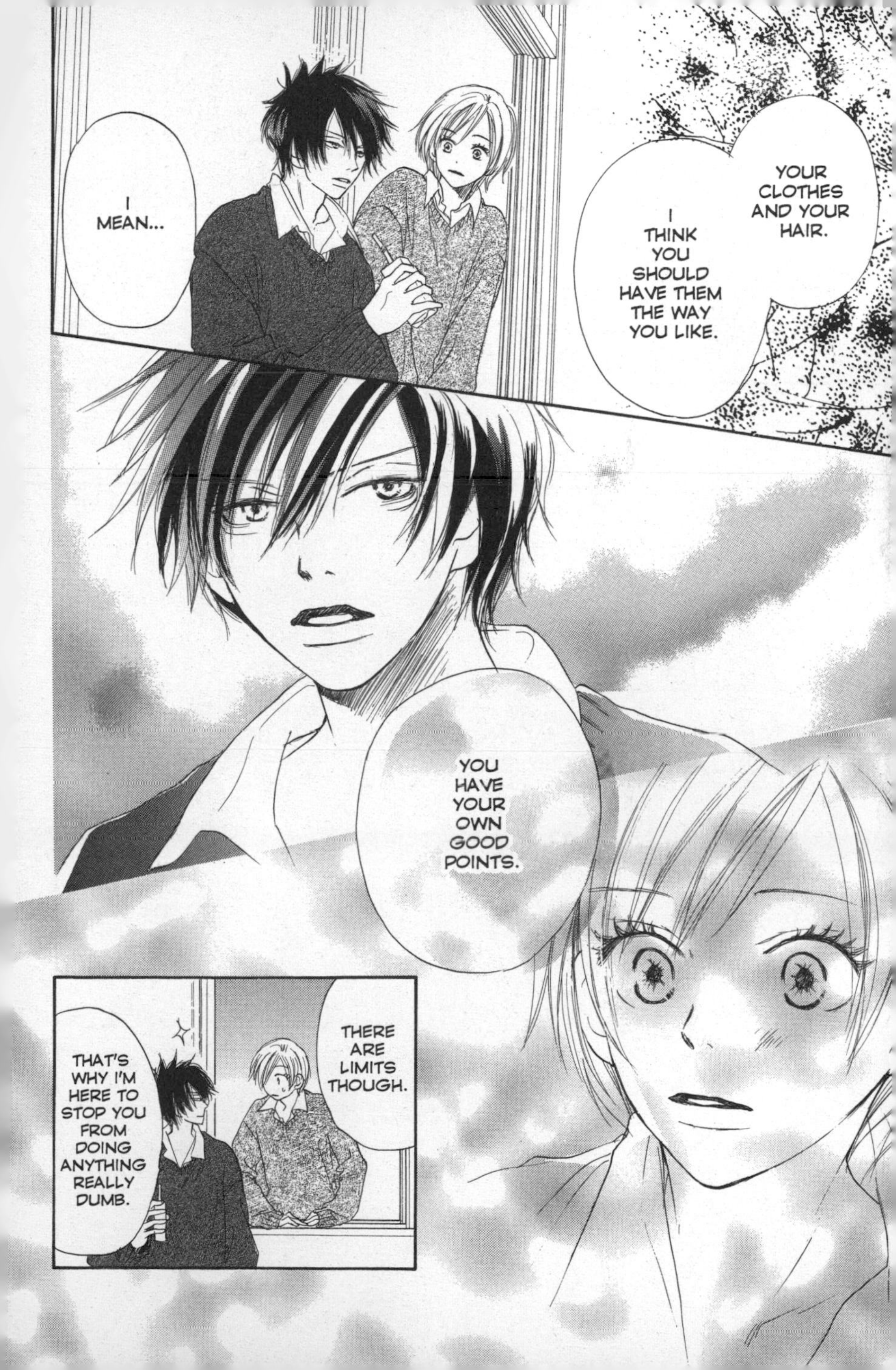
YOUR CLOTHES AND YOUR HAIR.
I THINK YOU SHOULD HAVE THEM THE WAY YOU LIKE.
I MEAN...
YOU HAVE YOUR OWN GOOD POINTS.
THERE ARE LIMITS THOUGH.
THAT'S WHY I'M HERE TO STOP YOU FROM DOING ANYTHING REALLY DUMB.

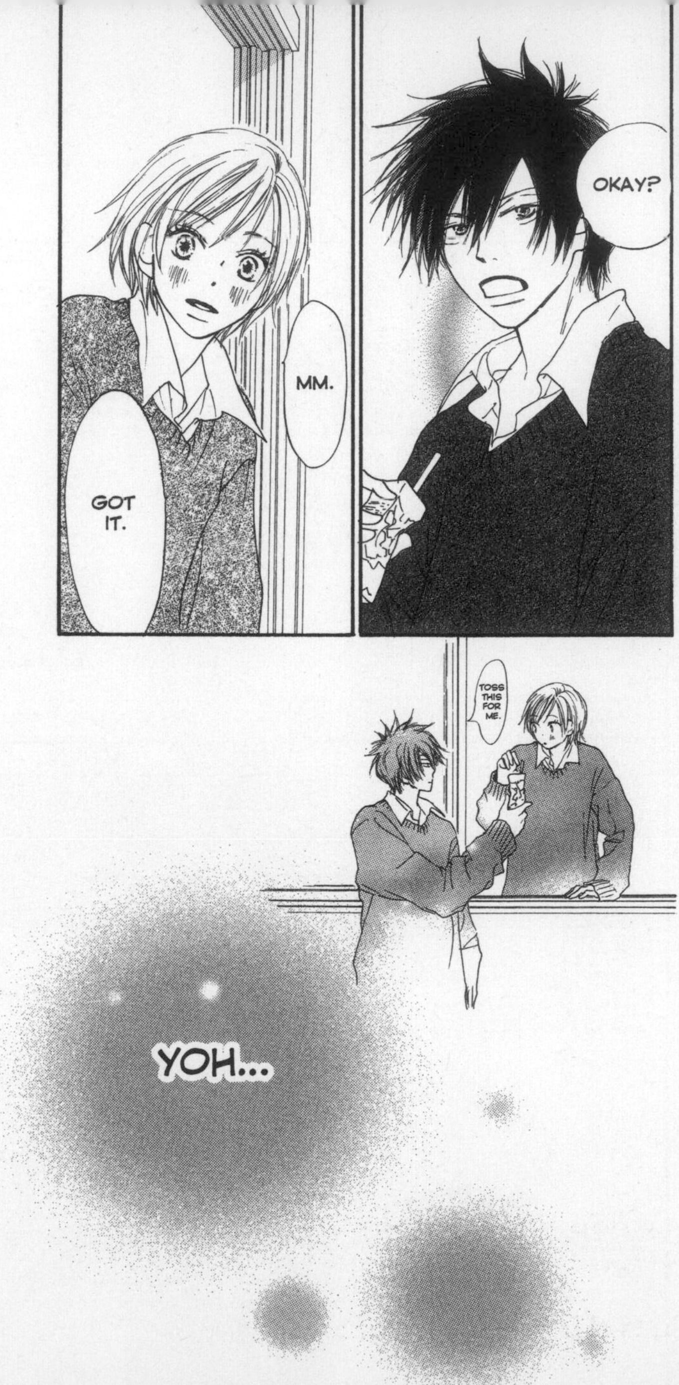
OKAY?
MM.
GOT IT.
TOSS THIS FOR ME.
YOH...

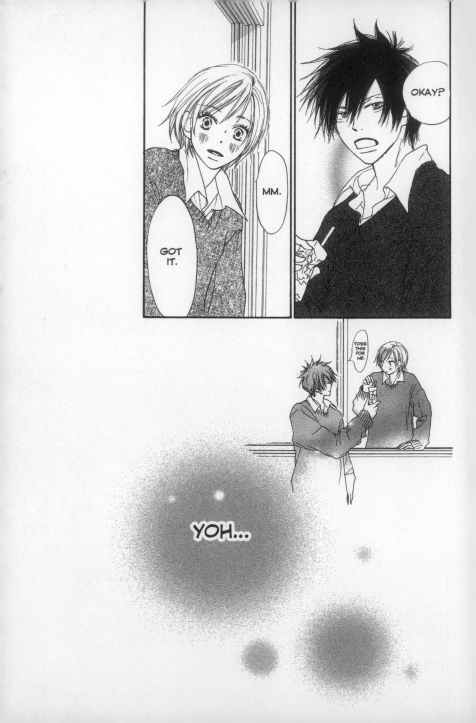

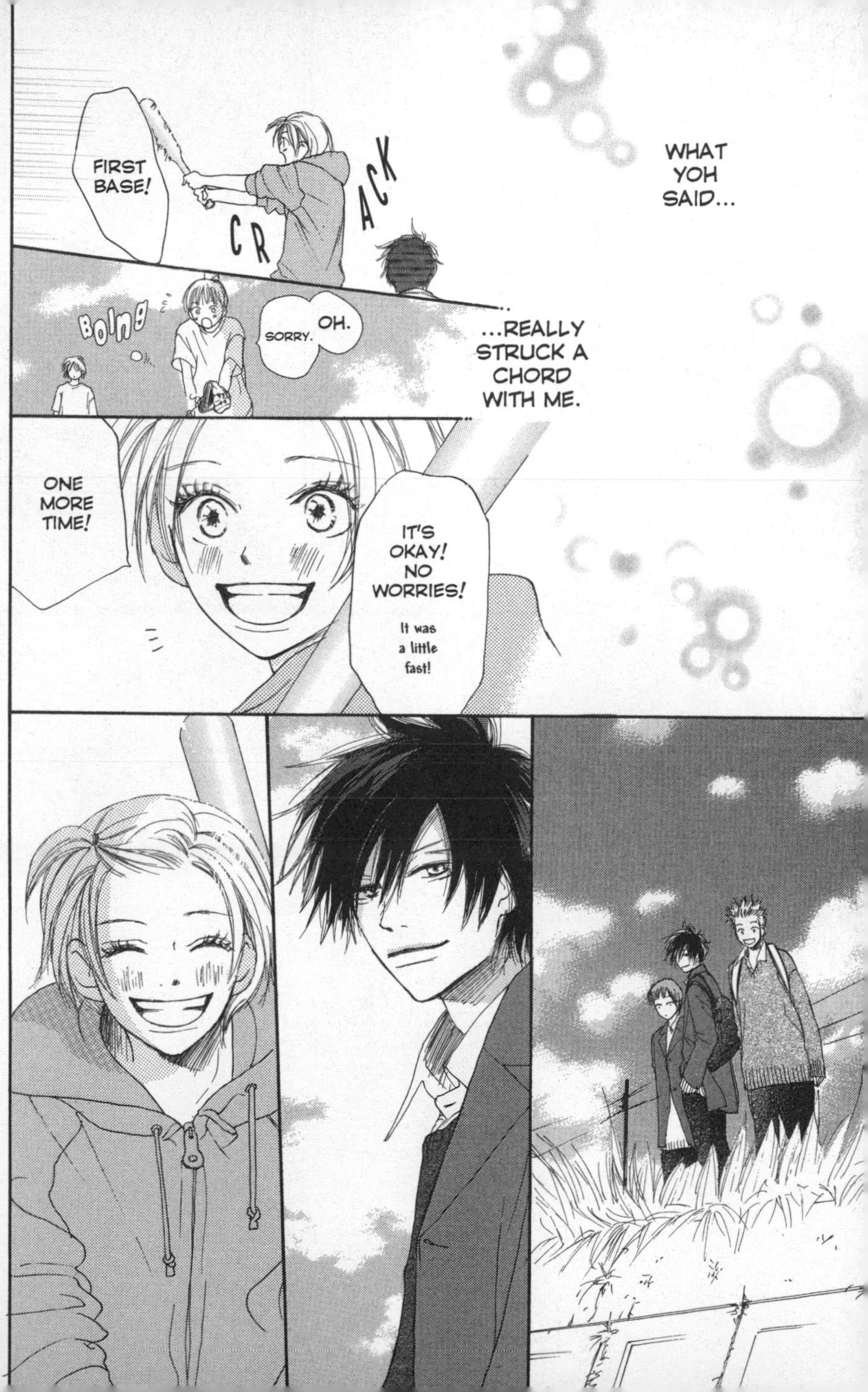
WHAT YOH SAID...
FIRST BASE!
CRACK
OH.
SORRY.
Boing
...REALLY STRUCK A CHORD WITH ME.
IT'S OKAY! NO WORRIES!
It was a little fast!
ONE MORE TIME!

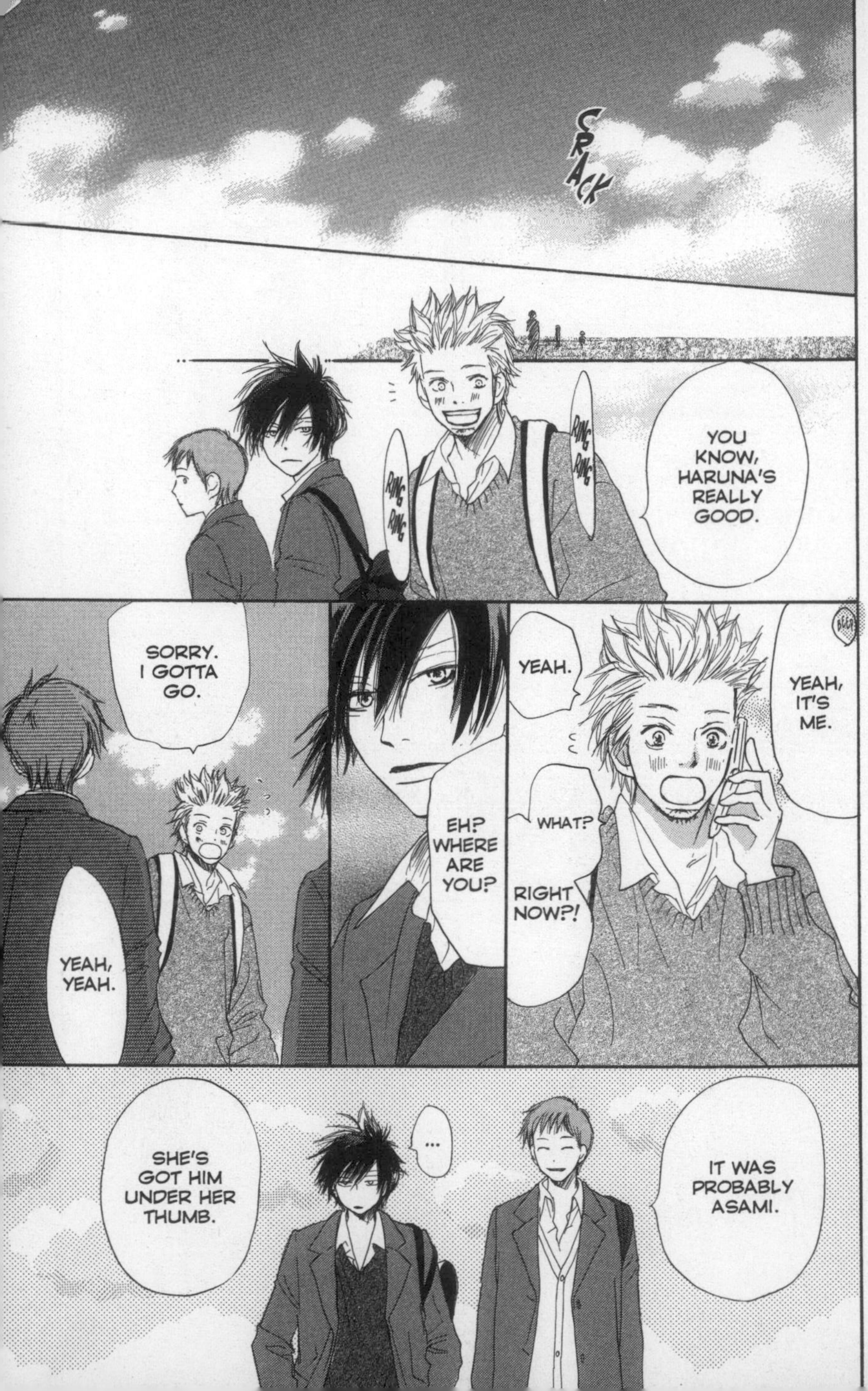
CRACK
YOU KNOW, HARUNA'S REALLY GOOD.
RING RING
RING RING
BEEP
YEAH, IT'S ME.
YEAH.
WHAT?
RIGHT NOW?!
EH? WHERE ARE YOU?
SORRY. I GOTTA GO.
YEAH, YEAH.
IT WAS PROBABLY ASAMI.
...
SHE'S GOT HIM UNDER HER THUMB.

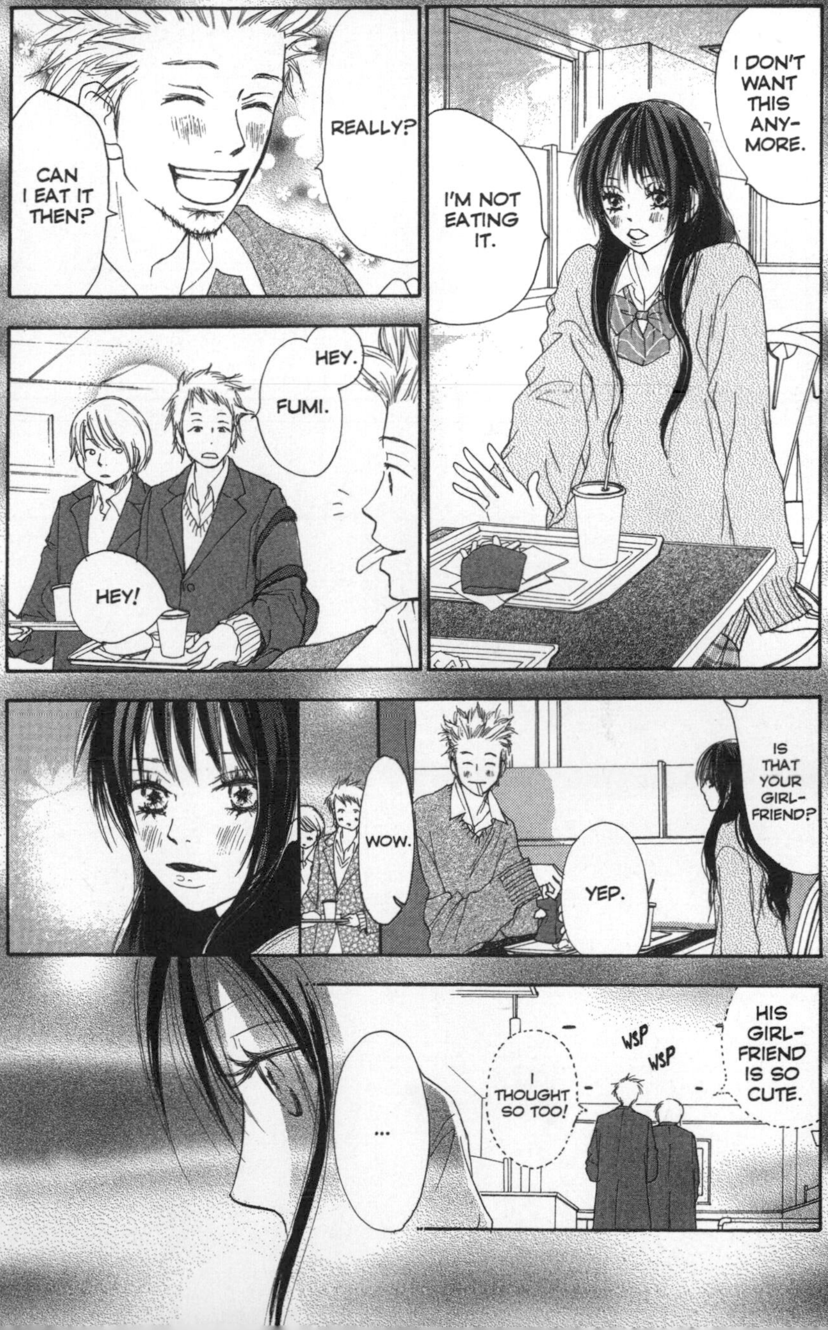
I DON'T WANT THIS ANYMORE.
I'M NOT EATING IT.
REALLY?
CAN I EAT IT THEN?
HEY.
FUMI.
HEY!
IS THAT YOUR GIRLFRIEND?
YEP.
WOW.
HIS GIRLFRIEND IS SO CUTE.
WSP
WSP
I THOUGHT SO TOO!
...

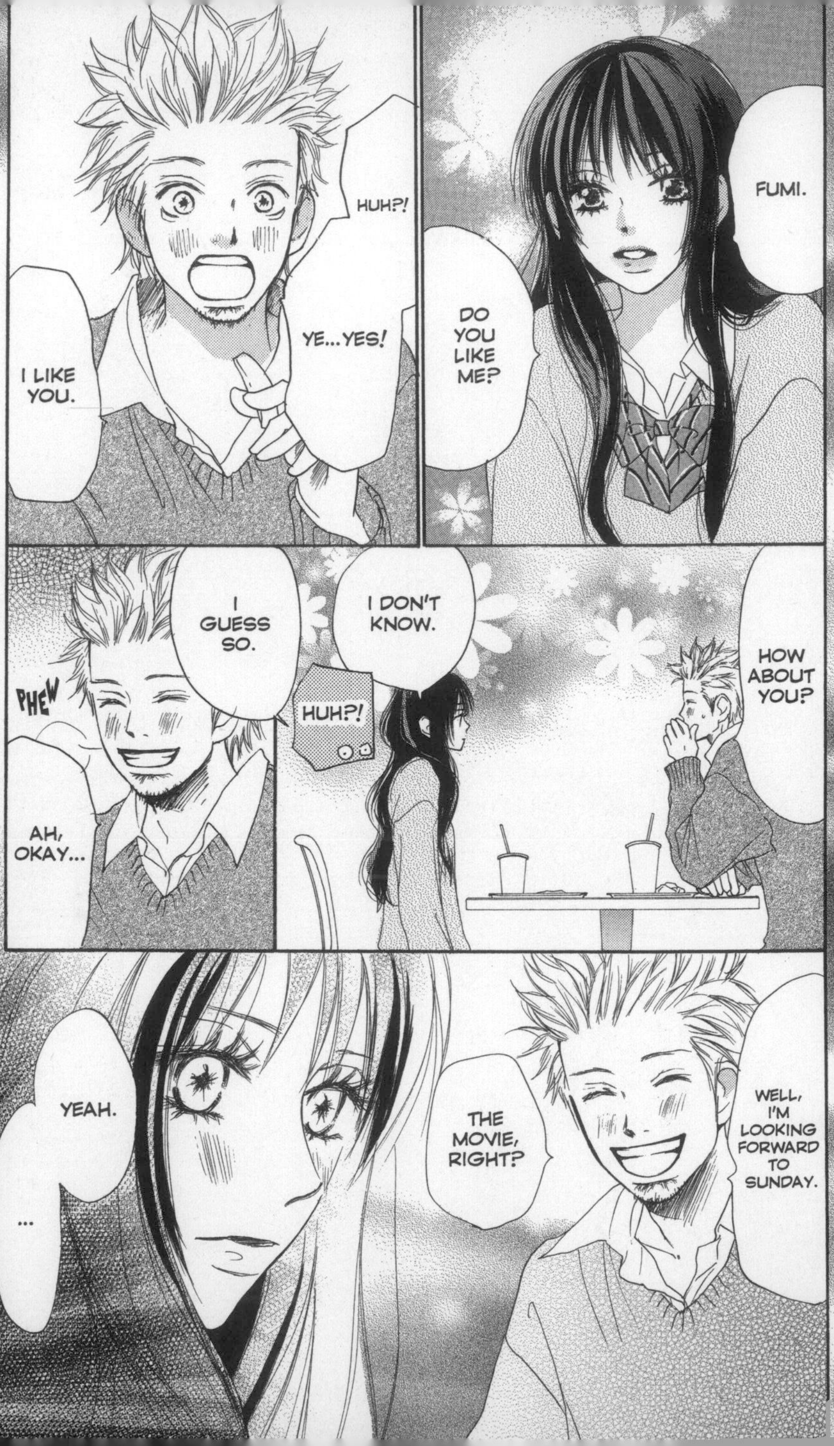
FUMI.
DO YOU LIKE ME?
HUH?!
YE...YES!
I LIKE YOU.
HOW ABOUT YOU?
I DON'T KNOW.
HUH?!
I GUESS SO.
PHEW
AH, OKAY...
WELL, I'M LOOKING FORWARD TO SUNDAY.
THE MOVIE, RIGHT?
YEAH.
...

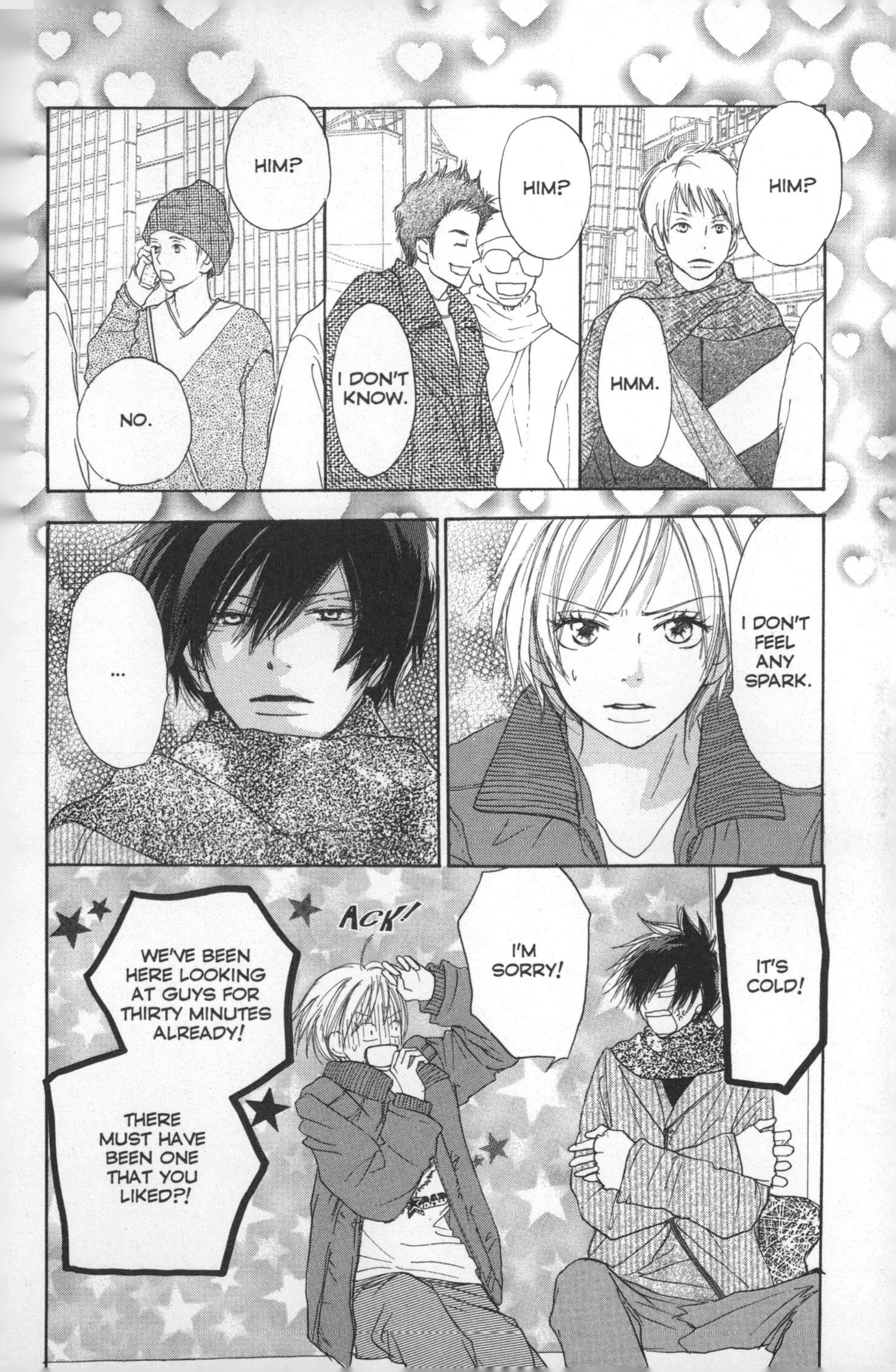
HIM?
HMM.
HIM?
I DON'T KNOW.
HIM?
NO.
I DON'T FEEL ANY SPARK.
...
IT'S COLD!
I'M SORRY!
ACK!
WE'VE BEEN HERE LOOKING AT GUYS FOR THIRTY MINUTES ALREADY!
THERE MUST HAVE BEEN ONE THAT YOU LIKED?!

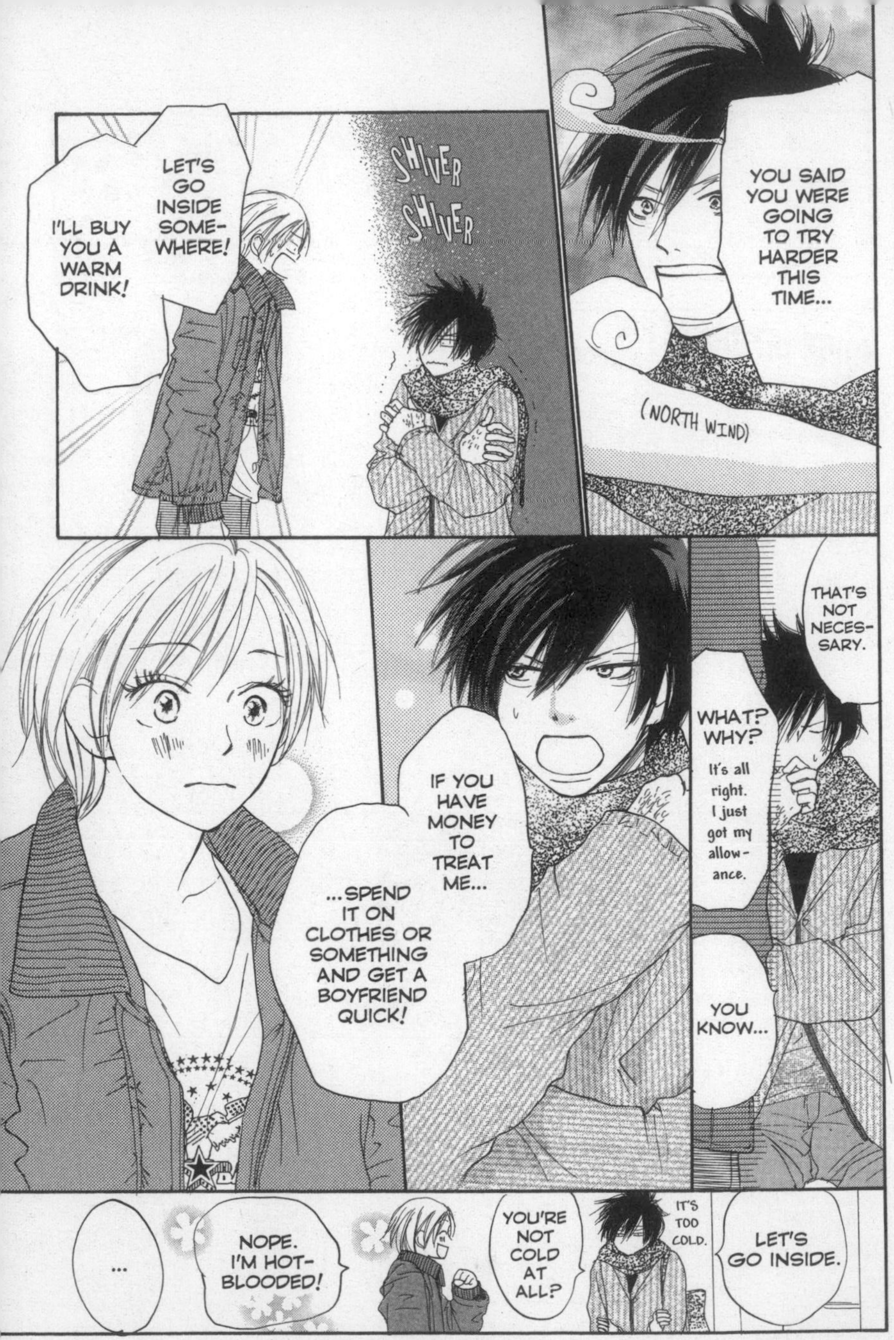
YOU SAID YOU WERE GOING TO TRY HARDER THIS TIME...
(NORTH WIND)
SHIVER SHIVER
LET'S GO INSIDE SOME-WHERE!
I'LL BUY YOU A WARM DRINK!
THAT'S NOT NECES-SARY.
WHAT? WHY?
It's all right. I just got my allow-ance.
YOU KNOW...
IF YOU HAVE MONEY TO TREAT ME...
...SPEND IT ON CLOTHES OR SOMETHING AND GET A BOYFRIEND QUICK!
LET'S GO INSIDE.
IT'S TOO COLD.
YOU'RE NOT COLD AT ALL?
NOPE. I'M HOT-BLOODED!
...

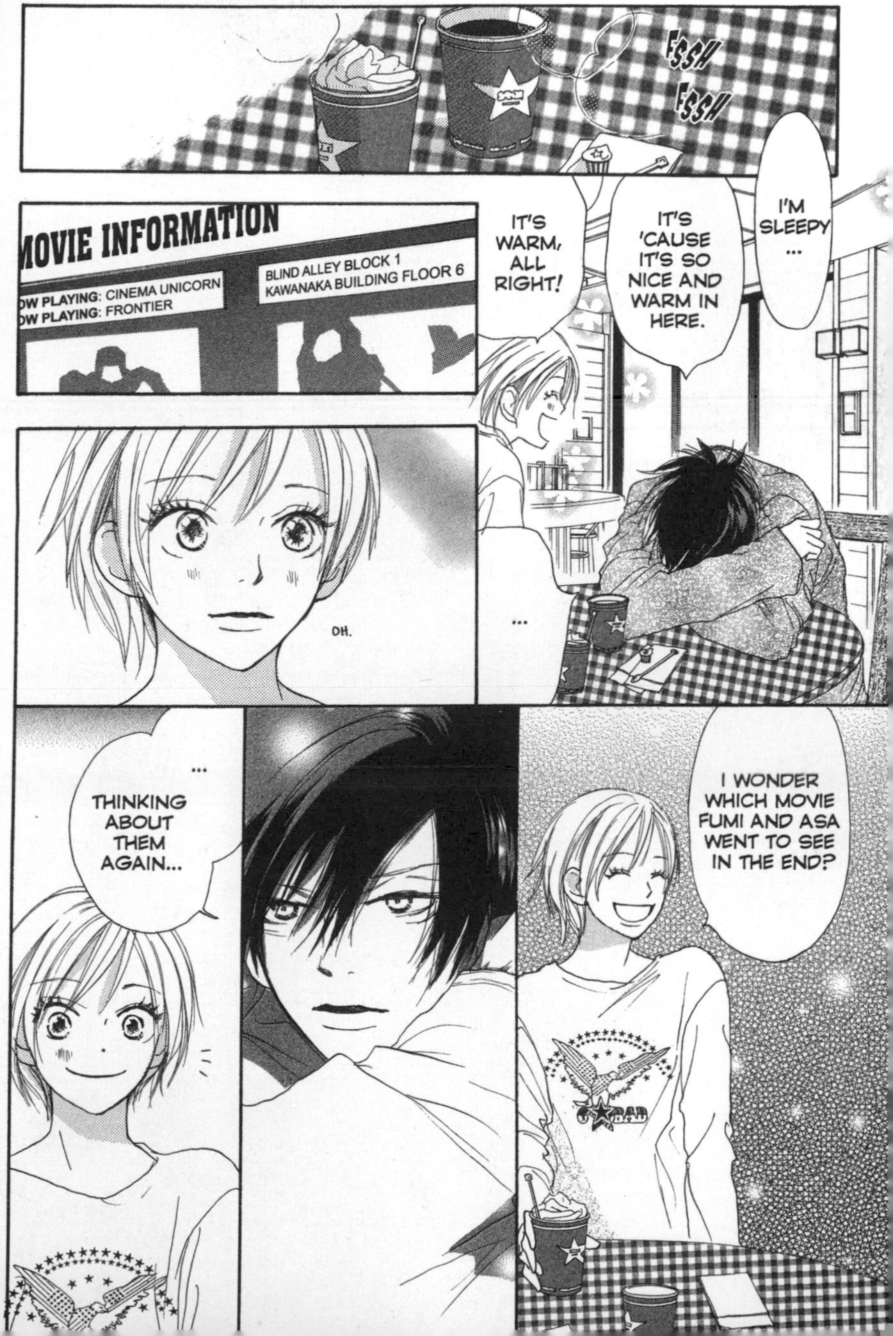
FSSH
FSSH
I'M SLEEPY...
IT'S 'CAUSE IT'S SO NICE AND WARM IN HERE.
IT'S WARM, ALL RIGHT!
...
MOVIE INFORMATION
OW PLAYING: CINEMA UNICORN
OW PLAYING: FRONTIER
BLIND ALLEY BLOCK 1
KAWANAKA BUILDING FLOOR 6
OH.
I WONDER WHICH MOVIE FUMI AND ASA WENT TO SEE IN THE END?
... THINKING ABOUT THEM AGAIN...

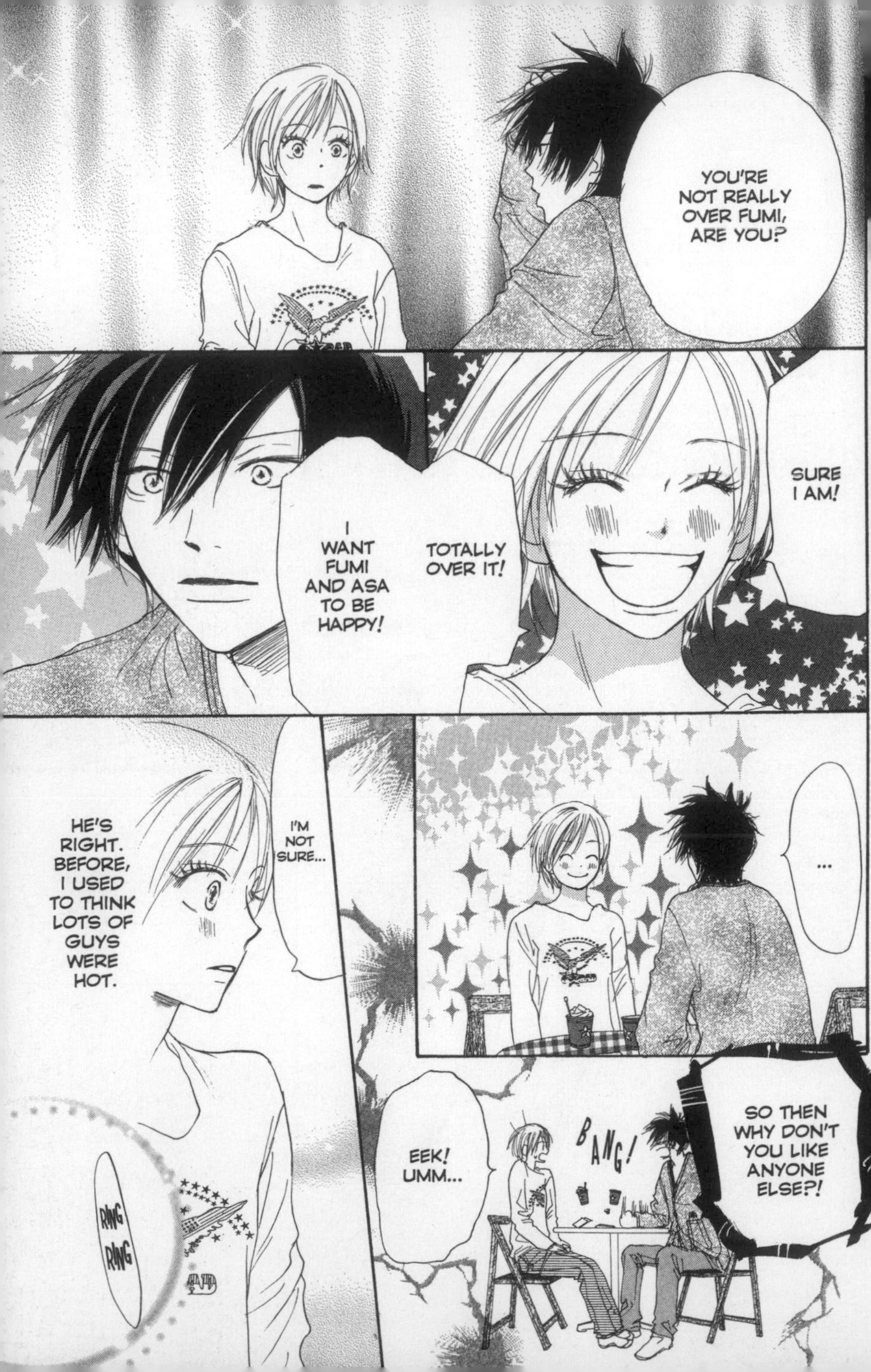
YOU'RE NOT REALLY OVER FUMI, ARE YOU?
SURE I AM!
TOTALLY OVER IT!
I WANT FUMI AND ASA TO BE HAPPY!
...
SO THEN WHY DON'T YOU LIKE ANYONE ELSE?!
BANG!
EEK! UMM...
I'M NOT SURE...
HE'S RIGHT. BEFORE, I USED TO THINK LOTS OF GUYS WERE HOT.
RING RING

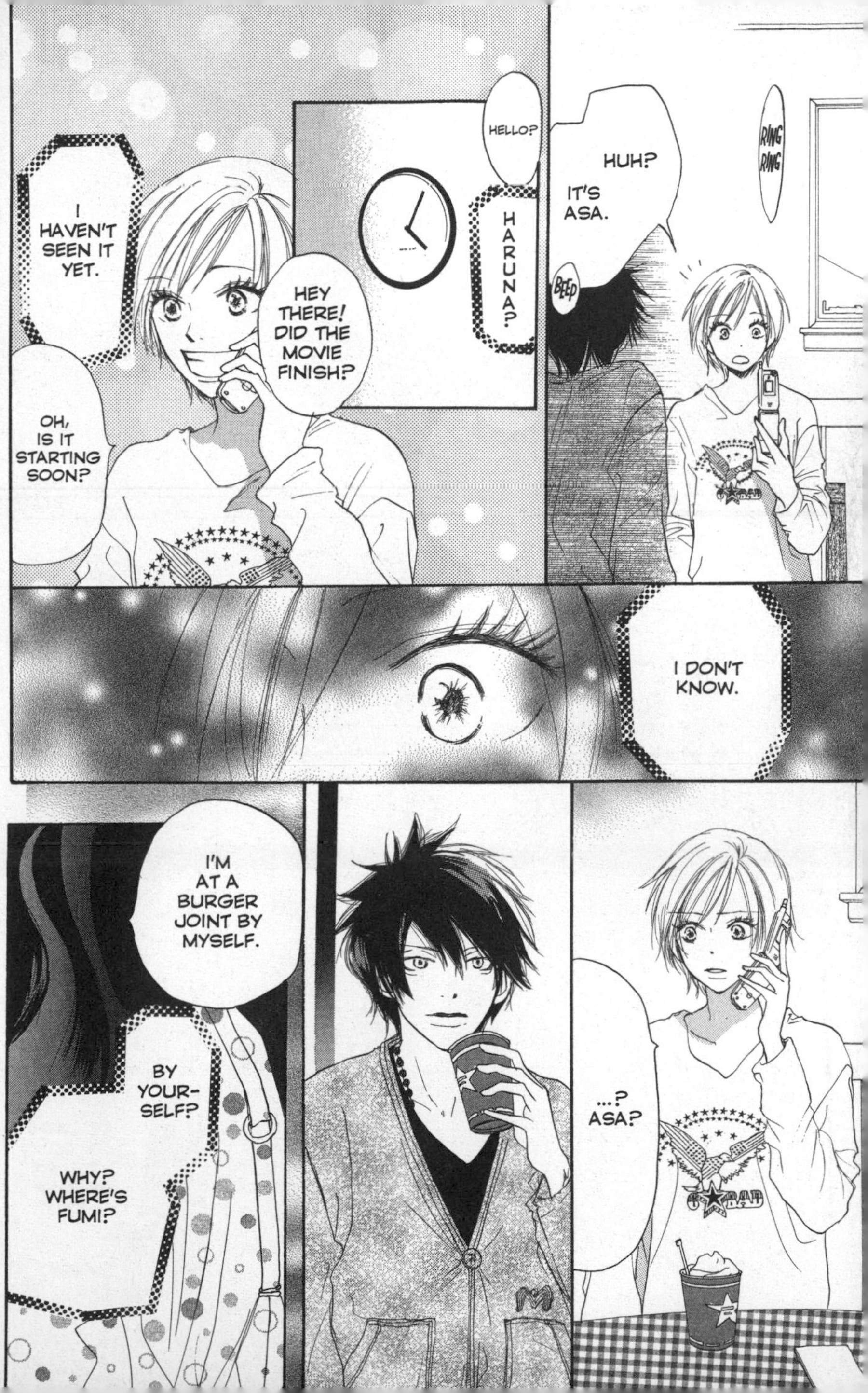
RING RING
HUH?
IT'S ASA.
BEEP
HELLO?
HARUNA?
HEY THERE! DID THE MOVIE FINISH?
I HAVEN'T SEEN IT YET.
OH, IS IT STARTING SOON?
I DON'T KNOW.
...? ASA?
I'M AT A BURGER JOINT BY MYSELF.
BY YOURSELF?
WHY? WHERE'S FUMI?

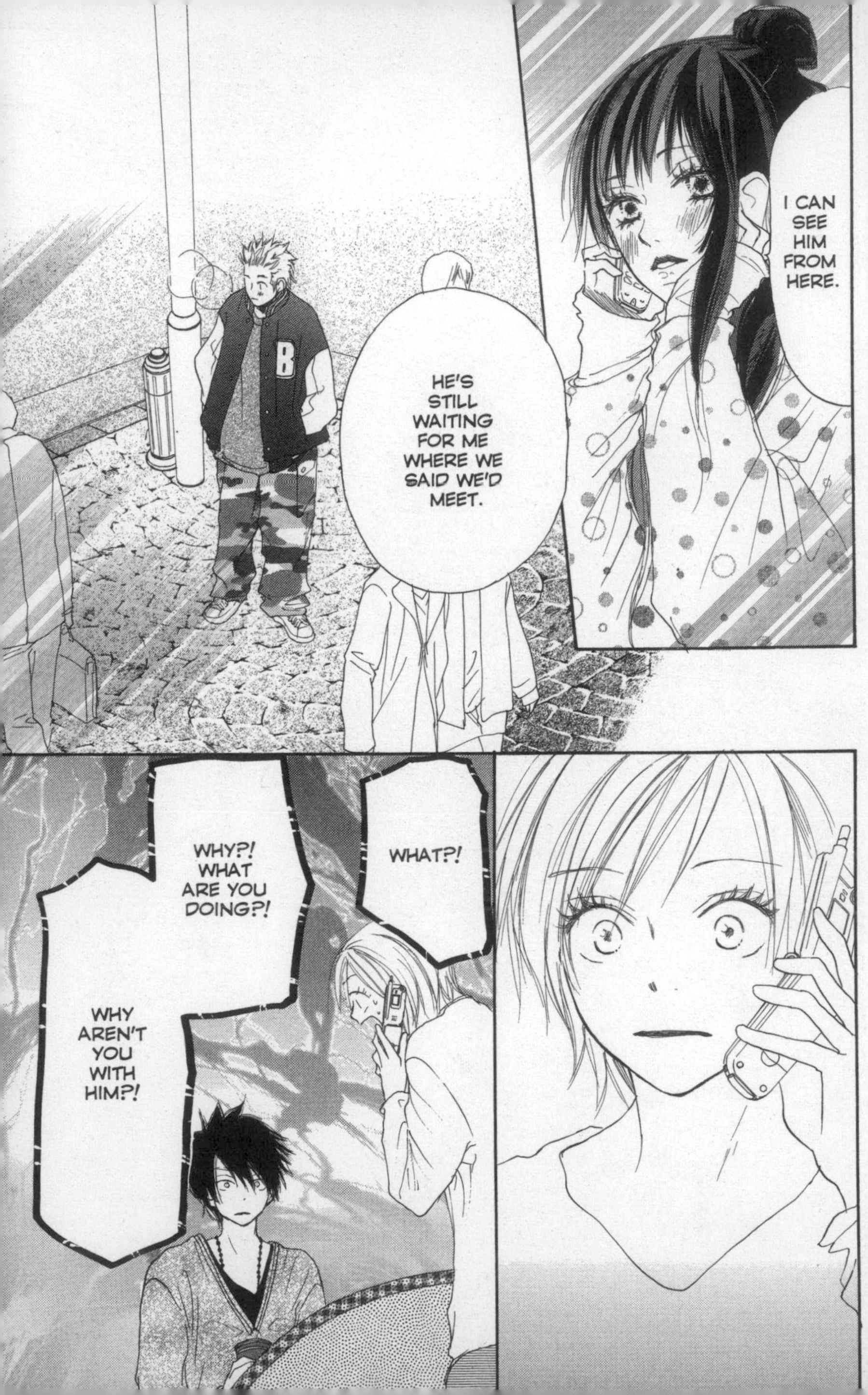
I CAN SEE HIM FROM HERE.
HE'S STILL WAITING FOR ME WHERE WE SAID WE'D MEET.
WHAT?!
WHY?! WHAT ARE YOU DOING?!
WHY AREN'T YOU WITH HIM?!

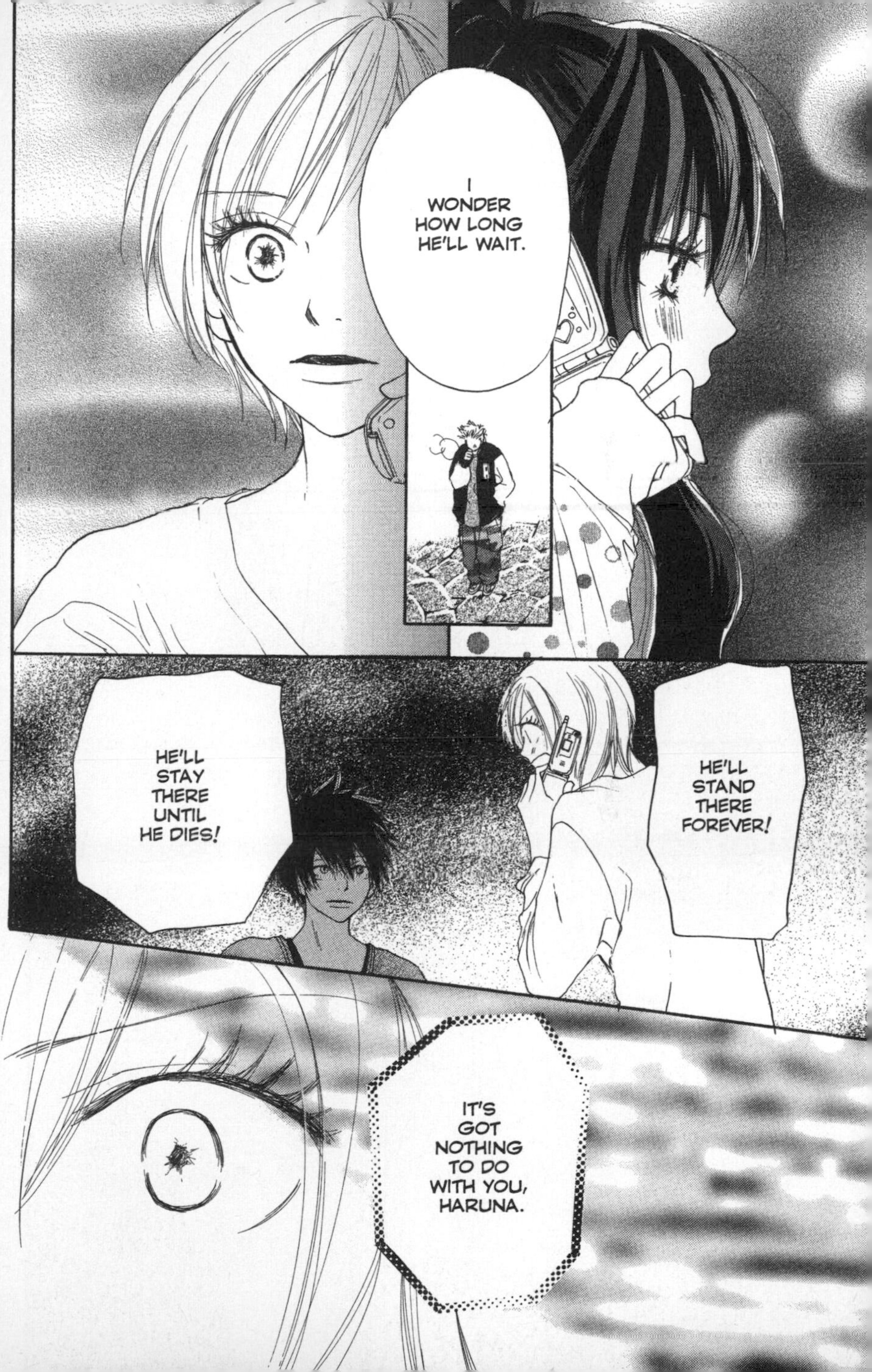
I WONDER HOW LONG HE'LL WAIT.
HE'LL STAND THERE FOREVER!
HE'LL STAY THERE UNTIL HE DIES!
IT'S GOT NOTHING TO DO WITH YOU, HARUNA.

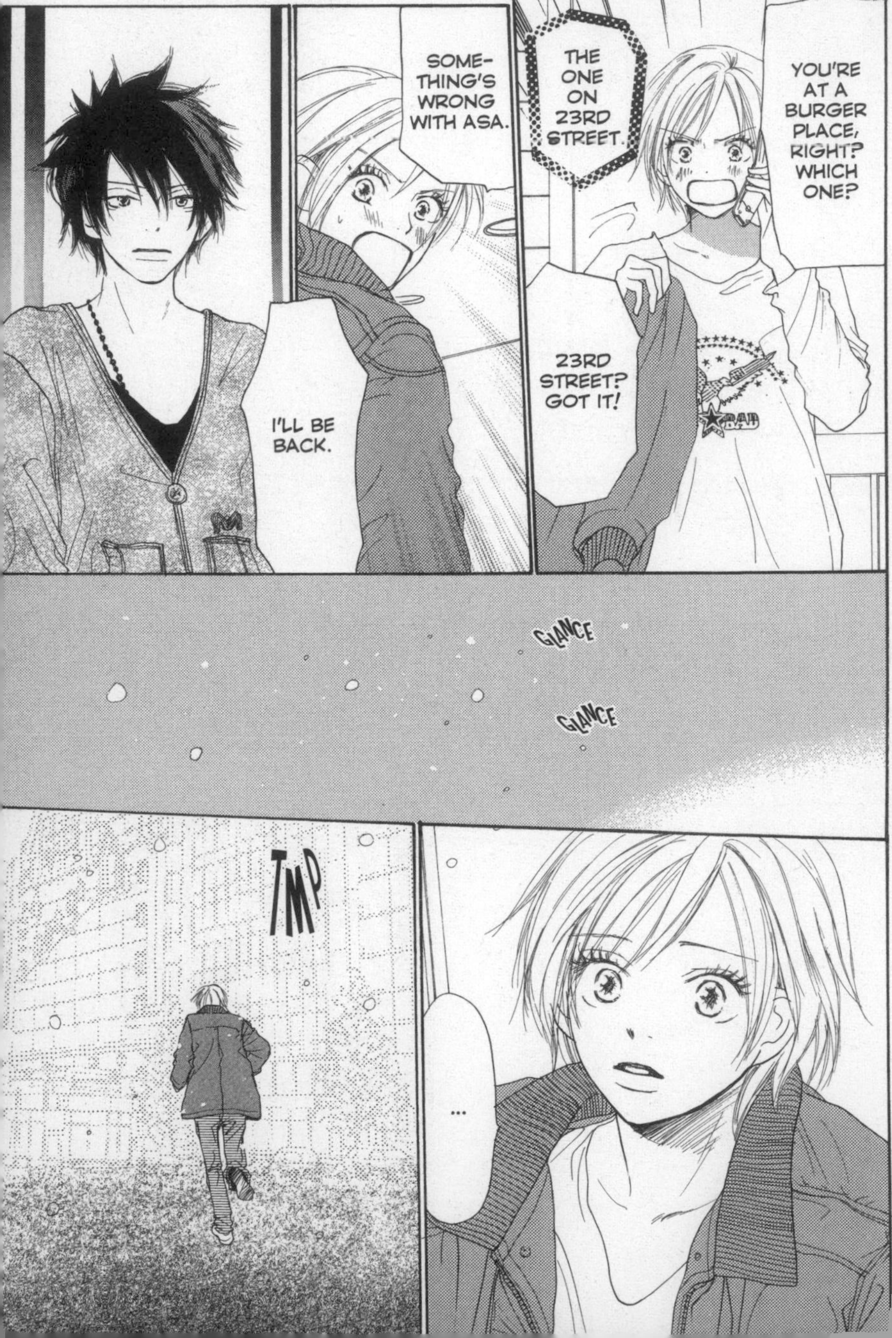
YOU'RE AT A BURGER PLACE, RIGHT? WHICH ONE?
THE ONE ON 23RD STREET.
23RD STREET? GOT IT!
SOME-THING'S WRONG WITH ASA.
I'LL BE BACK.
GLANCE
GLANCE
...
TMP

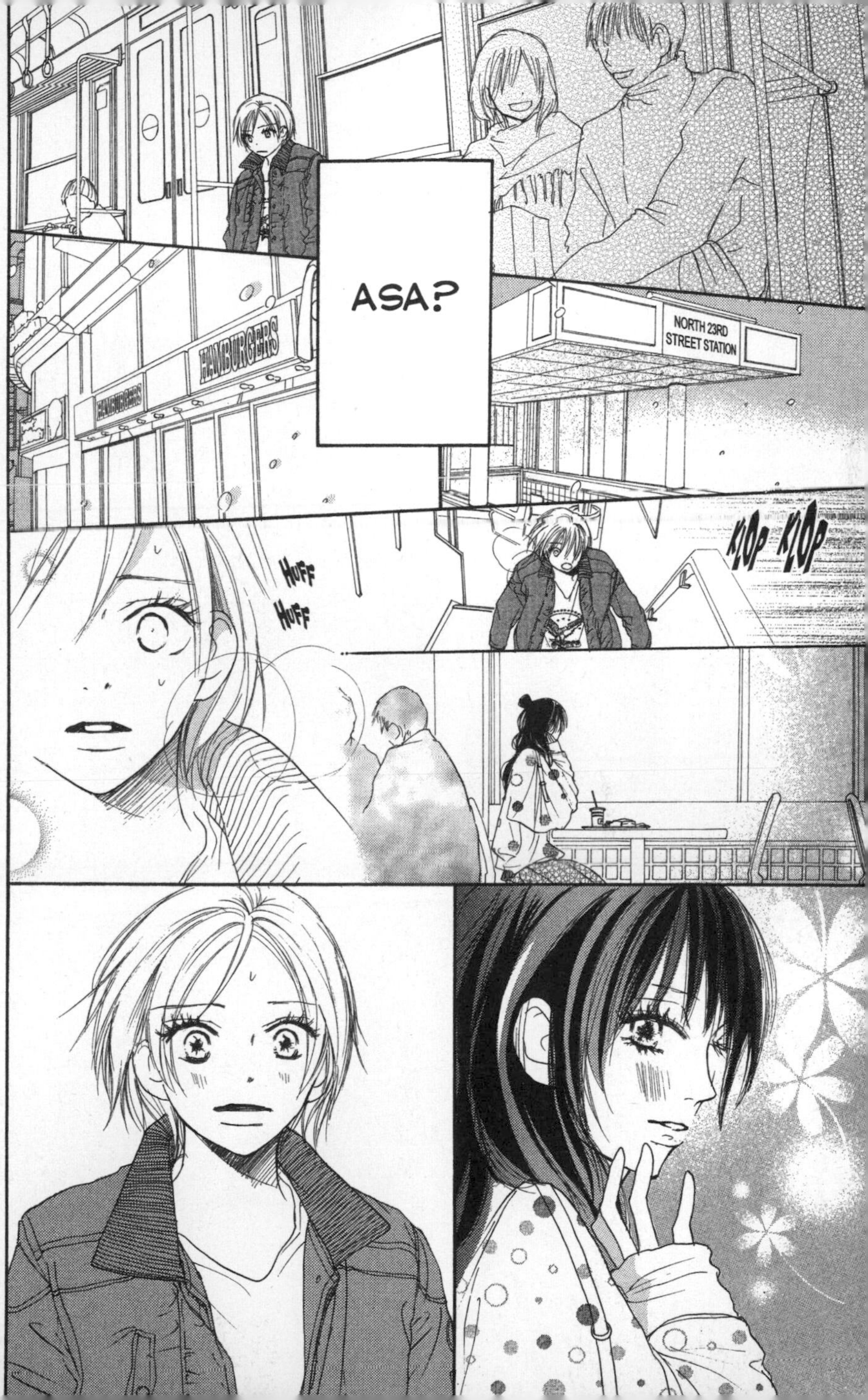
ASA?
NORTH 23RD STREET STATION
HAMBURGERS
HAMBURGERS
KLOP KLOP
HUFF HUFF

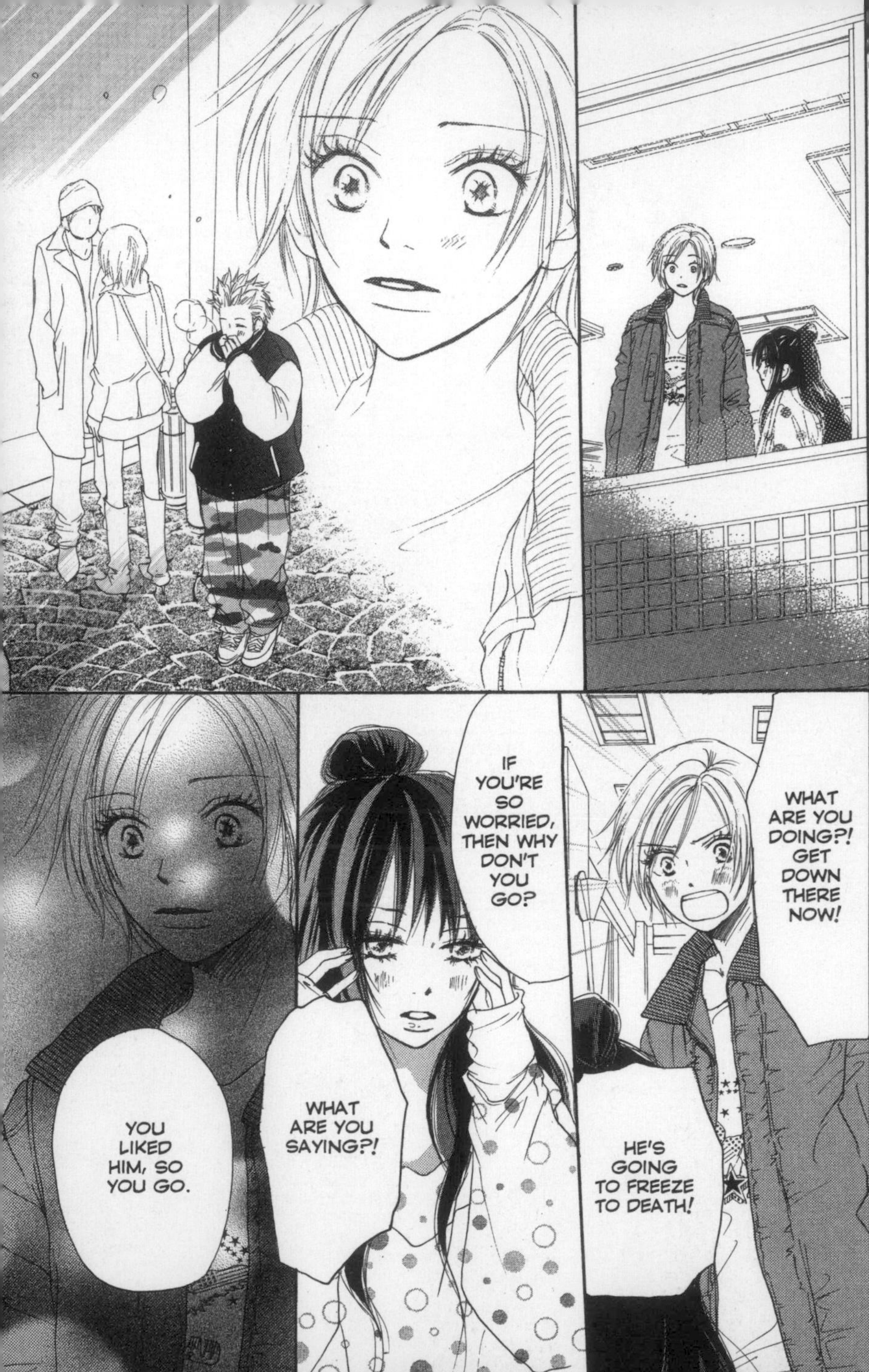
WHAT ARE YOU DOING?! GET DOWN THERE NOW!
HE'S GOING TO FREEZE TO DEATH!
IF YOU'RE SO WORRIED, THEN WHY DON'T YOU GO?
WHAT ARE YOU SAYING?!
YOU LIKED HIM, SO YOU GO.

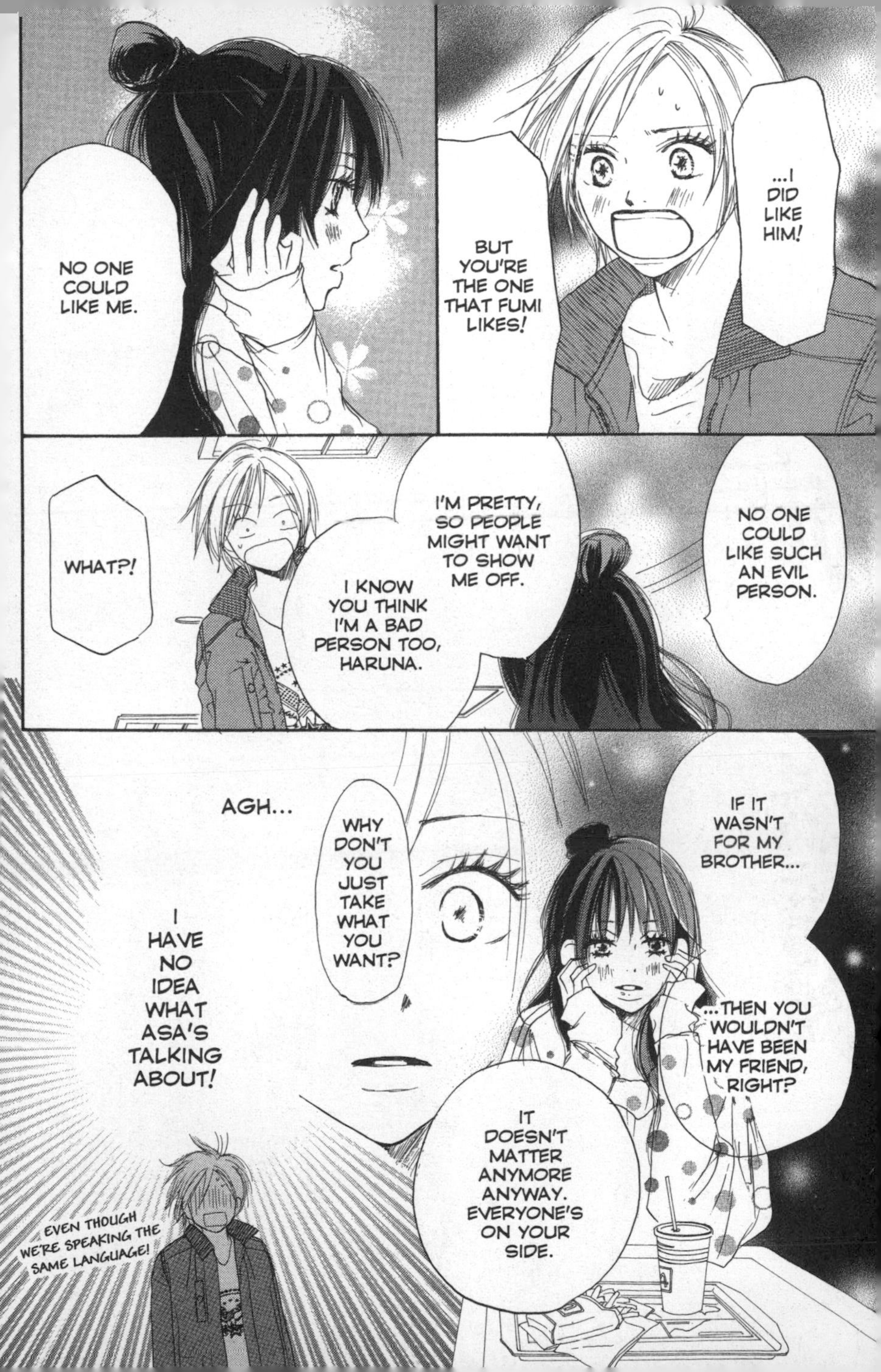
...I DID LIKE HIM!
BUT YOU'RE THE ONE THAT FUMI LIKES!
NO ONE COULD LIKE ME.
NO ONE COULD LIKE SUCH AN EVIL PERSON.
I'M PRETTY, SO PEOPLE MIGHT WANT TO SHOW ME OFF.
I KNOW YOU THINK I'M A BAD PERSON TOO, HARUNA.
WHAT?!
IF IT WASN'T FOR MY BROTHER...
...THEN YOU WOULDN'T HAVE BEEN MY FRIEND, RIGHT?
WHY DON'T YOU JUST TAKE WHAT YOU WANT?
AGH...
IT DOESN'T MATTER ANYMORE ANYWAY. EVERYONE'S ON YOUR SIDE.
I HAVE NO IDEA WHAT ASA'S TALKING ABOUT!
EVEN THOUGH WE'RE SPEAKING THE SAME LANGUAGE!

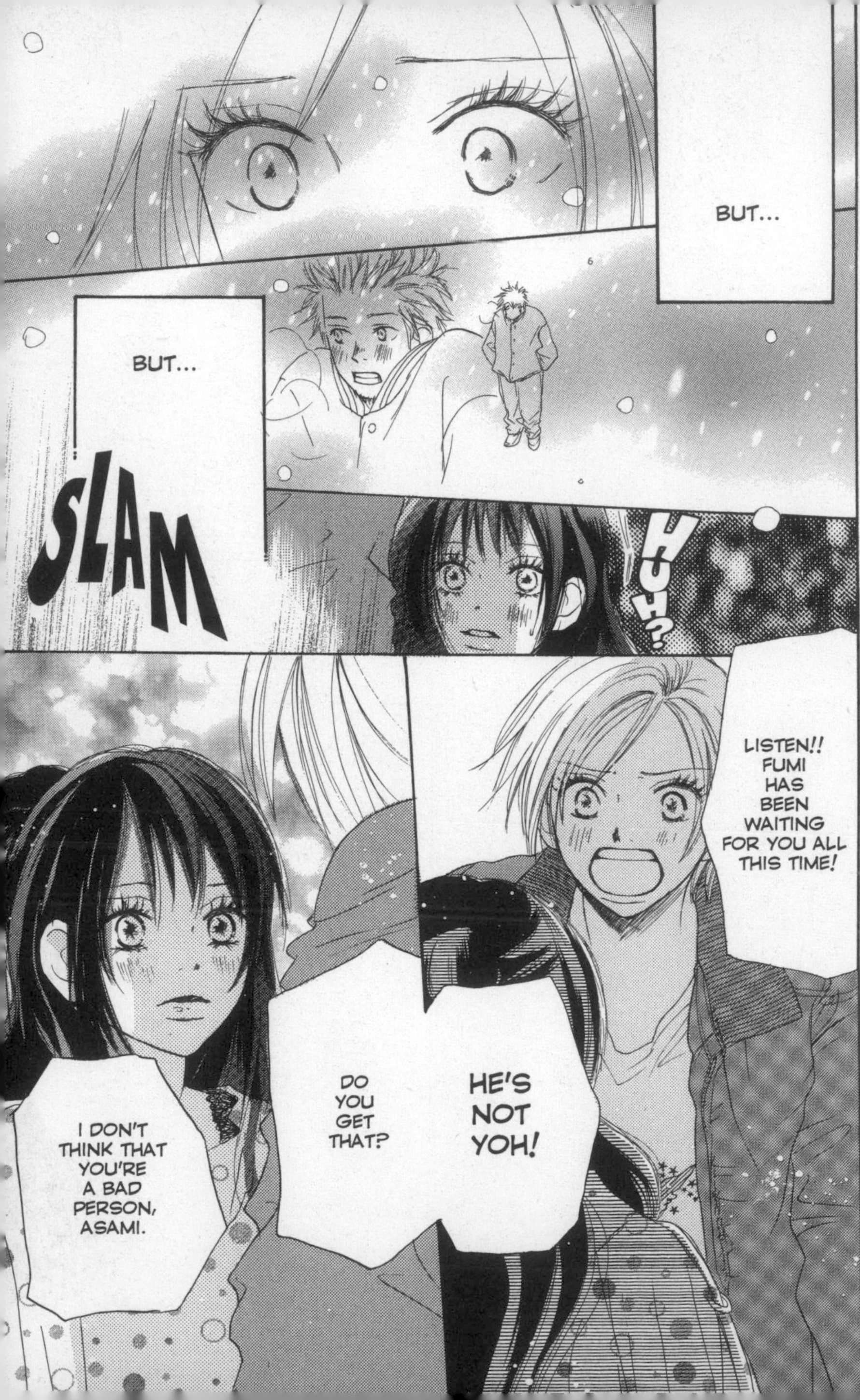
BUT...
BUT...
HUH?
SLAM
LISTEN!! FUMI HAS BEEN WAITING FOR YOU ALL THIS TIME!
HE'S NOT YOH!
DO YOU GET THAT?
I DON'T THINK THAT YOU'RE A BAD PERSON, ASAMI.

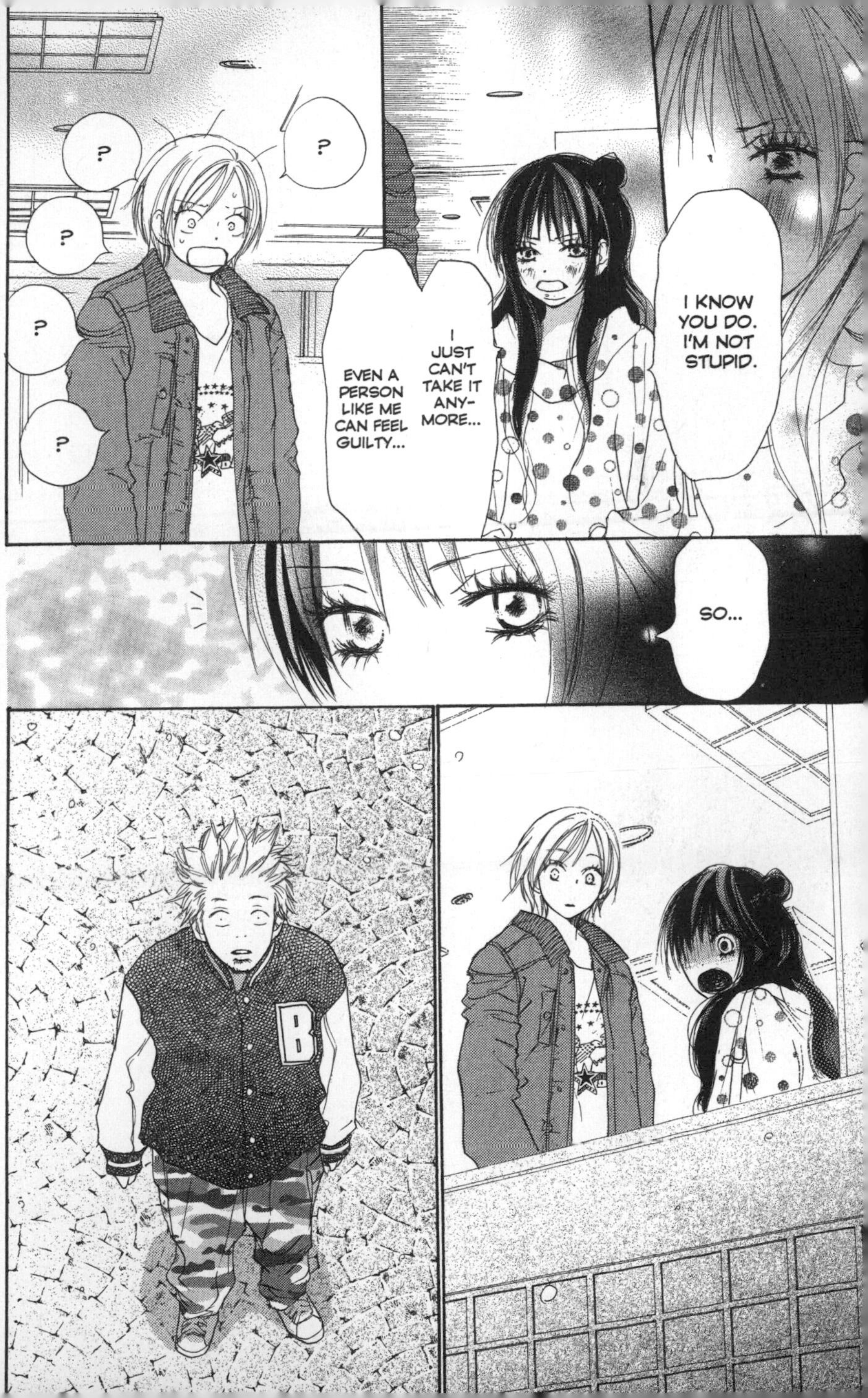
I KNOW YOU DO. I'M NOT STUPID.
I JUST CAN'T TAKE IT ANYMORE...
EVEN A PERSON LIKE ME CAN FEEL GUILTY...
?
?
?
?
?
SO...

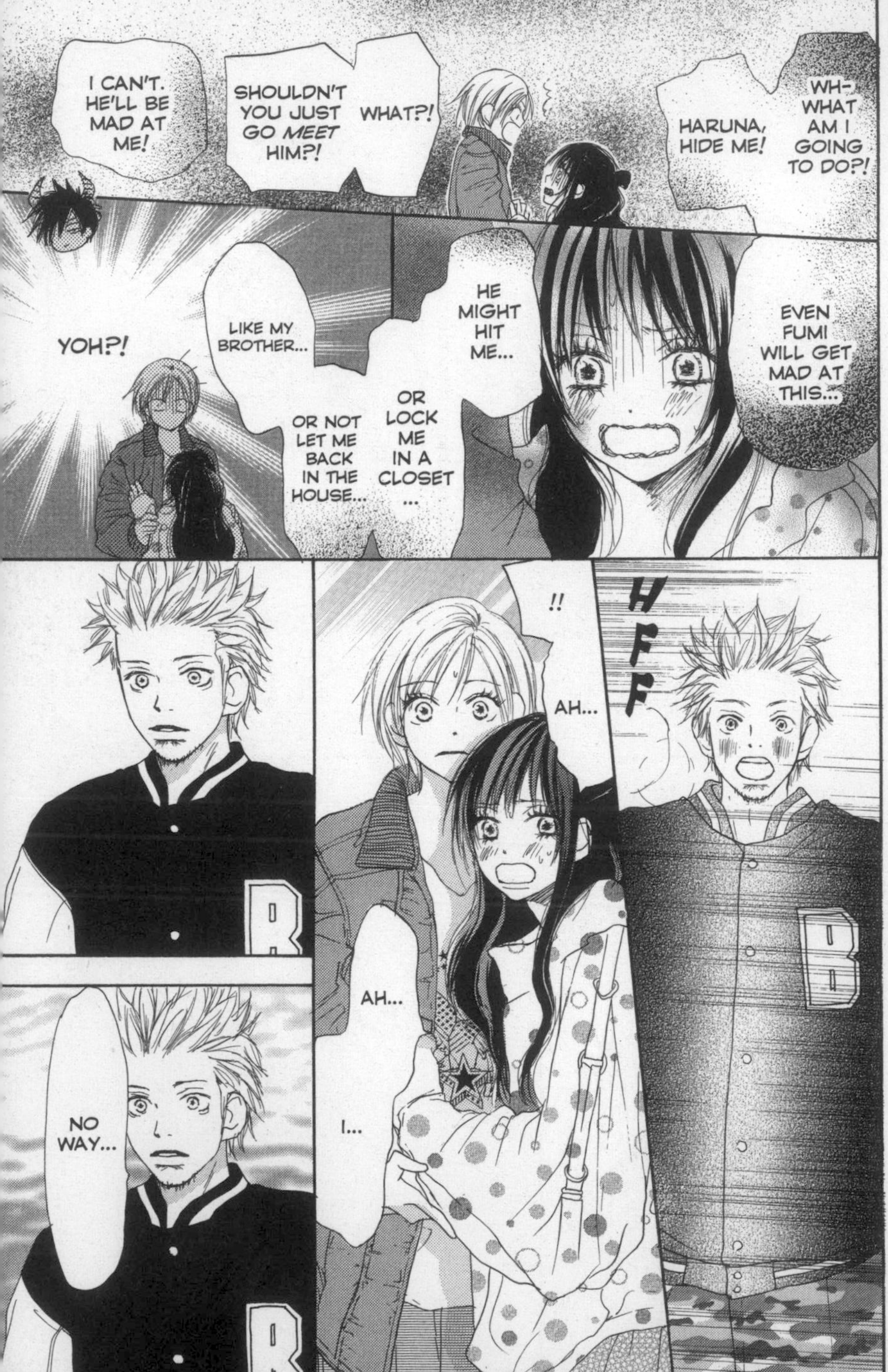
WH- WHAT AM I GOING TO DO?!
HARUNA, HIDE ME!
WHAT?!
SHOULDN'T YOU JUST GO *MEET* HIM?!
I CAN'T. HE'LL BE MAD AT ME!
EVEN FUMI WILL GET MAD AT THIS...
HE MIGHT HIT ME...
LIKE MY BROTHER...
OR LOCK ME IN A CLOSET ...
OR NOT LET ME BACK IN THE HOUSE...
YOH?!
HFF
!!
AH...
AH...
I...
NO WAY...

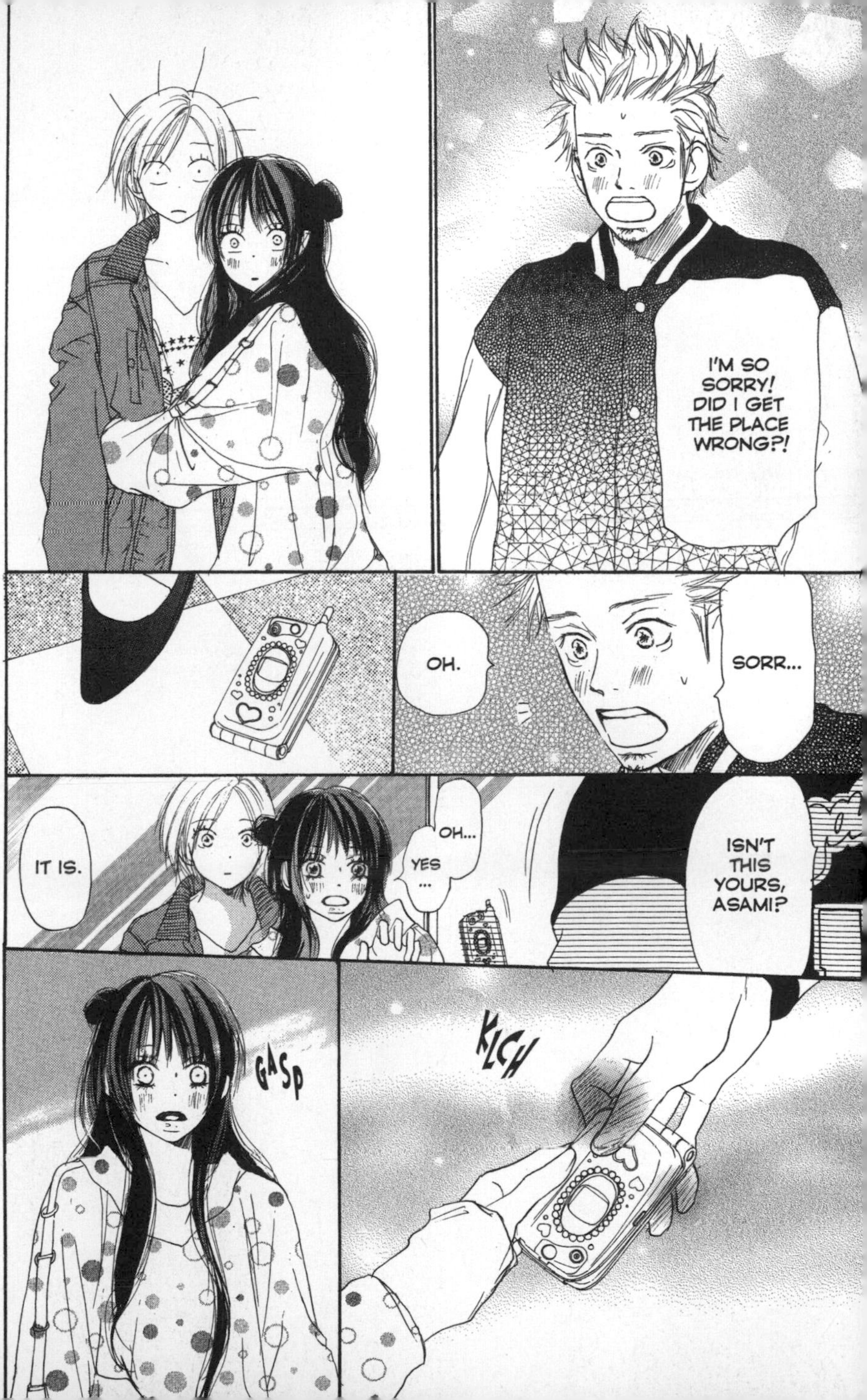
I'M SO SORRY! DID I GET THE PLACE WRONG?!
SORR...
OH.
ISN'T THIS YOURS, ASAMI?
OH... YES ...
IT IS.
KLCH
GASP

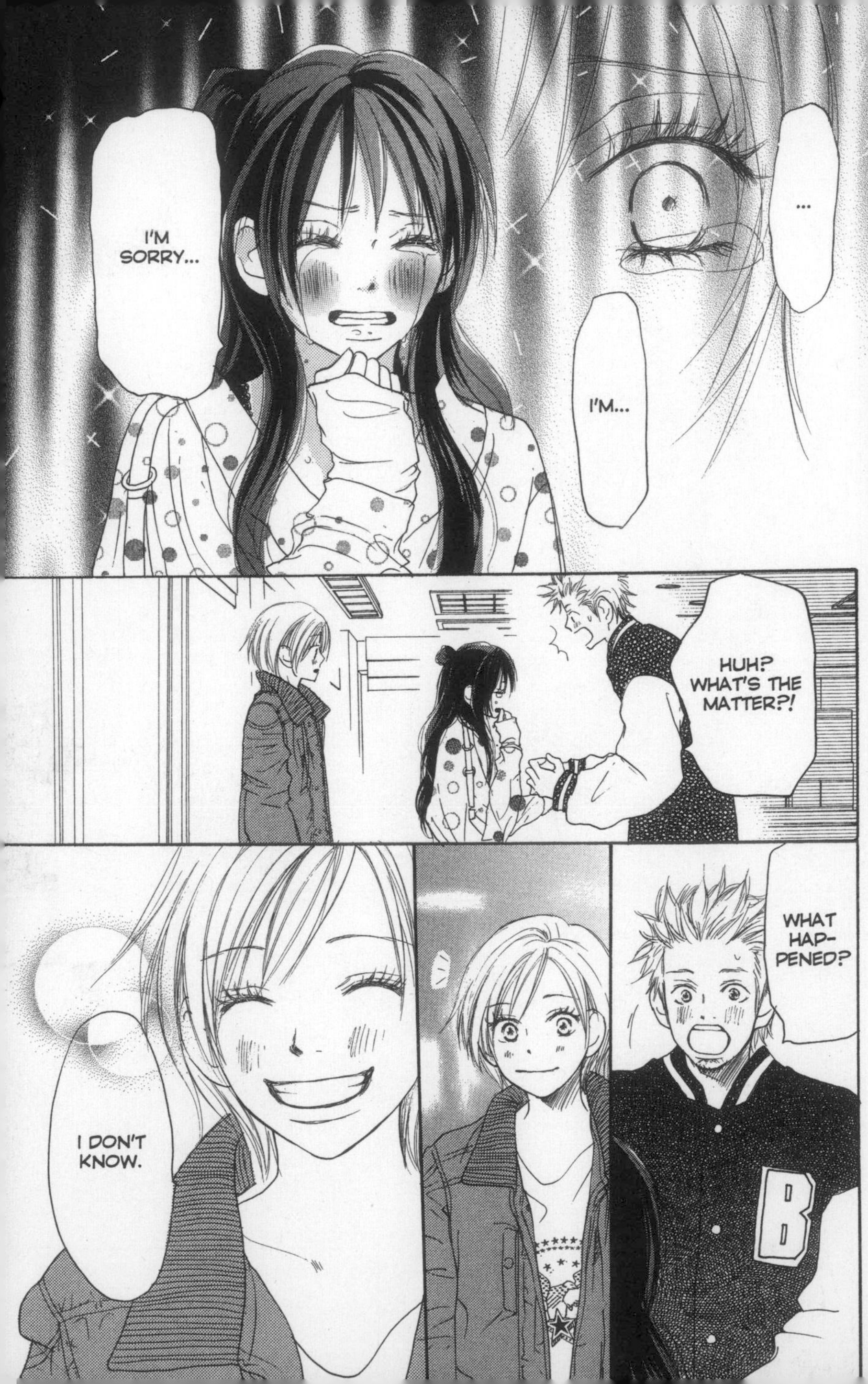
...
I'M...
I'M SORRY...
HUH? WHAT'S THE MATTER?!
WHAT HAP-PENED?
I DON'T KNOW.

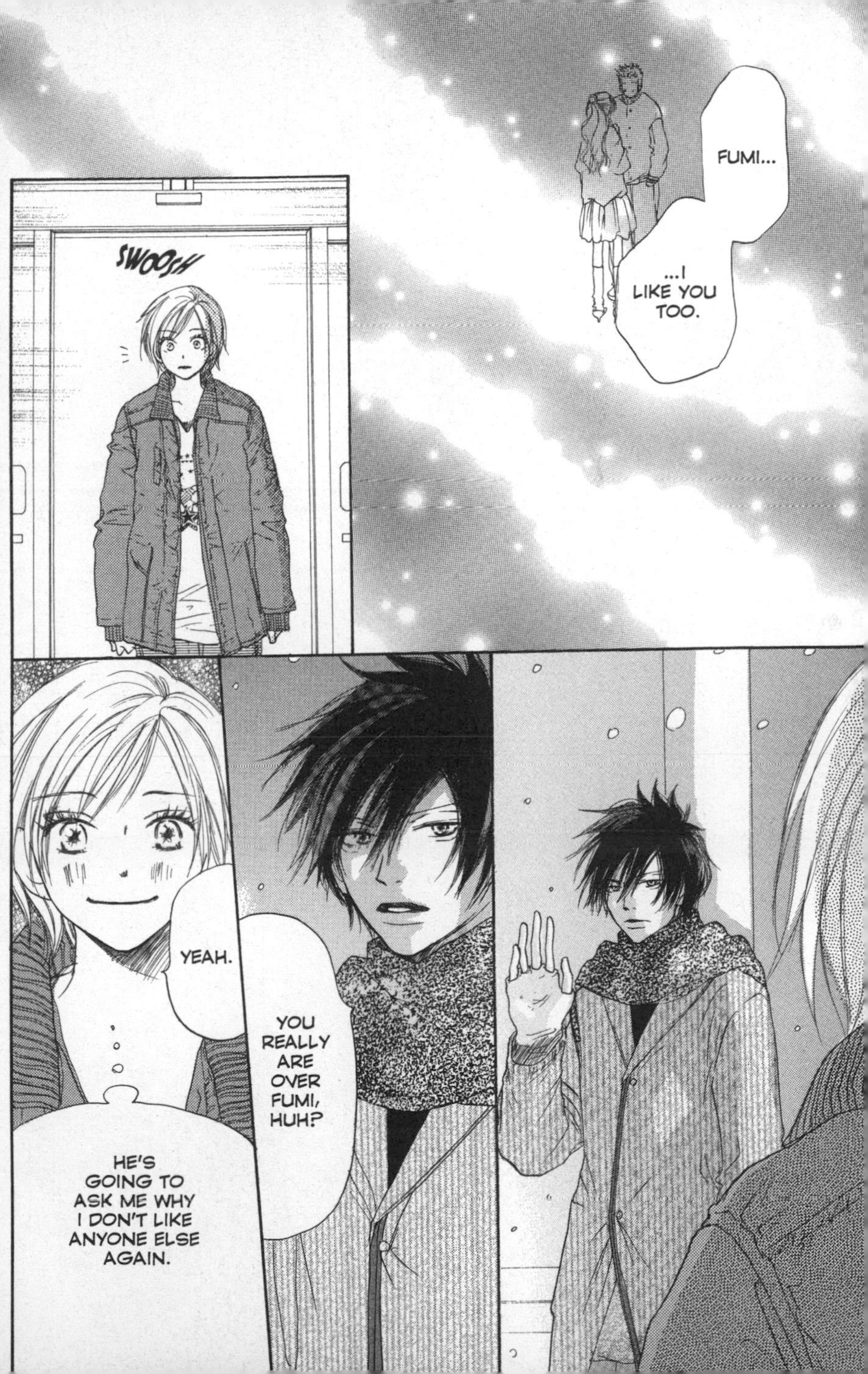
FUMI...
...I LIKE YOU TOO.
SWOOSH
YOU REALLY ARE OVER FUMI, HUH?
YEAH.
HE'S GOING TO ASK ME WHY I DON'T LIKE ANYONE ELSE AGAIN.

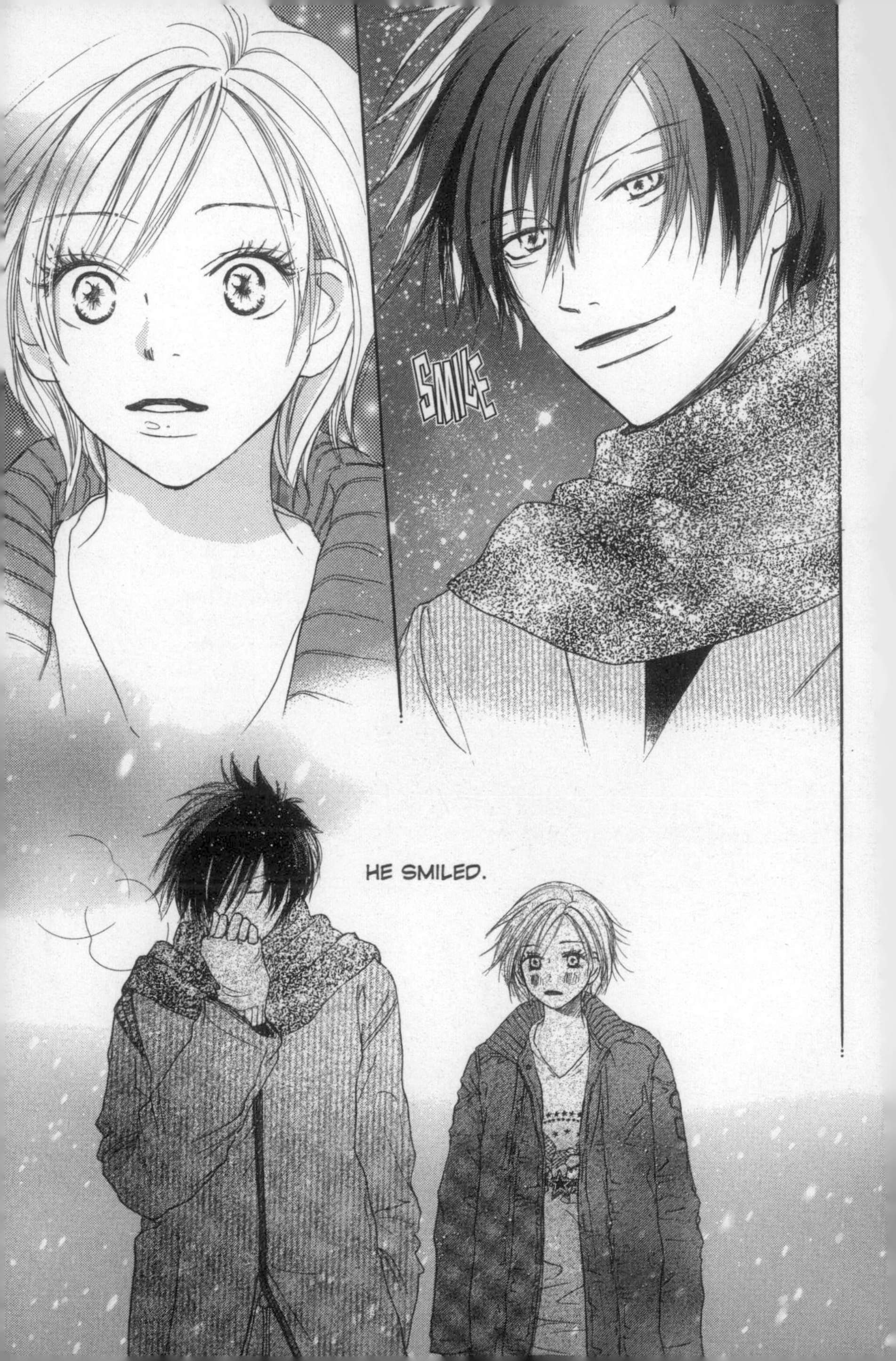
SMILE
HE SMILED.

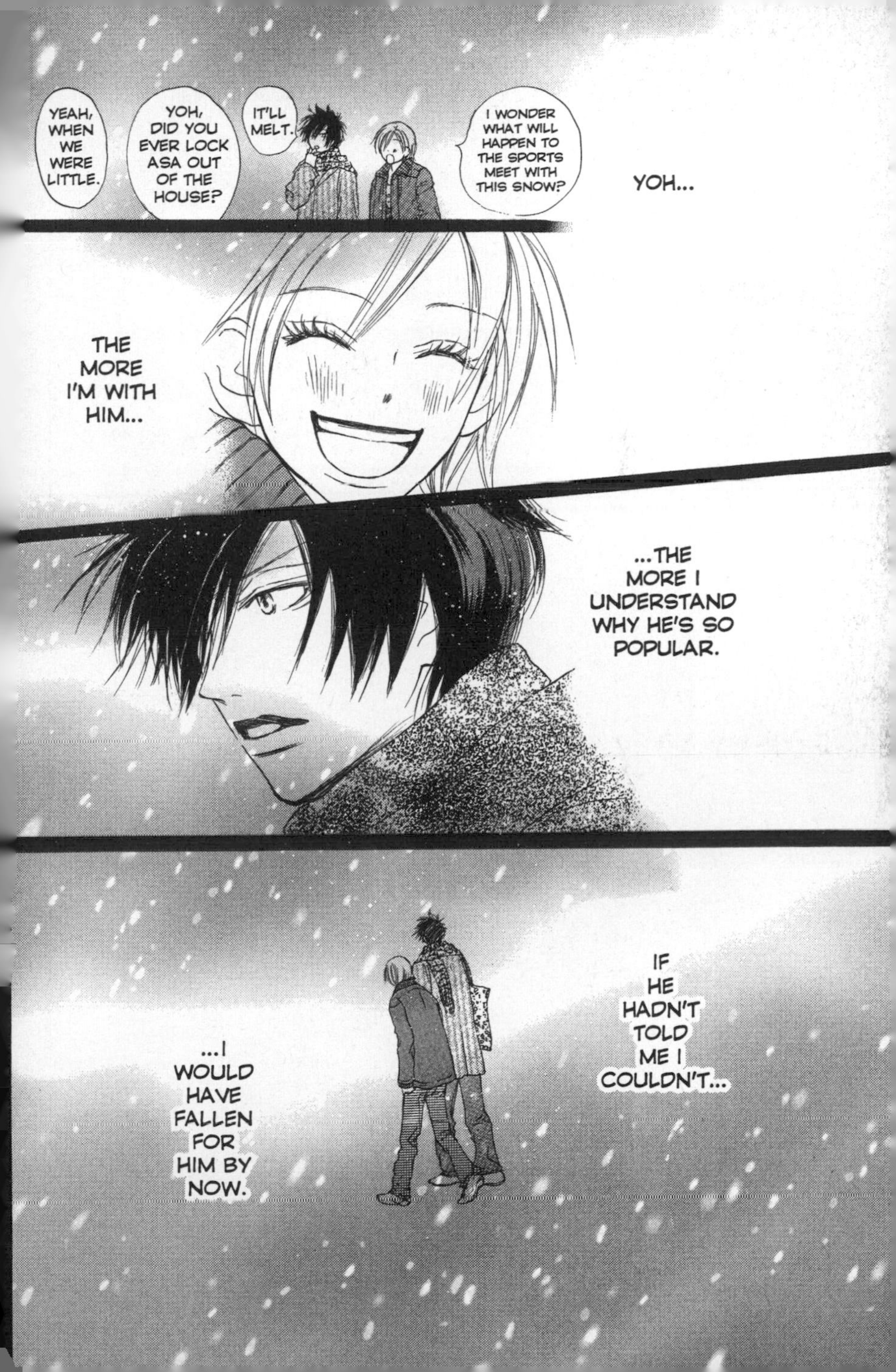
YOH...
I WONDER WHAT WILL HAPPEN TO THE SPORTS MEET WITH THIS SNOW?
IT'LL MELT.
YOH, DID YOU EVER LOCK ASA OUT OF THE HOUSE?
YEAH, WHEN WE WERE LITTLE.
THE MORE I'M WITH HIM...
...THE MORE I UNDERSTAND WHY HE'S SO POPULAR.
IF HE HADN'T TOLD ME I COULDN'T...
...I WOULD HAVE FALLEN FOR HIM BY NOW.

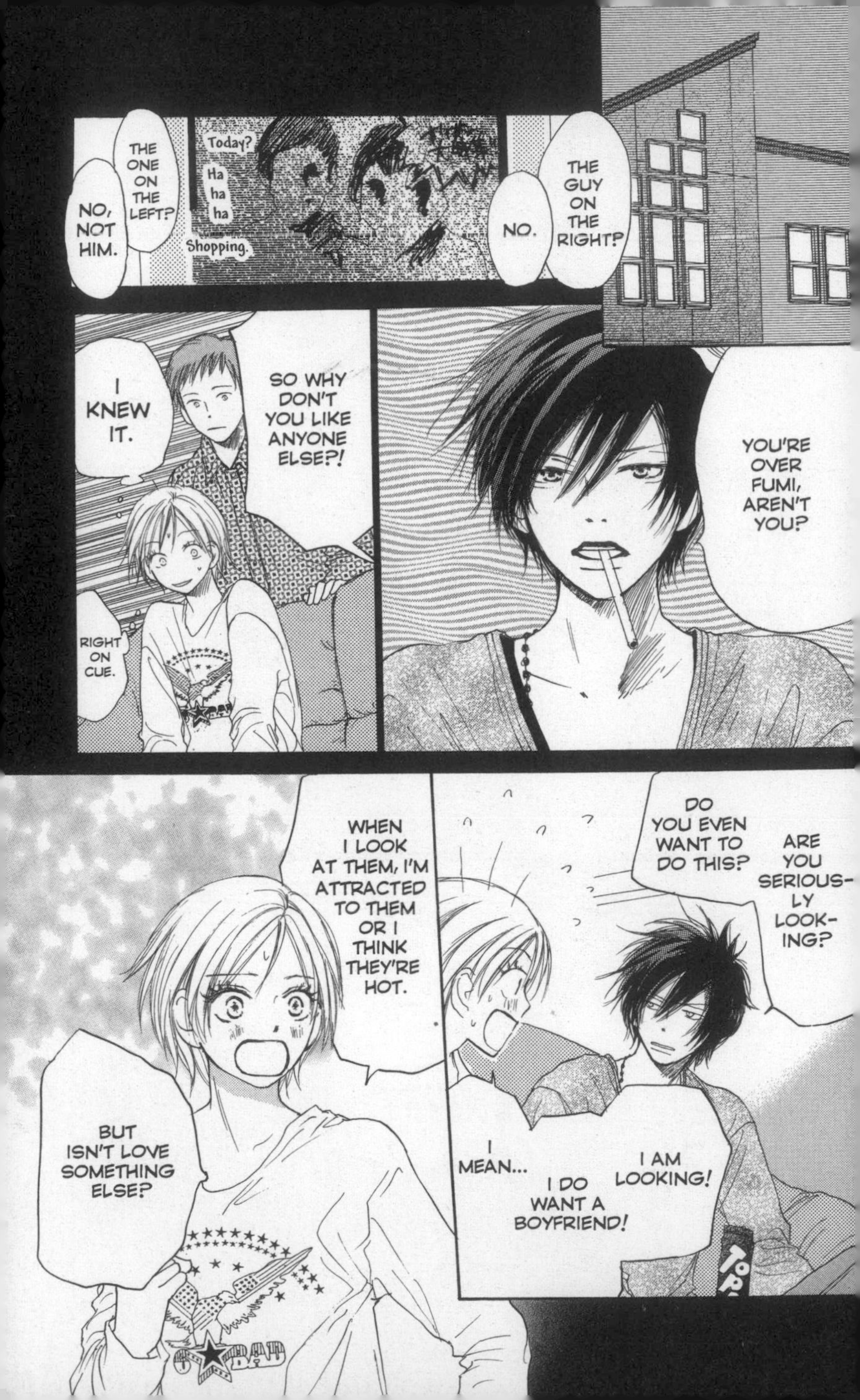
THE GUY ON THE RIGHT?
NO.
Today?
Ha ha ha
Shopping.
THE ONE ON THE LEFT?
NO, NOT HIM.
YOU'RE OVER FUMI, AREN'T YOU?
SO WHY DON'T YOU LIKE ANYONE ELSE?!
I KNEW IT.
RIGHT ON CUE.
DO YOU EVEN WANT TO DO THIS?
ARE YOU SERIOUS-LY LOOK-ING?
I AM LOOKING!
I DO WANT A BOYFRIEND!
I MEAN...
WHEN I LOOK AT THEM, I'M ATTRACTED TO THEM OR I THINK THEY'RE HOT.
BUT ISN'T LOVE SOMETHING ELSE?

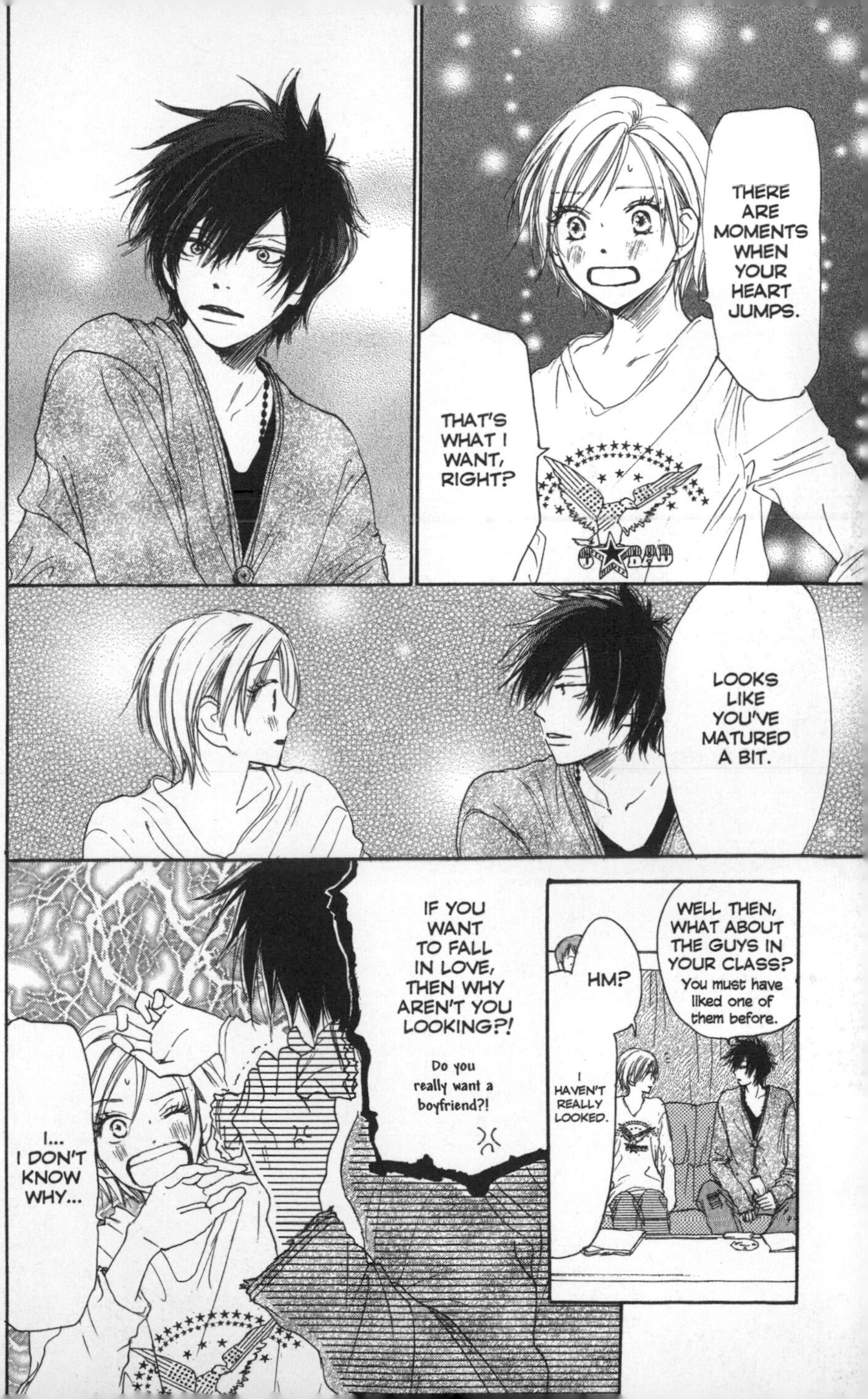
THERE ARE MOMENTS WHEN YOUR HEART JUMPS.
THAT'S WHAT I WANT, RIGHT?
LOOKS LIKE YOU'VE MATURED A BIT.
WELL THEN, WHAT ABOUT THE GUYS IN YOUR CLASS? You must have liked one of them before.
HM?
I HAVEN'T REALLY LOOKED.
IF YOU WANT TO FALL IN LOVE, THEN WHY AREN'T YOU LOOKING?!
Do you really want a boyfriend?!
I... I DON'T KNOW WHY...

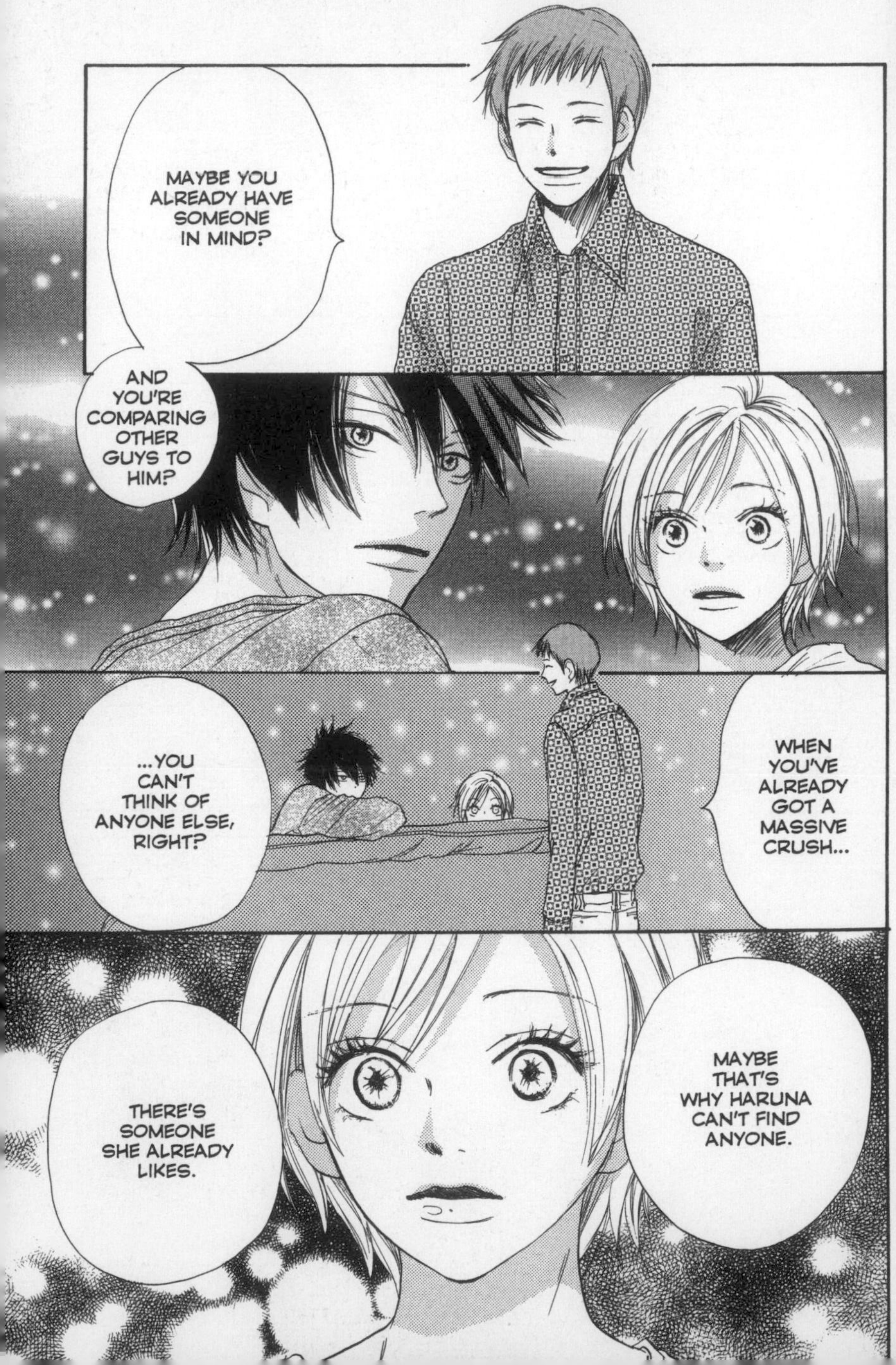
MAYBE YOU ALREADY HAVE SOMEONE IN MIND?
AND YOU'RE COMPARING OTHER GUYS TO HIM?
WHEN YOU'VE ALREADY GOT A MASSIVE CRUSH...
...YOU CAN'T THINK OF ANYONE ELSE, RIGHT?
MAYBE THAT'S WHY HARUNA CAN'T FIND ANYONE.
THERE'S SOMEONE SHE ALREADY LIKES.

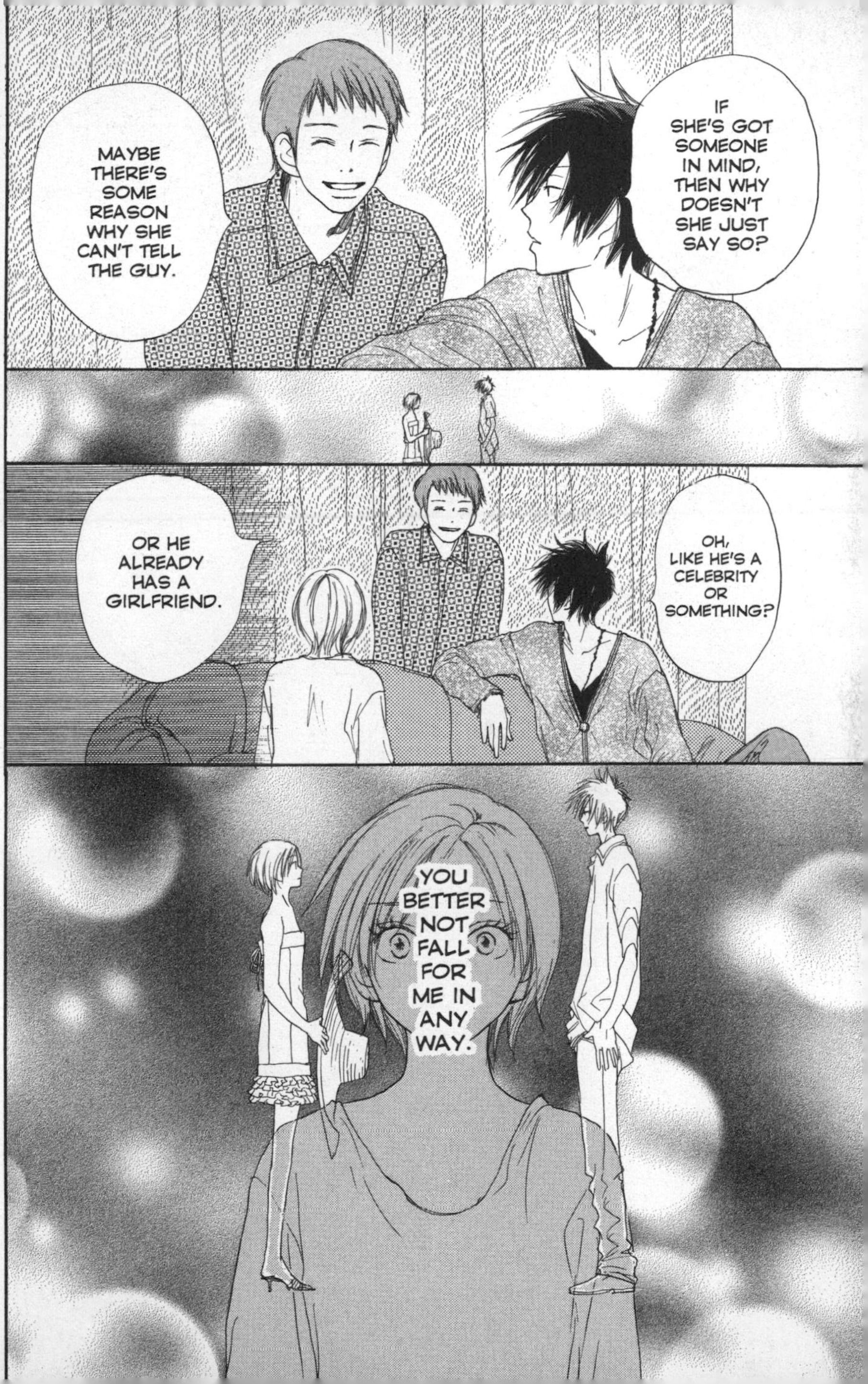
IF SHE'S GOT SOMEONE IN MIND, THEN WHY DOESN'T SHE JUST SAY SO?
MAYBE THERE'S SOME REASON WHY SHE CAN'T TELL THE GUY.
OH, LIKE HE'S A CELEBRITY OR SOMETHING?
OR HE ALREADY HAS A GIRLFRIEND.
YOU BETTER NOT FALL FOR ME IN ANY WAY.

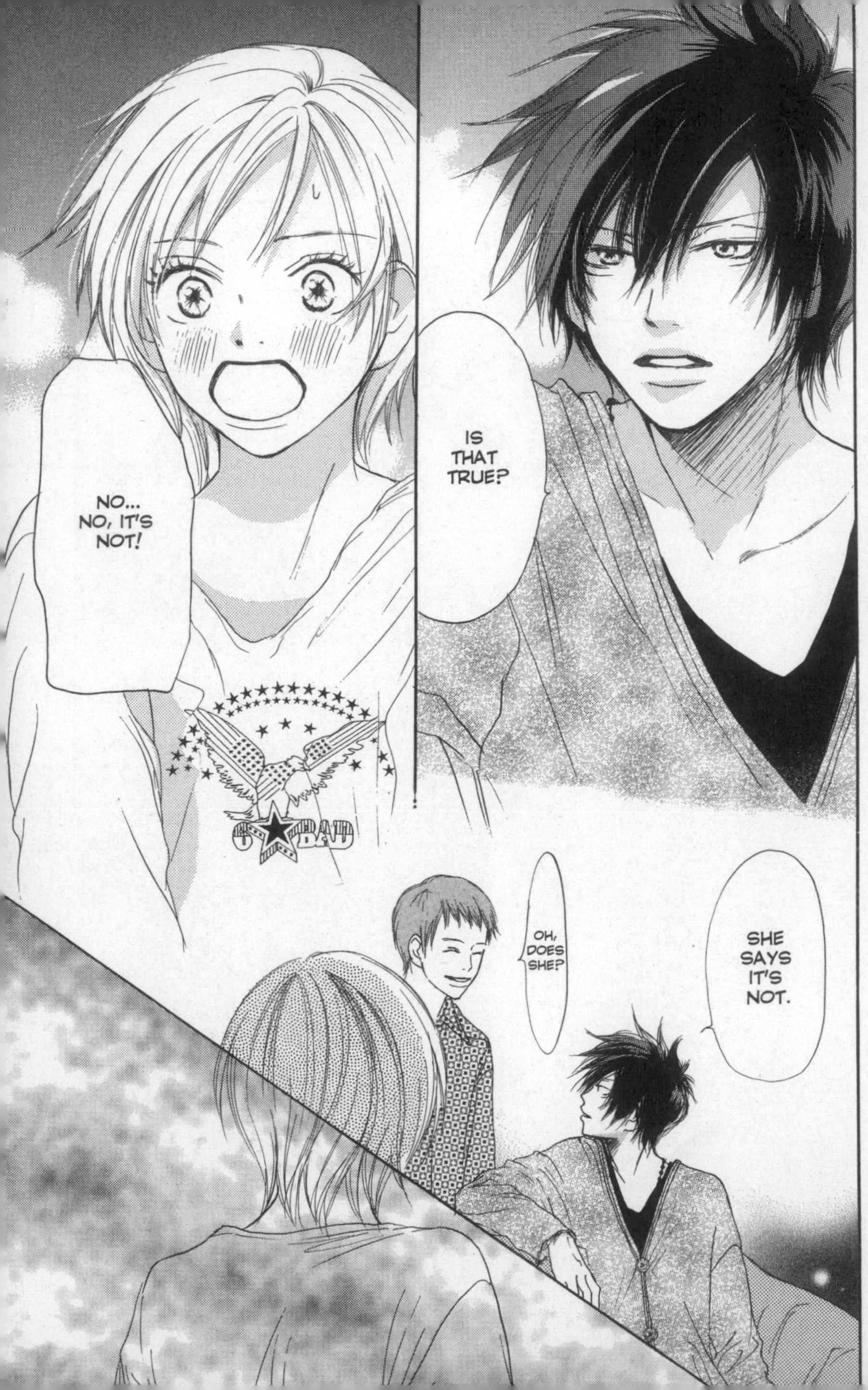
IS THAT TRUE?
NO... NO, IT'S NOT!
SHE SAYS IT'S NOT.
OH, DOES SHE?

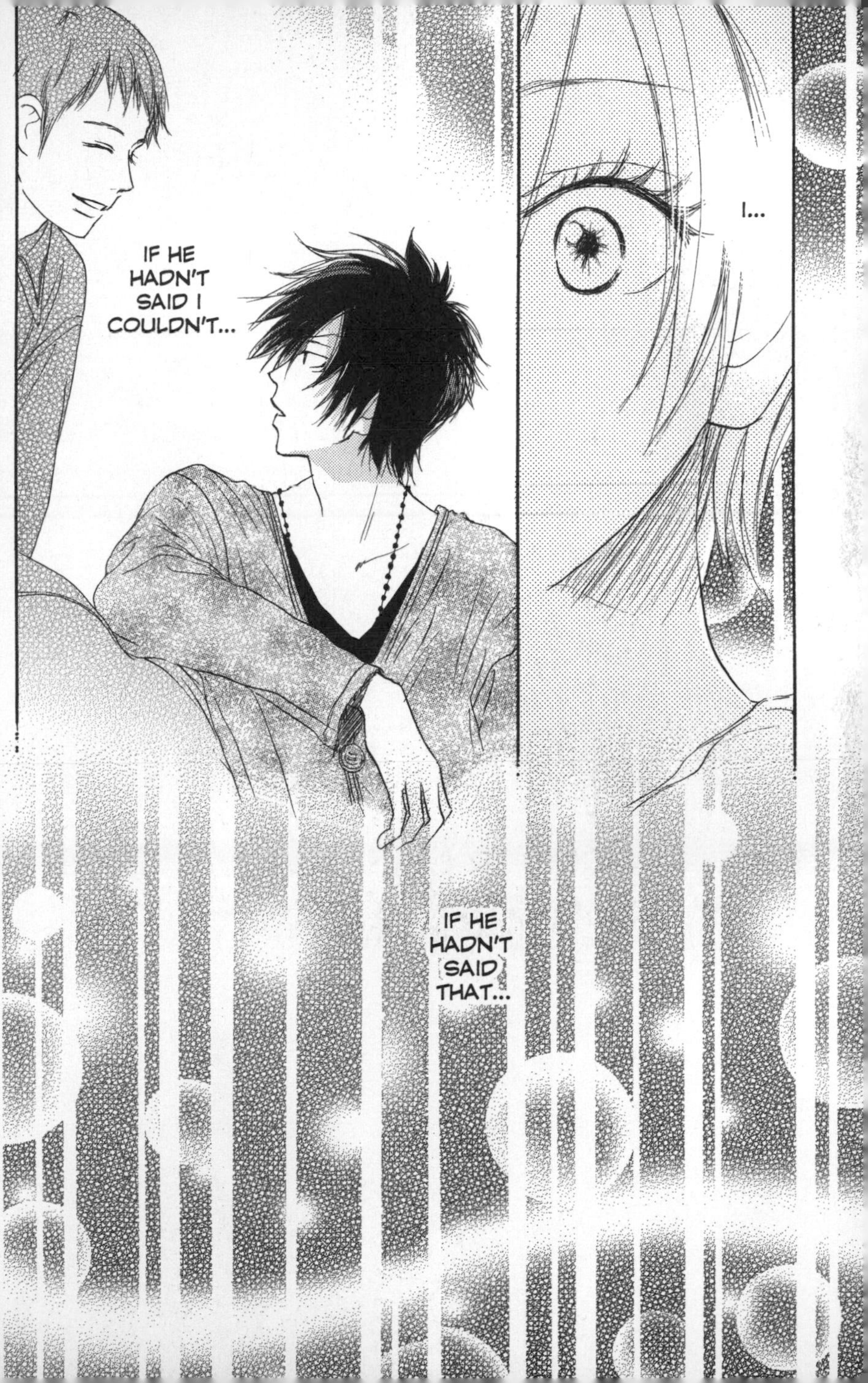
I...
IF HE HADN'T SAID I COULDN'T...
IF HE HADN'T SAID THAT...

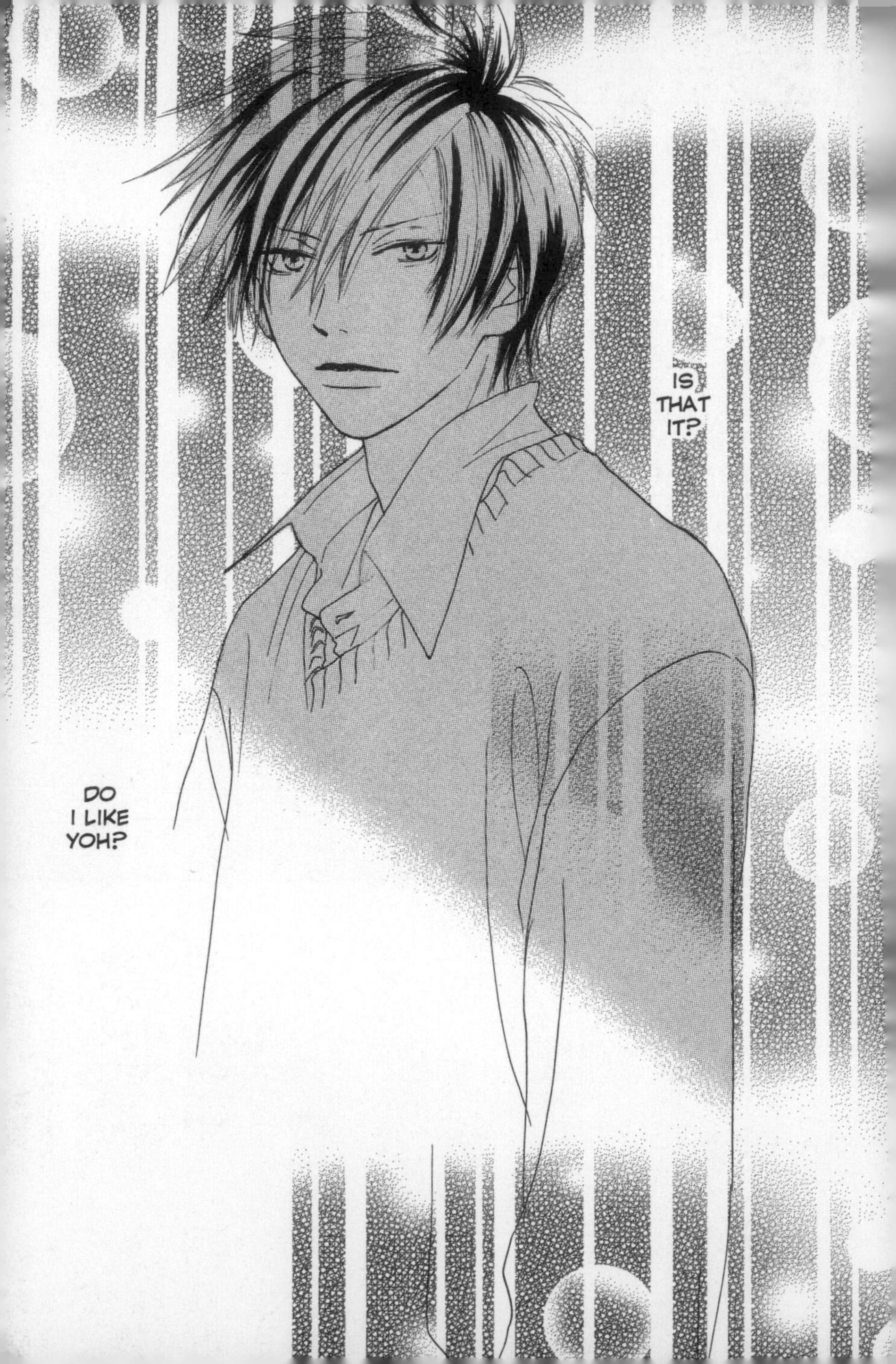
IS THAT IT?
DO I LIKE YOH?

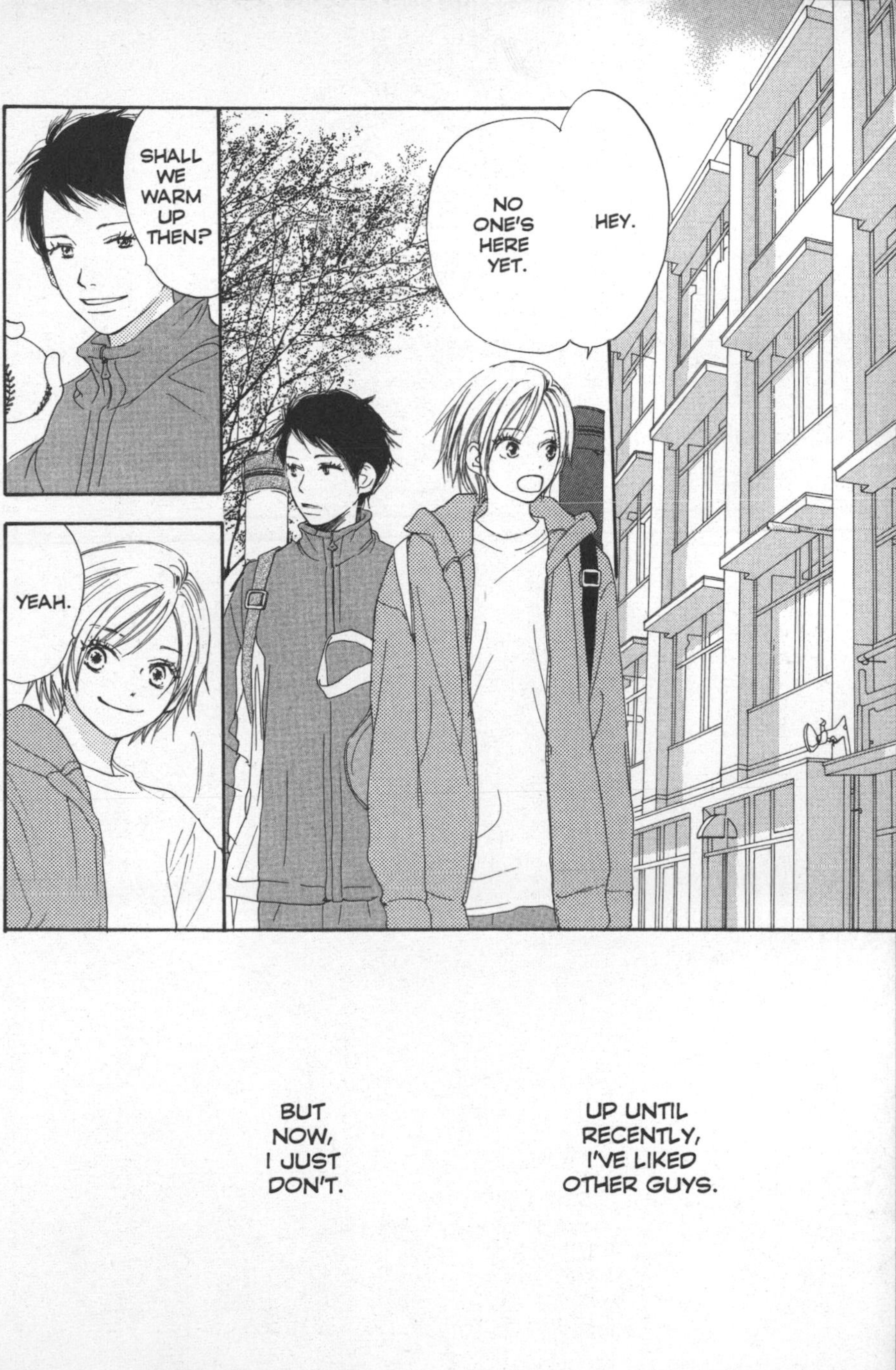
HEY.
NO ONE'S HERE YET.
SHALL WE WARM UP THEN?
YEAH.
UP UNTIL RECENTLY, I'VE LIKED OTHER GUYS.
BUT NOW, I JUST DON'T.

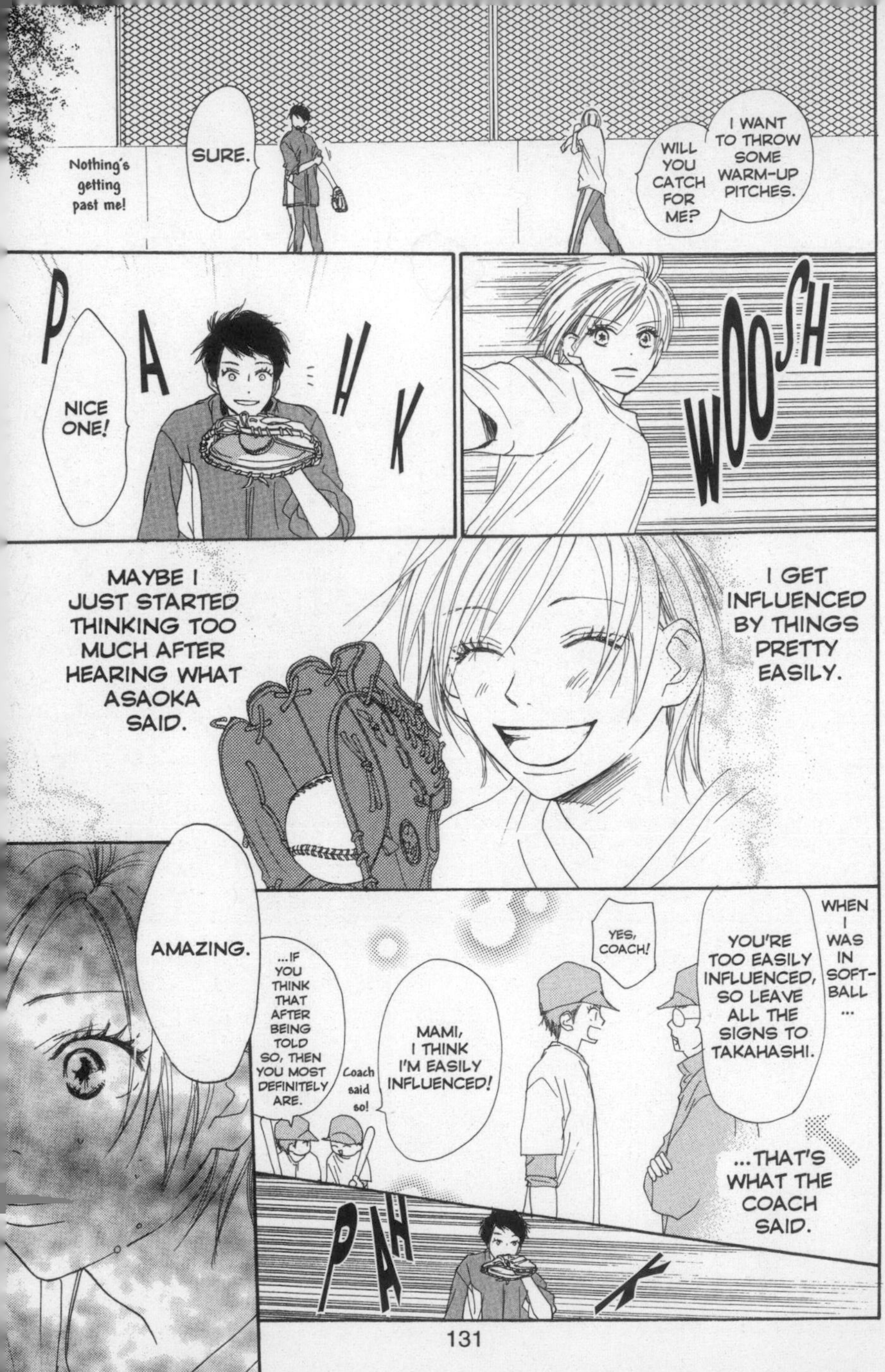
I WANT TO THROW SOME WARM-UP PITCHES.
WILL YOU CATCH FOR ME?
SURE.
Nothing's getting past me!
WOOSH
PAHK
NICE ONE!
I GET INFLUENCED BY THINGS PRETTY EASILY.
MAYBE I JUST STARTED THINKING TOO MUCH AFTER HEARING WHAT ASAOKA SAID.
WHEN I WAS IN SOFT-BALL...
YOU'RE TOO EASILY INFLUENCED, SO LEAVE ALL THE SIGNS TO TAKAHASHI.
YES, COACH!
MAMI, I THINK I'M EASILY INFLUENCED!
Coach said so!
...IF YOU THINK THAT AFTER BEING TOLD SO, THEN YOU MOST DEFINITELY ARE.
...THAT'S WHAT THE COACH SAID.
PAHK
AMAZING.

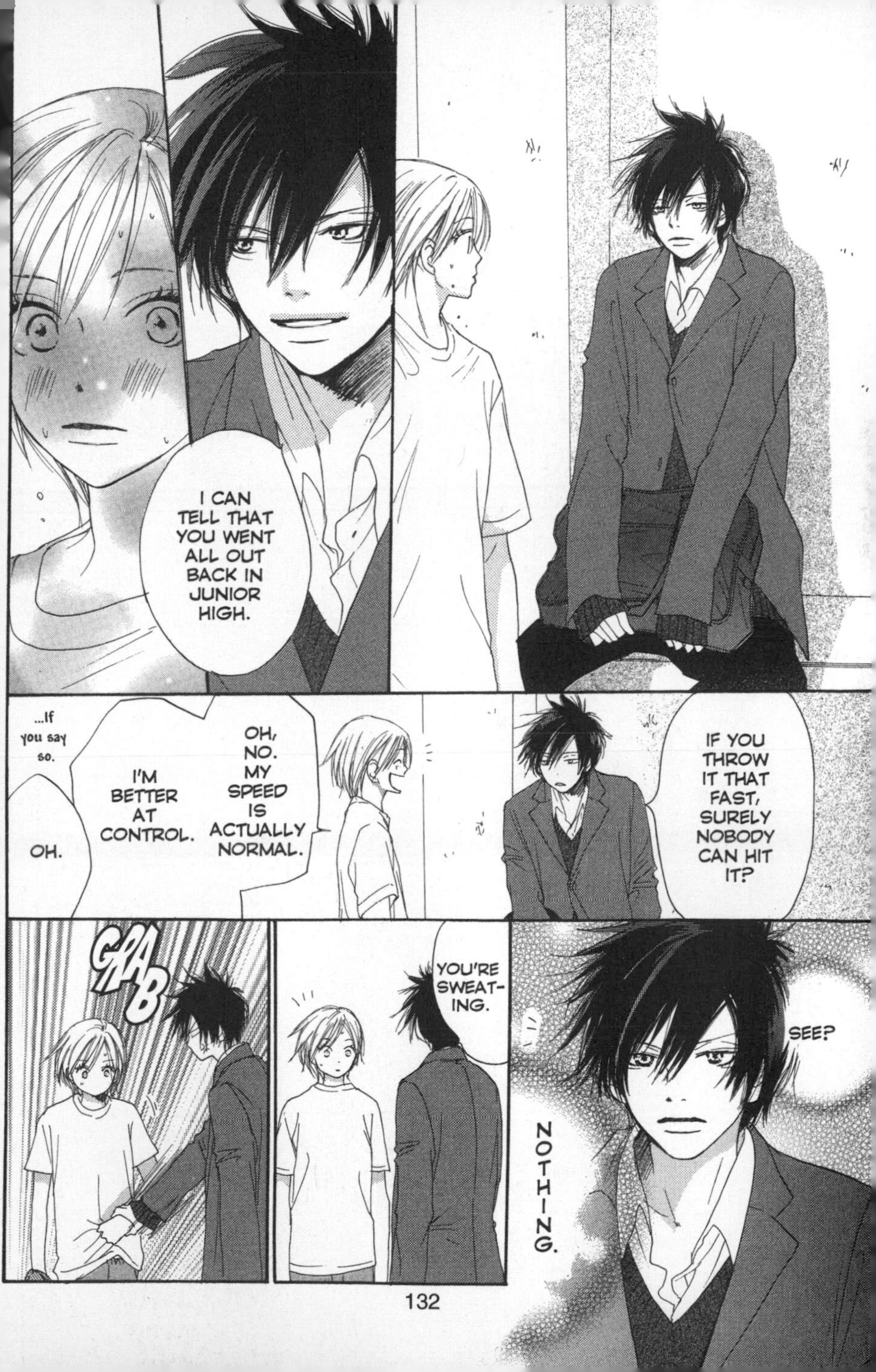
I CAN TELL THAT YOU WENT ALL OUT BACK IN JUNIOR HIGH.
IF YOU THROW IT THAT FAST, SURELY NOBODY CAN HIT IT?
OH, NO. MY SPEED IS ACTUALLY NORMAL.
I'M BETTER AT CONTROL.
OH.
...If you say so.
SEE?
NOTHING.
YOU'RE SWEAT-ING.
GRAB

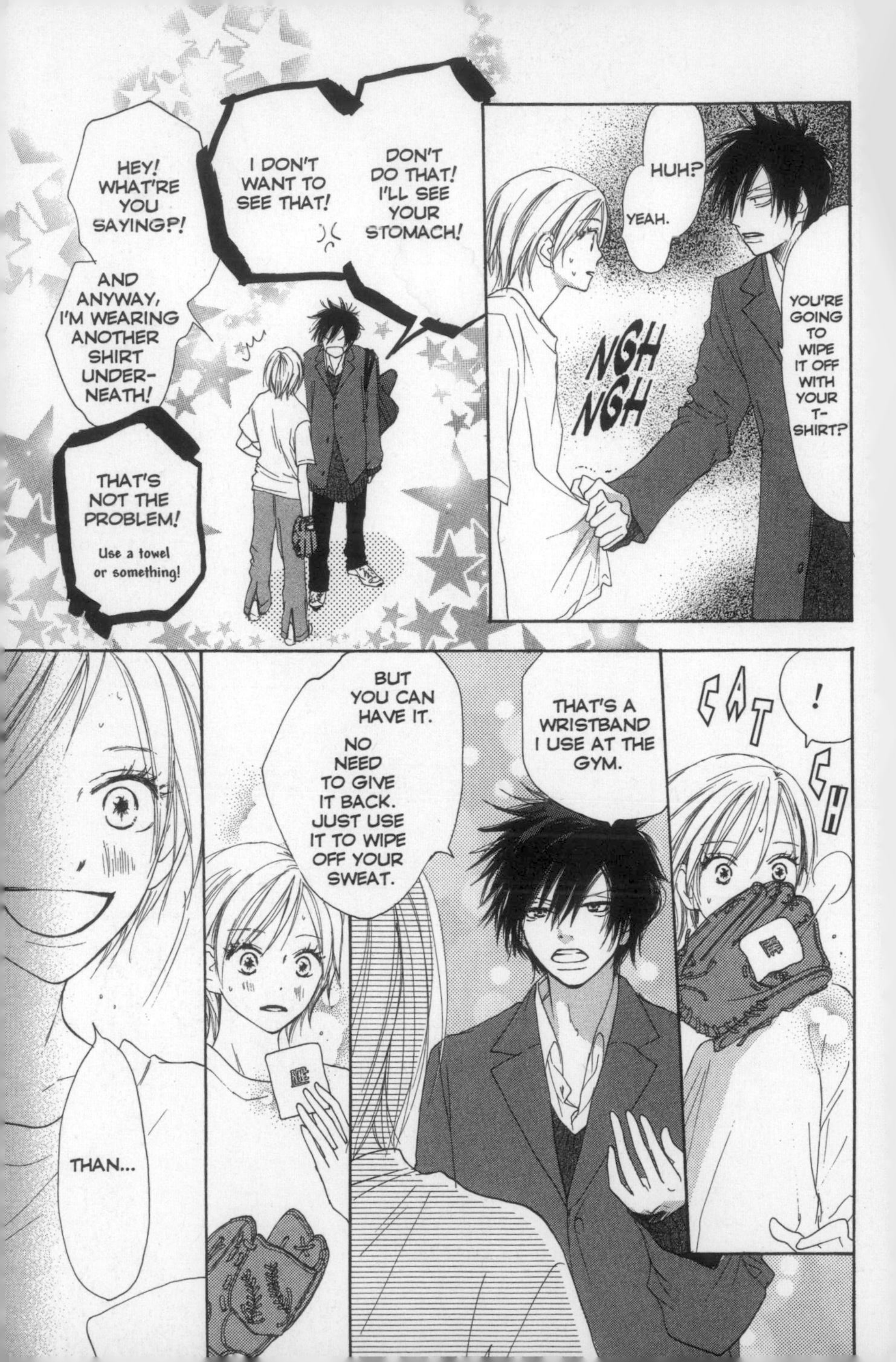
YOU'RE GOING TO WIPE IT OFF WITH YOUR T-SHIRT?
HUH?
YEAH.
NGH NGH
DON'T DO THAT! I'LL SEE YOUR STOMACH!
I DON'T WANT TO SEE THAT!
HEY! WHAT'RE YOU SAYING?!
AND ANYWAY, I'M WEARING ANOTHER SHIRT UNDER-NEATH!
THAT'S NOT THE PROBLEM!
Use a towel or something!
CATCH
!
THAT'S A WRISTBAND I USE AT THE GYM.
BUT YOU CAN HAVE IT.
NO NEED TO GIVE IT BACK. JUST USE IT TO WIPE OFF YOUR SWEAT.
THAN...

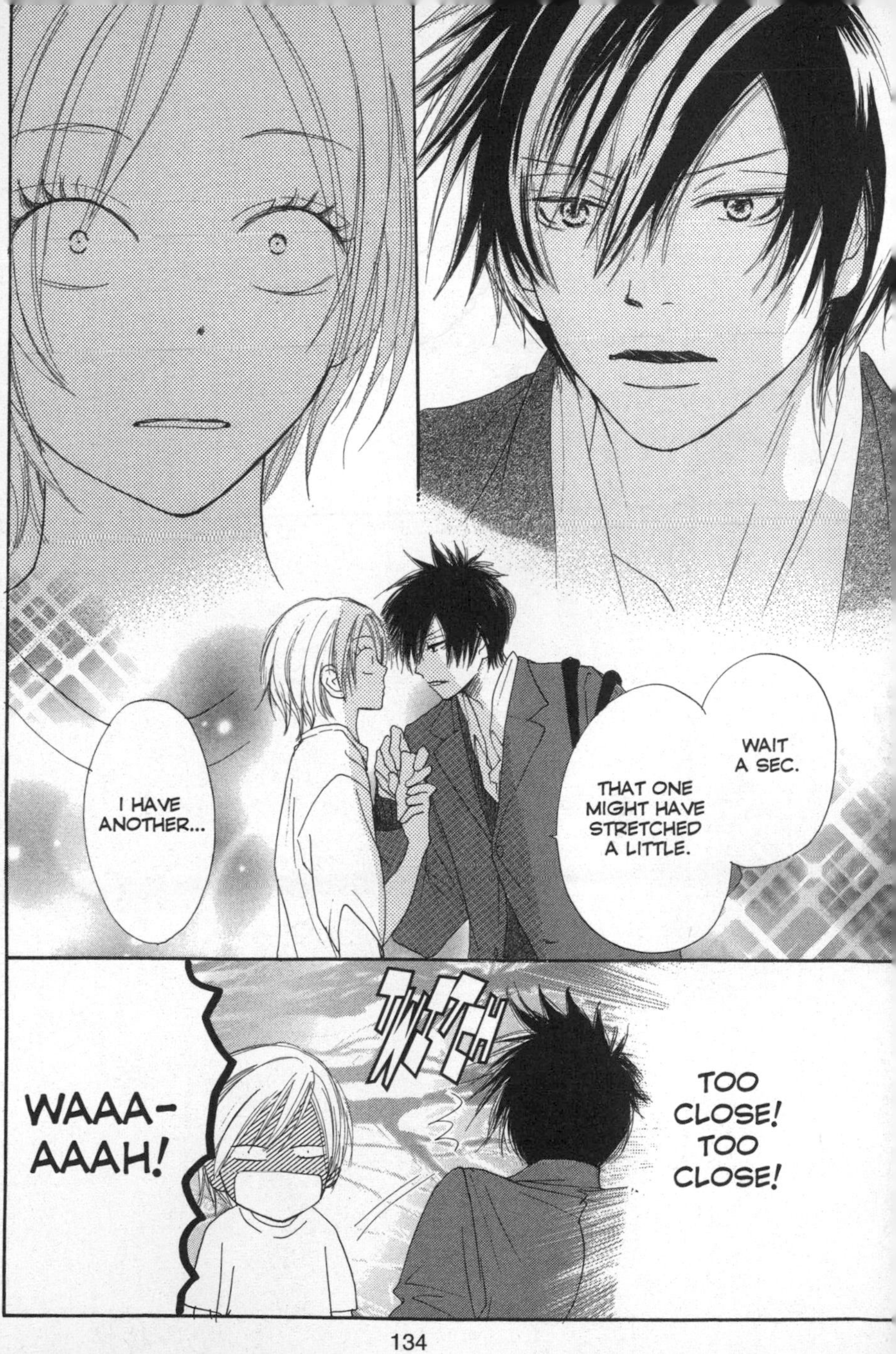
WAIT A SEC.
THAT ONE MIGHT HAVE STRETCHED A LITTLE.
I HAVE ANOTHER...
TOO CLOSE! TOO CLOSE!
WAAAA-AAAH!

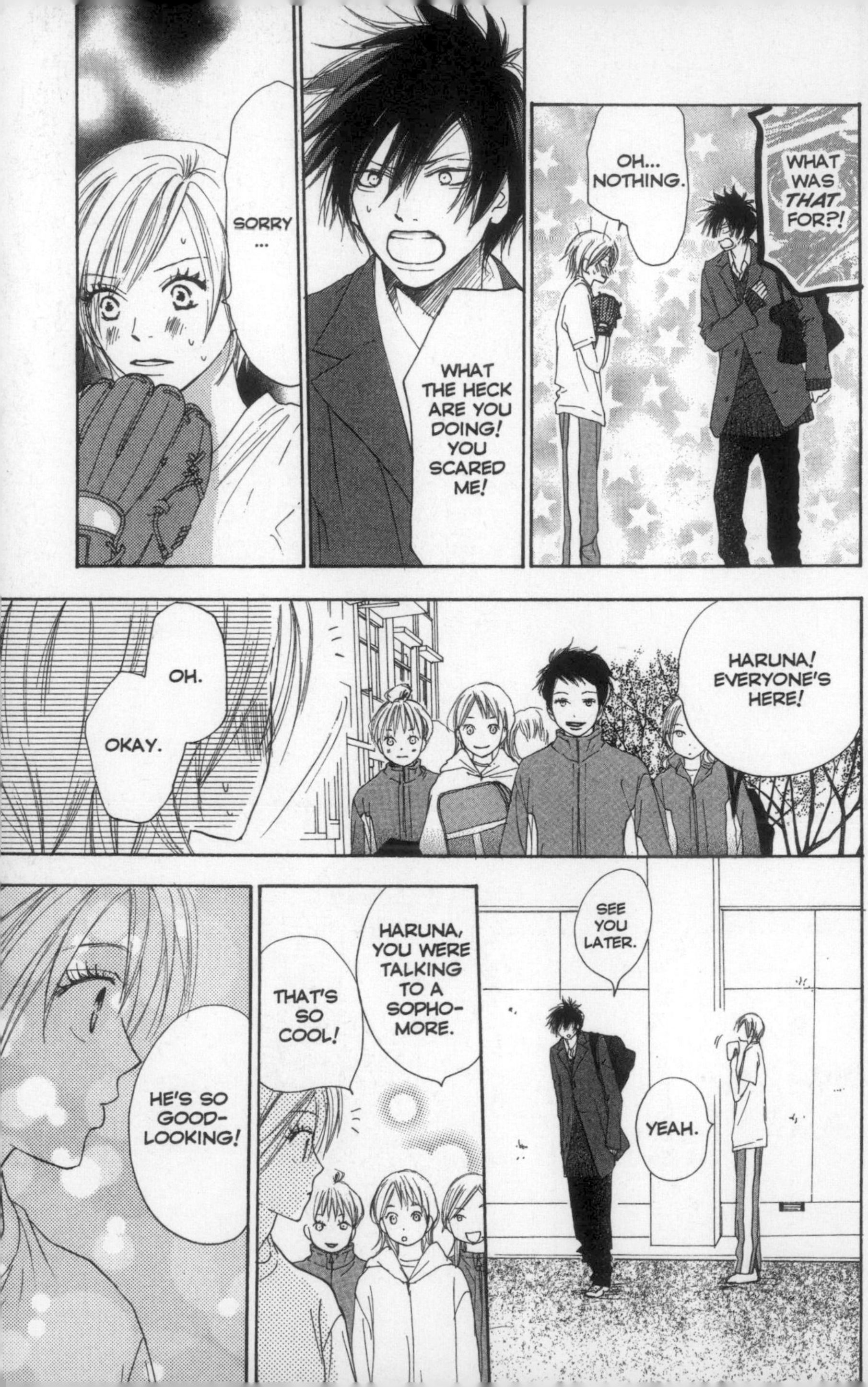
WHAT WAS *THAT* FOR?!
OH... NOTHING.
WHAT THE HECK ARE YOU DOING! YOU SCARED ME!
SORRY...
HARUNA! EVERYONE'S HERE!
OH.
OKAY.
SEE YOU LATER.
YEAH.
HARUNA, YOU WERE TALKING TO A SOPHOMORE.
THAT'S SO COOL!
HE'S SO GOOD-LOOKING!

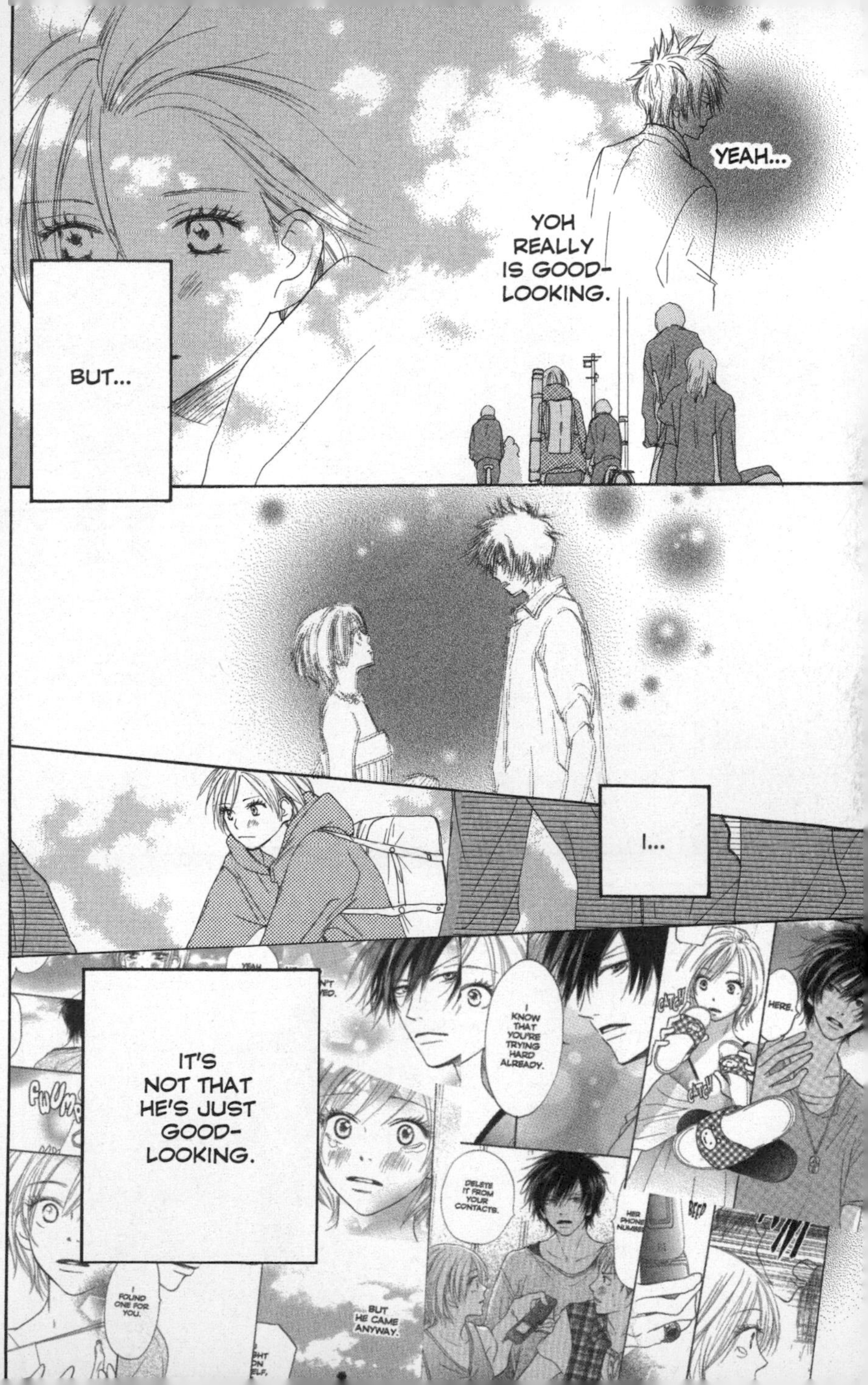
YEAH...
YOH REALLY IS GOOD-LOOKING.
BUT...
I...
HERE.
CATCH
I KNOW THAT YOU'RE TRYING HARD ALREADY.
IT'S NOT THAT HE'S JUST GOOD-LOOKING.
DELETE IT FROM YOUR CONTACTS.
BUT HE CAME ANYWAY.
I FOUND ONE FOR YOU.

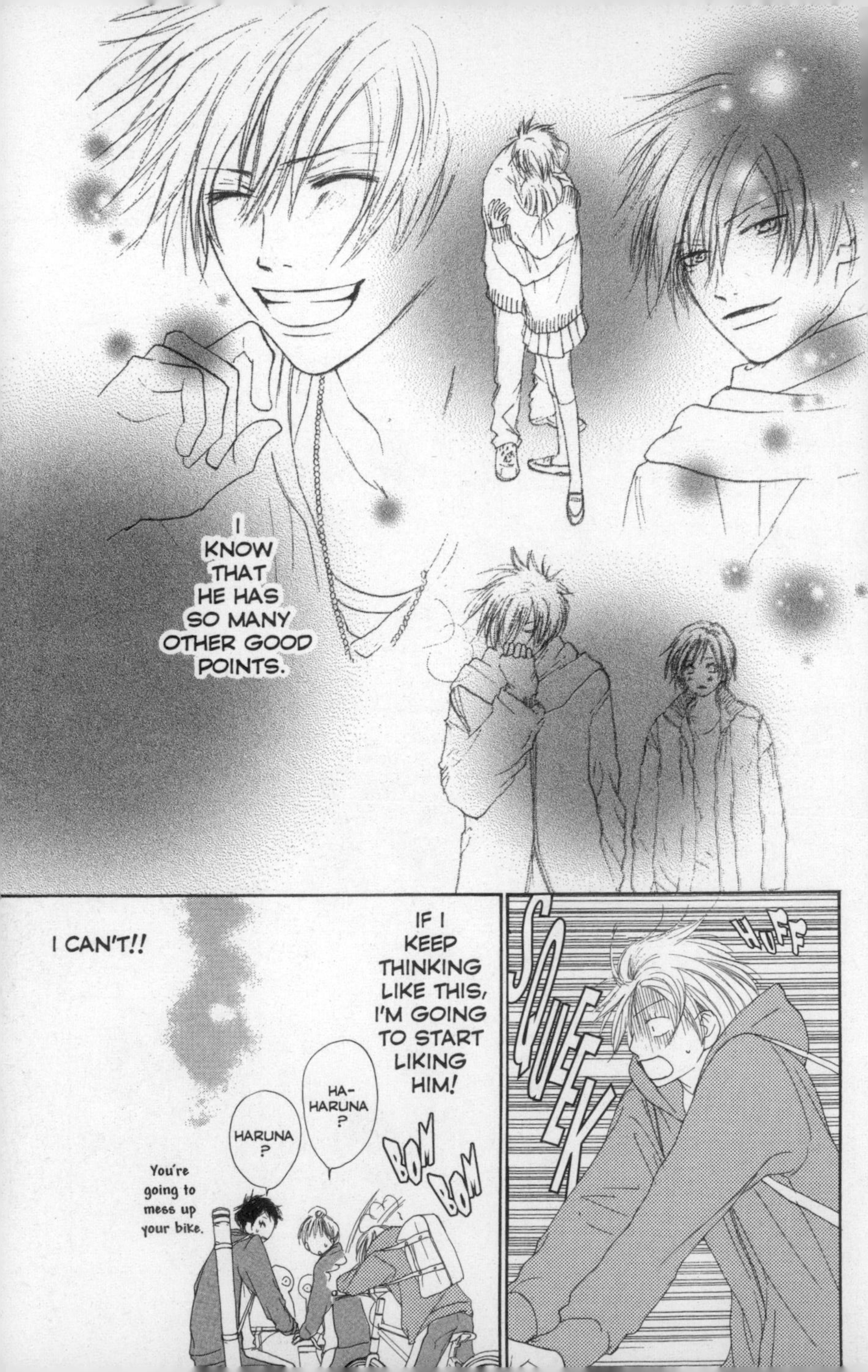

I KNOW THAT HE HAS SO MANY OTHER GOOD POINTS.
SQUEEEK
HUFF
IF I KEEP THINKING LIKE THIS, I'M GOING TO START LIKING HIM!
I CAN'T!!
BOM BOM
HA-HARUNA?
HARUNA?
You're going to mess up your bike.

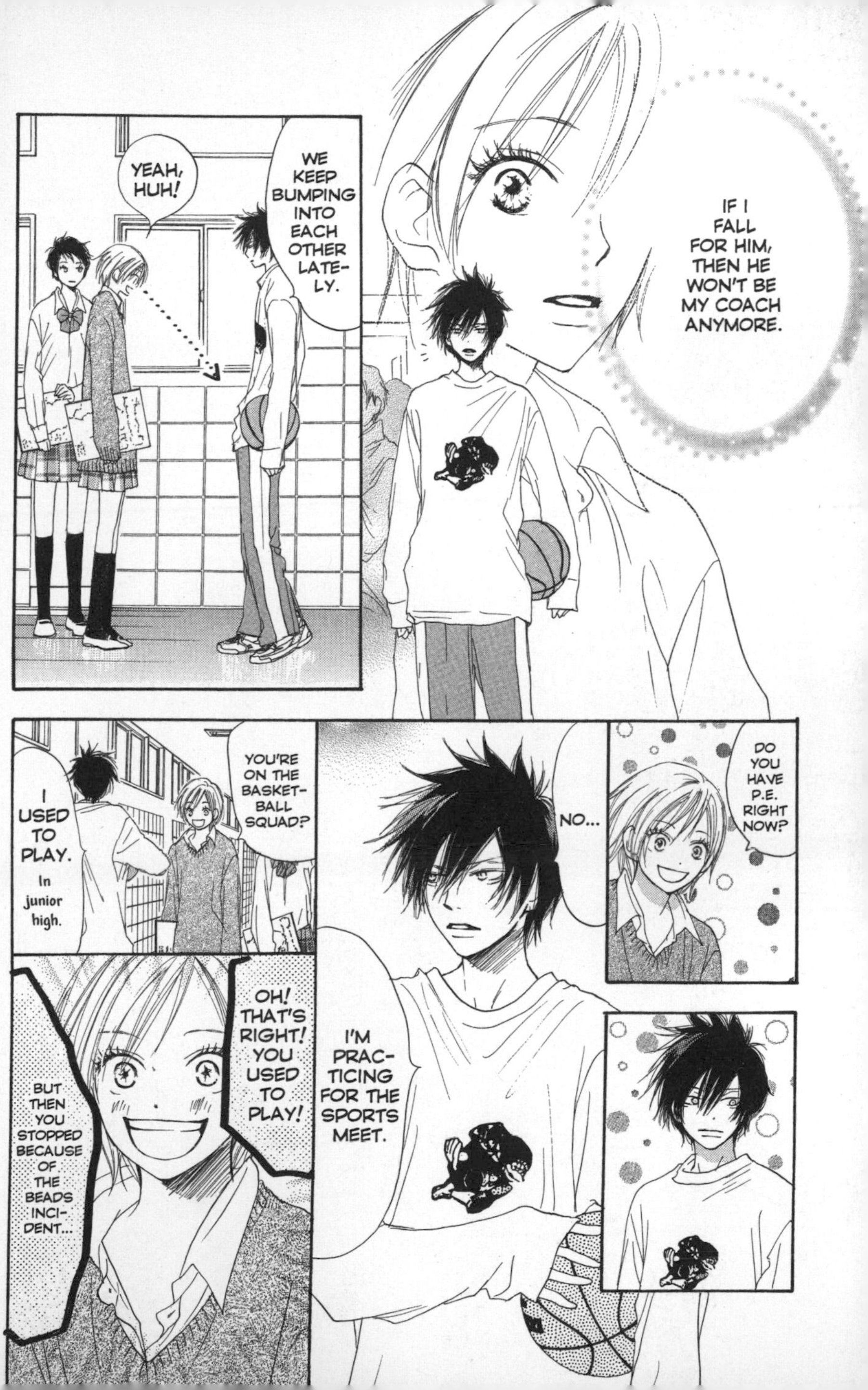

IF I FALL FOR HIM, THEN HE WON'T BE MY COACH ANYMORE.
WE KEEP BUMPING INTO EACH OTHER LATE-LY.
YEAH, HUH!
DO YOU HAVE P.E. RIGHT NOW?
NO...
I'M PRAC-TICING FOR THE SPORTS MEET.
YOU'RE ON THE BASKET-BALL SQUAD?
I USED TO PLAY.
In junior high.
OH! THAT'S RIGHT! YOU USED TO PLAY!
BUT THEN YOU STOPPED BECAUSE OF THE BEADS INCI-DENT...

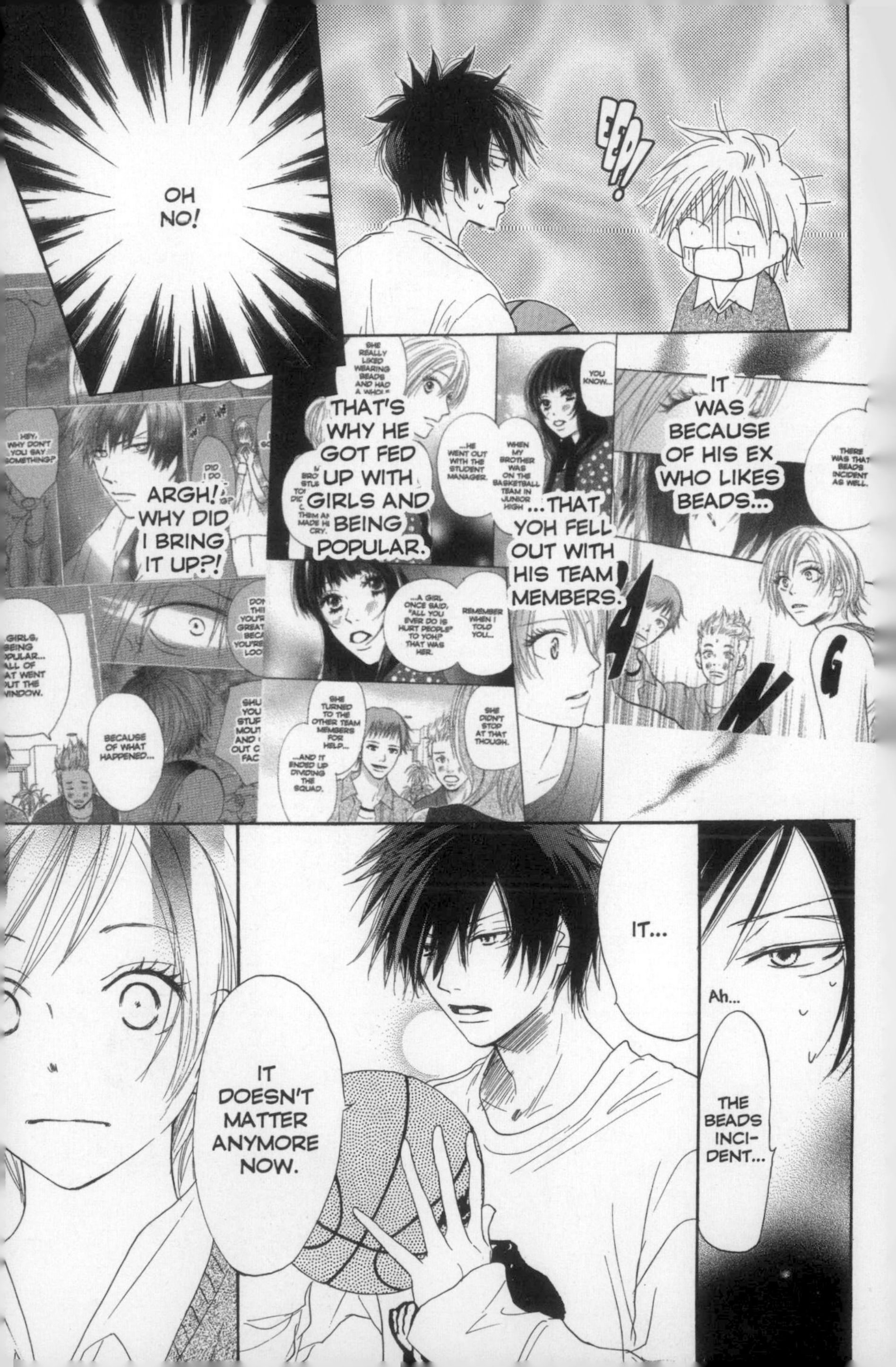
EEP!!
OH NO!
IT WAS BECAUSE OF HIS EX WHO LIKES BEADS...
THERE WAS THAT BEADS INCIDENT AS WELL.
YOU KNOW...
WHEN MY BROTHER WAS ON THE BASKETBALL TEAM IN JUNIOR HIGH
...HE WENT OUT WITH THE STUDENT MANAGER.
...THAT YOH FELL OUT WITH HIS TEAM MEMBERS.
SHE REALLY LIKED WEARING BEADS AND HAD A WHOLE
THAT'S WHY HE GOT FED UP WITH GIRLS AND BEING POPULAR.
REMEMBER WHEN I TOLD YOU...
...A GIRL ONCE SAID, "ALL YOU EVER DO IS HURT PEOPLE" TO YOH? THAT WAS HER.
SHE DIDN'T STOP AT THAT THOUGH.
SHE TURNED TO THE OTHER TEAM MEMBERS FOR HELP...
...AND IT ENDED UP DIVIDING THE SQUAD.
HEY, WHY DON'T YOU SAY SOMETHING?
ARGH! WHY DID I BRING IT UP?!
BECAUSE OF WHAT HAPPENED...
Ah...
THE BEADS INCI-DENT...
IT...
IT DOESN'T MATTER ANYMORE NOW.

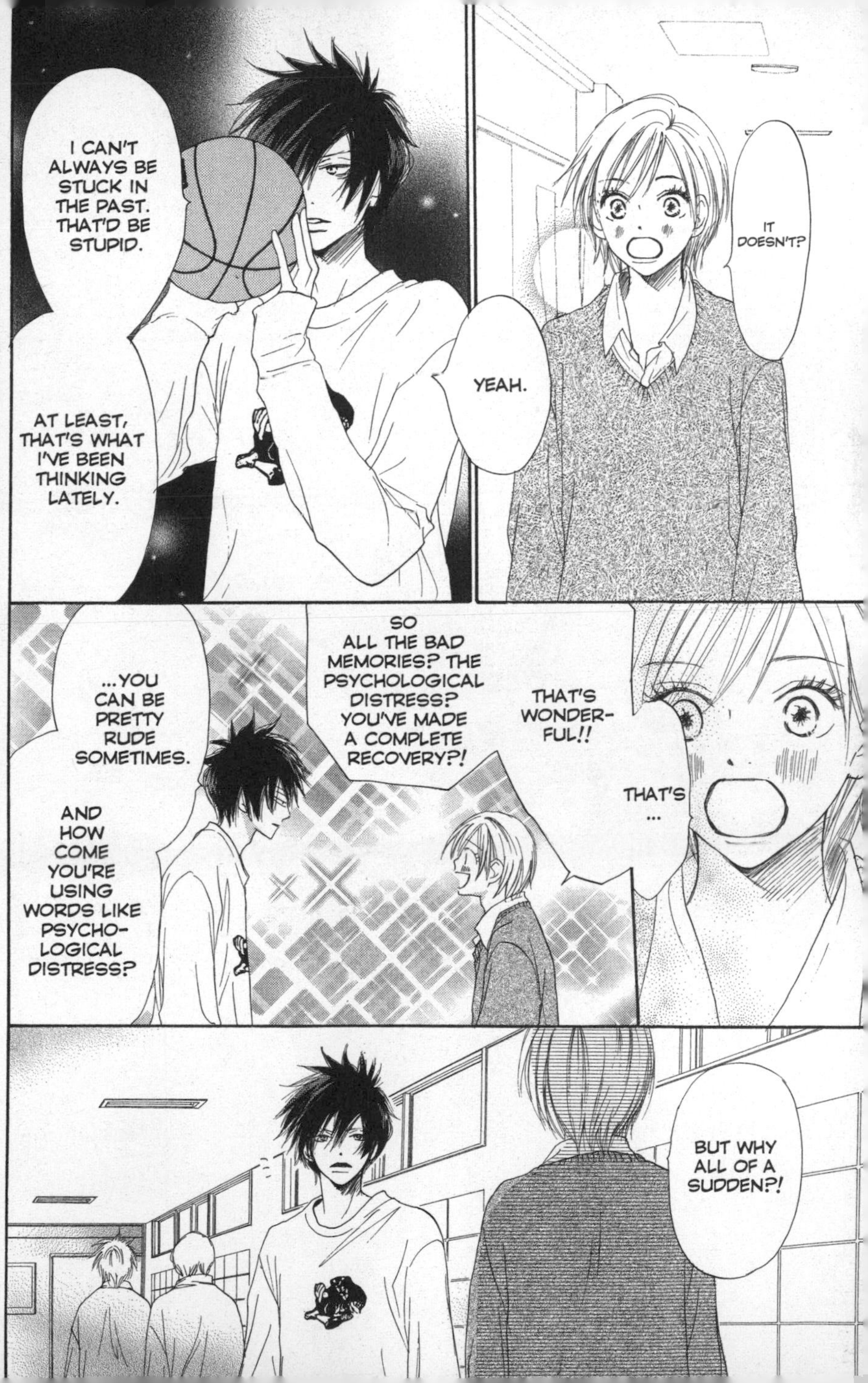
IT DOESN'T?
YEAH.
I CAN'T ALWAYS BE STUCK IN THE PAST. THAT'D BE STUPID.
AT LEAST, THAT'S WHAT I'VE BEEN THINKING LATELY.
THAT'S ...
THAT'S WONDER-FUL!!
SO ALL THE BAD MEMORIES? THE PSYCHOLOGICAL DISTRESS? YOU'VE MADE A COMPLETE RECOVERY?!
...YOU CAN BE PRETTY RUDE SOMETIMES.
AND HOW COME YOU'RE USING WORDS LIKE PSYCHO-LOGICAL DISTRESS?
BUT WHY ALL OF A SUDDEN?!

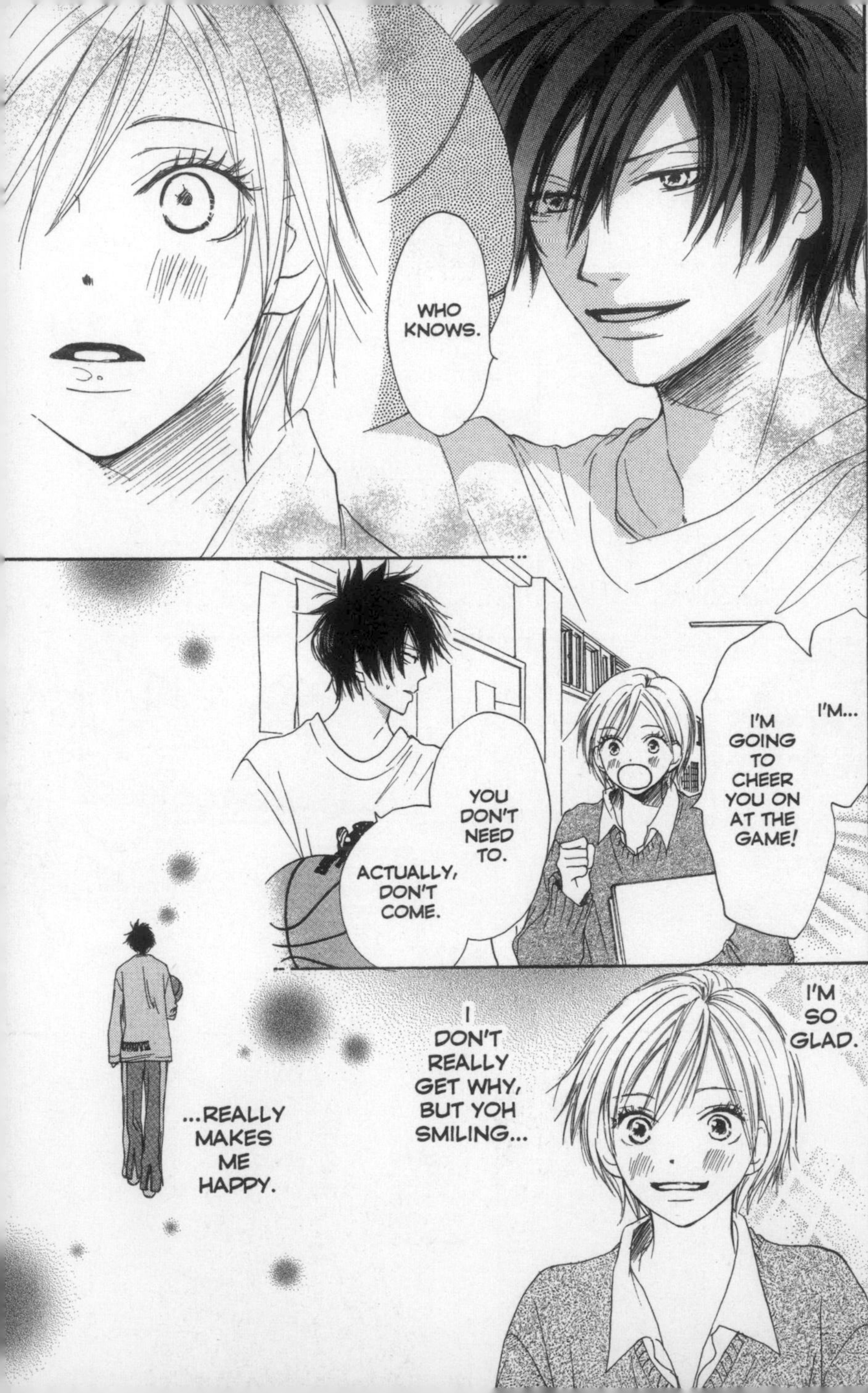
WHO KNOWS.
I'M...
I'M GOING TO CHEER YOU ON AT THE GAME!
YOU DON'T NEED TO.
ACTUALLY, DON'T COME.
I'M SO GLAD.
I DON'T REALLY GET WHY, BUT YOH SMILING...
...REALLY MAKES ME HAPPY.

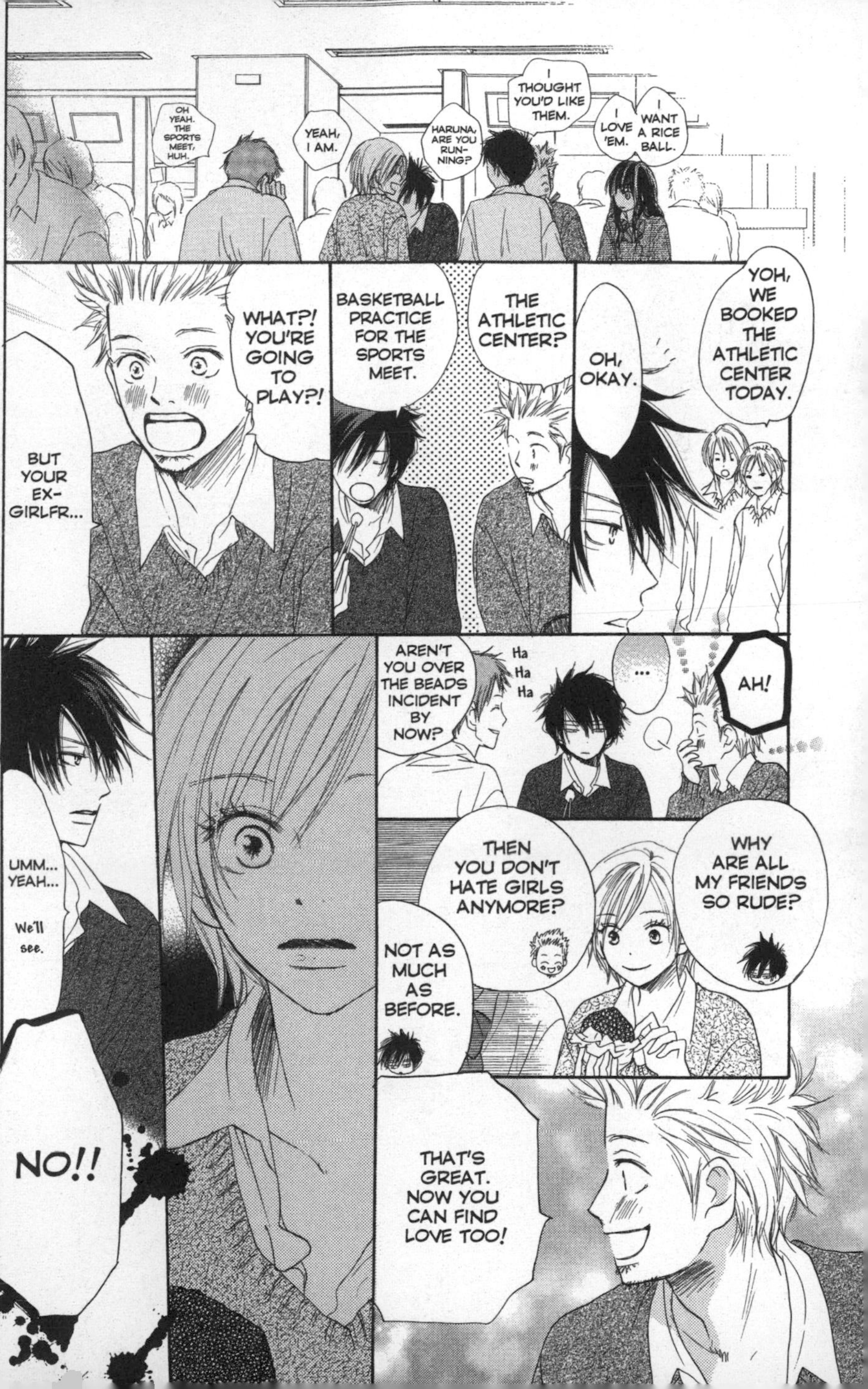
I WANT A RICE BALL.
I LOVE 'EM.
I THOUGHT YOU'D LIKE THEM.
HARUNA, ARE YOU RUNNING?
YEAH, I AM.
OH YEAH. THE SPORTS MEET, HUH.
YOH, WE BOOKED THE ATHLETIC CENTER TODAY.
OH, OKAY.
THE ATHLETIC CENTER?
BASKETBALL PRACTICE FOR THE SPORTS MEET.
WHAT?! YOU'RE GOING TO PLAY?!
BUT YOUR EX-GIRLFR...
AH!
...
Ha Ha Ha
AREN'T YOU OVER THE BEADS INCIDENT BY NOW?
WHY ARE ALL MY FRIENDS SO RUDE?
THEN YOU DON'T HATE GIRLS ANYMORE?
NOT AS MUCH AS BEFORE.
THAT'S GREAT. NOW YOU CAN FIND LOVE TOO!
UMM... YEAH...
We'll see.
NO!!

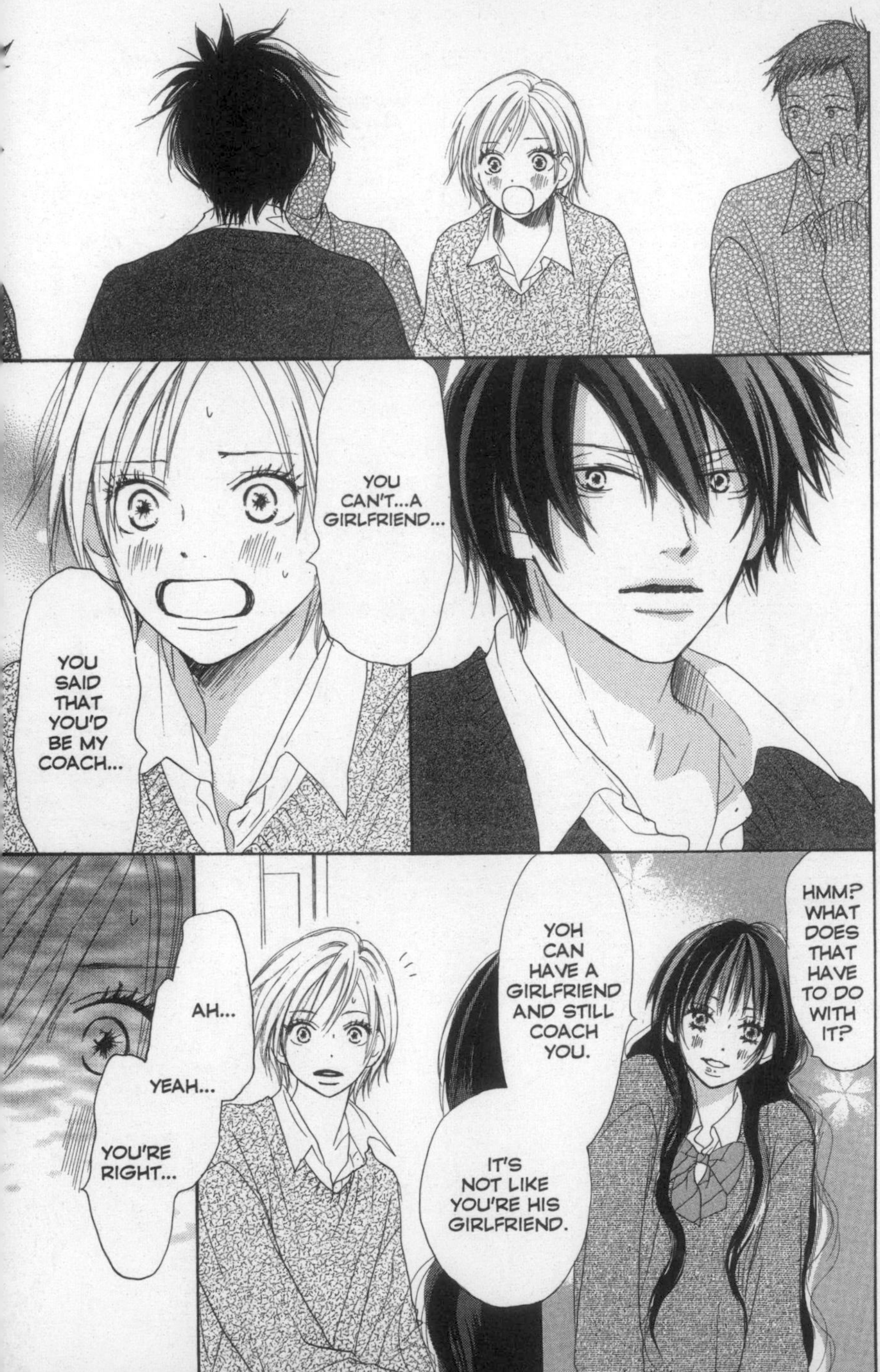
YOU CAN'T...A GIRLFRIEND...
YOU SAID THAT YOU'D BE MY COACH...
HMM? WHAT DOES THAT HAVE TO DO WITH IT?
YOH CAN HAVE A GIRLFRIEND AND STILL COACH YOU.
IT'S NOT LIKE YOU'RE HIS GIRLFRIEND.
AH...
YEAH...
YOU'RE RIGHT...

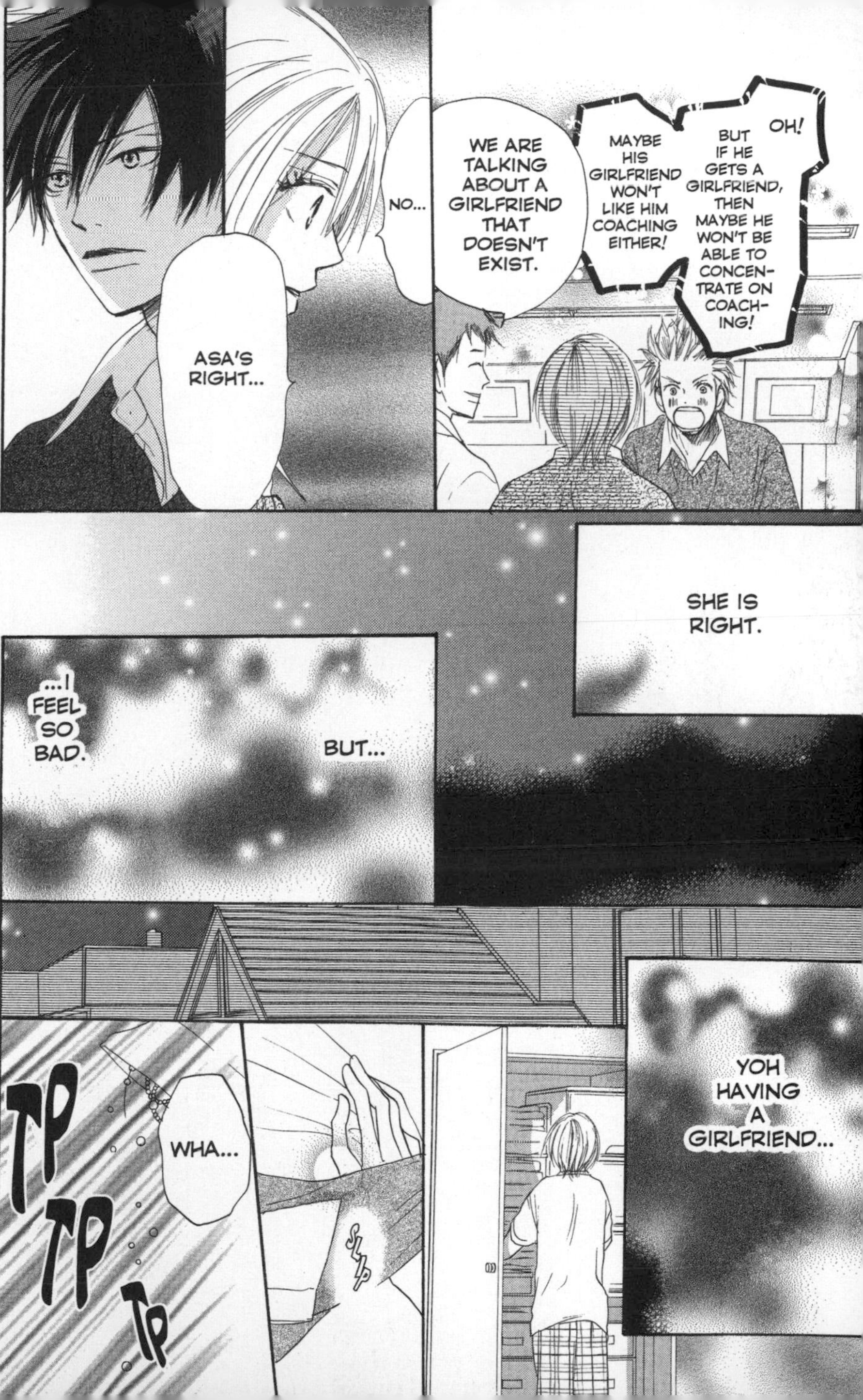
OH!
BUT IF HE GETS A GIRLFRIEND, THEN MAYBE HE WON'T BE ABLE TO CONCENTRATE ON COACHING!
MAYBE HIS GIRLFRIEND WON'T LIKE HIM COACHING EITHER!
WE ARE TALKING ABOUT A GIRLFRIEND THAT DOESN'T EXIST.
NO...
ASA'S RIGHT...
SHE IS RIGHT.
BUT...
...I FEEL SO BAD.
YOH HAVING A GIRLFRIEND...
SLIP
WHA...
TP TP TP

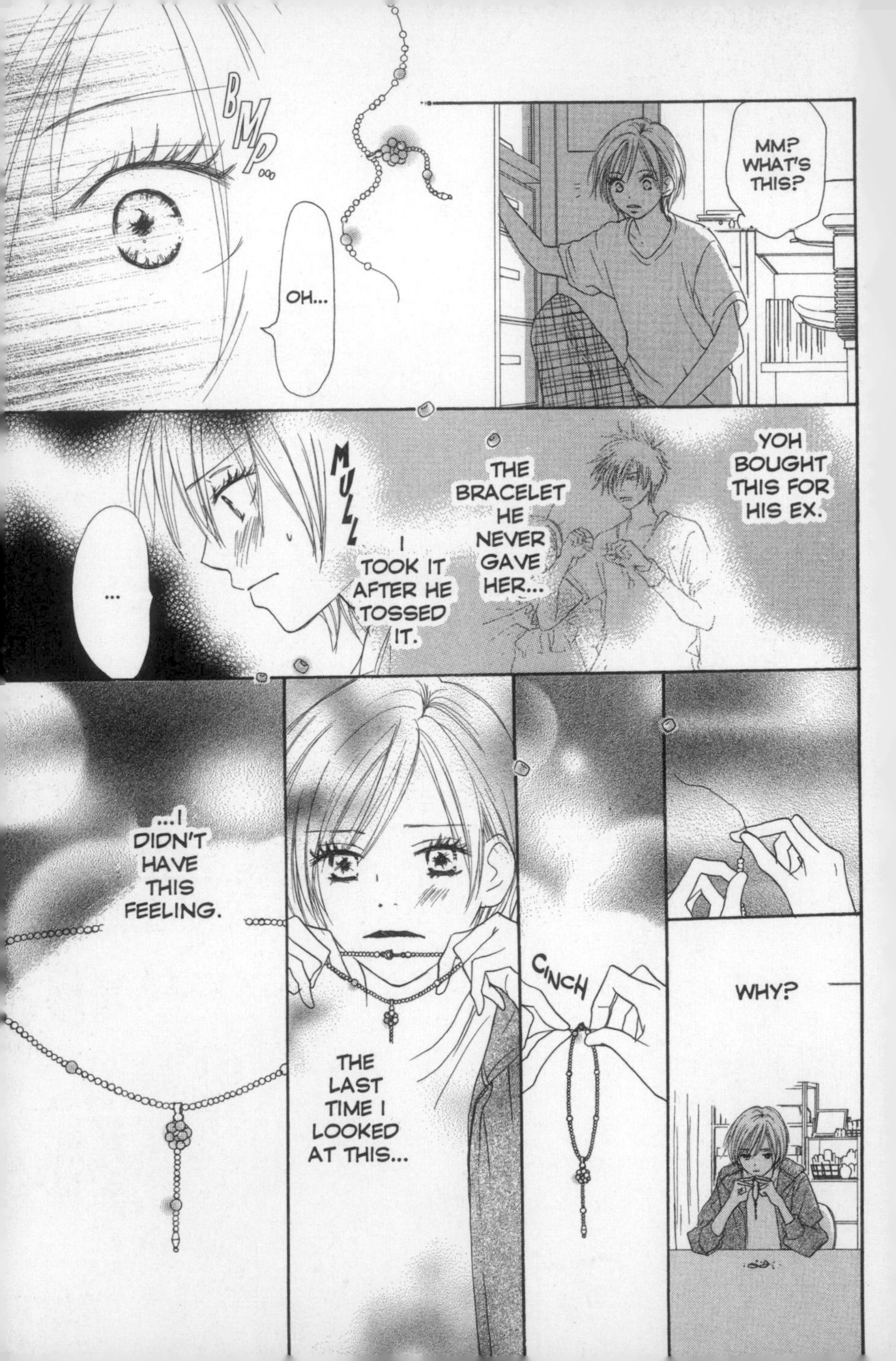
MM? WHAT'S THIS?
BMP...
OH...
YOH BOUGHT THIS FOR HIS EX.
THE BRACELET HE NEVER GAVE HER...
MULL
I TOOK IT AFTER HE TOSSED IT.
...
WHY?
CINCH
THE LAST TIME I LOOKED AT THIS...
...I DIDN'T HAVE THIS FEELING.

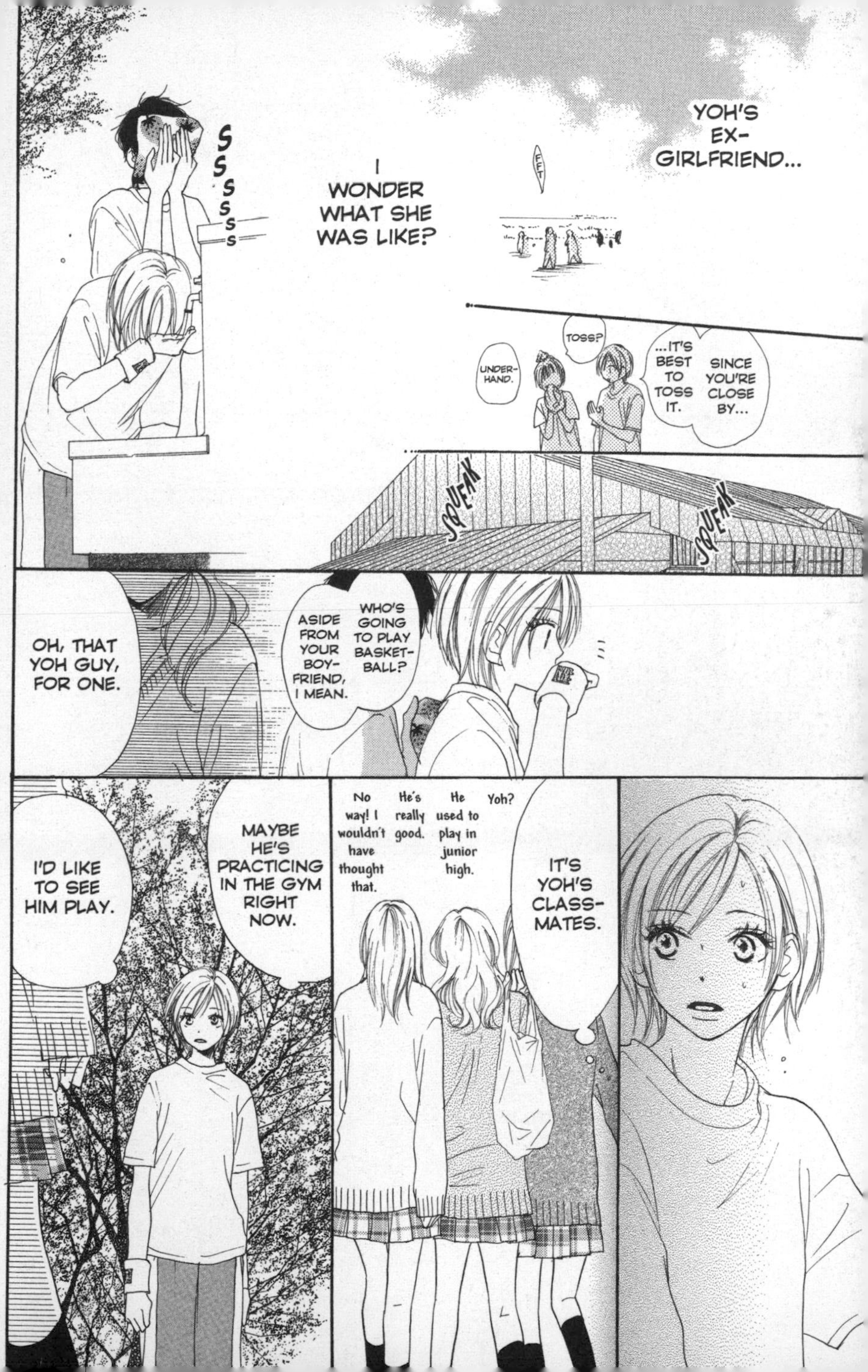
YOH'S EX-GIRLFRIEND...
FFT
I WONDER WHAT SHE WAS LIKE?
SINCE YOU'RE CLOSE BY...
...IT'S BEST TO TOSS IT.
TOSS?
UNDERHAND.
SQUEAK
SQUEAK
SSSSSS
WHO'S GOING TO PLAY BASKETBALL?
ASIDE FROM YOUR BOYFRIEND, I MEAN.
OH, THAT YOH GUY, FOR ONE.
IT'S YOH'S CLASSMATES.
Yoh?
He used to play in junior high.
He's really good.
No way! I wouldn't have thought that.
MAYBE HE'S PRACTICING IN THE GYM RIGHT NOW.
I'D LIKE TO SEE HIM PLAY.

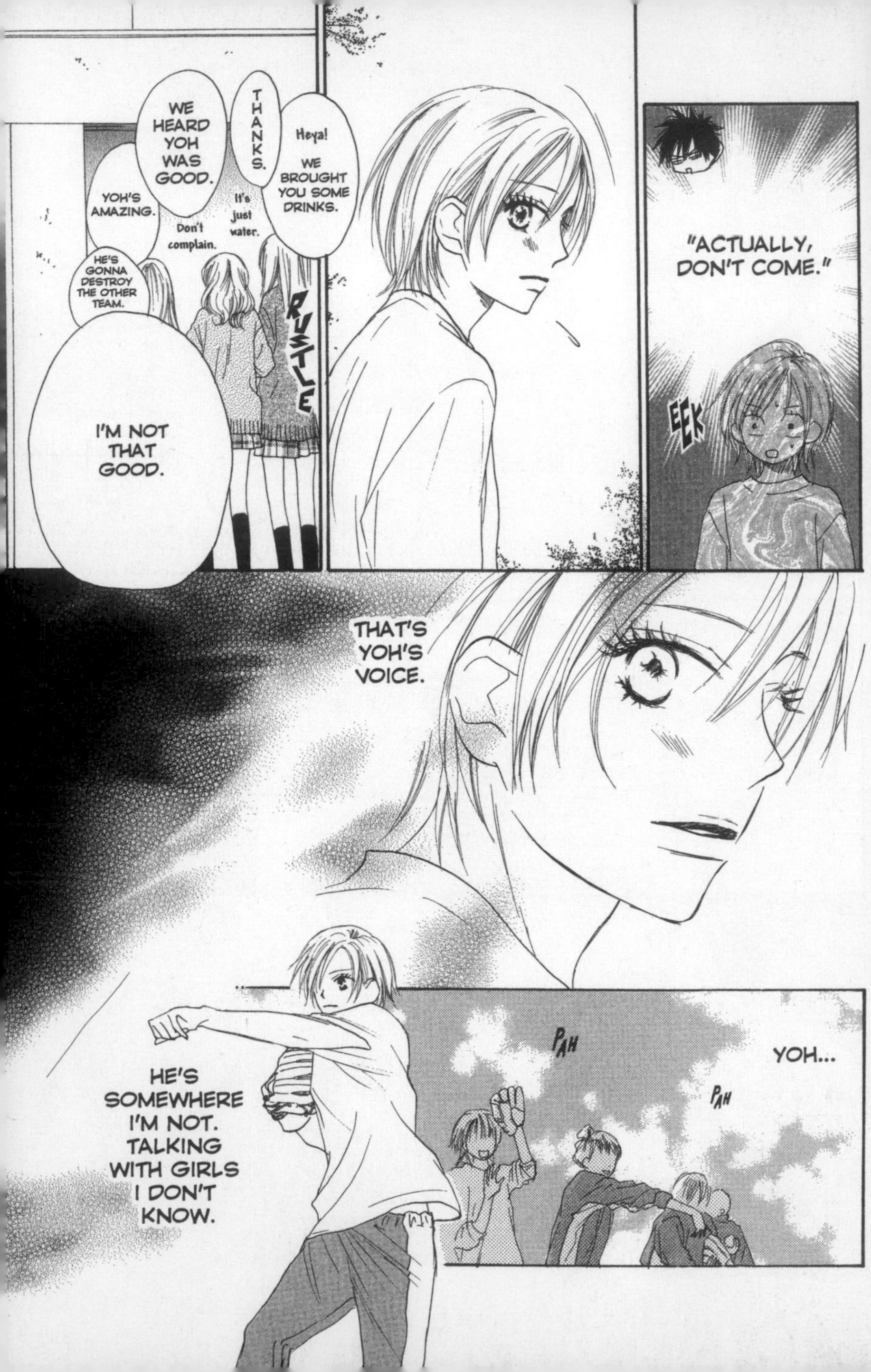
"ACTUALLY, DON'T COME."
EEK
Heya! WE BROUGHT YOU SOME DRINKS.
THANKS.
RUSTLE
It's just water.
WE HEARD YOH WAS GOOD.
Don't complain.
YOH'S AMAZING.
HE'S GONNA DESTROY THE OTHER TEAM.
I'M NOT THAT GOOD.
THAT'S YOH'S VOICE.
YOH...
PAH
PAH
HE'S SOMEWHERE I'M NOT. TALKING WITH GIRLS I DON'T KNOW.

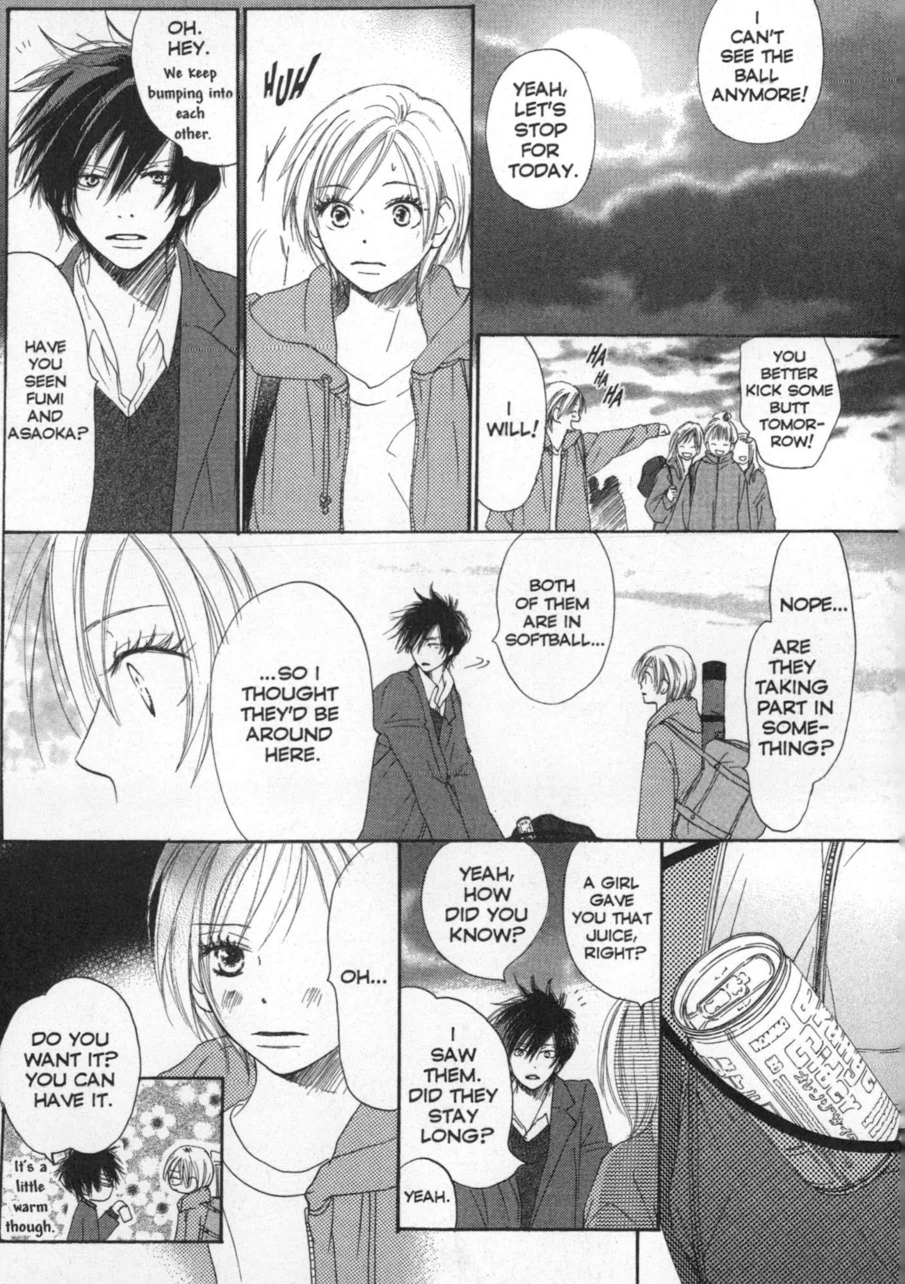
I CAN'T SEE THE BALL ANYMORE!
YEAH, LET'S STOP FOR TODAY.
YOU BETTER KICK SOME BUTT TOMOR-ROW!
HA HA HA
I WILL!
HUH
OH. HEY.
We keep bumping into each other.
HAVE YOU SEEN FUMI AND ASAOKA?
NOPE...
ARE THEY TAKING PART IN SOME-THING?
BOTH OF THEM ARE IN SOFTBALL...
...SO I THOUGHT THEY'D BE AROUND HERE.
A GIRL GAVE YOU THAT JUICE, RIGHT?
YEAH, HOW DID YOU KNOW?
I SAW THEM. DID THEY STAY LONG?
YEAH.
OH...
DO YOU WANT IT? YOU CAN HAVE IT.
It's a little warm though.

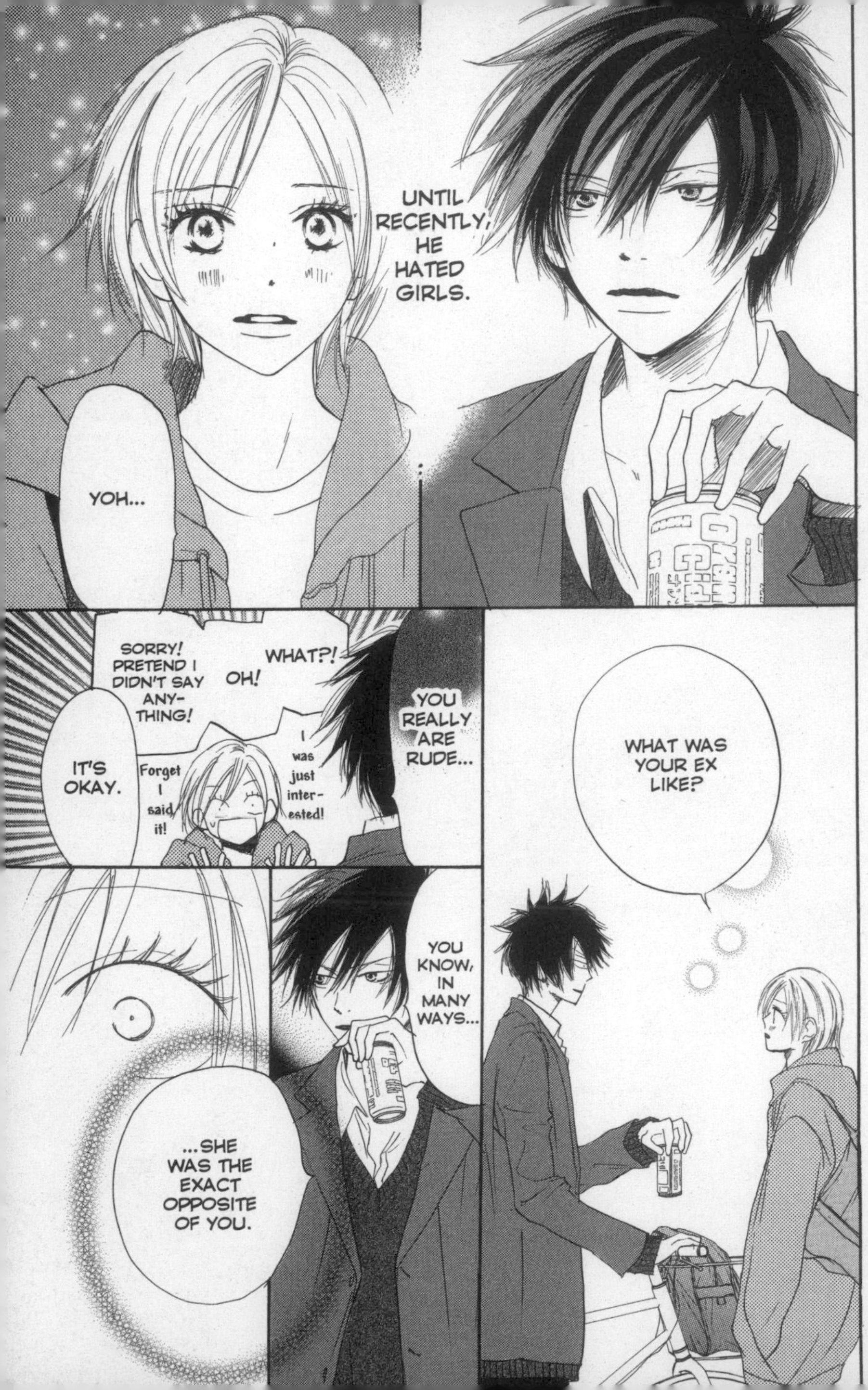
UNTIL RECENTLY, HE HATED GIRLS.
YOH...
WHAT WAS YOUR EX LIKE?
YOU REALLY ARE RUDE...
WHAT?!
OH!
SORRY! PRETEND I DIDN'T SAY ANYTHING!
I was just interested!
Forget I said it!
IT'S OKAY.
YOU KNOW, IN MANY WAYS...
...SHE WAS THE EXACT OPPOSITE OF YOU.

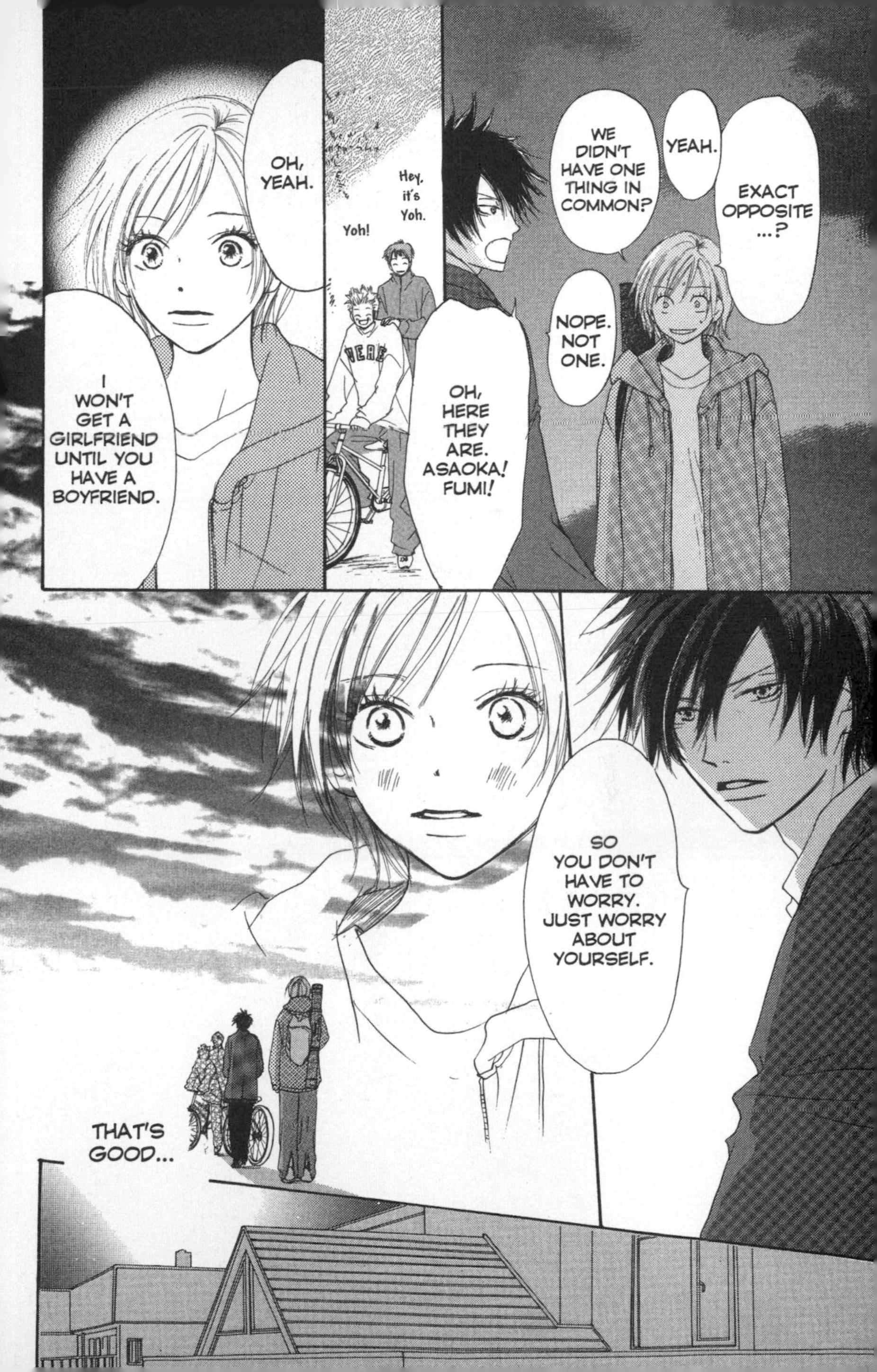
EXACT OPPOSITE ...?
YEAH.
WE DIDN'T HAVE ONE THING IN COMMON?
NOPE. NOT ONE.
Hey, it's Yoh.
Yoh!
OH, HERE THEY ARE. ASAOKA! FUMI!
OH, YEAH.
I WON'T GET A GIRLFRIEND UNTIL YOU HAVE A BOYFRIEND.
SO YOU DON'T HAVE TO WORRY. JUST WORRY ABOUT YOURSELF.
THAT'S GOOD...

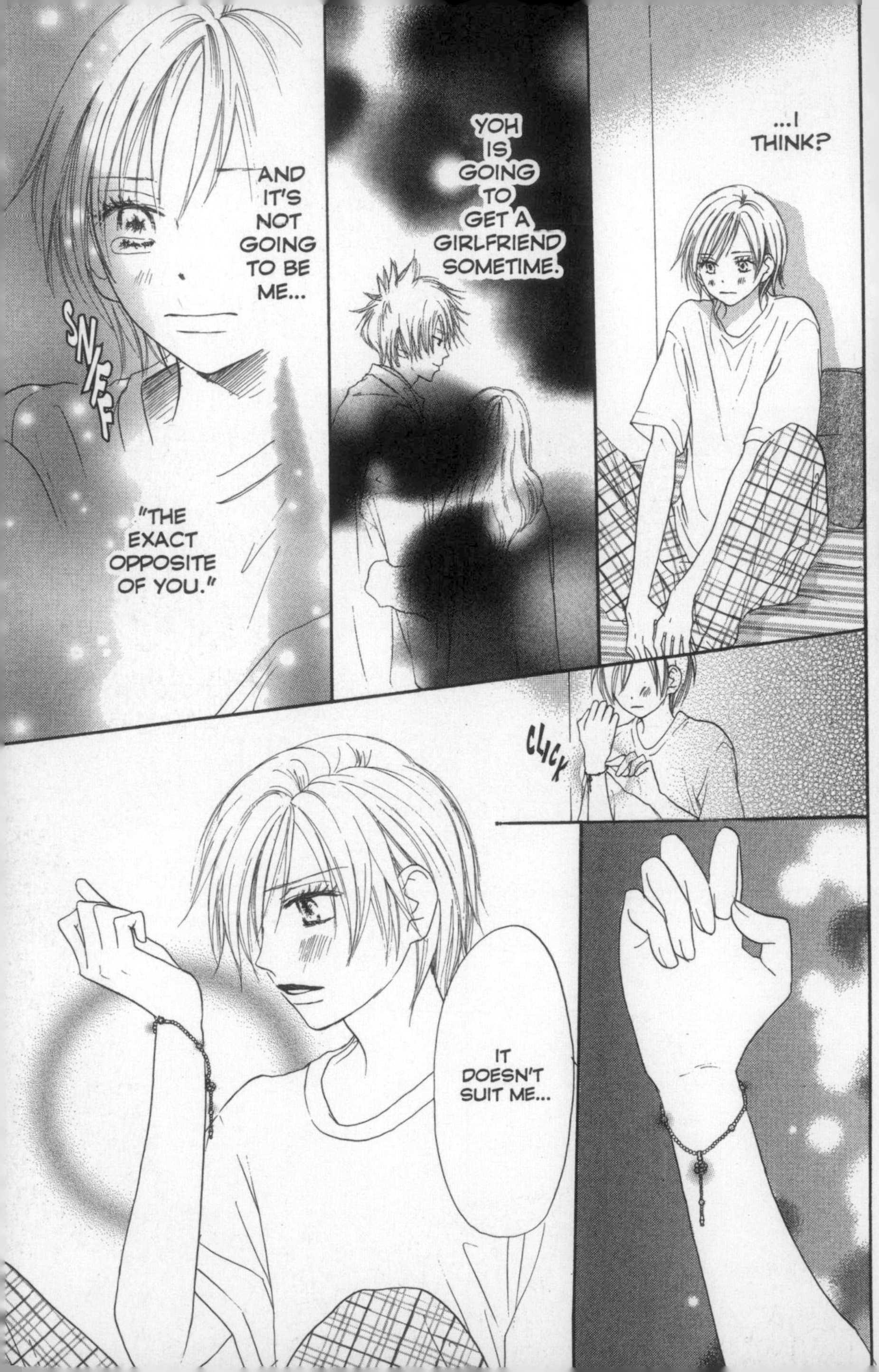
...I THINK?
YOH IS GOING TO GET A GIRLFRIEND SOMETIME.
AND IT'S NOT GOING TO BE ME...
SNIFF
"THE EXACT OPPOSITE OF YOU."
CLICK
IT DOESN'T SUIT ME...

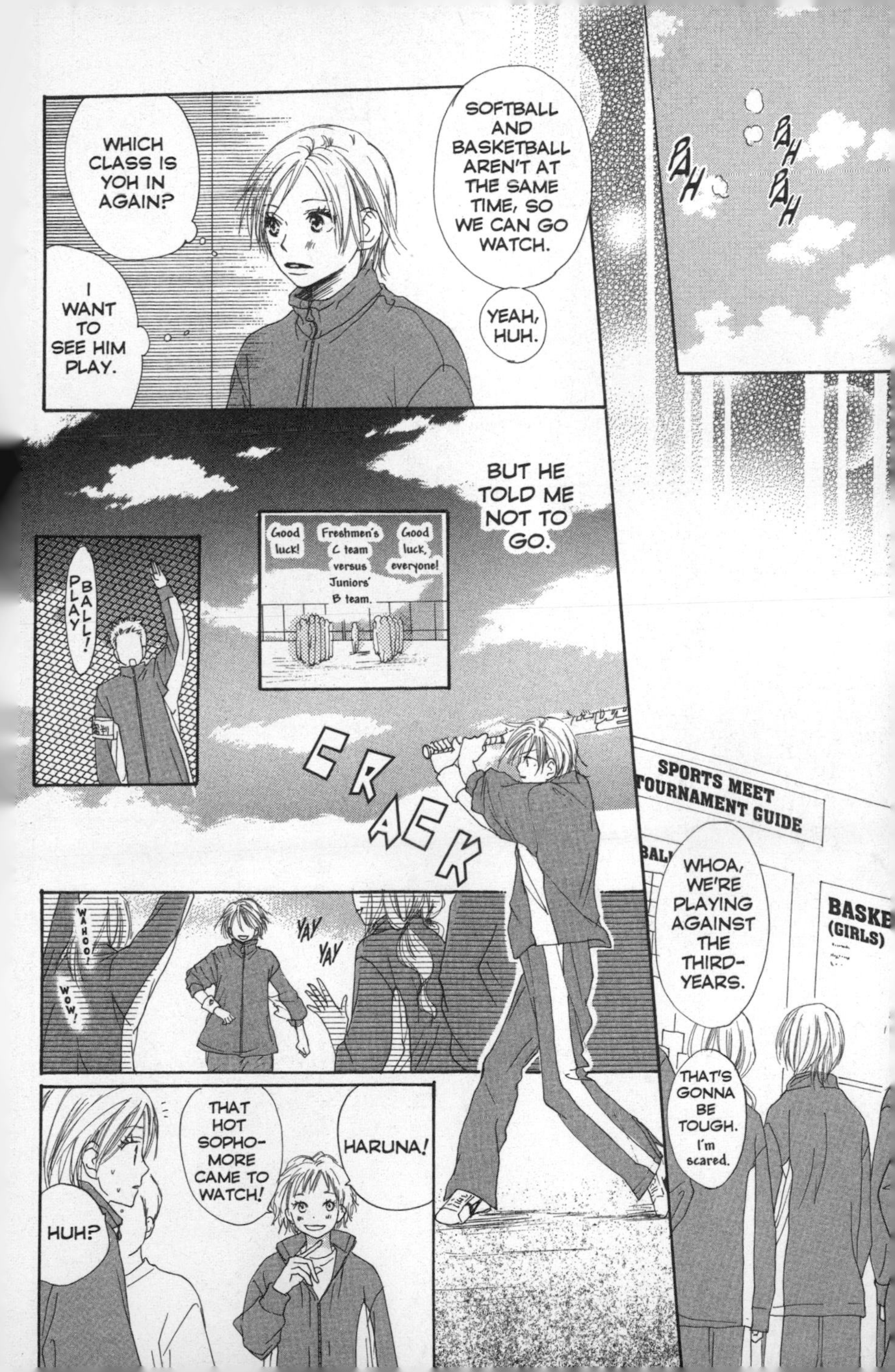
PAH
PAH PAH
SPORTS MEET TOURNAMENT GUIDE
(GIRLS)
WHOA, WE'RE PLAYING AGAINST THE THIRD-YEARS.
THAT'S GONNA BE TOUGH. I'm scared.
SOFTBALL AND BASKETBALL AREN'T AT THE SAME TIME, SO WE CAN GO WATCH.
YEAH, HUH.
WHICH CLASS IS YOH IN AGAIN?
I WANT TO SEE HIM PLAY.
BUT HE TOLD ME NOT TO GO.
Good luck, everyone!
Freshmen's C team versus Juniors' B team.
Good luck!
PLAY BALL!
CRACK
YAY YAY
WAHOO!
WOW!
HARUNA!
THAT HOT SOPHOMORE CAME TO WATCH!
HUH?

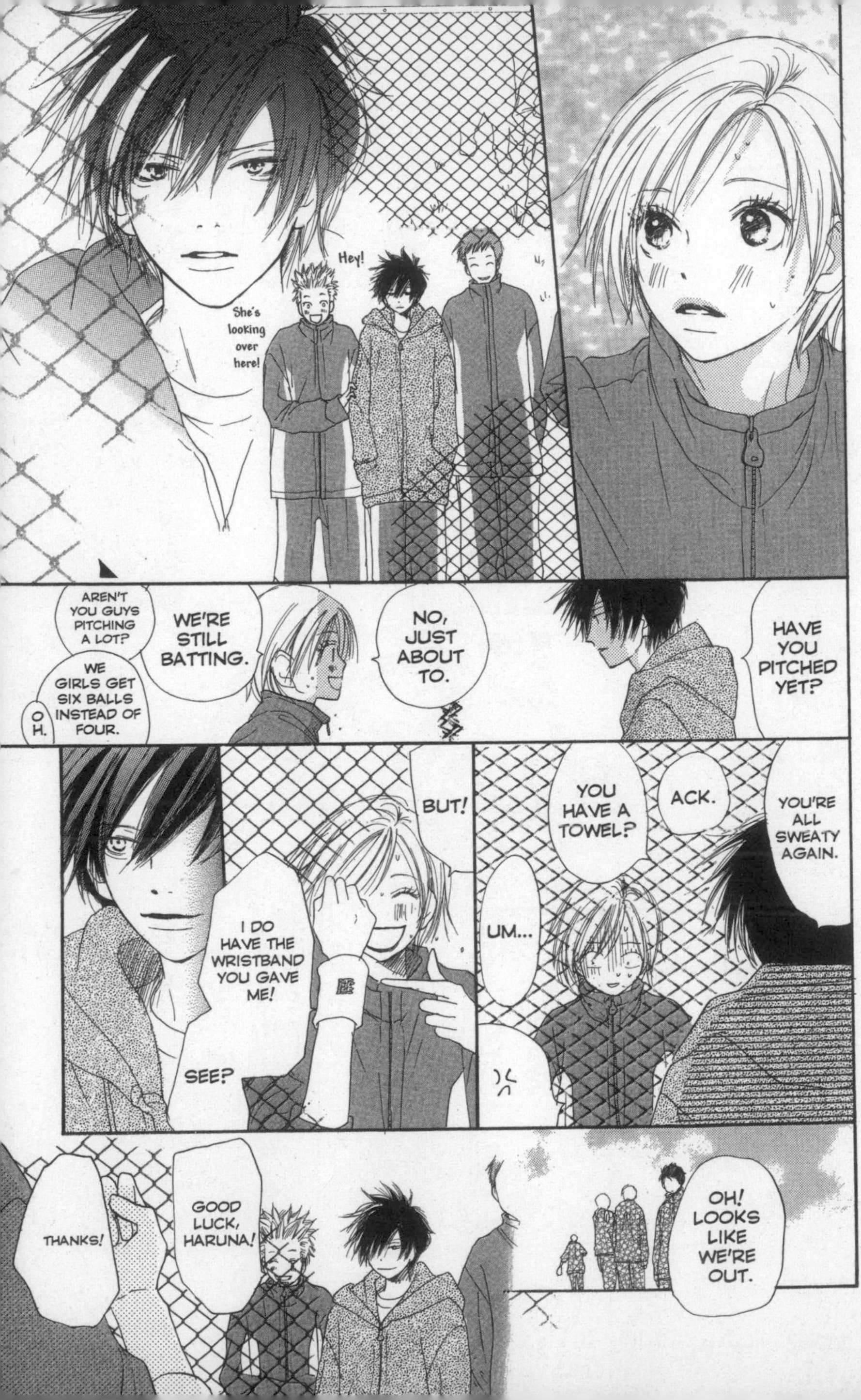
Hey!
She's looking over here!
HAVE YOU PITCHED YET?
NO, JUST ABOUT TO.
WE'RE STILL BATTING.
AREN'T YOU GUYS PITCHING A LOT?
WE GIRLS GET SIX BALLS INSTEAD OF FOUR.
OH.
YOU'RE ALL SWEATY AGAIN.
ACK.
YOU HAVE A TOWEL?
UM...
BUT!
I DO HAVE THE WRISTBAND YOU GAVE ME!
SEE?
OH! LOOKS LIKE WE'RE OUT.
GOOD LUCK, HARUNA!
THANKS!

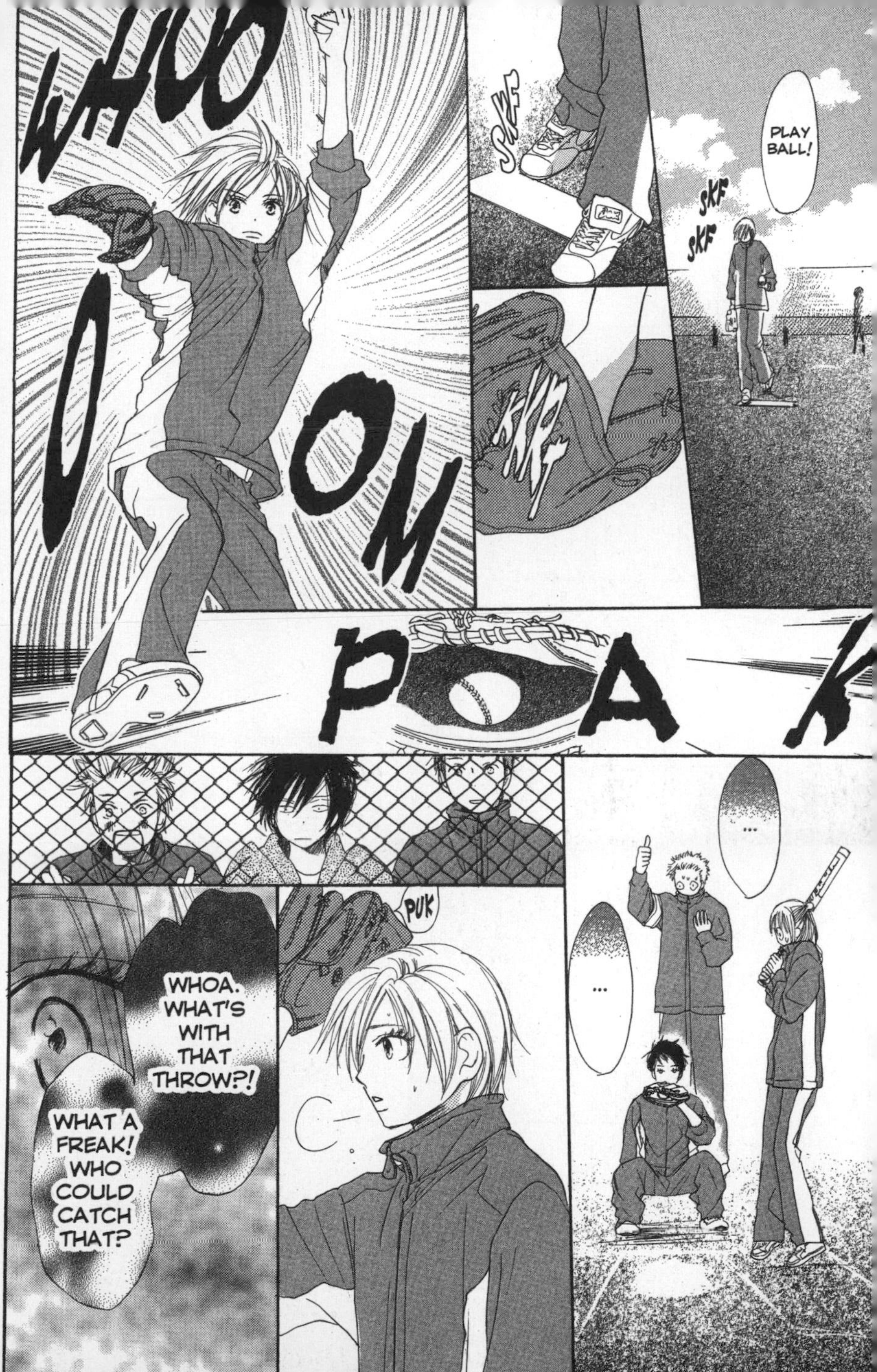

PLAY BALL!
SKF
SKF
SKF
KKR
WHOOOOM
POAK
...
...
PUK
WHOA. WHAT'S WITH THAT THROW?!
WHAT A FREAK! WHO COULD CATCH THAT?

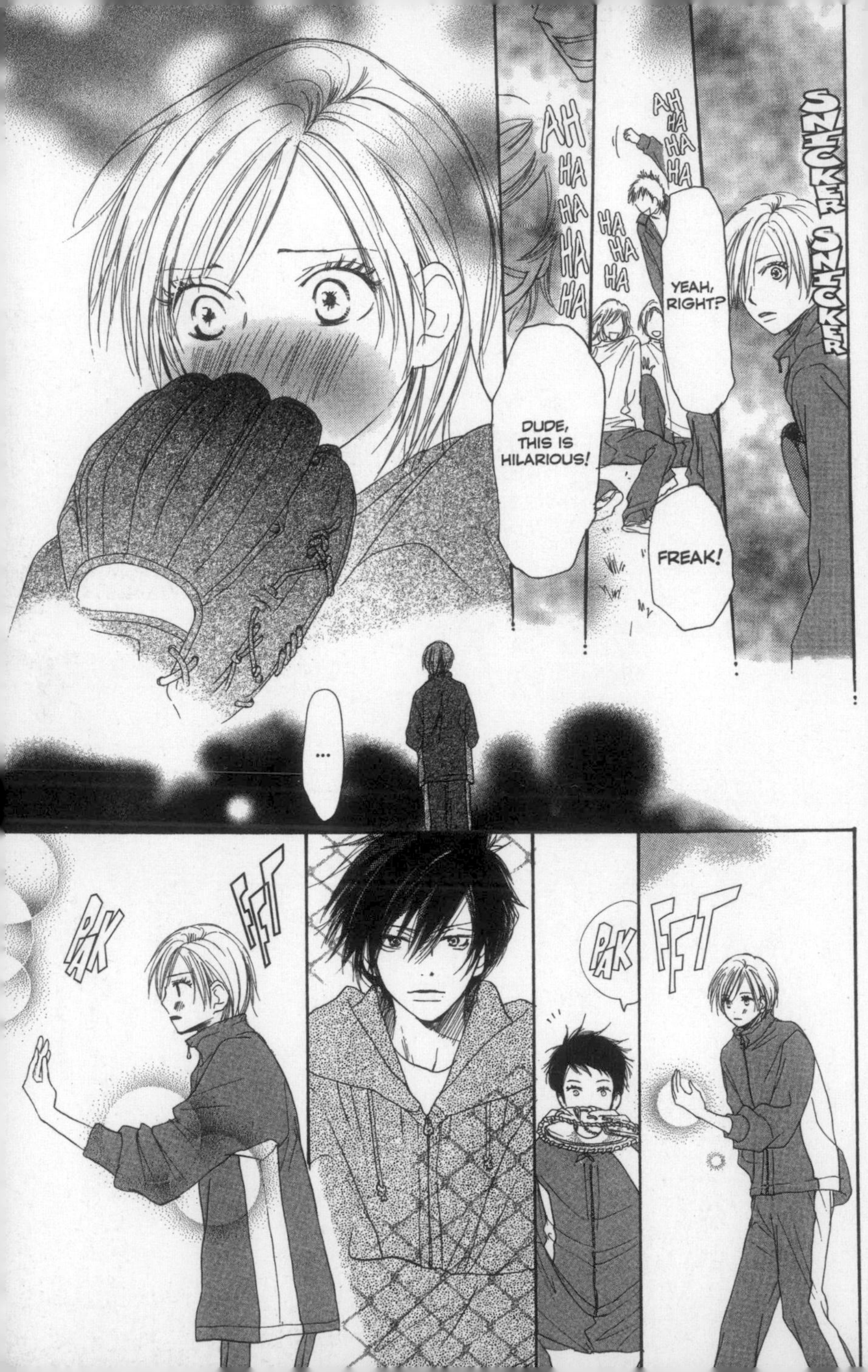
SNICKER SNICKER
AH HA HA HA HA
YEAH, RIGHT?
HA HA HA HA
AH HA HA HA HA HA
DUDE, THIS IS HILARIOUS!
FREAK!
...
PAK
FFT
PAK
FFT

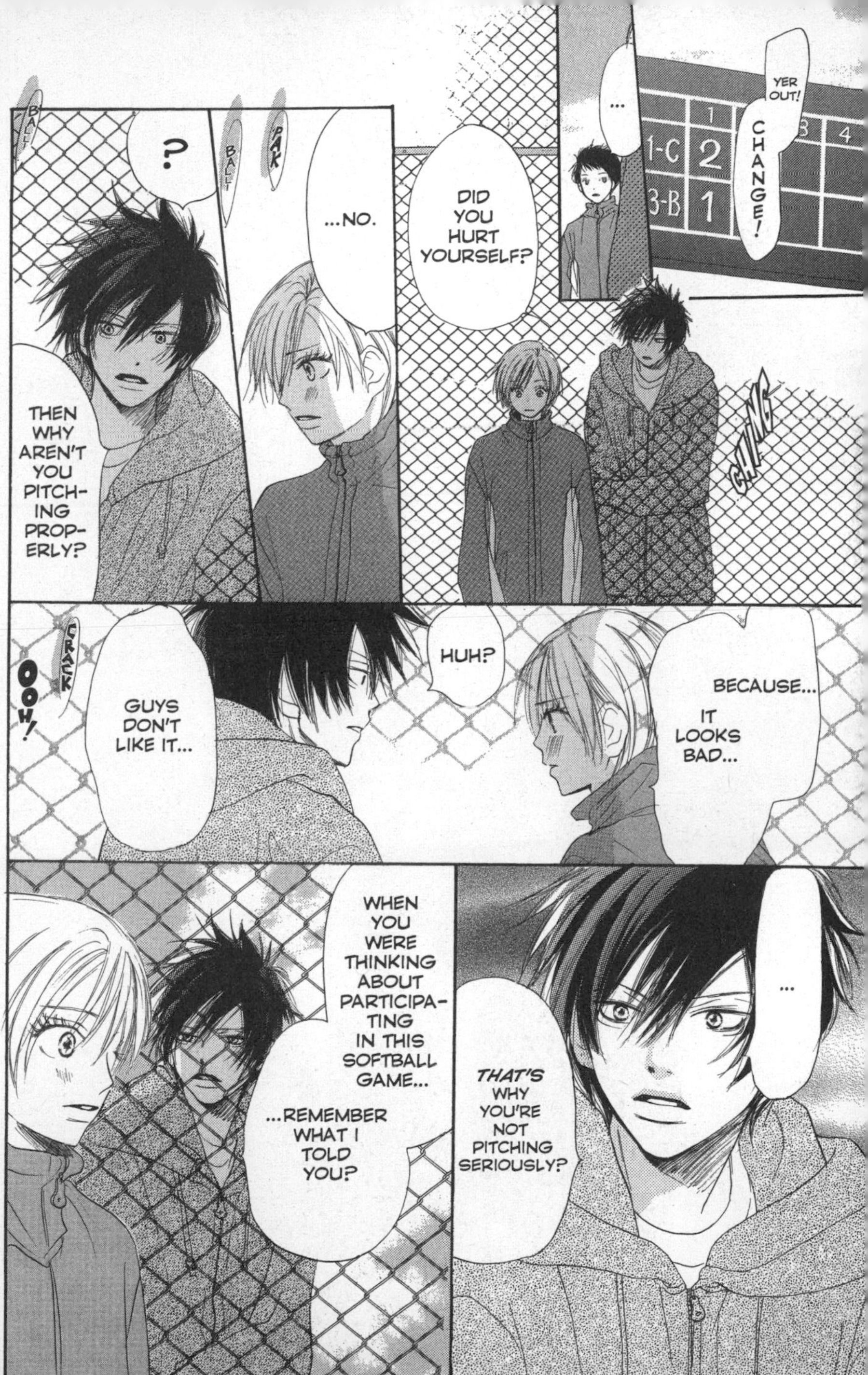

YER OUT!
CHANGE!
...
DID YOU HURT YOURSELF?
CHING
BALL
PAK
...NO.
BALL
?
THEN WHY AREN'T YOU PITCHING PROPERLY?
BECAUSE... IT LOOKS BAD...
HUH?
GUYS DON'T LIKE IT...
CRACK
OOOH!
...
THAT'S WHY YOU'RE NOT PITCHING SERIOUSLY?
WHEN YOU WERE THINKING ABOUT PARTICIPATING IN THIS SOFTBALL GAME...
...REMEMBER WHAT I TOLD YOU?

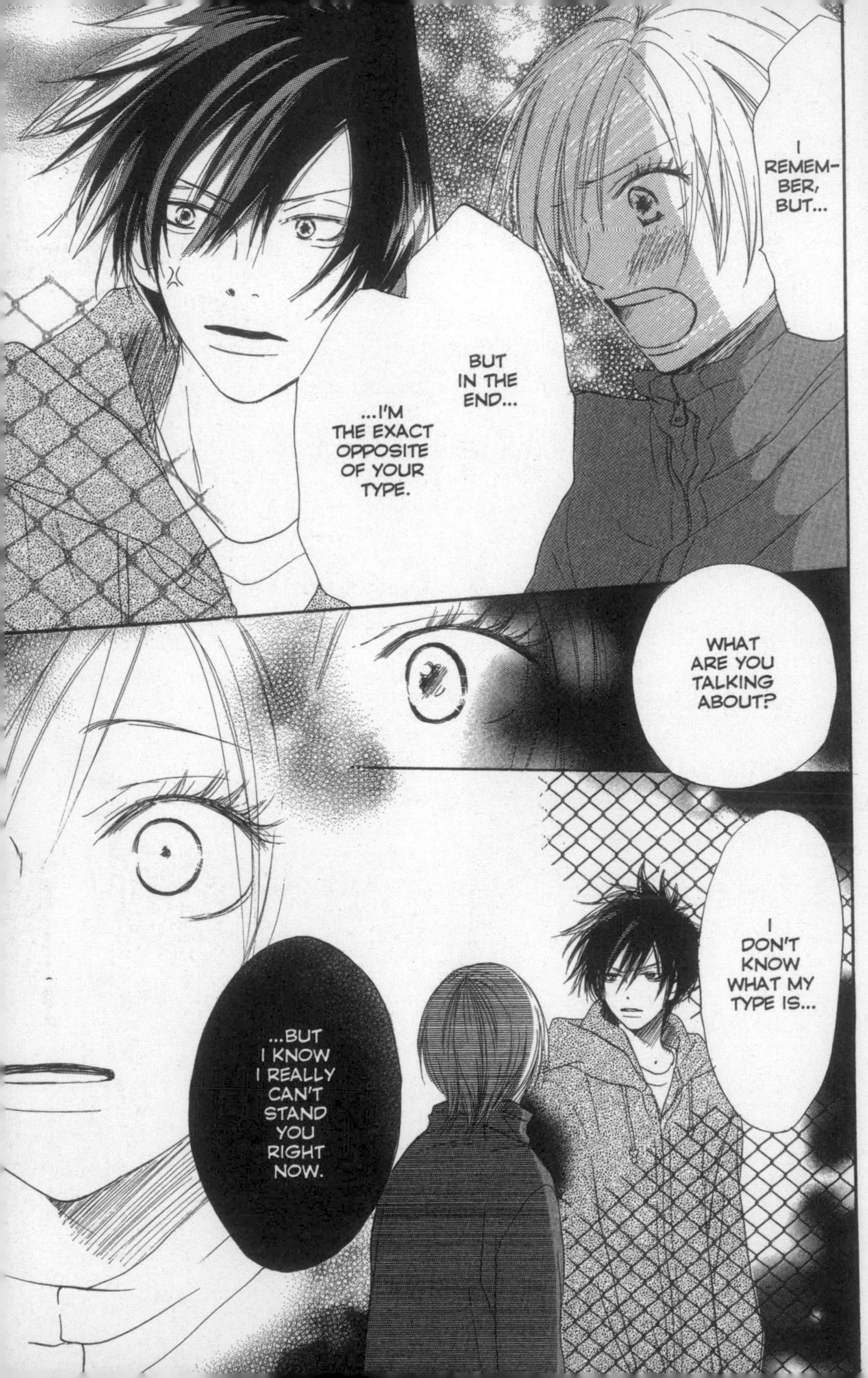
I REMEMBER, BUT...
BUT IN THE END...
...I'M THE EXACT OPPOSITE OF YOUR TYPE.
WHAT ARE YOU TALKING ABOUT?
I DON'T KNOW WHAT MY TYPE IS...
...BUT I KNOW I REALLY CAN'T STAND YOU RIGHT NOW.

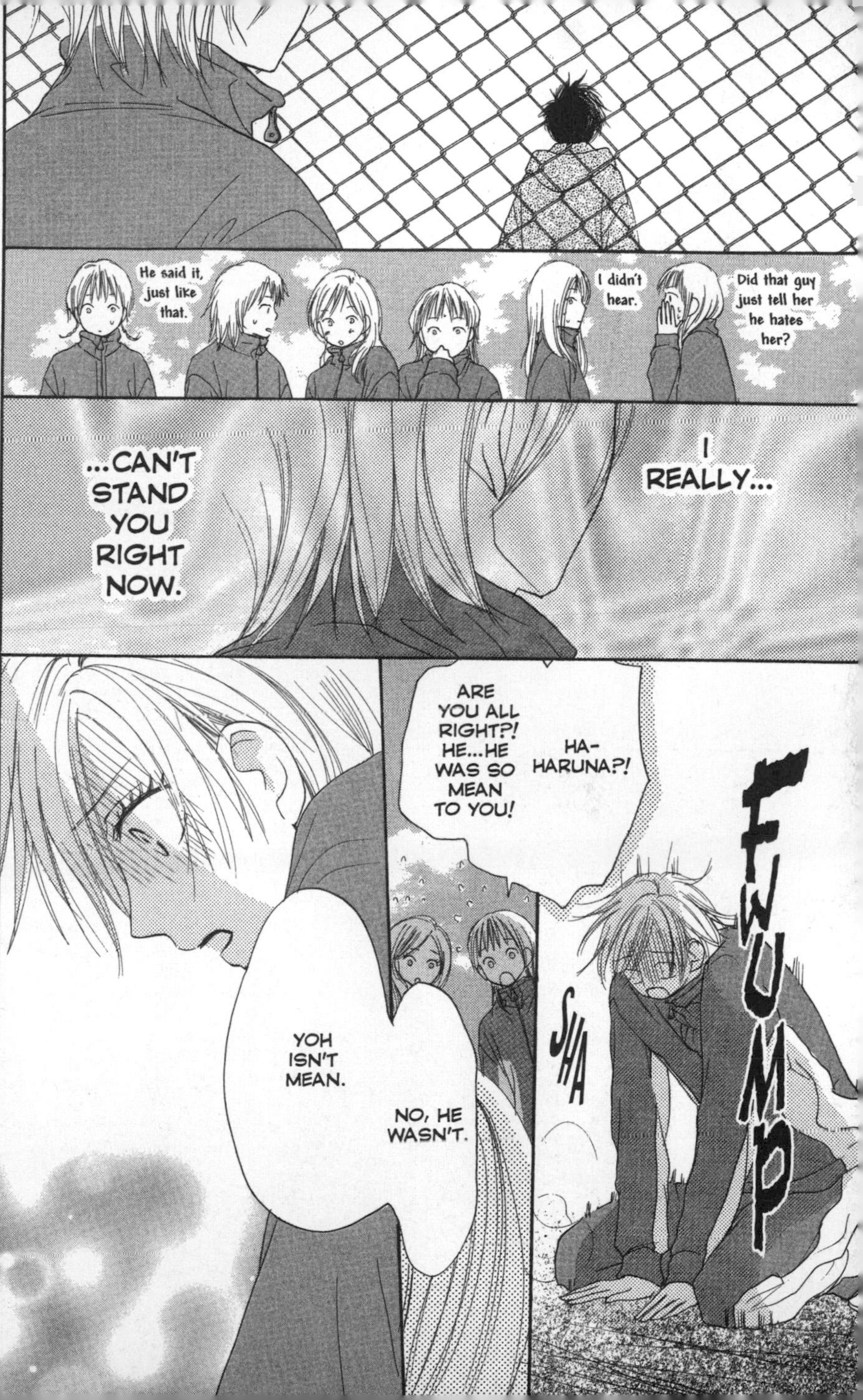
Did that guy just tell her he hates her?
I didn't hear.
He said it, just like that.
I REALLY...
...CAN'T STAND YOU RIGHT NOW.
FWUMP
SHA
HA-HARUNA?!
ARE YOU ALL RIGHT?! HE...HE WAS SO MEAN TO YOU!
YOH ISN'T MEAN.
NO, HE WASN'T.

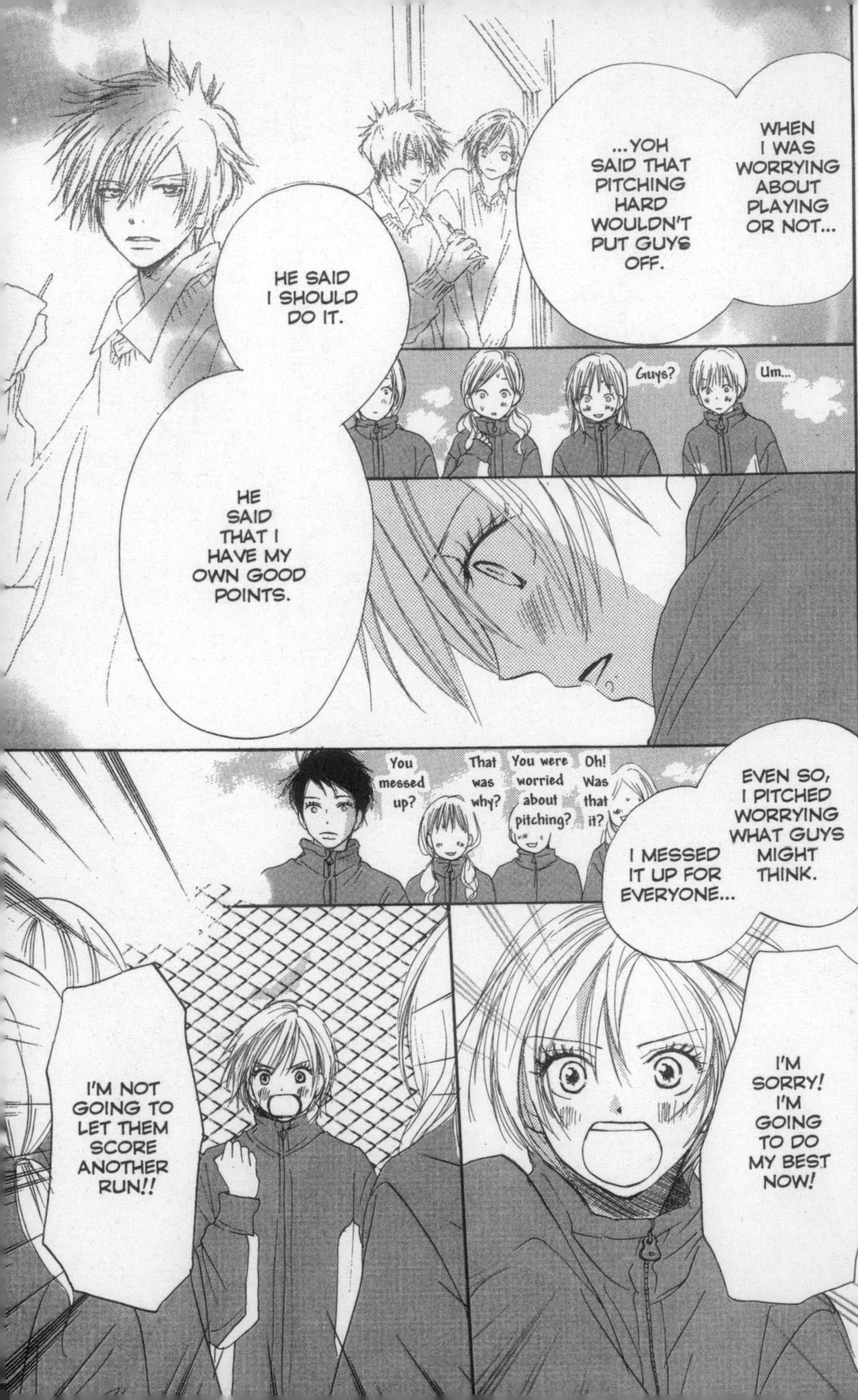
WHEN I WAS WORRYING ABOUT PLAYING OR NOT...
...YOH SAID THAT PITCHING HARD WOULDN'T PUT GUYS OFF.
HE SAID I SHOULD DO IT.
Um...
Guys?
HE SAID THAT I HAVE MY OWN GOOD POINTS.
EVEN SO, I PITCHED WORRYING WHAT GUYS MIGHT THINK.
I MESSED IT UP FOR EVERYONE...
Oh! Was that it?
You were worried about pitching?
That was why?
You messed up?
I'M SORRY! I'M GOING TO DO MY BEST NOW!
I'M NOT GOING TO LET THEM SCORE ANOTHER RUN!!

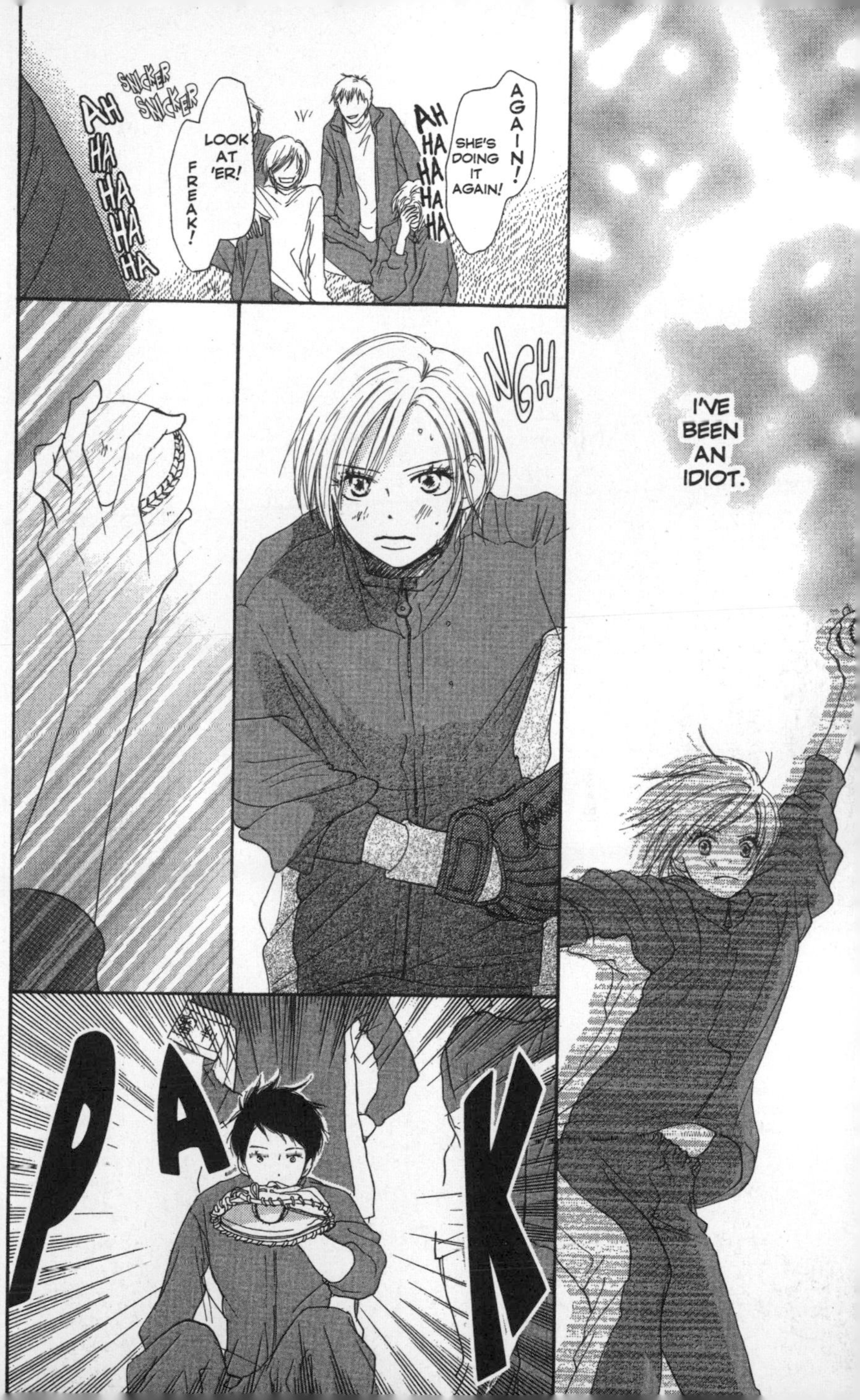
I'VE BEEN AN IDIOT.
AGAIN!
SHE'S DOING IT AGAIN!
AH HA HA HA HA HA
FREAK!
LOOK AT 'ER!
SNICKER SNICKER
AH HA HA HA HA HA
NGH
PAK

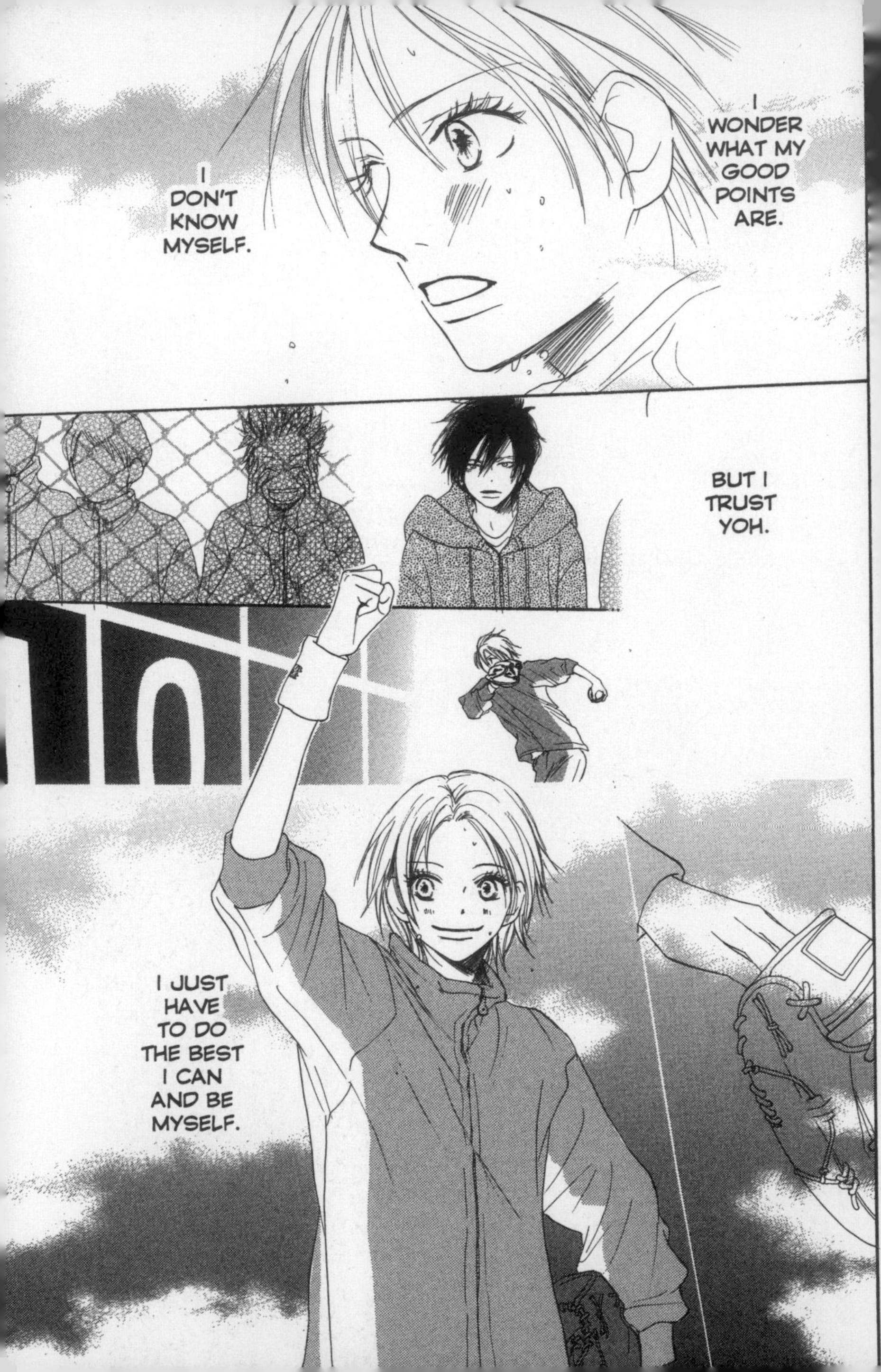
I WONDER WHAT MY GOOD POINTS ARE.
I DON'T KNOW MYSELF.
BUT I TRUST YOH.
I JUST HAVE TO DO THE BEST I CAN AND BE MYSELF.

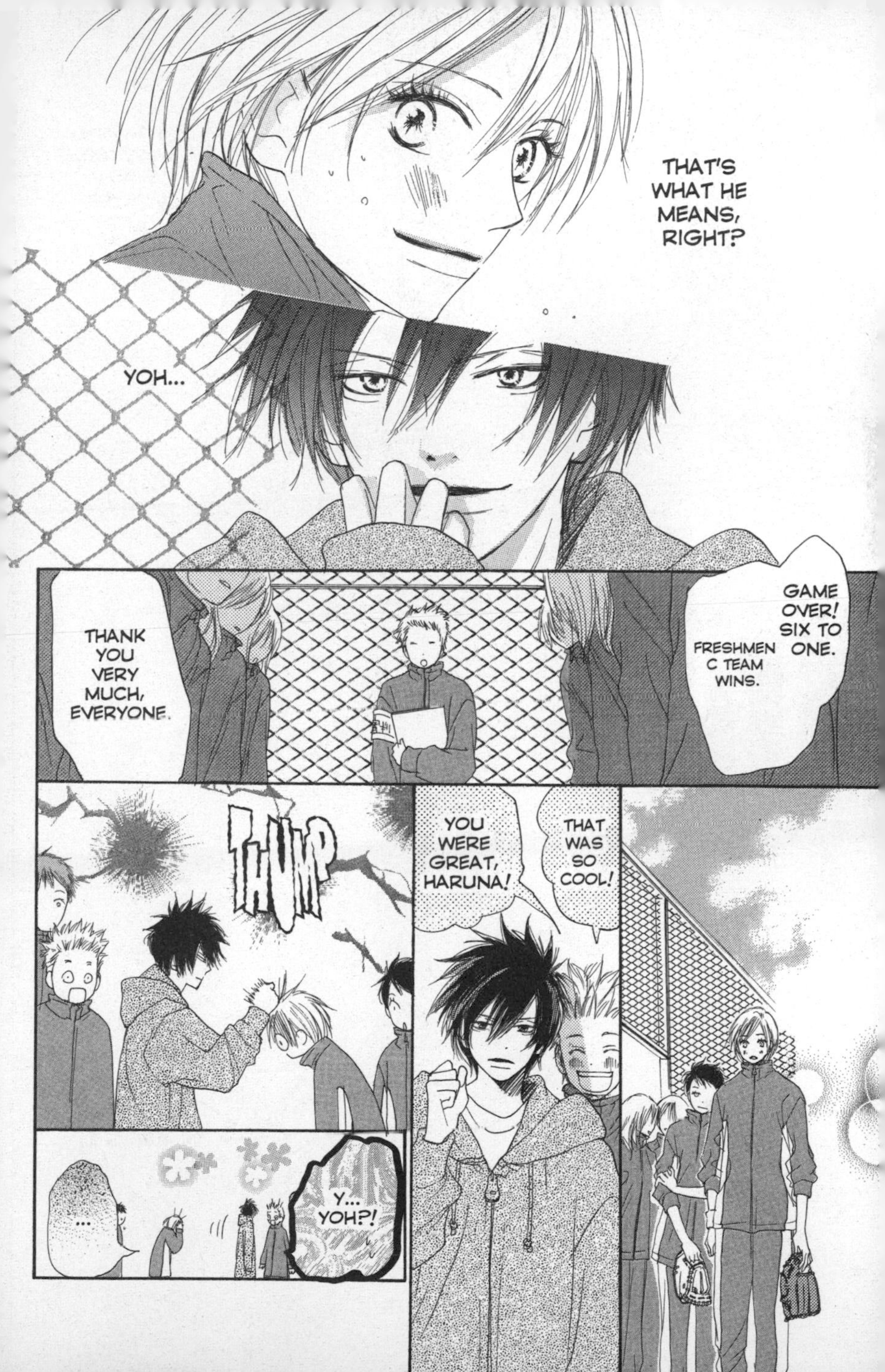
THAT'S WHAT HE MEANS, RIGHT?
YOH...
GAME OVER! SIX TO ONE.
FRESHMEN C TEAM WINS.
THANK YOU VERY MUCH, EVERYONE.
THAT WAS SO COOL!
YOU WERE GREAT, HARUNA!
THUMP
Y... YOH?!
...

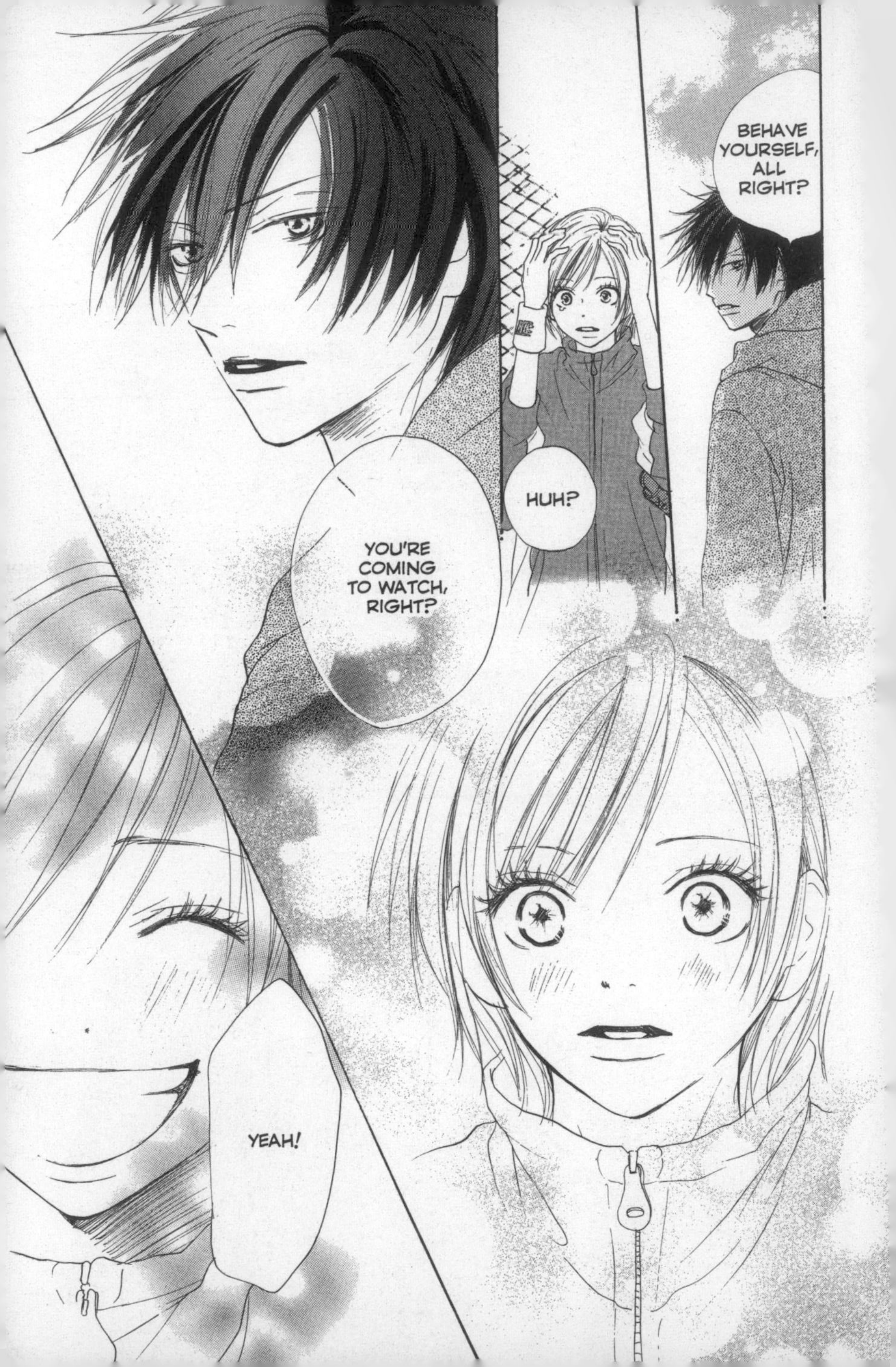
BEHAVE YOURSELF, ALL RIGHT?
HUH?
YOU'RE COMING TO WATCH, RIGHT?
YEAH!

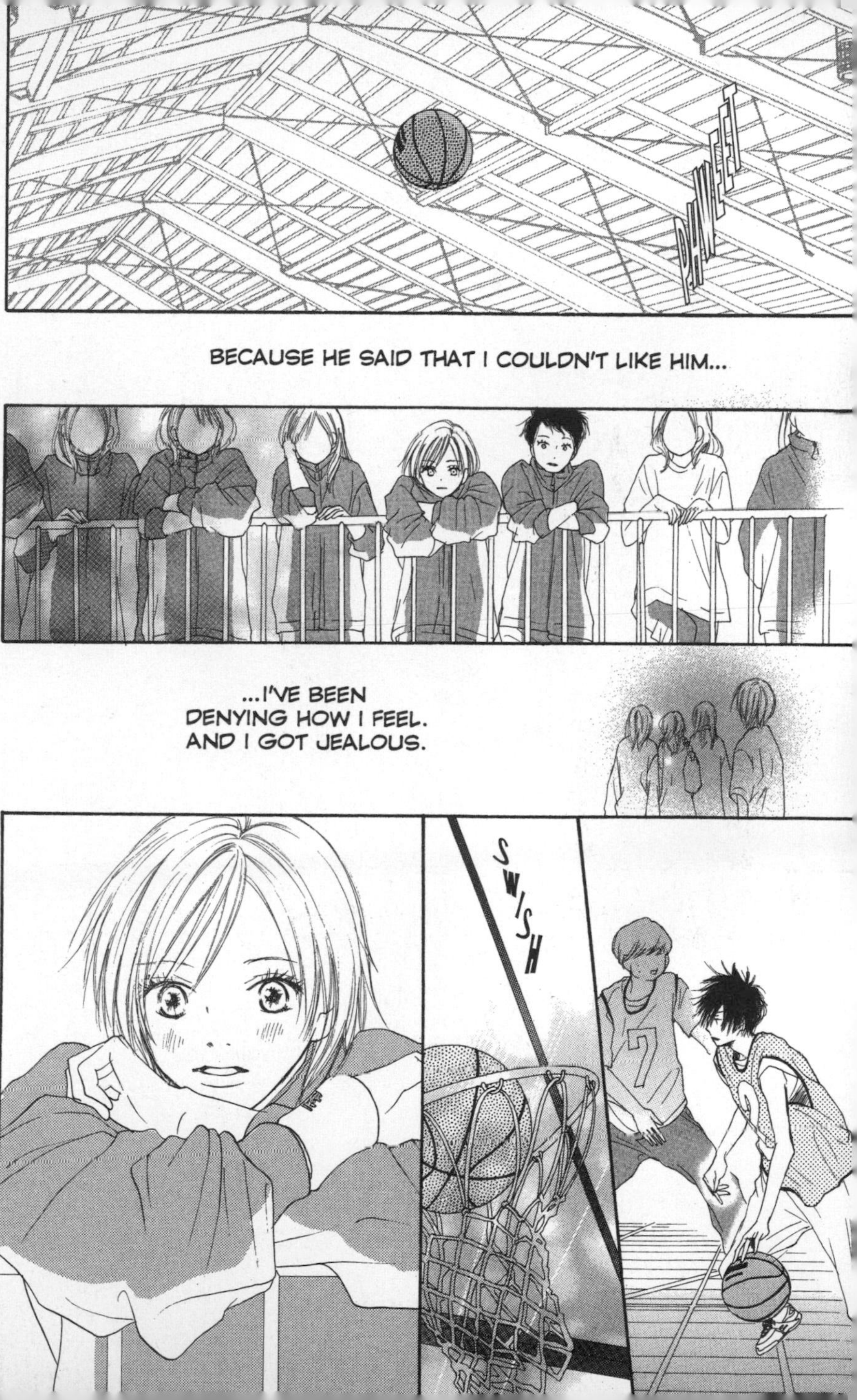
PHWEET
BECAUSE HE SAID THAT I COULDN'T LIKE HIM...
...I'VE BEEN DENYING HOW I FEEL. AND I GOT JEALOUS.
SWISH

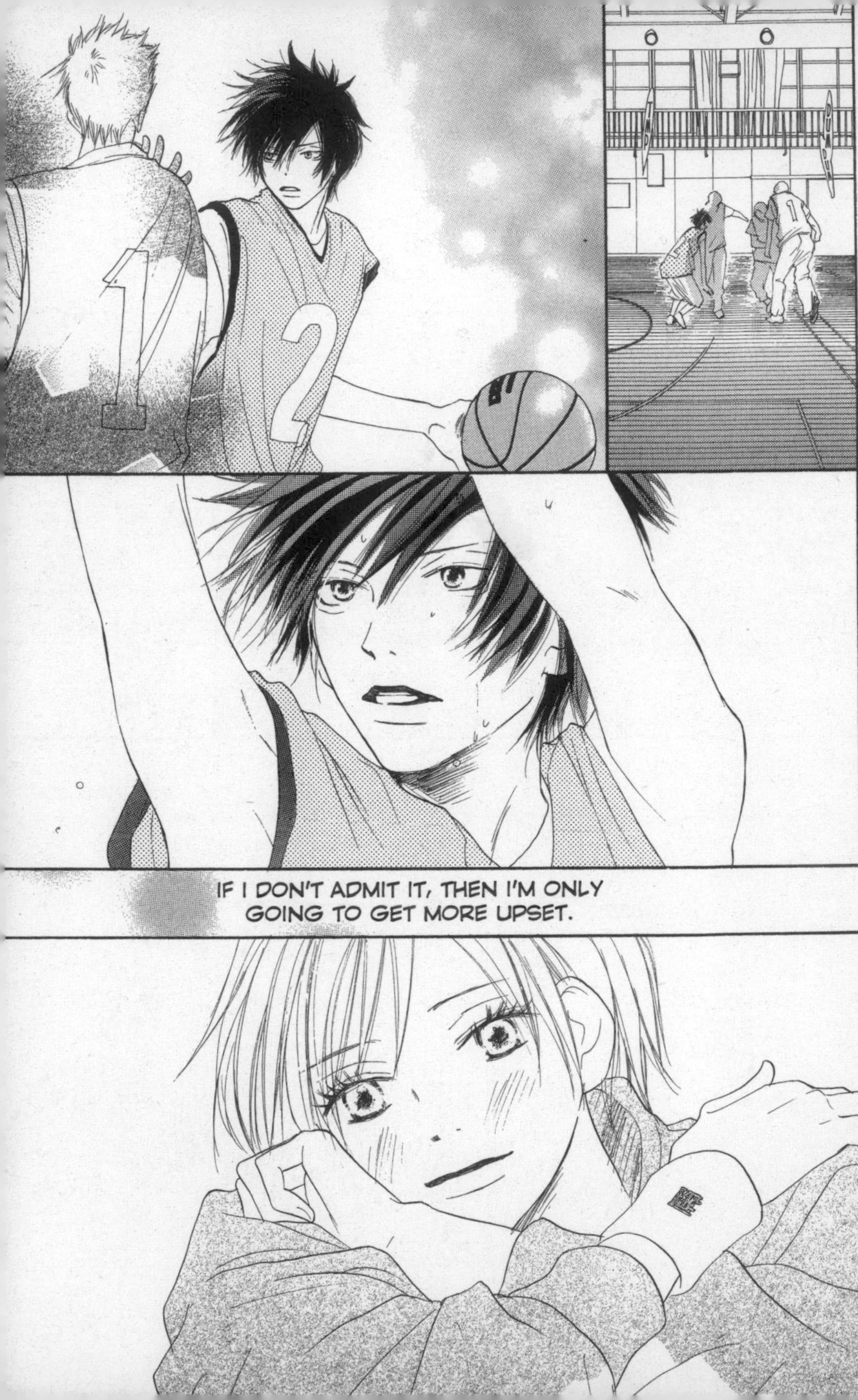
IF I DON'T ADMIT IT, THEN I'M ONLY GOING TO GET MORE UPSET.

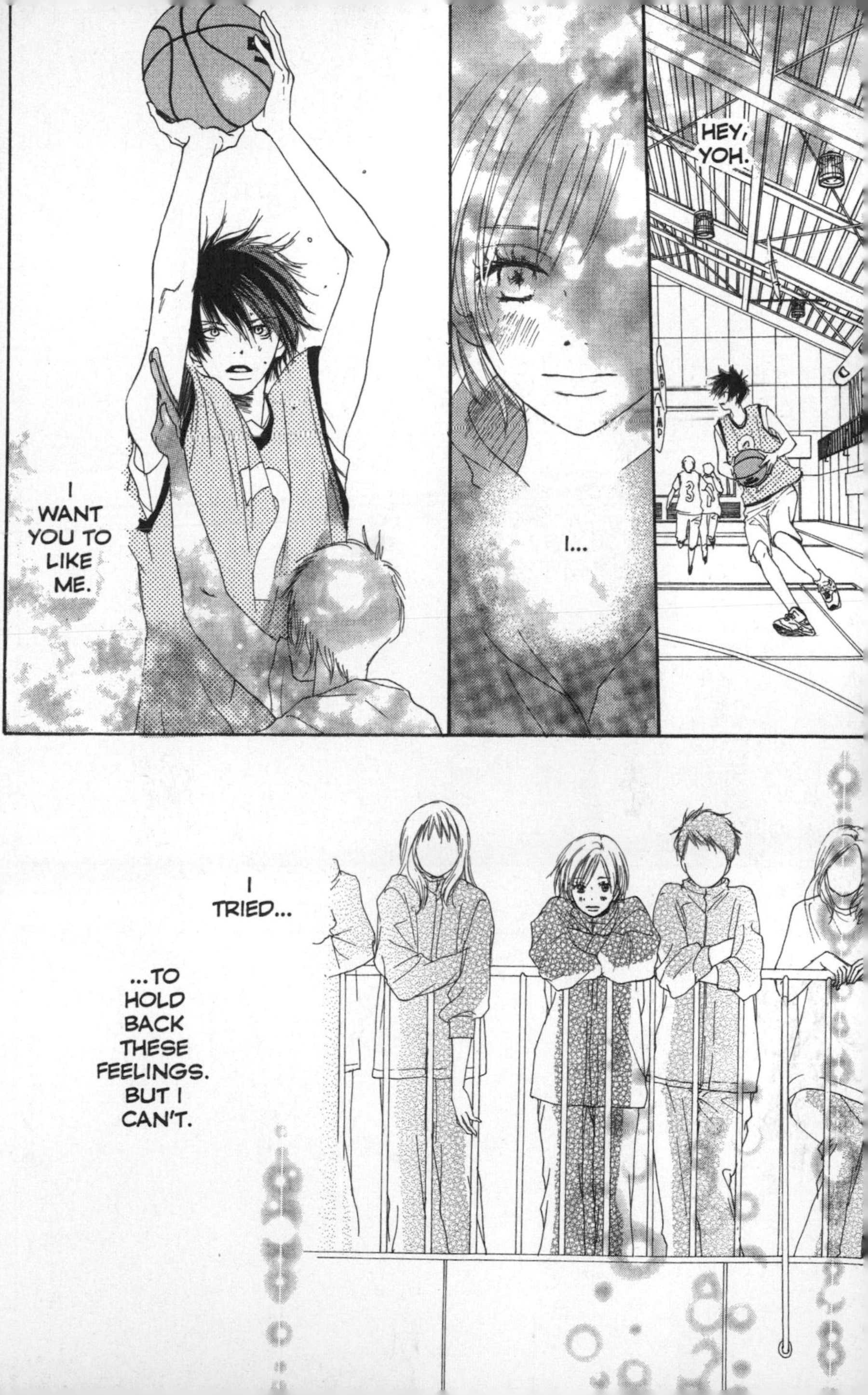

HEY, YOH.
TMP TMP
I...
I WANT YOU TO LIKE ME.
I TRIED...
...TO HOLD BACK THESE FEELINGS. BUT I CAN'T.

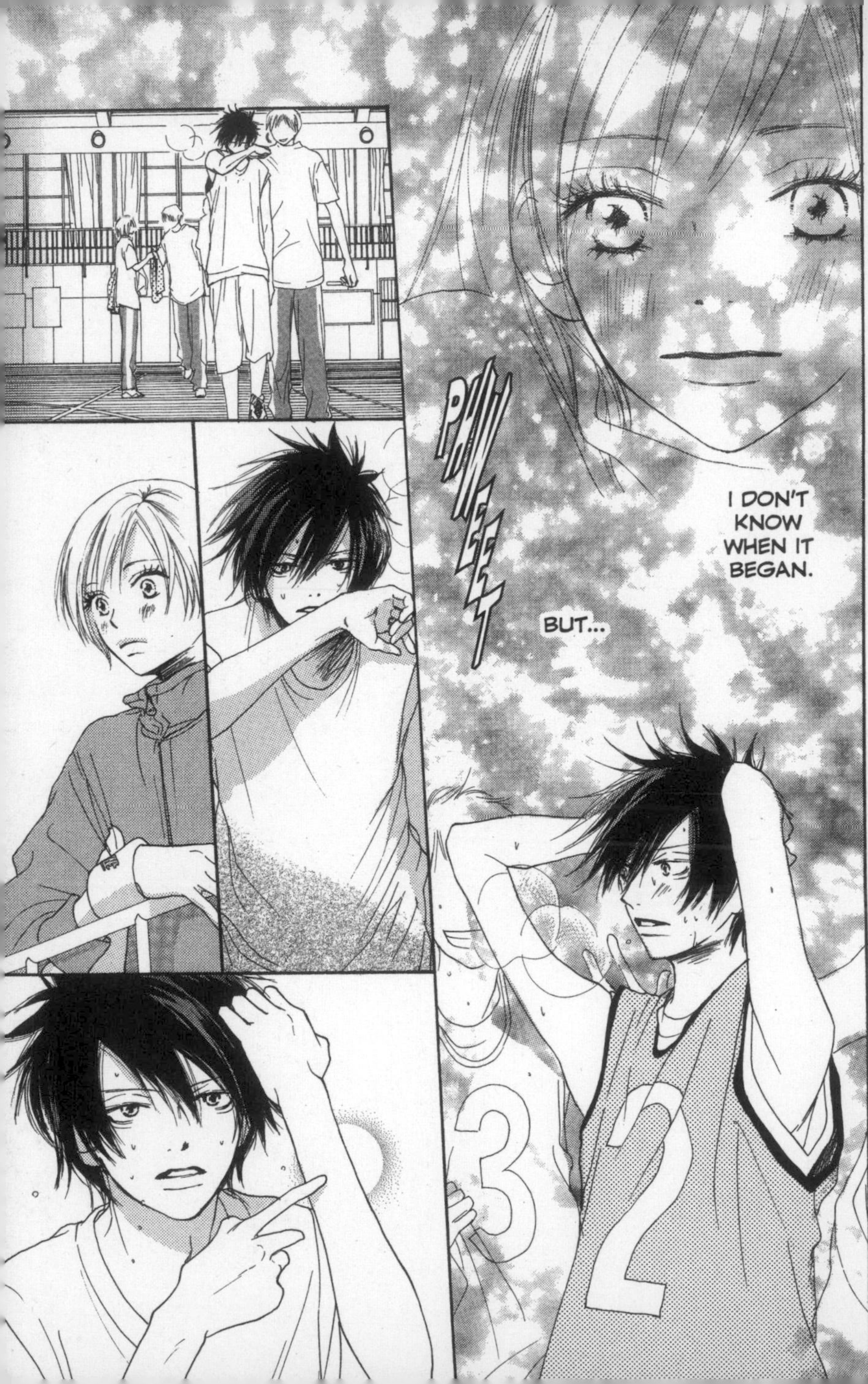
I DON'T KNOW WHEN IT BEGAN.
BUT...
PHWEET

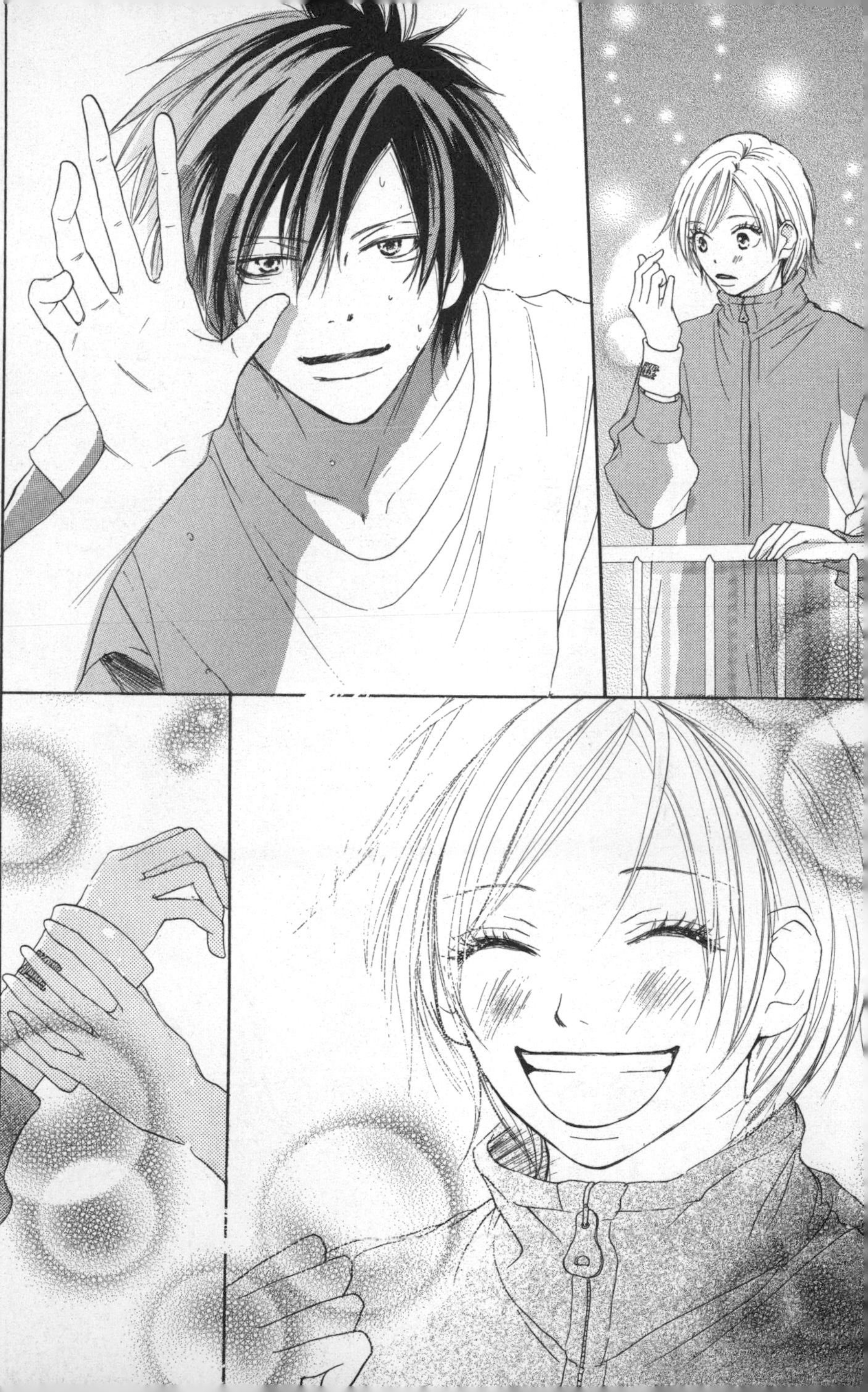

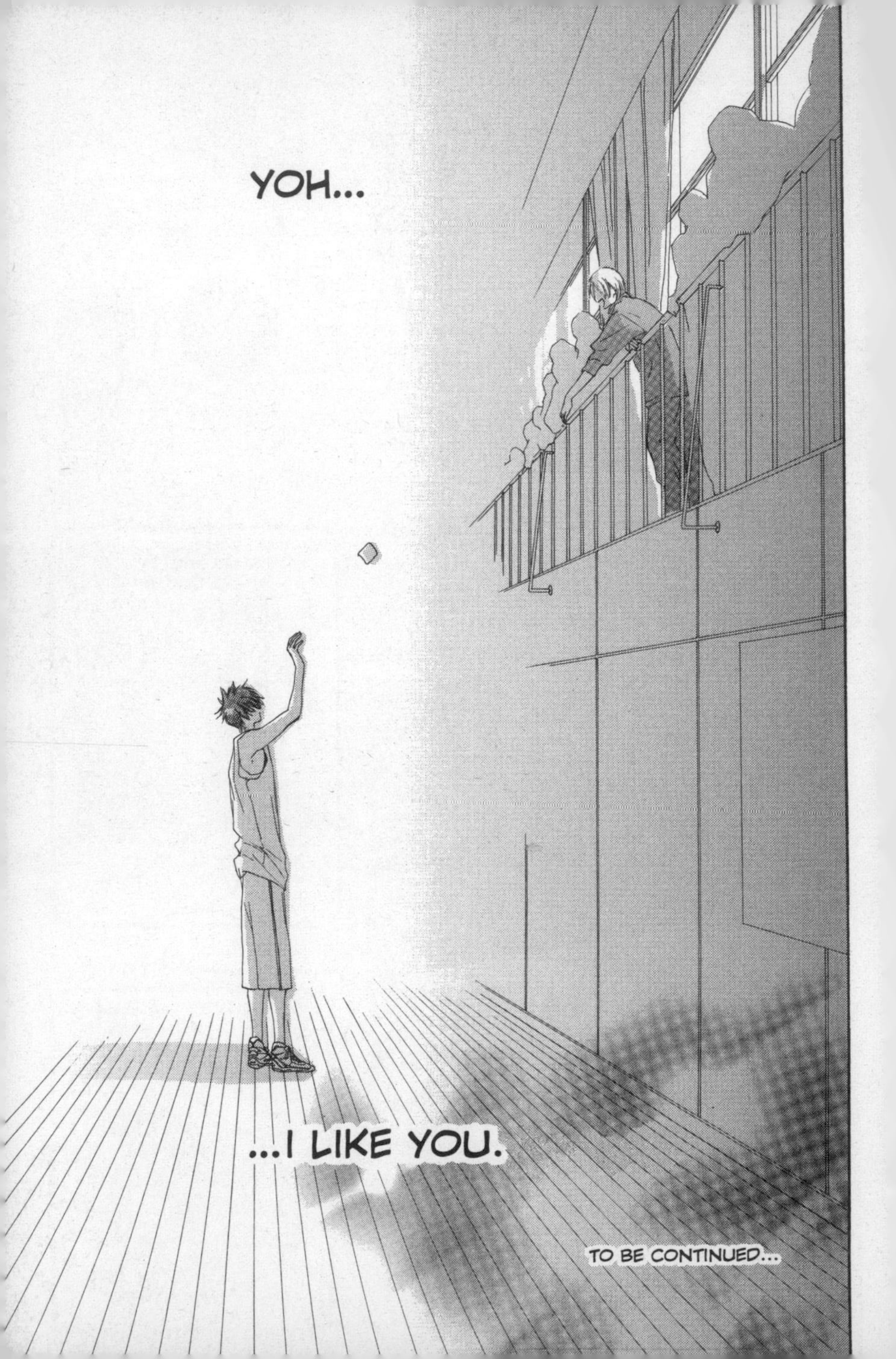
YOH...
...I LIKE YOU.
TO BE CONTINUED...

LESSON ON HOW TO BE HOT

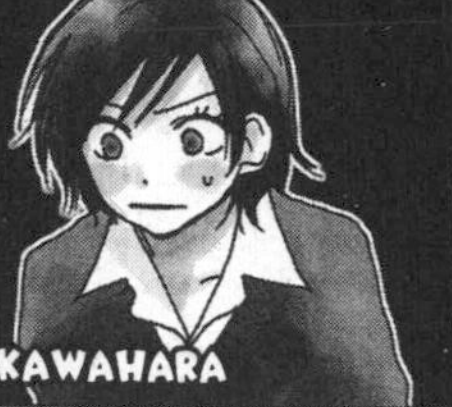

ILLUSTRATED BY: KAZUNE KAWAHARA

START

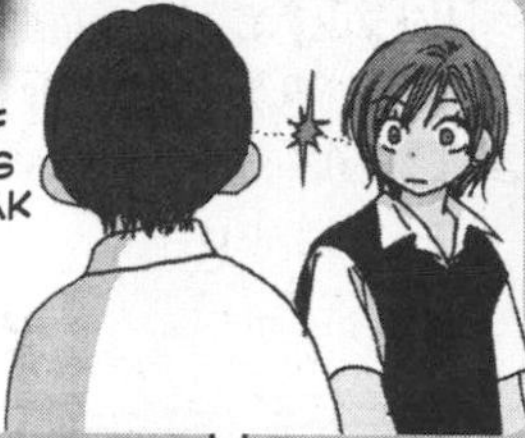

WHAT DO YOU DO IF YOU CATCH A GUY'S GAZE DURING BREAK TIME?
A: MAKE A JOKE
B: PRETEND NOT TO NOTICE

A
B

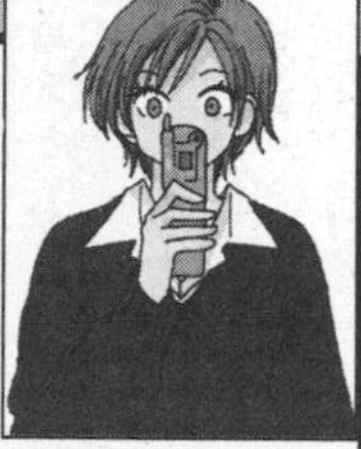

YOU GET A TEXT MESSAGE FROM YOUR FRIEND; HOW DO YOU REPLY?

A: TYPE EVERY LETTER IN PROPERLY
B: TYPE IT QUICKLY USING TXT SPK

WHAT DO YOU THINK IF ONLY YOUR FRIEND GETS HIT ON WHEN YOU'RE OUT SHOPPING?

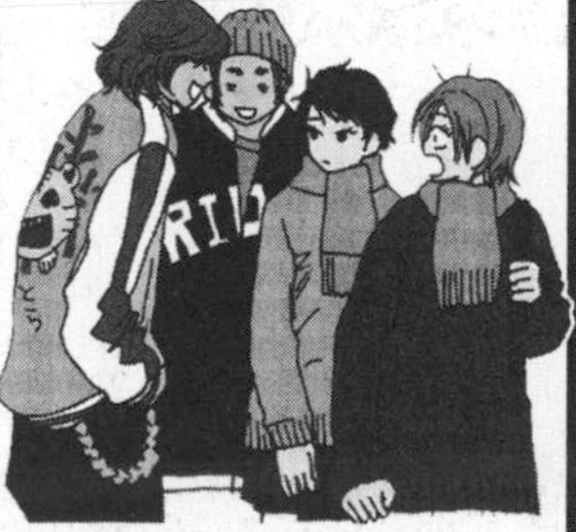

A: ARE THEY BLIND?!
B: WHAT'S WRONG WITH ME...

DO YOU ACT DIFFERENTLY IN FRONT OF YOUR GUY FRIENDS AND GIRL FRIENDS?

A: I DON'T ACT ANY DIFFERENTLY.
B: I'M A DIFFERENT PERSON!

YOU LIKE A GUY. WHAT DO YOU DO WHEN YOU FIND OUT THE TYPE OF GIRL HE LIKES?

A: USE IT AS REFERENCE
B: I TOTALLY CHANGE MYSELF TO BE THAT TYPE!

WHAT DO YOU DO TO KNOCK A GUY DEAD?

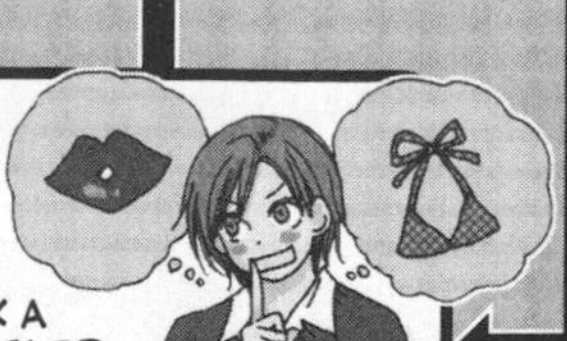

A: BEAUTIFUL LIPS
B: SHOW SOME CLEAVAGE

HOW MUCH HAIR DO YOU HAVE ON YOUR ARMS AND LEGS?

A: I SHAVE EVERY DAY, SO SILKY SMOOTH.
B: I FORGET TO SHAVE, SO PRETTY HAIRY.

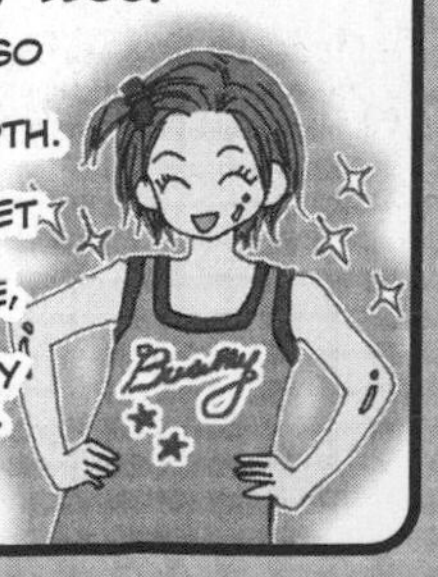

YOUR DATE CANCELS ON YOU; WHAT DO YOU DO?

A: MESSAGE A FRIEND
B: READ MANGA

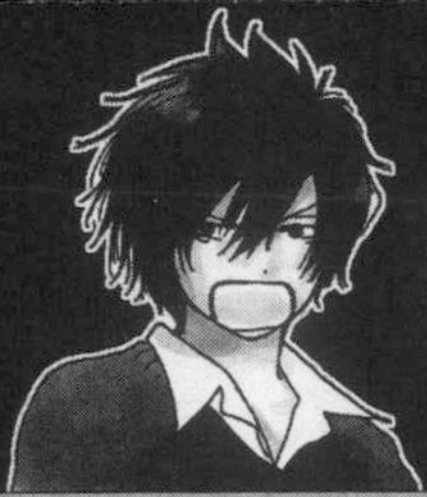

DEMON COACH YOH'S TEST AND

HOW DO YOU WRAP UP A PRESENT FOR A GUY?

A: SIMPLE AND PLAIN
B: PRETTY WITH BOWS

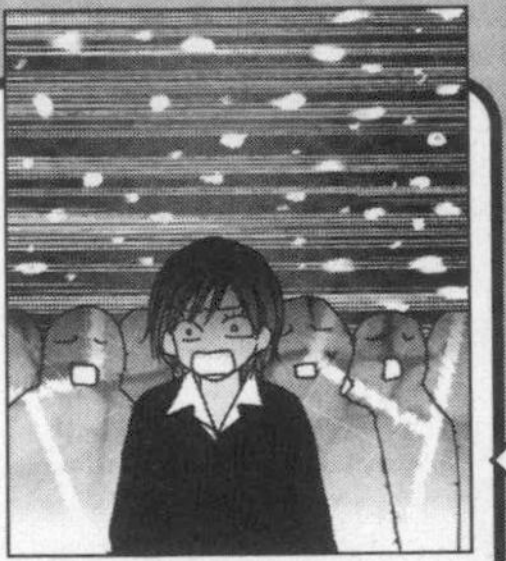

THE CLASS CLOWN MAKES FUN OF YOU!

A: LAUGH ALONG ANYWAY
B: SULK...

HOW MANY FUN THINGS DO YOU KNOW THAT YOU COULD SHARE WITH SOMEONE ELSE?

A: MORE THAN ONE
B: NOTHING...

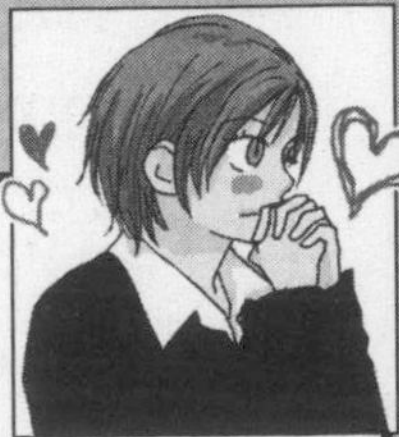

YOU GET WITH THE GUY YOU LIKE. WHAT DO YOU DO FIRST?

A: ASK FRIENDS FOR ADVICE.
B: WORRY ABOUT IT ON YOUR OWN.

YOH'S DIAGNOSIS AND ADVICE

EXPERT

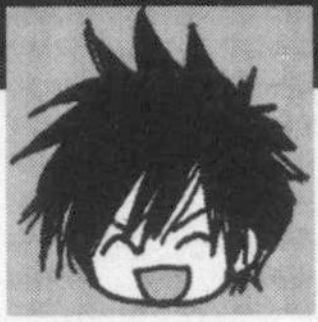

YOU'RE FUN AND POPULAR, SO LOTS OF GUYS FALL FOR YOU. YOU'RE ALSO GOOD AT GIVING ALL THE RIGHT SIGNS TO THE GUY YOU LIKE. YOU'RE PERFECT AS YOU ARE, SO DON'T CHANGE!

MASTER

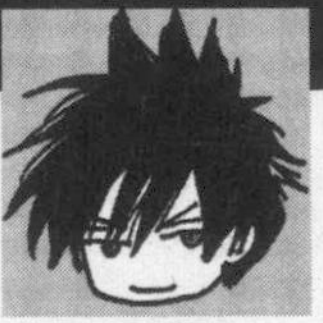

YOU'RE A GIRL THAT'S GOOD AT GETTING PEOPLE TO LIKE YOU. YOU KNOW WHEN TO LAUGH AND YOU EASILY MAKE FRIENDS, SO YOU'RE POPULAR WITH THE GUYS. JUST MAKE SURE YOU DON'T END UP "JUST A FRIEND." GO FOR IT!

AVERAGE

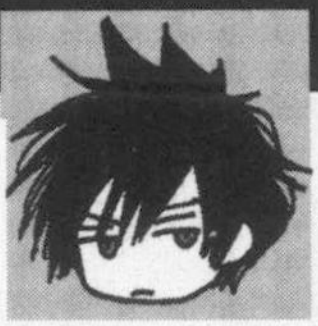

YOU HAVE YOUR OWN SPECIAL CHARMS, AND GUYS WHO NOTICE LIKE YOU. BUT YOU HOLD BACK A LITTLE, WHICH ISN'T GETTING YOU ANYWHERE. HAVE MORE CONFIDENCE IN YOURSELF AND YOU'LL GET THERE!

AMATEUR

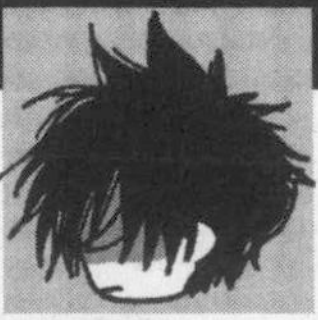

HEY, HEY! YOU'RE AS BAD AS HARUNA! YOU'RE TOTALLY CLUELESS. YOU DON'T KNOW YOUR OWN GOOD POINTS OR WHAT A GUY WANTS. IT'S GOOD TO BE INNOCENT, BUT YOU NEED TO STUDY ALONG WITH HARUNA!

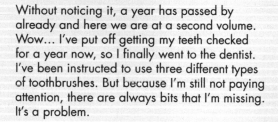

Without noticing it, a year has passed by
already and here we are at a second volume.
Wow... I've put off getting my teeth checked
for a year now, so I finally went to the dentist.
I've been instructed to use three different types
of toothbrushes. But because I'm still not paying
attention, there are always bits that I'm missing.
It's a problem.

– Kazune Kawahara

Kazune Kawahara is from Hokkaido prefecture
and was born on March 11th (a Pisces!). She
made her manga debut at age 18 with *Kare no
Ichiban Sukina Hito* (His Most Favorite Person).
Her other works include *Sensei!*, serialized in
Bessatsu Margaret magazine. Her hobby is
interior redecorating.

HIGH SCHOOL DEBUT
VOL. 2
Shojo Beat Edition

STORY & ART BY
KAZUNE KAWAHARA

Translation & Adaptation/Translation By Design - Gemma Collinge
Touch-up Art & Lettering/Mark Griffin
Design/Izumi Hirayama
Editor/Amy Yu

KOKO DEBUT © 2003 by Kazune Kawahara
All rights reserved.
First published in Japan in 2003 by SHUEISHA Inc., Tokyo.
English translation rights arranged by SHUEISHA Inc.

The stories, characters and incidents mentioned in this publication are
entirely fictional.

Printed in the U.S.A.

Published by VIZ Media, LLC
P.O. Box 77010
San Francisco, CA 94107

10 9 8 7 6 5
First printing, March 2008
Fifth printing, February 2014

www.viz.com   www.shojobeat.com

SURPRISE!

You may be reading the wrong way!

It's true: In keeping with the original Japanese comic format, this book reads from right to left—so action, sound effects and word balloons are completely reversed. This preserves the orientation of the original artwork—plus, it's fun! Check out the diagram shown here to get the hang of things, and then turn to the other side of the book to get started!

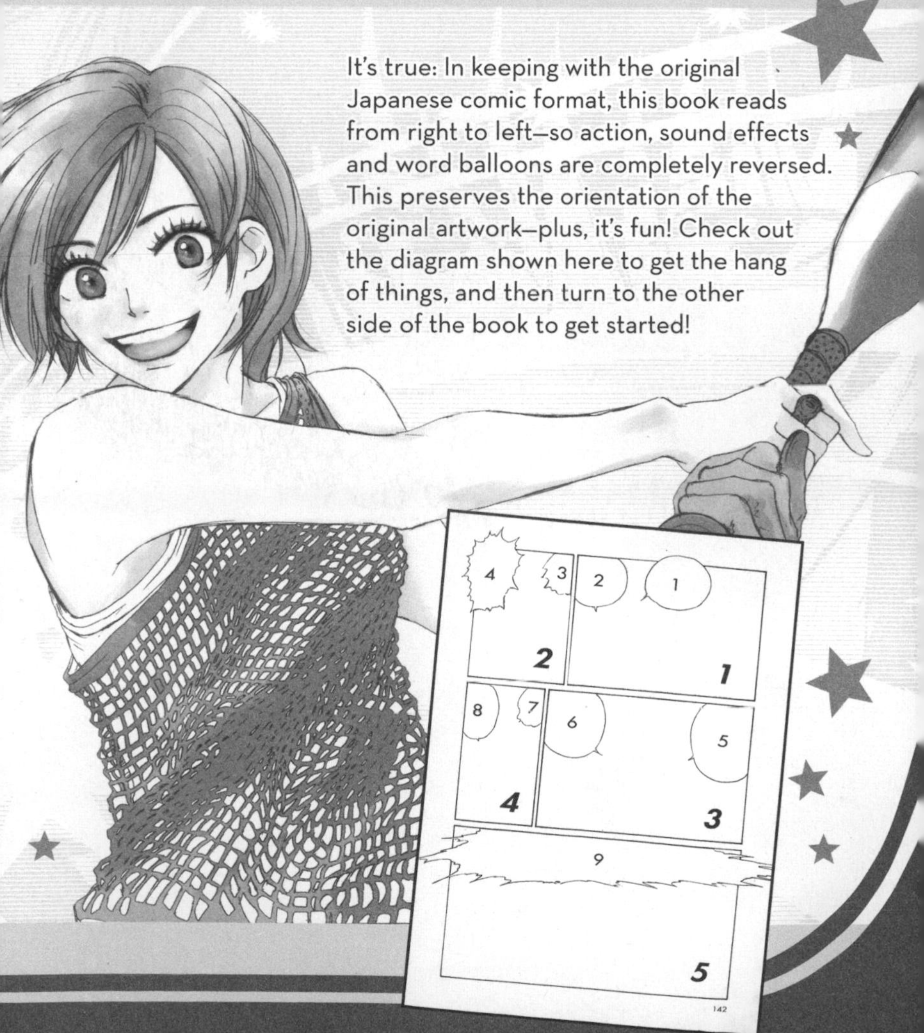
1
2
3
4
1
2
5
6
7
8
3
4
9
5